MODERN
RUSSIAN THEOLOGY

BUKHAREV SOLOVIEV
BULGAKOV

MODERN RUSSIAN THEOLOGY

BUKHAREV SOLOVIEV BULGAKOV

Orthodox Theology in a New Key

Paul Valliere

T&T CLARK
EDINBURGH

T&T CLARK LTD
59 GEORGE STREET
EDINBURGH EH2 2LQ
SCOTLAND

www.tandtclark.co.uk

First published 2000

ISBN 0 567 08755 7

British Library Cataloguing-in-Publication Data
A catalogue record for this book is available from the British Library

Typeset by Fakenham Photosetting Limited, Fakenham, Norfolk
Printed and bound in Great Britain by Bookcraft Ltd, Avon

To Marjo

Negli occhi porta la mia donna Amore,
Per che si fa gentil ciò ch'ella mira.

Note

The italicized passages in quotes from Russian sources are in italics in the sources themselves unless otherwise noted.

Contents

Preface

In this book I seek to demonstrate the vitality and enduring significance of the ideas of a group of modern Russian Orthodox theologians. I proceed mainly through a close reading of the primary sources, letting each thinker speak for himself.

All translations from Russian and other languages are my own, unless otherwise noted. Transliteration follows the system of the Library of Congress except in the rendering of Russian names, where I opt for more conventional English spelling, e.g. Dostoevsky rather than Dostoevskii. Referring to Bulgakov after his ordination, however, I write Father Sergii, as this form is now widely used in English-language writing on Bulgakov. In bibliographical references the original Russian spelling is always honored.

I use the New Revised Standard Version of the Bible to render biblical quotations in the original Russian sources except where this would violate the author's meaning or a crucial traditional reading. In such cases I translate directly from the Slavonic or Russian. I thank the National Council of the Churches of Christ in the United States of America for permission to quote the NRSV.

Of the many people to whom I am indebted for inspiration and ideas, I must first mention Father Alexander Schmemann and Father John Meyendorff, the teachers who introduced me to the study of Orthodox theology. Can anyone imagine finer guides? I am particularly grateful to them for encouraging me to explore a theological path different from their own. May their memory be eternal.

I also wish to thank my teacher James A. Martin, Jr for first lessons, delivered long ago, in the dialogue between philosophy and theology.

Koichi Shinohara of McMaster University has helped me in more ways than he knows since our conversation in the fall of

1989 when I first imagined this book. Bea de Bary Heinrichs has also contributed to this project from the start.

I am indebted to many Orthodox friends who by counsel and example have helped me understand, to the extent that I do, the material presented in this book. I am especially indebted to Vladimir Zelinsky, Michael Meerson, Natasha Kostomarova, Aleksandr Simkin, Hegumen Innokenty Pavlov, Evgeny Rashkovsky, Ioann Miroliubov, Aleksandr Geronimus, Leonid Kishkovsky, Vera Shevzov, Vigen Guroian and Charles and Natalie Ashanin.

My project could not have proceeded without the regular exchange of ideas and work in progress with wonderful colleagues in the American Association for the Advancement of Slavic Studies, especially Judith Deutsch Kornblatt, Richard F. Gustafson, Bernice Glatzer Rosenthal, Caryl Emerson, James P. Scanlan, George L. Kline, Edward Kasinec, Randall Poole and Catherine Evtuhov. I am also grateful for the constructive criticism of my work by Stratford Caldecott and his associates at T&T Clark.

I shall not attempt to name the colleagues and students at Butler University who have contributed to this book. Suffice it to say that, for me, a deep sense of intellectual community, renewed daily, is the supreme pleasure of academic life. I am also grateful to the administration of the university, especially Geoffrey Bannister, Paul Yu and Margriet Lacy, for the sabbatical leaves and other support granted to me. A semester as Visiting Sabbatical Professor at The General Theological Seminary in New York allowed me to begin work on this book. For that semester and for his good counsel since then, I am grateful to Bob Wright. I also thank my many friends at Christian Theological Seminary in Indianapolis for their help.

The clergy and people of the Episcopal Diocese of Indianapolis have been a constant source of inspiration and guidance. I am deeply indebted to Ted Jones, Anne Shelburne Jones, and Bob Giannini.

Most of all I thank Marjo, Dan and Joanna, Eleanor and John for their love and patience.

Indianapolis
Christmas, 1999

Introduction

The material presented in this book is drawn from a stream of Orthodox Christian thought which arose in nineteenth-century Russia, flourished in the early twentieth century and figured prominently on the Orthodox theological scene as late as the 1930s. Calling it a 'Russian school,' Alexander Schmemann described its approach to the theological task in the following terms:

> Orthodox theology must keep its patristic foundation, but it must also go 'beyond' the Fathers if it is to respond to a new situation created by centuries of philosophical development. And in this new synthesis or reconstruction, the western philosophical tradition (source and mother of the Russian 'religious philosophy' of the nineteenth and twentieth centuries) rather than the Hellenic, must supply theology with its conceptual framework. An attempt is thus made to 'transpose' theology into a new 'key,' and this transposition is considered as the specific task and vocation of Russian theology.[1]

A few of the thinkers whom Schmemann thus characterizes, such as Vladimir Soloviev, Nikolai Berdiaev, Pavel Florensky and Sergei Bulgakov, have been known in the West at least by name for a long time. The content of their thought, on the other hand, is not well-understood except perhaps in the case of Berdiaev, whose concise and translatable works enjoyed great popularity in Europe and America until about the 1970s. The names of most other figures of the modern Russian school, such

[1] 'Russian Theology: 1920–1972, An Introductory Survey,' *St Vladimir's Theological Quarterly* 16 (1972):178. Schmemann used the phrase 'Russian school' to refer to this stream of thought in 'Role of Honour,' *St Vladimir's Seminary Quarterly* 2 (1954):6.

as Sergei and Evgeny Trubetskoi, Mikhail Tareev, Lev Karsavin, Semyon Frank, A.V. Kartashev, Georgy Fedotov, Lev Zander and Vasily Zenkovsky, are recognized by no more than a handful of western theologians. Aleksandr Bukharev (Archimandrite Feodor), the pioneer of Orthodox theology 'in a new key,' is not well-known even among Orthodox theologians. This book offers a detailed exposition of the thought of three of the best thinkers of the Russian school beginning with Bukharev.

The theology of the Russian school grew out of the need to relate the Orthodox faith to what is usually called a modern or free society, that is to say, a society consisting of relatively autonomous, unharmonized spheres of activity operating outside the tutelage of church or state. The Russians were the first eastern Christian people to wrestle with the problem of Orthodoxy and modernity because a society of the modern type began to develop in Russia earlier than in other Orthodox lands. There were a number of reasons for Russia's precedence, of which political independence, great-power status in Europe, and the social and educational reforms of Peter the Great and Catherine the Great in the eighteenth century were the most important.

That the Russians were the first Orthodox people who struggled to be modern did not mean they were prepared for the task. The opposite was the case. The Russians had no models, positive or negative, to guide them – that is to say, no Orthodox Christian models. In western Christendom a comparable process had been going on for a long time. Westerners had centuries of experience with religious change in the Renaissance, Reformation and Enlightenment to guide them; and in any case modernity was a product of their own civilization. The Russians, as an eastern Christian people, could not appropriate the western experience with an easy conscience. Few people in nineteenth-century Russia doubted that the preservation of a distinctive Orthodox civilization counted for something in the grand scheme of things, for to think otherwise would have been tantamount to regarding the holy Orthodox faith as a historical accident. Yet there were no precedents to which Orthodox Russians could look. For better or worse, they were on their own.

The issues themselves were not unique to Russia. The Russian school grappled with the challenges facing all faith communities in modern times, such as the tension between tradition and freedom, the challenge of modern humanism, the mission of the church to modern society, the status of dogma in modern intellectuality and the significance of religious pluralism. The universality of these issues along with the role of western philosophical ideas in forging modern civilization in the first place led to the engagement with modern philosophy which Schmemann notes as a fundamental characteristic of the Russian school. This engagement reflected an interest in philosophy not just as a specialized academic pursuit but in the most basic sense of the word: the quest for *sophia*, for wisdom, for insight into the meaning of life. Challenged and also energized by modernity, the Russian school sought to reconstruct the Orthodox theological tradition, to move beyond patristic Orthodoxy to a philosophic Orthodoxy for new times.

Michael Meerson, a present-day Orthodox theologian reviving the project of the Russian school, offers a helpful supplement to Schmemann's description by linking the Russian school to the 'anthropological paradigm shift' in modern theology.[2] Meerson is referring specifically to modern reconstructions of trinitarianism, but his observation applies more generally. The Russian school was the representative in the Orthodox world of an approach to theology which emerged in many parts of Christendom in modern times. It has been described as an approach *von unten nach oben* ('from human beings and the world to God') rather than *von oben nach unten* ('from God to human beings and the world').[3] Or one could simply say it relies on anthropological analogies to express theological truths. Here theology takes as its starting point not the mystery of God but the enigma of the human being, not revelatory tradition alone but the complicated dialogue between

---

[2] Michael Aksionov Meerson, *The Trinity of Love in Modern Russian Theology: The Love Paradigm and the Retrieval of Western Medieval Love Mysticism in Modern Russian Trinitarian Thought (from Solovyov to Bulgakov)* (Quincy, IL: Franciscan Press, 1998), p. xvi.

[3] The phraseology is Karl Barth's as rendered by Wilhelm Pauck, *Harnack and Troeltsch: Two Historical Theologians* (New York: Oxford University Press, 1968), pp. 41–2.

tradition and human experience. In Russia the perplexing relationship between Orthodoxy and the modern world served both as a metaphor and as an actual venue for this dialogue.

Schmemann was exposed to the Russian school as a student at the Orthodox Theological Institute of Saint Sergius in Paris, where many leading Russian Orthodox thinkers had found a home following the upheavals of the Russian Revolution. Indeed the methods and goals of the Russian school commanded the loyalty of most of the founding faculty of Saint Sergius, which opened its doors in 1925. By the mid-1930s, however, a different approach to the Orthodox theological task began to take shape. Led by Georges Florovsky and Vladimir Lossky, the new group rejected the notion of going beyond patristic Orthodoxy. As Schmemann summarized their position:

> The tragedy of Orthodox theological development is viewed here precisely as a drifting away of the theological mind from the very spirit and method of the Fathers, and no reconstruction or new synthesis are thought possible outside a creative recovery of that spirit. 'The style of the Patristic age cannot be abandoned. This is the only solution for contemporary theology. There is no one modern idiom which can unite the Church.'[4]

The Neopatristic school, as the new approach came to be called, effectively sidelined the Russian school by the late 1940s, partly because of its own dynamism, partly because of the natural attrition of Russian-school thinkers. The Russian school found it difficult to reproduce itself in emigration because of its connection with a Russian civilization which had been either destroyed by the Russian Revolution or isolated behind the

---

[4] Schmemann, 'Russian Theology: 1920–1972,' p. 178. The quoted matter is from Georges Florovsky. Pursuing the contrast between the two approaches, Schmemann adds 'neither of these two trends was organized into a disciplined "school" and that a great variety of emphases existed within each one of them' (p. 179). This is quite true, but the operative term in Schmemann's caveat is 'disciplined.' Neither the Russian nor the Neopatristic stream was a disciplined school in the sense of being institutionalized or centrally directed. Nevertheless, that one is dealing with two schools of thought in the usual sense of the phrase is perfectly clear from Schmemann's description. Moreover, the variety that existed within each school, while considerable, was never so great as to obscure the basic differences.

insuperable barriers erected by the Soviet state. The Neopatristic initiative, by contrast, found an audience among the younger generation of diaspora Russians who recognized their future lay in the West. It was helped along also by western converts to Orthodoxy who shared its passion for the liturgical, ascetical and mystical traditions of the fathers. By the middle of the twentieth century the ascendancy of the Neopatristic school was secure. Almost no one in the Orthodox world talked any longer about going 'beyond the fathers.'

To make matters worse, not all Orthodox scholars who remembered the Russian school regarded it fondly. The most influential critic was Georges Florovsky, author of what is still after fifty years the most detailed and stirring study of Russian theology, *The Paths of Russian Theology*.[5] In his book Florovsky deals with Russian school thinkers at length but from a one-sided point of view. He presents the history of pre-revolutionary Russian theology as the story of the alienation of the Orthodox mind from its sources, arguing that theology in Russia was patterned on western academic traditions, such as Roman Catholic scholasticism and Protestant pietism or moralism, but almost never on 'the mind of the fathers.' A process of self-correction began with the retrieval of patristic sources by Metropolitan Filaret (Drozdov) and others in the nineteenth century; but progress was hampered by many obstacles, including the steady stream of intellectual imports from the West. Florovsky rejected the notion Orthodox theology required any sort of alliance with modern philosophy. He championed tradition-based patristic Orthodoxy, not philosophic Orthodoxy.

Not all critics were as severe as Florovsky, but his assessment carried enough weight to cause most Neopatristic theologians to avoid close identification with the Russian school. As for the giants who could not be ignored, such as Soloviev, Florensky, Bulgakov, Berdiaev and a few others, attention was given only

---

[5] Georgii Florovskii, *Puti russkogo bogosloviia*, 3rd ed., preface by J. Meyendorff (Paris: YMCA-Press, 1983). The first edition appeared in 1937. English trans.: *Ways of Russian Theology*, trans. Robert L. Nichols, vols 5–6 of *The Collected Works of Georges Florovsky*, ed. Richard S. Haugh (Belmont, Massachusetts: Nordland Publishing Company, 1979; Vaduz: Büchervertriebsanstalt, 1987). All references in this study are to the third Russian edition.

to those aspects of their thought which could be harmonized with Neopatristic concerns. The rest was ignored.

At the dawn of the twenty-first century, however, there are good reasons for undertaking a fresh examination of the Russian school. Besides the scholarly objective of rendering a fairer account of modern Orthodox theology, there is the intellectual imperative of bringing a sense of balance to a theological scene long dominated by the Neopatristic approach. While no one who loves Orthodox theology would deny the extraordinary contributions of the Neopatristic school, one may wonder whether its unchallenged hegemony has been a good thing. Neopatristic thinkers are theological classicists, like Roman Catholic Neo-Thomists and Protestant Neo-Orthodox theologians. To the extent that classicism means patterning theology on historic sources, it is an ingredient of the theological task in every age. Yet there is an important difference in the role classicism has played in modern Orthodoxy as compared with western communions. In modern Roman Catholicism and Protestantism classicists have usually had plenty of critics to contend with, whereas in Orthodox theology the Neopatristic school has had the field more or less to itself for decades. So commanding is the dominance of the Neopatristic school that even the theological dialogue between Orthodoxy and the western churches since the middle of the twentieth century has been a dialogue between various western theologies on the one hand and Neopatristic Orthodoxy on the other. Many observers think of modern Orthodox theology and Neopatristic theology as one and the same. The existence of principled alternatives in Orthodox theology is rarely suspected.

Recent changes in the Orthodox world provide another reason for a fresh look at the Russian school. The revolutions of 1989–91, sweeping away the Soviet imperium, ushered in a period of openness, experimentation and reconstruction throughout the Orthodox world. In Russia, Ukraine, Romania, Georgia and many other countries, Orthodox people enjoy unprecedented liberty to reform their church, their society and themselves. But reformers need landmarks. Where are Orthodox people to look for guidance of a theological kind on issues such as free markets, new republics, constitution-making, ethnic relations, religious pluralism, gender roles, poverty, crime and a host of other contemporary problems? They will not find it in Neopatristic sources for the most part. The Russian school, on the other hand, dealt with contemporary problems all the time because its overarching concern was to promote the engagement of Orthodox believers with the modern world in all sectors – politics, society, economy, education, science, the arts and so on.

A final reason for studying the thought of the Russian school is that it is indispensable background for understanding the theological scene in Russia today. Theological reflection started to reconstitute itself in Russia during the 1960s and 1970s when intellectuals, many of them converts to Orthodoxy, began recovering the abandoned legacy of pre-revolutionary Russian civilization including the thought of the Russian school. At the same time a new generation of Orthodox activists helped create the Soviet human rights movement and, to that end, brought a whole new set of social, political and cultural issues to the theological forum.[6] While neither the intellectuals nor the activists were ever of one mind theologically, by returning the problem of Orthodoxy's relation to the modern world to the theological agenda they resurrected the project of the Russian school. In many cases the linkage was quite direct, as the new thinkers made a close reading of the original texts of the Russian school. This was the case with the much revered Aleksandr Men as well as with younger intellectuals such as Michael Meerson, Evgeny Barabanov, Vladimir Zelinsky and many others.

After the fall of the Soviet Union the theological situation in Russia became more complicated. Western sources of all kinds including Neopatristic works poured in, and a larger segment of the population began participating in theological discussion.

---

[6] For samples of these discussions in English, see *The Political, Social and Religious Thought of Russian 'Samizdat': An Anthology*, ed. Michael Meerson-Aksenov and Boris Shragin, trans. Nickolas Lupinin (Belmont, Massachusetts: Nordland Publishing Company, 1977). Two essay collections from the period are indispensable sources for the study of Russian Orthodox thought in recent times: *Iz-pod glyb: sbornik statei* (Paris: YMCA-Press, 1974); and *Samosoznanie: sbornik statei*, ed. P. Litvinov, M. Meerson-Aksenov and B. Shragin (New York: Izdatel'stvo 'Khronika', 1976). The former is available in English: Alexander Solzhenitsyn *et al.*, *From Under the Rubble*, trans. A.M. Brock *et al.* under the direction of Michael Scammell, with intro. by Max Hayward (Boston and Toronto: Little, Brown and Company, 1975).

However, the fact that Russian Orthodox intellectuals redis-covered the indigenous Russian school before most other sources became readily available affects the way in which the new sources are being received in Russia today. Moreover, the reception is taking place in conditions that differ as profoundly from the Paris of the 1930s as from pre-revolutionary Russia. One who wishes to understand contemporary Russian theology must take all this background into account and still be prepared for surprises. The world of twenty-first century Russian Orthodox theology is unlikely to embody the Neopatristic ideal of a consensus founded on the mind of the fathers.

In this book the thought of the Russian school is presented through an analysis of three of its leading expositors: Aleksandr Matveevich Bukharev (Archimandrite Feodor, 1824–71), Vladimir Sergeevich Soloviev (1853–1900) and Sergei Nikolaevich Bulgakov (1871–1944). Each receives detailed attention in his own right, but recurrent themes are also examined, as these best demonstrate the continuity of the Russian school. The focus is on the theology itself, that is to say, on what Russian-school thinkers actually believed and taught as the Orthodox faith. While a history of the Russian school is needed, this book is not it. Historical background is supplied only to the extent necessary for appreciating the theology.

Bukharev, Soloviev and Bulgakov have been selected to represent the beginning, middle and end of the Russian school, respectively. Bukharev (Archimandrite Feodor) represents the beginning in that he was Russian Orthodoxy's first modern theologian, that is to say, the first Russian theologian who recognized modernity as a theological problem and placed the problem at the center of his work. Bukharev was not the first Russian Orthodox thinker of the modern age. Chaadaev, Odoevsky, Khomiakov, Kireevsky and other lay aristocrats who created modern Russian religious philosophy in the first half of the nineteenth century preceded him. But Archimandrite Feodor represents the starting point of the Russian school better than the lay philosophers because he was a church theologian. He was educated in Orthodox theological schools and spent most of his career in ecclesiastical institutions, whereas the aristocrats were cosmopolitan intellectuals nurtured as much by western European culture as by Russian Orthodoxy. Feodor's theology has the virtue (for our purposes) of being completely home-grown.

Feodor was also a church theologian in the substantive sense of taking Orthodox dogma as the framework for his thought. He did not think *about* Orthodox dogma but *by means of it*. He would not have known how to proceed in any other way. The lay philosophers, by contrast, came to the Orthodox dogmatic tradition, if at all, from an intellectual starting point outside of it. Ivan Kireevsky (1806–56), for example, developed his ideas first of all through reflection on the philosophy of Schelling, with whom he studied in Munich. He did not discover the riches of Orthodox theology until, back in Russia, his wife observed Schelling's ideas 'had long been familiar to her from the works of the Church Fathers.'[7] Kireevsky took her testimony to heart and began to investigate his native tradition. Archimandrite Feodor did not have to discover Orthodox dogmatics; for him modernity was the great discovery.

Vladimir Soloviev represents the middle of the Russian school, not just chronologically but because he was the crucial mediator between home-grown Orthodoxy and modern critical thought. Soloviev came from a distinguished academic family and received an excellent education. A philosophical idealist, he was profoundly interested in religion. His extensive writings inspired a reorientation of Russian philosophy to religious questions at the end of the nineteenth century.

The resonance between Archimandrite Feodor's theology and Soloviev's thought, which we will demonstrate through an analysis of their works, has particular significance for understanding the Russian school. Soloviev was not acquainted with Archimandrite Feodor or directly influenced by his work. By the time Soloviev's career began, Feodor had died and his legacy was eclipsed for reasons that will be explained later. Yet there is a deep congruence between these two men's visions of Orthodoxy in the modern world. It is not a congruence of style or method. Archimandrite Feodor's works have dogmatic profundity but little philosophical sophistication. Soloviev's

---

[7] V.V. Zenkovsky, *A History of Russian Philosophy*, trans. George L. Kline, 2 vols (New York: Columbia University Press, 1953), 1:212.

philosophical expertise is evident on every page of his writings, but he was not a church theologian. Indeed, the status of Orthodox dogma in his thought is a problem that will require explication. In spirit and substance, however, Bukharev and Soloviev shared a great deal. This commonality may be cited as evidence the Russian school did not depend on direct affiliation but grew out of a set of problems and promptings which had deep roots in the situation of modern Orthodoxy.

Sergei Bulgakov's relation to Soloviev, by contrast, was a case of affiliation. Bulgakov belonged to the first generation of Russian intellectuals inspired by Soloviev. The two men never collaborated, for Soloviev was dead by the time Bulgakov began taking a serious interest in him. But once Bulgakov discovered Soloviev's thought, he embraced it enthusiastically.

The differences between Soloviev and Bulgakov are as important as the continuities, however. Bulgakov was much more closely connected with the everyday life of the Orthodox Church than Soloviev. He grew up in a clerical family in provincial Russia and spent almost four years at Orel Theological Seminary studying for the priesthood. Distressed by 'the philistinism and spiritual enslavement which saturated the pores of church life all around him,'[8] he abandoned his calling before completing the degree. But his decision was not forever. After a successful career as an economist during which he also made important contributions to religious philosophy, Bulgakov was ordained in 1918. In his second career, spent mainly in exile, he devoted himself to dogmatic theology.

In Bulgakov's work, then, the theology of the Russian school, which took shape in Archimandrite Feodor's dogmatic vision and negotiated a critical turn in Soloviev's religious philosophy, came full circle and returned to dogmatics. As the thinker who gathered up the manifold riches of the Russian school and bore them into the church as an intellectual offering, Bulgakov represents the culmination of the movement.

Bulgakov also represents the end in the historical sense, for the Russian school was doomed at home and losing its

---

[8] Sergii Bulgakov, *Avtobiograficheskie zametki*, posthumous ed., preface and notes by L.A. Zander (Paris: YMCA-Press, 1946), p. 35.

audience abroad by the time he finished his work. The fresh shoots that broke through the soil in Soviet Russia in the 1960s and 1970s were the beginning of a new history, not without precedent, but not an organic outgrowth of the earlier movement, either.[9]

Note on Translation: 'The Humanity of God'

In this book I experiment with a new translation of a key term in the vocabulary of the modern Russian school: *bogochelovechestvo*. The word is usually translated 'Godmanhood,' here 'the humanity of God.'[10] Since readers already acquainted with Russian thought might wonder at my departure from tradition or at the absense of semantic parallelism between the Russian original and my English phrase, a word of explanation is in order. Let me say at the outset, however, that I regard my translation as a means of advancing discussion of a difficult concept, not as a solution which every interpreter will necessarily wish to adopt.

Bogochelovechestvo is an abstract noun formed from *Bogochelovek*, God-human, a name for Christ the incarnate Word of God. *Bogochelovechestvo* is the sum of the conditions, qualities and characteristics united in the person of the God-human.

The traditional English translation gives the appearance of being a literal semantic equivalent of the Russian: *Bog* (God) +

---

[9] 'When we survey our church life today,' wrote one of the new Orthodox thinkers in 1980, '[we see] almost no cultural or even personal ties stretching from that time to our own.' Vladimir Zelinskii, *Prikhodiashchie v tserkov'* (Paris: La Presse Libre, 1982), p. 10.

[10] I introduced 'the humanity of God' for *bogochelovechestvo* in a paper at the Conference on Russian Religious Thought at the University of Wisconsin in 1993. For the published version see 'Sophiology as the Dialogue of Orthodoxy with Modern Civilization,' *Russian Religious Thought*, ed. Judith Deutsch Kornblatt and Richard F. Gustafson (Madison: The University of Wisconsin Press, 1996), pp. 176–92. Boris Jakim's 'divine humanity' is another creative contribution to the discussion. See Vladimir Solovyov, *Lectures on Divine Humanity*, trans. Boris Jakim (Hudson, New York: Lindisfarne Press, 1995). Michael Meerson utilizes both Jakim's and my translations as well as 'God's humanity' to good effect in *The Trinity of Love in Modern Russian Theology*. I depart from my translation only when *bogochelovechestvo* occurs with a possessive, in which case I follow Jakim, e.g. *Ego bogochelovechestvo*, 'His divine humanity' (referring to Christ).

chelovek (man) + nominalizing ending = *bogochelovechestvo* (Godmanhood). But the equation is flawed. For one thing, *chelovek* has no gender implications in Russian; it means human being, not man (male). The distinction is important in an environment that has grown sensitive to issues of gender. Also, manhood is unsatisfactory for *chelovechestvo*, which is the Russian word for humanity. The erasure of humanity from *bogochelovechestvo* is an especially grave violation of the original term because, as we shall see, the concept of *bogochelovechestvo* was the vehicle for a principled and profound Orthodox Christian humanism. Another strike against Godmanhood is its lack of resonance. The word is an ungraceful semantic isolate in English, lacking vibrancy and associations.

One option, of course, would be not to translate *bogochelovechestvo* but to use the Russian term while explaining what it means. This solution might make sense for a gathering of Slavists, but it cannot be recommended to those who wish to acquaint a wider audience of English-speakers with the riches of modern Russian theology. True, words sometimes escape their linguistic boundaries. The term 'sobornost', to cite an example from Russian theology, seems to have established itself in the English-speaking world, although I suspect that most non-specialist readers still need a gloss to make sense of it.[11] It seems obvious, however, that *bogochelovechestvo* cannot be accommodated in English. One look at it is enough to discourage all but the most adventurous Anglophones. Beyond that, outright borrowing is not always the best solution to problems of translation. There is a danger in such cases that use of the foreign term will encourage an attitude of exoticism or esoterism, as if the substance of the concept in question were unique, existing outside the common store of human knowledge and belief. For the same reason I have not adopted translations based on the patristic Greek vocabulary from which *bogochelovechestvo*

---

[11] Jaroslav Pelikan, for example, concludes the final volume of *The Christian Tradition* with a chapter entitled 'The Sobornost of the Body of Christ.' See *Christian Doctrine and Modern Culture (since 1700)*, vol. 5 of *The Christian Tradition: A History of the Development of Doctrine* (Chicago and London: The University of Chicago Press, 1989). The term 'sobornost' appears in *Webster's Third New International Dictionary* (1981).

ultimately derives (theandry, theanthropy).[12] The thinkers of the modern Russian school addressed the problems of the Universal Church and of universal humanity. To convey their thought in resonant theological English may be difficult, but it is worth the effort, for even a modicum of success will demonstrate the broad scope of their message. In any case I am confident that Bukharev, Soloviev and Bulgakov would have strongly approved of an American theologian writing about them in the idiom of English-speaking theology rather than using language that necessarily confines them to the world of Russian Orthodoxy.

Some colleagues with whom I have discussed 'the humanity of God' object that the phrase overhumanizes, one might say 'domesticates', *bogochelovechestvo*.[13] They also point out that the English word 'humanity', besides referring to the condition of being human, can⌣mean 'kindness' or 'humaneness', a concept for which a different, albeit closely related word is used in Russian (*chelovechnost'*). There is merit in these criticisms;

---

[12] For a roster of the Greek words with references to the patristic sources, see *A Patristic Greek Lexicon*, ed. G.W.H. Lampe (Oxford: The Clarendon Press, 1961), beginning with *theandria*. It should be noted that *theandria, theanthrôpia* and their derivatives occur relatively rarely in patristic sources and usually indicate Origenist or Monophysite tendencies. The attitude of the fifth-century Orthodox bishop Quintianus is typical: *ei tis theanthrôpian legei, kai ouchi theon kai anthrôpon mallon legei, anathematizesthô* ('If anyone says theanthropy rather than saying God *and* human being, let him be anathematized'; *Patrologia Graeca*, ed. Migne, 85:1740). The most prominent case involving these terms was the effort by Emperor Heraclius, Patriarch Sergius of Constantinople and Patriarch Cyrus of Alexandria in the seventh century to reconcile the Monophysites to Orthodoxy by offering the formula *mia theandrikê energeia* ('one divine-human activity') to describe the activity of Christ the God-human. The effort broke down over objections from Rome as well as from many eastern theologians. In any case, nowhere in the annals of patristic theology is there an example of a theological system founded on *theandria* or *theanthrôpia*. Theologies of the humanity of God are modern constructs, examples of the reconstructionism characteristic of the Russian school.

[13] In *The Domestication of Transcendence: How Modern Thinking About God Went Wrong* (Louisville: Westminster John Knox Press, 1996) William Placher introduced this term to describe modern interpretations of Christian doctrine that diminish the sense of the transcendence or otherness of God. Placher would probably regard all forms of theology *von unten nach oben* as suffering from this defect. But of course he was not familiar with the theology of the Russian school, nor have most other western theologians reckoned with it.

but, as I shall argue, they apply not just to my translation but to the concept of *bogochelovechestvo* as formulated by the Russian school in the first place. My exposition will show the Russian school forged the concept of the humanity of God precisely for the purpose of promoting a humanizing approach to theology and a more humane ecclesiastical culture. Many contemporary scholars fail to detect this motive in *bogochelovechestvo* because they view the term through the prism of Neopatristic theology. The Neopatristic school focuses on the concept of theosis (deification) and subordinates the whole gamut of anthropological values to it. In the Russian school the humanity of God is connected first of all with kenosis, the self-emptying of God in the incarnation, a connection that was still clear as late as the 1930s in Bulgakov's dogmatic theology. But I am running ahead of myself. The documentation for my position is in the book.

Readers familiar with twentieth-century Protestant theology will recognize the allusion to a famous essay by Karl Barth in my 'humanity of God' and may wonder why a bow in Barth's direction opens a book dedicated to an anthropological and philosophic tradition in theology. Of all modern theologians Barth was the most trenchant and persistent critic of theology 'from below.' As readers of Barth know, however, *The Humanity of God* (1956) marked a moment of self-criticism late in his career. While in no sense retracting the vindication of the transcendence of God which forms the heart of his theology, Barth acknowledged his position had its limitations, the chief one being that 'the *humanity* of God did not quite come into its rights' in his work. He advised those who were responsible for the next stage of theological culture to revisit the theme which he dispatched too peremptorily. At stake is a basic theological truth which Barth states with characteristic clarity: 'Since God in His deity is human, [theological] culture must occupy itself neither with God in Himself nor with man in himself but with the man-encountering God and the God-encountering man and with their dialogue and history, in which their communion takes place and comes to fulfillment.'[14] These words, which could

---

[14] Karl Barth, *The Humanity of God*, trans. John Newton Thomas and Thomas Wieser (Richmond, Virginia: John Knox Press, 1960), p. 55.

have been written by Soloviev or Bulgakov, nicely summarize the meaning of *bogochelovechestvo*. While Barth did not work out a theology of the humanity of God, his testimony is good authority for taking a close look at three Russian Orthodox theologians who did.

PART I

BUKHAREV: ORTHODOXY AND THE MODERN WORLD

I

The Making of a Renewalist

PROPHETIC PROMPTINGS

Aleksandr Matveevich Bukharev was born into a village deacon's family in Tver Province in 1824.[1] His father, like most rural clergy, divided his time between serving the church and cultivating a small plot of land. The living was a poor one, which put a strain on relations between husband and wife. Yet Aleksandr's childhood seems to have been happy. He was especially close to his father, whom he eulogized as a paragon of evangelical benevolence.[2]

---

[1] For a synopsis of Bukharev's life and work see P. Znamenskii, 'Vmesto vvedeniia. O zhizni i trudakh Aleksandra Matveevicha (arkimandrita Feodora) Bukhareva,' in Arkhimandrit Feodor (A.M. Bukharev), *O pravoslavii v otnoshenii k sovremennosti* (St Petersburg: Sinodal'naia tipografiia, 1906), pp. v–xxviii. The essay first appeared as 'Pechal'noe dvadtsatipiatiletie,' *Pravoslavnyi sobesednik*, 1896. A more detailed portrait is offered by Elisabeth Behr-Sigel, *Alexandre Boukharev: Un Théologien de l'Église orthodoxe russe en dialogue avec le monde moderne. Introduction et Lettres à Valérien et Alexandra Lavrski*, preface by Olivier Clément (Paris: Éditions Beauchesne, 1977), Introduction, pp. 27–98. An excellent account of the crisis in Archimandrite Feodor's career is provided by A.M. Belorukov, 'Vnutrennii perelom v zhizni A. M. Bukhareva,' *Bogoslovskii vestnik*, 1915, nos 10–12:785–867. A rich selection of biographical and autobiographical material including an unfinished portrait by Pavel Florensky is found in *Arkhimandrit Feodor (A.M. Bukharev): pro et contra. Lichnost' i tvorchestvo arkhimandrita Feodora (Bukhareva) v otsenke russkikh myslitelei i issledovatelei. Antologiia*, ed. B.F. Egorov, N.V. Serebrennikov, and A.P. Dmitriev, Seriia 'Russkii Put'' (St Petersburg: Izdatel'stvo Russkogo Khristianskogo gumanitarnogo instituta, 1997). This volume also contains the most complete bibliography of works by and about Bukharev, pp. 766–92. Most sources report the year of Bukharev's birth as 1822. For 1824 see Gregory L. Freeze, 'Die Laisierung des Archimandriten Feodor (Bucharev) und ihre kirchenpolitischen Hintergründe: Theologie und Politik im Russland der Mitte des 19. Jahrhunderts,' *Kirchen im Osten: Studien zur osteuropäischen Kirchengeschichte und Kirchenkunde* 28 (1985):28, n. 7.

[2] Behr-Sigel, *Alexandre Boukharev*, pp. 35–9.

A sickly but intellectually precocious child, Aleksandr received his elementary education at the district ecclesiastical school and was admitted to Tver Seminary at the relatively early age of fifteen. Completing the course at the head of his class in 1842, he proceeded to Moscow Theological Academy. Upon graduation in 1846 he was tonsured with the name of Feodor and stayed on at the academy as an instructor of biblical studies. He was promoted to professorial rank in 1852 and to the monastic rank of archimandrite the following year.

Moscow Theological Academy was a stimulating place to be in the period of Bukharev's residence. The most eminent members of the faculty were A.V. Gorsky (1812–75), one of Russia's greatest church historians, and F.A. Golubinsky (1797–1854), a philosophical theologian and gifted expositor of German idealism who has been called 'the founder of Russian theistic philosophy.'[3] Golubinsky was the teacher who first inspired Feodor's optimism toward modern thought as a resource, even an ally, for Orthodox theology.[4]

The influence of Metropolitan Filaret of Moscow on Archimandrite Feodor was also very significant. Filaret (Drozdov, 1782–1867) had been rector of St Petersburg Theological Academy and was genuinely interested in theological

---

[3] S. Glagolev, 'Golubinskii Feod. Aleksandr.,' *Bogoslovskaia entsiklopediia* (St Petersburg, 1900–11), 4:490. For brief discussions of Golubinsky's contribution to philosophical theology in Russia see Zenkovsky, *A History of Russian Philosophy*, 1:300–6, and Florovskii, *Puti russkogo bogosloviia*, pp. 238–41.

[4] Golubinsky's impact on Bukharev is described by Behr-Sigel, *Alexandre Boukharev*, pp. 45–6. In view of my discussion of Soloviev's and Bulgakov's sophiology later in this work, it is interesting to note Father Pavel Florensky, himself a sophiologist, traced the origins of sophiological speculation in Russian theology to Golubinsky and counted Bukharev as well as Soloviev among Golubinsky's heirs in this respect. See Florensky's letter to Luk'ianov in S.M. Luk'ianov, *Materialy k biografii V. S. Solov'eva* (Petrograd, 1916–21), 1:344, n. 662, quoted in S.M. Solov'ev, *Zhizn' i tvorcheskaia evoliutsiia Vladimira Solov'eva* (Brussels: Izdatel'stvo Zhizn' s Bogom, 1977), p. 90. Golubinsky's legacy is an example of the impact of western thought on modern Russian Orthodox theology resulting from the institution of higher theological schools in Russia by Peter the Great. As Marc Raeff has observed, 'It is the particular character of this clerical education that in large part explains the penetration of the ideas of Leibnizian rationalism, of *Naturphilosophie* and the attraction of Romanticism as well as synergetic utopianism.' 'Georgij Florovskij historien de la culture religieuse russe,' *Cahiers du monde russe et soviétique* 29 (1988):565.

scholarship, especially biblical studies. He kept a watchful eye on Moscow Academy, and his good will was an important factor affecting the advancement of a young biblical scholar. Filaret's dogmatic theology, expressed primarily in his sermons, also played an important role in Bukharev's formation. The metropolitan's theology of the cross, with its stress on Christ as the sacrificial Lamb of God, was one the main sources of Archimandrite Feodor's dogmatic vision.[5]

Between 1849 and 1854 three exegetical essays by Feodor appeared anonymously in *Appendices to the Works of the Holy Fathers*.[6] These were his only publications while on the faculty of Moscow Theological Academy, although they were by no means his only writings. His output was substantial, but most of it was too daring for the theological press of the pre-reform era. Feodor's penchant for drawing out the implications of biblical theology for the contemporary ecclesiastical and social scene was especially troubling to his supervisors, for commentary on contemporary events, whatever its content, was feared because of the controversy it might precipitate.

Three Letters to N.V. Gogol, composed in 1848, is an example of the kind of work that was beginning to alienate Feodor from his superiors in church and state.[7] The letters were prompted by Gogol's *Selected Passages from Correspondence with Friends*, an anthology of the author's views on a wide range of social, political and ecclesiastical issues published in 1846.[8] In *Selected Passages* Gogol addressed his public as a

---

[5] 'As for his [theological] views, [Bukharev] was closest to Filaret of Moscow, as he himself always admitted. The basic idea of his "system" – his whole teaching on the love of the Cross – was taken from Filaret. And even his fateful work on the Apocalypse was not conceived without Filaret's indirect influence. [The Apocalypse] was the Metropolitan of Moscow's favorite book.' Florovskii, *Puti russkogo bogosloviia*, p. 347. An article on Filaret by Bukharev was published posthumously: 'O Filarete, mitropolite moskovskom, kak plodotvornom dvigatele razvitiia pravoslavno-russkoi mysli,' *Pravoslavnoe obozrenie*, 1884, 1:717–49.

[6] See n. 23 below.

[7] The letters were published twelve years later: [Arkhimandrit Feodor], *Tri pis'ma k N. V. Gogoliu, pisannye v 1848 godu* (St Petersburg: V tipografii morskogo ministerstva, 1860). Feodor's reports on personal encounters with Gogol appear on pp. 5–6 and p. 138, note. See also Behr-Sigel, *Alexandre Boukharev*, pp. 51–2.

[8] Nikolai Gogol, *Selected Passages from Correspondence with Friends*, trans. Jesse Zeldin (Nashville: Vanderbilt University Press, 1969).

zealous Orthodox Christian, advancing the view that modern Russia's problems could be solved only by a vital and active Orthodox faith. The book scandalized Gogol's secular-minded admirers. It also unsettled conservative Orthodox who viewed the mingling of secular and ecclesiastical affairs with alarm. Some charged Gogol with 'spiritual pride'; others wondered, 'Why should a spiritual man get mixed up in the affairs and confusions of secular thought and literature, what does a theological point of view have in common with worldly letters?' Feodor tells us that this question was directed also at him for taking an interest in Gogol's work.[9] There could be no question of *Three Letters to N.V. Gogol* seeing the light of day at the time. Monks were expected to avoid controversy. It made no difference that Feodor wrote to defend a prominent Orthodox layman who had witnessed to his faith before a critical, secular-minded audience.

The reason Orthodox conservatives took umbrage at Gogol's and Feodor's publicism in spite of its Orthodox content is clear enough. To ask Orthodox believers to address the problems of modern Russia implied a number of assumptions which the authorities resisted: There *were* problems in modern Russia, the Orthodox Church was not already doing everything it was supposed to be doing to solve these problems, and the solutions might require some new arrangements in church and state.

The tone of *Three Letters to N.V. Gogol*, while not extreme, is sharp. Feodor casts Orthodox Russia as a contemplative eastern Mary who, in contrast to the busy western Martha, has put aside all earthly cares for the sake of salvation. As a result Russia has preserved the holy Orthodox faith, for which the country is to be commended; but from long inactivity Russia's people have become passive and defensive with respect to their faith:

> Russian people, sensing the incomparable value of the treasure entrusted to them, trembled for it, thought only about how best to preserve it and fell into a kind of one-sidedness. The thought lodged in their soul that they would

[9] *Tri pis'ma k N.V. Gogoliu*, pp. 3–5.

perform the whole of their task simply by preserving the heavenly treasure; they lost sight of the fact that they were supposed to use this treasure, to put it to work, to multiply the talents given them through their own labor. They began to fall asleep spiritually. This, at least, is how I understand the thought of [Gogol's] rather dark utterance: 'the mass began to doze.' And how they dozed! What insensate stagnation descended upon the country – everywhere to some extent, but particularly in the remote corners and out-of-the-way places of Russia![10]

'Stagnation' (*zastoi*) was hardly a flattering term, especially as Feodor applied it not just to Russian material culture but to the country's spiritual condition as well.

Three Letters to N.V. Gogol was not the only work which Feodor failed to get published at the time of its composition. Several others were withheld from publication, of which the most important were a series of essays on the letters of Paul and the first chapters of a commentary on the canonical Apocalypse. In both of these cases Metropolitan Filaret made the decision.[11]

The Apocalypse commentary, begun in the early 1850s, was an important outlet for Feodor's prophetic promptings. The Revelation of John, with its dramatic vision of a persecuted, vindicated and radiantly victorious church, had a special appeal for a renewalist. With its mysterious historical allegories it also inspired Feodor to ponder the mission of the Orthodox Church in world history, a question which took on a new urgency for thoughtful Orthodox Russians in the period 1848–54.

In 1848–49 revolutions engulfed much of Europe. While Russia remained calm domestically, military intervention against the revolution in the Austrian empire embroiled the country directly in the upheaval. The result, contrary to the expectations of the Russian government, was the rapid deterioration of relations with the western powers culminating in the declaration of war by England, France and Turkey in the spring of 1854. During the next two years Russia endured invasion, a painful siege and a humiliating peace. The events had an

---

[10] *Tri pis'ma k N.V. Gogoliu*, p. 30; cf. pp. 28–9.
[11] Znamenskii, 'Vmesto vvedeniia,' pp. vii–viii, x–xi.

enormous impact on Russian public opinion and hastened the coming of the Great Reforms. Church opinion was also affected, for the Crimean conflict was drenched in religious symbolism. Originating in a dispute between Russia and France over control of Christian shrines in the Holy Land, the confrontation brought Roman Catholic France, Protestant England and Islamic Turkey into league against Orthodox Russia. The confessional contours of the event – Orthodoxy against the allied forces of heterodoxy and heresy – were an open invitation to prophetic speculation.

Of course prophecy requires a prophet, and Feodor did not claim to be one. However, he believed he had found a worthy seer in Petr Tomanitsky (1782–1866), a supernumerary priest who lived a marginal existence in New Jerusalem, a suburb of Uglich on the Volga north of Moscow.[12] Father Petr was a 'fool-for-Christ' (*iurodivyi*), whose unconventional practices made him an outsider to the established ministry of the Orthodox Church but endeared him to the simple folk and occasionally to educated Orthodox seeking revitalization. As a young married priest Father Petr had conducted an ostensibly normal ministry in New Jerusalem; but after his wife's premature death his behavior took an idiosyncratic turn. He was careless with church funds, did not get along with his deacons and showed signs of mental instability. The ecclesiastical consistory of Uglich stripped him of official duties in 1814. Later he spent some time in an insane asylum before settling down to the vocation of holy man and freelance spiritual advisor.

Father Petr drew upon the full repertoire of Russian folk piety. He liked to pray in the open air on the bank of the Volga, refused to wear the black cassock of a priest, did not take communion but gave wine to his spiritual children in his own quarters, told fortunes by manipulating pebbles, sticks and iron filings, and rendered prophetic interpretations of domestic and world events. Feodor turned to Father Petr for spiritual guidance frequently after 1849. During the Crimean War he sought Petr's interpretation of the conflict and became convinced this irregular priest was the apocalyptic 'mind that

---

[12] For a biographical portrait of Father Petr and a detailed account of his relationship with Archimandrite Feodor see Belorukov, 'Vnutrennii perelom.'

24

has wisdom' (Rev. 17:9) who knows the secret dispositions of Providence regarding the whore of Babylon and her beast. From this fixed point Feodor constructed a chronology which assigned the allegories of Revelation 1–16 to the historical past and the remainder of the book to the future, with the Crimean drama as the first stage of God's judgment upon the whore.[13]

While the irrationality of Feodor's views is surprising, his relationship with Father Petr fits a pattern of behavior that can be seen throughout his career. Feodor was drawn to individuals with something fresh to say concerning the vocation of Orthodoxy in their time. Gogol, who in his own way was as strange a man as Father Petr, was one of these. Feodor also rose to the defense of Ivan Iakovlevich Koreisha, a Moscow fool-for-Christ whom a critic had attacked in the press as a false prophet and dangerous influence on those – mostly women – who went to him for advice. Feodor praised Ivan Iakovlevich for relating the gospel to the concrete, everyday concerns of Orthodox people and found nothing theologically offensive in his ministry in spite of the fact he conducted it from his cell in an insane asylum. The critic, unmoved by Feodor's apologia, replied with a theological criterion of his own: 'We know that prophets do not exist nowadays, and thus everyone who appears to be one is a false prophet.'[14]

In his relationship with Father Petr, Archimandrite Feodor liked to cast himself in the role of a proud, scholarly 'Pharisee' forced to learn humility from one who embodied 'child-likeness in Christ.' The friendship endured. As late as 1863, on the eve of his marriage, Bukharev took his fiancée, Anna Sergeevna Rodyshevskaia, to meet Father Petr. The young noblewoman was shocked by the elder's rudeness, the coarseness of his entourage and Bukharev's self-abasement in his presence.[15]

In the fall of 1854 Archimandrite Feodor left Moscow Academy to become dean of students (*inspektor*) at Kazan Theological Academy. At Kazan he also served as a professor of

---

[13] Belorukov, 'Vnutrennii perelom,' pp. 841–2.
[14] I. Pryzhov, *Zhitie Ivana Iakovlevicha, izvestnogo proroka v Moskve* (St Petersburg, 1860), p. 29. This source also contains Archimandrite Feodor's reply to Pryzhov, dated October 23, 1860: 'Neskol'ko zamechanii po povodu stateiki v 'Nashem vremeni' o mnimom lzheproroke,' pp. 31–45.
[15] Belorukov, 'Vnutrennii perelom,' pp. 815–21; 827, n. 102.

dogmatic theology. The shift in academic field was not unusual for the time, as the boundaries between theological disciplines were not as rigid as they would become later in the century with the growing professionalization of academic theology. Moreover, the change was compatible with Feodor's strengths. His work has lasting value chiefly because of its dogmatic content.

As dean of students Feodor was the head disciplinarian at the Academy. Discipline in the theological schools of the time was understood more or less in military terms. The rules were strict, and harsh punishments were the order of the day. Feodor could not have been less suited to his role. Nervous, emotional, physically unimposing and immensely gentle, he was anything but the stereotypical *inspektor*. His leniency was appreciated by the students, but it brought him into conflict with the administration of the academy. After a change of rectors in 1857, relations worsened. In 1858 Feodor asked to retire to a monastery, a request which he had made twice before during his years at Kazan. Instead of being sent to a monastery, however, Feodor was transferred to St Petersburg and appointed to the ecclesiastical censorship committee. His career in the theological schools was over.

However unsuccessful it may have been in terms of professional advancement, the deanship at Kazan provided Feodor with an opportunity to witness in a public way to the core values of his theology. Father P.V. Znamensky (1836–1910), a student of Feodor's and later professor of church history at Kazan, describes the connection between Feodor's theology and his daily work as follows:

Continually absorbed in his ideas, [Archimandrite Feodor] applied his scholarly and profound view of the Old Covenant in relation to the New to the system of academic life that existed at the time. He viewed the whole disciplinary system of the previous inspectorate as a kind of legalistic tutelage which had no place and was even sinful in the new age of grace, a tutelage based on the dead letter of law without spirit, on an old-testamental fear devoid of the love and liberty of the children of God and operating for the sake of outward appearances. This nervous and impressionable man did not hide these thoughts even from his students. They in turn strongly hoped that in his deanship there would be a weakening of the strict regimen that had held sway before, and in this hope they were not disappointed. By nature and even more by conviction, [Feodor] simply could not present himself in a domineering manner, as all inspectors before him had done. Viewing his service as divine service and, in the spirit of his theological system, conforming himself to the Only-Begotten, he assumed in his own person 'the form of a student,' so to speak, he tried to live the students' life as a member of one body and one little church with them, he viewed everything pertaining to the students as pertaining also to him and to Christ, he reckoned even the students' faults as his own and grieved over them as over his own, as if [these faults] manifested his own deadness and distance from the Only-Begotten. He approached all students with the same tenderness and love, treating those in whom he saw something amiss even more benevolently than the well-behaved. The first time one student appeared before him to be disciplined, the youth stopped outside the threshold of the dean's office and waited in the anteroom, as had long been the custom. Father Feodor took him by the hand and, leading him into the office, observed with a smile, 'It's obvious you are a child of the Law.'[16]

Feodor provides an early example of what one might call liberal pedagogy in Russia, although to him it was simply the Lamb's pedagogy: if Christ assumed 'the form of a slave' (Phil. 2:7) for the sake of humanity, should not a Christian dean assume the form of a student when ministering to his charges?

The theme of divine pedagogy, or *paideia*, was already prominent in Feodor's *Three Letters to N.V. Gogol*. There the essential point was that 'God's saving love in Christ' is not an abstract ideal or external rule, but an indwelling presence, a 'heavenly guest' and 'inner teacher' imparting divine things to the one in whom it resides. 'Everything that positively and progressively expresses all-creative love and wisdom becomes a

---

[16] P. Znamenskii, *Istoriia kazanskoi dukhovnoi akademii za pervyi (dorefor-mennyi) period ee sushchestvovaniia (1842–1870 gody)*, 3 vols (Kazan: Tipografiia imperatorskogo universiteta, 1891–2), 1:129–30.

teacher' for the person who heeds the divine pedagogy; 'the most insignificant of people can be a teacher for him; the most foolish thing shows its wise aspect to him; and the whole universe before him stands as a single, open book of doctrine.'[17]

This 'universe' includes the world of human culture and those who create it. In *Selected Passages from Correspondence with Friends* Gogol stressed the role the creative artist could play in the moral and spiritual education of a people. Feodor takes up the point enthusiastically in *Three Letters to N.V. Gogol*. The key to artistic creativity, he believes, lies in the capacity of the artist 'to hear and proclaim the love that creates and directs all things.' All works that engage this love, which is to say all 'genuine' works of art, have the power to raise our thoughts to God and lead us by degrees 'out of our banal and dead existence to the radiant and life-giving sphere of Christianity.' This is the case, Feodor insists, even when the artist is 'a foreigner, an adherent of another faith or even a pagan.'[18] In other words, while only Christians may be in a position to understand the divine vocation of art in the fullest sense, genuine art is at all times part of the divine *paideia*. 'Even the most secular poem or art in general, while remaining within its sphere, serves Christ in its own way by sensing and reflecting His light as it shines even in simple human and earthly [things].'[19]

In *Selected Passages from Correspondence with Friends* Gogol adduced an example of this truth in a review of the Russian translation of Homer's *Odyssey* by the distinguished poet Vasily Zhukovsky (1783–1852). Though a pagan and a polytheist, Homer can serve as a spiritual educator for a Russian Orthodox person by teaching him

> that in any case he should not lose heart, as Ulysses did not lose heart when in all his difficult and grave moments he called out in his heart, without doubting that by this interior call within himself he was creating an interior prayer to God, which in moments of distress every man accomplishes, even he who has no understanding of God.[20]

[17] *Tri pis'ma k N.V. Gogoliu*, pp. 17–18.
[18] *Tri pis'ma k N.V. Gogoliu*, p. 47.
[19] *Tri pis'ma k N.V. Gogoliu*, p. 57.
[20] Gogol, *Selected Passages*, p. 35.

Feodor seconds Gogol's proposition by observing that the great church father Gregory the Theologian (Nazianzus), had made the same point fifteen hundred years earlier when 'he said of the *Odyssey* that it is from start to finish an encomium of virtue.'[21] The comparison is suggestive, for while Feodor's and Gogol's view of art owed an obvious debt to Romantic theories popular in their century, the patristic tradition, imbued with the Greek idea of the divine *paideia*, provided support for it as well.[22]

MESSIANIC TEXTS

Feodor's first published works, 'On the Second Psalm' and 'On the Second Part of the Book of the Holy Prophet Isaiah,' appeared in *Appendices to the Works of the Holy Fathers* in 1849 and 1850, respectively.[23] *Appendices* was a theological yearbook supplementing a series of Russian translations of primary sources of patristic theology.[24] Until the 1860s it was the only scholarly theological periodical published in Moscow. The title of the yearbook was a clear statement of the way in which its sponsors viewed the task of theology: theological scholarship was a series of footnotes on patristic tradition. This view was not uncreative at the time because the revival of patristic studies was a dynamic development in nineteenth-century Russian Orthodox theology. The publication of primary sources of patristic theology in modern Russian trans-lation was indispensable to this revival, and the yearbook of

---

[21] *Tri pis'ma k N.V. Gogoliu*, p. 52, note.

[22] On the concept of *paideia* in early patristic literature see Werner Jaeger, *Early Christianity and Greek Paideia* (Cambridge: The Belknap Press, Harvard University Press, 1961).

[23] [Ieromonakh Feodor], 'O vtorom psalme,' *Pribavleniia k izdaniiu tvorenii sviatykh ottsev v russkom perevode*, pt 8 (Moscow: V tipografii V. Got'e, 1849):353–403; 'O vtoroi chasti knigi sv. proroka Isaii,' ibid., pt 9 (1850):79–131. A third essay, on Paul's letter to the Philippians, appeared later: 'O poslanii apostola Pavla k Filippiitsam,' ibid., pt 13 (1854): 121–35.

[24] *Pribavleniia k tvoreniiam sv. ottsev*, 48 vols (Moscow, 1843–91). An index covering most of the series was published: *Ukazatel' statei, pomeshchennykh v Pribavleniiakh k tvoreniiam sv. ottsev za 1843–1864, 1871, 1872, 1880–1886 gody* (Moscow: Tipografiia M.G. Volchaninova, 1887).

supplementary essays significantly expanded the scope of the series.

Of course many of the essays published in *Appendices to the Works of the Holy Fathers* were not appendices at all but free-standing compositions on a variety of theological topics. This was certainly true of Feodor's contributions. Far from being glosses on patristic exegesis of the biblical texts under scrutiny, Feodor's essays are good examples of a new biblicism in nineteenth-century Russian Orthodox theology. The author examines each biblical text in its own right, paying attention to its historical context and distinctive message. He makes frequent use of different versions of the biblical text to expose problems or propose solutions. He regularly consults the Hebrew text, often preferring it to the Septuagint and Slavonic tradition. Occasionally he refers to the work of modern western scholars (De Wette, Eichhorn, Gesenius and others), although his references do not indicate more than minimal competence in German. References to patristic commentaries are common but not copious, and Feodor sometimes adduces them to document differences of opinion among the fathers themselves. The Bible is the most quoted source. All quotations are in Slavonic, as Feodor was writing at a time when the ban on vernacular Russian versions of scripture was still absolute. The awkwardness of the official policy is plain to see, since Feodor's essays were written in modern Russian and presuppose an audience interested in Bible study.

In most cases, Feodor's included, nineteenth-century Russian biblicism did not involve radical criticism. Radical criticism may be defined as that which does not just investigate the conditions under which the Bible was produced but interrogates the church dogmas which traditionally provided the framework for interpreting the Bible. Far from questioning the dogmatic framework, Feodor was guided by it. Indeed, he was not so much a biblical theologian as a dogmatic theologian; or better, he did not make the distinction.

With respect to dogma Feodor was a pre-critical thinker. While radical critics of the Bible employ historical analysis to relativize dogmatic claims, Feodor believed history supports dogma. Commenting on Psalm 2, for example, he discusses the issue of the identity of the 'son' whom God addresses in verse 7:

' "You are my son; today I have begotten you."' Feodor knows that 'certain modern interpreters' take the son to refer to actual kings of Judah (David or Solomon), but he adduces 'historical considerations' that rule out this interpretation. For example, the psalm speaks of a rebellion of nations and peoples against the son; but when Feodor examines the rebellions against David and Solomon as reported in the books of Samuel and Kings, he finds no case that corresponds precisely to the scenario described by the psalmist. Concluding the son cannot be one of the kings of Judah, he decides that Psalm 2 must refer to the eternal Son of God, Jesus Christ, whose rejection by rebellious humanity was foreseen by the divinely inspired psalmist David.[25] Obviously, history serves as a handmaiden to dogma in this exegesis.

In 'On the Second Part of the Book of the Holy Prophet Isaiah' Feodor addresses the issue of the integrity of the canonical book of Isaiah. His aim is to refute the theory that the canonical book is in fact two books: one by the pre-exilic Isaiah of Jerusalem (eighth–seventh centuries BCE), the other by an unidentified exilic or post-exilic prophet (sixth century BCE).[26] Feodor believes the entire book of Isaiah was the work of Isaiah of Jerusalem. The problem which he must explain is that beginning with Isaiah 40 the prophet discourses on events and personages of the end of the Babylonian exile, such as King Cyrus of Persia. The historical discrepancy can be solved, Feodor maintains, if we consider the prophecies from Cyrus' point of view. If the prophecies depicting the fall of Babylon, the rise of Persia and the liberation of captive Israel issued from one of his contemporaries, Cyrus would not have taken them seriously. He was a pagan king, not an Israelite, and had no reason to heed the word of the God of Israel. Since he embraced the prophecies as the words of the true God, he must have done so because he knew these prophecies were delivered before his time and merited trust because they were actually determining his fate.[27] Feodor does not stop to consider that the biblical picture of Cyrus as the servant of God might not conform with

---

[25] 'O vtorom psalme,' pp. 354–8.
[26] Isaiah 40–55 are regarded by most scholars as the book of Deutero-Isaiah.
[27] 'O vtoroi chasti knigi proroka Isaii,' pp. 88–90.

the historical personage. His concern is to defend the autonomy of prophecy. 'Imagining the Prophet of the second part [of Isaiah] as no more than a poet-historian, the sophists have entangled themselves in contradictions . . . The point is that the writer was not a poet-historian but a Prophet.'[28] The 'sophists' are the western biblical scholars who question the integrity of the canonical book.

Several of the main themes of Feodor's mature theology are evident in his early essays. First, the choice of subject matter demonstrates an interest in triumphalist, messianic prophecy. Psalm 2 prophesies the triumph of Israel's anointed king over the rulers of the earth. Deutero-Isaiah prophesies the liberation of Israel from Babylonian captivity. Feodor interprets both prophecies in christological and ecclesiological terms: they concern the destiny of Christ and the Orthodox Church. The prophecies also anticipate the visions of the canonical Apocalypse. The 'rod of iron' with which the anointed king will rule the nations (Ps. 2:9) reappears in Christ's promise to his suffering church in Revelation 2:26–8: 'To everyone who conquers and continues to do my works to the end, I will give authority over the nations; to shepherd them with an iron rod, as when clay pots are shattered – even as I also received authority from my Father.'[29] Deutero-Isaiah's scenario is recapitulated in John's vision of the fall of 'Babylon the great' and the triumph of the saints in Revelation 18–19.

Another important theme in Feodor's theology is the twofold sovereignty of Christ. 'As Savior and Redeemer of the world appointed from eternity, Christ is the universal King of grace Who has received gracious authority over all people – Jews and Gentiles.'[30] In other words, the grace of Christ, while universal, embraces two distinct communities: Jews and 'the nations,' or Gentiles. Feodor finds the distinction everywhere in the history of salvation. So, for example, when he considers the nations and peoples who conspire against the Lord and his anointed in

[28] 'O vtoroi chasti knigi proroka Isaii,' p. 121; cf. p. 114, where Feodor refers to De Wette as a 'sophist' (*mudrovatel'*).
[29] 'O vtorom psalme,' pp. 362–4.
[30] 'O vtorom psalme,' p. 373.

Psalm 2, he sees them not as generic rebels but as Gentiles and Jews, respectively:

> 'Nations and peoples': the Septuagint, following the Hebrew, puts *ethnê kai laoi*. For the most part, and especially when they are used together, these words signify Gentiles and Israelites, respectively. For example, 'Rejoice, nations, with His people,' i.e. with God's people (Deut. 32:43). Hence also in the New Testament these words are used in the same sense, e.g. 'a light for revelation to the Gentiles and for glory to your people Israel' (Lk 2:32).[31]

In later works, as we shall see, Feodor often allegorizes the distinction between Jews and Gentiles, creating 'spiritual Jews' and 'spiritual Gentiles' alongside historic Jews and Gentiles. Allegorization generalizes the dichotomy. For Feodor, individuals and communities never respond to 'the King of grace' in a general way but always as Jews or Gentiles. Whether they accept God's grace or reject it, and whether they do so fervently or lukewarmly, they do it in a Jewish or a Gentile way, as at Christ's Passion the Gentiles 'raged' while the Jews 'plotted in vain.' The sovereignty of Christ is always twofold.

It is nevertheless possible to speak of the integral humanity of Christ when this refers to the incarnation. The incarnation, or humanity of God in Christ, is a third important theme in Feodor's theology. The concept is pre-philosophic in Feodor's works, although some of his applications anticipate the philosophical development that comes to fruition in Vladimir Soloviev's *Lectures on the Humanity of God*. In 'On the Second Psalm' Feodor sees the incarnation as the key to understanding the 'most remarkable' verse in the psalm: 'I will tell of the decree of the Lord: He said to me, "You are my son; today I have begotten you"'(v. 7). Are these words addressed to Christ in his divinity or in his humanity? It must be the latter, Feodor argues, since in the next verse the Lord says, 'Ask of me, and I will make the nations your heritage, and the ends of the earth your possession,' words that can only be addressed to Christ in his humanity because in his divinity he is already Lord of the ends of the earth. Yet that which the human Christ hears proclaimed

---

[31] 'O vtorom psalme,' pp. 365–6.

is nothing less than his divine personhood: 'You are my son, today I have begotten you.' As a result Christ's humanity is glorified and introduced into divinity.

In neither of his first published essays does Feodor offer observations on contemporary life. Nevertheless, from the concluding pages of 'On the Second Part of the Book of the Holy Prophet Isaiah' one can infer the direction in which he was headed. He calls to mind the crisis of the Israelite theocracy in Isaiah of Jerusalem's time. The northern kingdom of Israel had fallen, the kingdom of Judah was surrounded by enemies. The cultic sacrifices had lost their connection with living faith and become ritualistic. As for the people and king of Judah, Isaiah tells us their hearts 'shook as the trees of the forest shake before the wind' (7:2) in view of the dangers threatening the house of David. 'Clearly,' writes Feodor, 'there was a crying need in the [Israelite] Church for new, clearer and more exact revelations of the grace to come, for the reinvigoration of a prototypical church organization which was losing its vital significance. It was this great need of the Church, this real demand on the part of believers that the great Prophet Isaiah satisfied with the second part of his book. A spirit of comfort and encouragement pervades the entire part.'[32]

The preaching of comfort, courage, renewal and 'grace to come' to a theocracy and church debilitated by formalistic religiosity and outside threats: this was Feodor's view of Isaiah's calling in old Israel and of his own calling in modern Russian Orthodoxy. To link the two ministries explicitly he needed only the freedom to draw analogies between sacred history and the contemporary world. When the day of freedom came, Feodor was ready to prophesy to his contemporaries. The prophetic word, after all, is always a word for today.

[32] 'O vtoroi chasti knigi sv. proroka Isaii,' pp. 128–9.

2

Orthodoxy and the Modern World

When Feodor arrived in St Petersburg in 1858 to take up his assignment as an ecclesiastical censor, he found himself in a position to get some of his works published. As a member of the committee charged with reviewing manuscripts by church authors, he could now make his case from the inside. He also benefited from the spirit of the age. A liberal atmosphere pervaded Russia, and especially St Petersburg, following the accession of Tsar Alexander II in 1855. The Great Reforms were at hand, and Russians were discussing their problems with unprecedented freedom. It was a good time and a good place to be a renewalist.

In 1860, with the help of the editors of *Strannik* (*The Pilgrim*), one of the new theological journals which sprang up during the reform period, Feodor brought out his best known work, *On Orthodoxy in Relation to the Modern World*.[1] A collection of essays on the titular theme, *On Orthodoxy* created a sensation in the Orthodox reading public by proposing the Orthodox Church open a dialogue with the forces of 'modernity' (*sovremennost*').[2] The idea had been dear to Feodor

---

[1] Arkhimandrit Feodor, *O pravoslavii v otnoshenii k sovremennosti, v raznykh stat'iakh*, Izdanie 'Strannika' (St Petersburg: V Tipografii Torgovogo Doma S. Strugovshchikova, G. Pokhitonova, N. Vodova i Ko., 1860). The book was reprinted early in the twentieth century: Arkhimandrit Feodor (A.M. Bukharev), *O pravoslavii v otnoshenii k sovremennosti*, Besplatnoe prilozhenie k zhurnalu 'Tserkovnyi Golos' za 1906 god (St Petersburg: Sinodal'naia tipografiia, 1906). All references to *O pravoslavii* in the present study are to the 1860 edition.

[2] Archimandrite Feodor was not the only Orthodox churchman to call for a dialogue with the forces of modernity. The same idea inspired the Moscow priests who launched *Pravoslavnoe obozrenie* (*The Orthodox Review*) in 1860 and the academic theologians who contributed to the flourishing theological press in Russia after 1860. Vera Shevzov has told the story of *Pravoslavnoe obozrenie*

since the 1840s; but it was new to most Orthodox people, and many considered it dangerous.

Feodor's most outspoken critic was V.I. Askochensky (1813–79), editor of *Domashniaia beseda* (*Family Conversation*).[3] Askochensky had a background in theology, having taught patrology at Kiev Theological Academy, but in the 1850s he turned to journalism. The polemical atmosphere of the Russian press suited him. As criticism of the church and other pillars of Russian tradition intensified, Askochensky employed the same crude tools to defend Orthodoxy as the secularist radicals used to attack it. Toward Archimandrite Feodor he harbored a grudge because of the latter's allegedly critical attitude toward *Domashniaia beseda* on the censorship committee. But the antipathy went deeper. A journalistic street-fighter, Askochensky could not abide the saintly archimandrite's openness to the world outside the Orthodox community. When Archimandrite Feodor used the pages of a secular journal, *Syn otechestva* (*Son of the Fatherland*), to reply to some of Askochensky's criticisms, Askochensky pointed out the journal was edited by a Roman Catholic (A.V. Starchevsky) and complained that Feodor 'may have wished to show by this that in the name of modernity and civilization Orthodoxy can make peace with Catholicism and even Judaism.'[4] When Archimandrite Feodor wrote that all human beings should be regarded as icons created in the image of God and hence worthy of honor, Askochensky exclaimed: 'What? So gypsy girls, prostitutes, Jews and Can-Can dancers are all icons of God

---

in two excellent unpublished papers: '*Pravoslavnoe obozrenie* 1860–1870: An Overview' and '*Pravoslavnoe obozrenie* and the Academic Theologians' View on Orthodoxy and "Modernity" in the 1860s.' The latter was presented at the Second International Scientific and Ecclesiastical Conference on the Millennium of the Baptism of Russia, Moscow, May, 1987. The best study of the institutional (as distinct from cultural, philosophical and theological) aspects of clerical liberalism in the period is Gregory L. Freeze, *The Parish Clergy in Nineteenth-Century Russia: Crisis, Reform, Counter-Reform* (Princeton: Princeton University Press, 1983).
[3] For a biographical sketch of Askochensky see Behr-Sigel, *Alexandre Boukharev*, p. 60, n. 89.
[4] Quoted by P.V. Znamenskii, *Pravoslavie i sovremennaia zhizn': polemika 60-kh godov ob otnoshenii pravoslaviia k sovremennoi zhizni (A.M. Bukharev)* (Moscow: 'Svobodnaia Sovest'', 1906), pp. 25–6.

Himself and worthy of honor? Lord, have mercy! This is blatant iconoclasm, which has now spoken its final word.'[5]

Askochensky's vituperative attacks on Archimandrite Feodor disturbed the peace of the central church administration, for whom any debate about the church's role in society was a bad sign. The assignment of blame – did it belong to Askochensky for his attacks on a clerical author or to Feodor for writing *On Orthodoxy* in the first place? – became a matter of bureaucratic infighting. The Bukharev Affair had begun. It would end in 1863 when Feodor requested release from holy orders and was defrocked.[6]

On Orthodoxy is a collection of sixteen essays on a wide variety of topics. Three essays (2, 11, 14) bear the common title, 'On the Modern World in Relation to Orthodoxy.' They form a single composition which Feodor divided up and distributed to enhance the thematic unity of the collection. 'On the Modern World in Relation to Orthodoxy' offers a brief sketch of the main periods of church history from earliest days to the Enlightenment with observations on the relevance of each period for the modern situation. Feodor proceeds similarly in most of the other essays. Taking a topic from scripture or church history he expostulates on it in the light of the challenges and opportunities facing Orthodoxy in the modern world.[7]

---

[5] Quoted by Znamenskii, *Pravoslavie i sovremennaia zhizn'*, pp. 70–1.

[6] The best account of the Bukharev Affair is P.V. Znamenskii, *Pravoslavie i sovremennaia zhizn'*; see n. 4 above. This work first appeared in *Pravoslavnyi sobesednik*, 1902, nos 4–6, 9–11 and came out as a separate monograph under the title *Bogoslovskaia polemika 1860-kh godov ob otnoshenii pravoslaviia k sovremennoi zhizni* (Kazan, 1902). Richer in biographical detail is the account by A.M. Belorukov, 'Vnutrennii perelom.' The only treatment based on archival sources is Gregory L. Freeze, 'Die Laisierung des Archimandriten Feodor.' See also Behr-Sigel, *Alexandre Boukharev*, and Florovskii, *Puti russkogo bogosloviia*, pp. 344–9.

[7] The long first essay, 'The Twelve Feasts of the Church,' draws primarily on liturgical material. The largest group of essays, in keeping with Feodor's scholarly background, treat biblical topics: 'On Characteristic Features of the Outlook and Way of Life of the Old Testament Person' (3), 'On the Divine Legislation through the Holy Prophet and Godseer Moses' (4), 'On the Temptation of Our Lord Jesus Christ by the Devil in the Wilderness' (5), 'The Apostle Paul's Teaching on the Anti-Christ' (6) and 'The Unbelief and Persuasion of the Apostle Thomas' (15). Two essays deal with the unhappy and politically sensitive matter of Orthodox–Old Believer relations: 'Pedagogical Notes on the Preparation and Education of Promising Workers for the Conversion of the Erring' (12) and 'The Instruction of Schismatics through the Gospel' (13). One of the most important essays in the

The disparity of the contents of *On Orthodoxy* initially obscures the focus of the book, but the patient reader will come to appreciate a unity which is no less convincing for being achieved by indirect means. Rather than laying out his theological vision in abstract terms, Feodor articulates it anew in each topical context. The result is a basic congruence between the overall proposition of *On Orthodoxy*, namely the call for a fresh engagement between Orthodoxy and the modern world, and authorial method. *On Orthodoxy* does not have a clear beginning or end. It starts, stops and starts again many times. In a sense the book is all middle. In this respect it replicates the experimental and dialogical character of Feodor's project.

THE BURIED TREASURE

Feodor begins the lead essay of *On Orthodoxy*, 'The Twelve Feasts of the Church,' by quoting a discourse of Filaret of Moscow on the parable, 'The kingdom of heaven is like treasure hidden in a field' (Mt 13:44). In the metropolitan's allegory the field represents the individual human being; the deep place where the treasure is buried, the human heart; the treasure itself, 'the new life from God' bestowed by the indwelling Holy Spirit. All Christians, regenerated by baptism, possess this treasure, yet not all make use of it. 'The imperishable seed does not germinate in us, does not flower, does not bear fruit.'[8] Archimandrite Feodor takes up Filaret's allegory but applies it beyond the pietistic framework in social, national and ecclesiastical contexts. The Russian people received the gift of regeneration by accepting Orthodoxy in the time of Vladimir. But just as Christian individuals sometimes fail to own the gift truly, so do Christian nations. The thought fills Feodor with alarm:

---

book, 'The Appearance of Christ to the World (Ivanov's Painting)' (9), is unique in that it treats a work by a nineteenth-century Russian artist. The remaining essays are 'On Principles in Everyday or Civic Affairs' (7), 'The Gospel Read at Thanksgiving Services for the Royal Family' (8), 'A Sermon Preached in Lent at the Burial of a Student' (10) and a brief 'Conclusion' (16).

[8] 'Beseda vysokopr. Filareta, mitrop. Mosk., o *novom rozhdenii svyshe*,' quoted in 'Dvanadesiatye tserkovnye prazdniki,' *O pravoslavii*, p. 3.

Whence comes this terrible misfortune which removes us from the state of Christ the New Adam and returns us to the state of the Old Adam (even though we left it at the time of baptism and, as a nation, at the time of Vladimir, Equal of the Apostles)? Does it come from the non-Orthodox West, or from our own inattention and infidelity to the real power of Orthodoxy – something which also harms the West to which we have a duty to reveal the value of Orthodoxy? Whichever is the case, we need to try as hard as we can, both as individuals and collectively as a society, to find a way out of a misfortune so destructive of our present and future life[9]

Throughout *On Orthodoxy* Feodor presses the same case: Orthodoxy is a heavenly treasure, but Orthodox people obscure the fact by apathy, lack of faith and failure to share the treasure with their neighbors, including the West. Feodor summons his fellow Orthodox 'not to bury but to use' the gift entrusted to them. He exhorts them to remember the truth of Christ is not their private possession but 'a treasure for the whole world, and consequently that we who possess this treasure are debtors before the whole world.'[10] He reminds his fellow Russians that they bear particular responsibility for the Orthodox cause because Russia, alone among the eastern Christian countries, is strong and independent. Yet when Feodor ponders the question, 'What is the present condition of the new Israel?,' he sadly concludes 'both in spirit and in power, it is in many respects the same as that of [old] Israel when it was oppressed by the Gentiles in Egypt.'[11] How have things come to such a pass?

As Feodor analyzes it, the breakdown of the evangelical mission in Orthodoxy mirrors the twofold structure of the original revelation. It will be recalled that Christ and the Gospel were not revealed to a generic humanity, but to Jews and Gentiles, respectively. Christ was given as 'a light for revelation to the Gentiles and for glory to your people Israel' (Lk 2:32).

---

[9] 'Dvanadesiatye tserkovnye prazdniki,' *O pravoslavii*, pp. 4–5.
[10] 'Ob osobennostiakh v obraze vozzreniia i zhizni vetkhozavetnogo cheloveka,' *O pravoslavii*, pp. 90–2.
[11] 'O Bozhestvennom zakonodatel'stve chrez sv. proroka i Bogovidtsa Moiseia,' *O pravoslavii*, p. 134; cf. p. 142.

Feodor ponders the duality of Simeon's utterance in a meditation on the Feast of the Presentation (Candlemas):

> St Simeon greeted the God-child whom he had met and taken into his arms as 'a light for revelation to the Gentiles and for glory to your people Israel.' Now, you know that even in the Christian world (and sometimes even among us Orthodox) there is a certain moral and spiritual tendency in which people show zeal only for the letter of God's law, the letter of Orthodoxy, as the Jews did in their day. Then there is another tendency which, in the various fields of thought and in social, domestic and private life, leads people to take as their vital principle of action not Christ, but ideas and norms drawn from outside of Him, and sometimes even unbridled passions pure and simple.
>
> The first tendency can rightly be called spiritually Jewish, the second, spiritually Gentile, for the spirit and power of Judaism and paganism, respectively, precisely characterize the designated tendencies. I need not say how harmful and destructive both of these tendencies are – the one causing the Jews to crucify Christ, the other leading the Gentiles to fall away from God and persecute His Church.[12]

Feodor's account of the failure of Orthodox witness in his day relies heavily on this scheme, which is in effect a scheme for Orthodox Christian self-criticism. The Jews and Gentiles whom it holds up for reproach are not the real Jews and Gentiles of Feodor's day but the 'spiritual' Jews and Gentiles in the Orthodox Church. When the church falls short of its missionary vocation, the two communities incorporated in its fellowship revert to type and thereby distort the gospel. The 'spiritually Jewish' distortion takes the form of the reduction of the gospel to a religion of the letter, a self-righteous, legalistic, non-missionary Orthodoxy. The 'spiritually Gentile' distortion occurs when Orthodox people engage in secular pursuits without seeking the presence of Christ in the world or even thinking of him at all. The two tendencies represent opposite ways of responding to the relation between church and world,

---

[12] 'Dvanadesiatye tserkovnye prazdniki,' *O pravoslavii*, p. 22.

but they produce the same result: burying the treasure which is Orthodoxy.

The 'spiritually Jewish' tendency subverts the spirit of the gospel by a strict construction of the letter. A formal, loveless system of Orthodox religious observances replaces the love of Christ for the world. Feodor calls the approach Jewish because it appears to him to resemble the piety of the scribes and Pharisees as described in the New Testament. Feodor cites Paul's explanation of the phenomenon: 'For, being ignorant of the righteousness that comes from God, and seeking to establish their own, they have not submitted to God's righteousness' (Rom. 10:3).[13] Self-righteousness gives the lie to the saving gift of 'the universal King of grace.' It is a difficult attitude to overcome because it is based on a kind of faith:

> Every other obstacle or failure of mind and spirit, since it does not relate directly to faith or to the orientation of one's faith, can easily be detected and corrected in the light of pure faith. But when obstacles and errors creep into the mind and attitude of a person's own faith, that person does not detect them; and what goes undetected cannot be corrected.[14]

In other words, the Orthodox rigorist is the last person to see how far he stands from Christ's love for the world.

Objectively considered, the rigorist does not love the world but hates it. For him the problem of 'Orthodoxy in relation to the modern world' is easily solved: the modern world is to be rejected and Orthodoxy shielded from the winds of change. Feodor believes this attitude takes Orthodoxy back to the pre-evangelical dispensation. He compares Orthodox rigorists to John the Baptist, whose stern message of repentance and ascetical lifestyle befitted the forerunner of Christ but not those who have received the gift of Christ.[15] He sees the rigorists as

---

[13] 'Dvanadesiatye tserkovnye prazdniki,' O pravoslavii, p. 11.
[14] 'O sovremennosti v otnoshenii k pravoslaviiu,' O pravoslavii, pp. 51–2.
[15] 'Dvanadesiatye tserkovnye prazdniki,' O pravoslavii, pp. 11–12, 26–7. In the second reference Feodor discusses the incident reported in Mk 2:18–20, where people ask Jesus, 'Why do John's disciples and the disciples of the Pharisees fast, but your disciples do not fast?' Feodor interprets the passage to support his view that the faith commanded by Jesus is 'quite different from the strict and jealous spirit of John.'

backing away from Christ to the religion of Moses and Elijah, although the real Moses and Elijah have already joined Christ on Mount Tabor and become 'partakers of the glory and light of Christ's Transfiguration.' In the Tabor light 'all ecclesiastical laws and institutions ... which our formalism has reduced to a dead, old-covenantal state come to life and stand revealed in all their gracious power and glory.' Rather than feeling weighed down by problems, Christians should rejoice and exclaim with the witnesses of the transfiguration, 'It is good for us to be here' (Mk 9:5).[16]

Feodor is not deterred by the objection that a rigorist, world-rejecting piety can be found in the Christian dispensation, such as in the heroic witness of the early Christian martyrs. A careful examination of their example, he believes, upholds his critique of latter-day Orthodox rigorism. He points out that the world in which he and his contemporaries live is for the most part not a place where Orthodox Christians risk their lives for the faith. If, like the martyrs, they wish to participate in the Passion of Christ, they must do so in some other way than by physically suffering for Orthodoxy. What might this be?

The clue lies in the Passion itself. Christ did not reject the world but endured it as the Lamb of God, lovingly taking its sins upon himself. Those who would imitate the way of the martyrs in the modern world should do so by manifesting the love of the Lamb toward all people, even the enemies of Orthodoxy. Zeal without love, on the other hand, is actually a form of complacency:

> If we do not share the spirit and attitude of the Lord's love by which, as the Word of God puts it (Gal. 3:13), 'he became a curse for us' sinful and wayward human beings, then our firm faith, however zealous, will not be far removed from spiritual complacency, a complacency more or less connected with the censure of other people for their deficiencies and errors with regard to faith. Our zeal against all that is hostile to Christ will not be far removed from a repugnant and frightening spirit of intolerance. Guided and inspired by such dispositions, our actions will certainly not be a fruitful seed for

---

[16] 'Dvanadesiatye tserkovnye prazdniki,' O pravoslavii, p. 28.

Christianity but will quickly desiccate all that is alive and fruitful in Christianity. Yes, ours is a time when a person may campaign for Christ in word, but upon closer inspection one sees that many a [fighter] campaigns confidently and self-righteously for the dead letter of one or another verity without wishing to know the true spirit of Christ [in the matter]. This amounts to judaizing in Christianity.[17]

If the age of the martyrs should not be cited to support a loveless rigorism, neither should the age of the ecumenical councils that succeeded it. To be sure, the church fathers displayed uncompromising rigor in the definition and defense of Orthodox dogma, but one must keep in mind that 'those who struggled for Orthodoxy in the period of the ecumenical councils stood not for the dead letter of faith but for the actual power of the union of human beings with God in Christ.' The fathers were concerned with the real salvation of the human race. 'And as the zeal of these fighters for Orthodoxy was animated explicitly by love of humankind in pursuit of human salvation, so it was combined with the extreme care, tolerance and self-denial of love.'[18] Rigorism without love, on the other hand, is a kind of blasphemy against the Holy Spirit. It amounts to supposing 'that the Spirit can no longer imbue believers with the mind and disposition of that same love of Christ for human beings and for the world [by which Christ emptied himself for the sake of the world] . . . as if nowadays the truth of Christ only condemns and rejects the sinful world rather than graciously guiding and saving it.'[19] As Feodor reads the record, then, church history does not support the rigorist or 'spiritually Jewish' approach to Orthodoxy.

The 'spiritually Gentile' attitude trades the power of the gospel for 'Gentilism' or 'paganism' (*iazychestvo* in Russian translates both). Today one would say 'secularism,' a word that did not exist in Feodor's vocabulary. The challenge posed by secularism concerns the relationship of faith to the spheres of life in the world, such as family, nation, state, arts and sciences.

[17] 'O sovremennosti v otnoshenii k pravoslaviiu,' *O pravoslavii*, pp. 54–5.
[18] 'O sovremennosti v otnoshenii k pravoslaviiu,' *O pravoslavii*, pp. 62–3; cf. pp. 56–7.
[19] 'O sovremennosti v otnoshenii k pravoslaviiu,' *O pravoslavii*, p. 67.

The Gentile view is these matters lie beyond the purview of the church, that the principles by which they are structured cannot be derived from the gospel. Feodor sees this view as contrary to the biblical faith in both the Old Covenant and the New:

> Especially as far as the life of the family, nation and state is concerned, in the Old Covenant it all formed a context which elevated the believer to a vision, albeit from afar, of the grace of Christ to come and to the appropriation of the blessings of grace. As for us who already know and possess in Christ the very essence of grace and truth, we can and must build and develop our own familial, national and political order on the basis of Christ's truth and grace, directly and fully self-consciously.'[20]

Feodor believes the same about the arts and sciences. He finds exciting examples of inspired artists and thinkers in the Old Testament, such as Bezalel, constructor of the tabernacle, whom God filled with his Spirit and with 'knowledge in every kind of craft, to devise artistic designs, to work in gold, silver, and bronze, in cutting stones for setting, and in carving wood, in every kind of craft' (Ex. 35:31–3).[21] And of course Moses grew up among the Egyptians and mastered their learning. The all-embracing nature of Christ's truth is even more evident to Feodor in the New Covenant, for in Christ 'are hidden all the treasures of wisdom and knowledge' (Col. 2:3). When Orthodox people exempt the concerns of worldly life from the sovereignty of Christ they become in effect 'the same fleshly people as the other children of Adam and Eve.'[22] Christians are not called to be latter-day Gentiles any more than they are called to be latter-day Jews. They are called to new life in Christ in every sphere of their existence.

Yet when Feodor looked at his church and his society he saw plenty of Gentiles. On the one hand there were Russians who

---

[20] 'Ob osobennostiakh v obraze vozzreniia i zhizni vetkhozavetnogo cheloveka,' *O pravoslavii*, p. 89.
[21] 'O Bozhestvennom zakonodatel'stve chrez sv. proroka i Bogovidtsa Moiseia,' *O pravoslavii*, pp. 140–1.
[22] 'Ob osobennostiakh v obraze vozzreniia i zhizni vetkhozavetnogo cheloveka,' *O pravoslavii*, p. 90.

considered themselves Orthodox but did not take Orthodoxy into account in a principled way when managing secular affairs. Feodor convicts them of 'hypocrisy toward their own conscience.' The fervent love of God, 'strong as death' (Song of Songs 8:6), cannot bear such ambivalence. Other Russians were Gentiles because they had lost their faith and embraced some other ultimate principle. Interestingly, Feodor shows more patience and charity toward these unbelievers than toward the 'hypocrites.' But he cautions them against accepting one or another theory of the nature of things 'on blind faith,' only to discover later it falls short. They would do better to investigate the actual ground of things because this inquiry will eventually lead them to Christ. Feodor is convinced

> our truly innate, spiritual ideas about truth and goodness, about beauty and being, and the truly supreme laws of our reason are fundamentally and essentially luminous and shining indications of 'the Light that enlightens every human being who comes into the world' (Jn 1:9), namely, Christ the Divine Word, the foundation of all things; [they are] indications of our spiritual nature even in its present state of disorder and alienation from God.[23]

Feodor's conviction is a very old one in Christian theology, going back at least as far as the second-century Apologists. Christ, the focal point and head of the church, is also 'the light that enlightens every human being who comes into the world,' the source of all goodness, truth and beauty. The Christian faith is cosmic and universal.

If this is so, Orthodox Christians should act accordingly, approaching the Gentiles in their midst with spiritual and intellectual generosity. The problem was that many Orthodox found it difficult to relate to unbelievers in this way. Unbelief was a relatively new phenomenon in Russia in the middle of the nineteenth century, and most Orthodox people saw it as a malignancy. Always on the look-out for the positive, Feodor saw unbelief as presenting an occasion for self-criticism and renewal among the Orthodox:

[23] 'O Bozhestvennom zakonodatel'stve chrez sv. proroka i Bogovidtsa Moiseia,' *O pravoslavii*, pp. 142–4.

How is it that this misfortune [unbelief] has in many respects crept in among us Orthodox? Is it not precisely to keep us from spiritual pride toward other nations, the pride from which old Israel perished so terribly? But even without this we as Orthodox Christians should know that Orthodoxy, the truth of Christ unadulterated by falsehood, is a treasure for the whole world; consequently that we who possess this treasure are debtors before the whole world – debtors who will be judged along with all the nations at the Last Judgment of Christ if we do not try to disclose, adequately and accessibly for all people, the true and universal significance of the treasure of Orthodoxy which we possess. Or is this inattention to the illuminating treasure – so strange as to be incomprehensible, yet so usual among us – nothing less, perhaps, than a sign of our spiritual immaturity?[24]

Moreover, Feodor does not see the Gentile interest in worldly life as a totally negative thing any more than he condemns the Judaic concern for purity of faith. He believes his secular-minded contemporaries for the most part 'have not deliberately turned away from God's truth; they simply love the systems of this world with a special energy, they are concerned with the means, the conveniences and the proper ordering of earthly life, they wish to busy themselves with the world as it actually is in this life, and furthermore (let us give them their due) they try to go about their business in a sound and rational way.' Is it 'contrary to God's truth and love' for Christians 'to descend to this [secular] condition?' How could it be, Feodor wonders, when 'Christ himself, in order to raise earth-bound humanity to heaven, came down from heaven to earth?' If Christ was not concerned with the salvation of 'everything on earth,' why did he teach his followers to pray, 'Thy will be done on earth as in heaven?'[25]

In short, the treasure of Orthodoxy is not a transcendental or heavenly vision, but communion with the Word of God incarnate. 'The whole truth of the New Covenant, and also of

---

[24] 'Ob osobennostiakh v obraze vozzreniia i zhizni vetkhozavetnogo cheloveka,' *O pravoslavii*, pp. 91–2.
[25] 'O Bozhestvennom zakonodatel'stve chrez sv. proroka i Bogovidtsa Moiseia,' *O pravoslavii*, pp. 135–6.

all Orthodox church life,' is contained in 'that love by which the consubstantial Son of God took the whole of human nature into the unity of His Person for the salvation of human beings, and in this [human] nature was revealed as the Lamb of God who takes away the sins of the world, bearing even unto death the burden of all our errors and crimes, as if he himself were guilty of them all.'[26] Christ, the Word made flesh, is the measure of Orthodox truth. Secularists and Orthodox rigorists alike fall short of it, the former by failing to see the world in relation to its divine ground and destiny, the latter by shunning and condemning the world. Both stances are one-sided. The task of incarnational theology is to widen the view on both sides, for 'as long as the judaic spirit holds us in its fetters, that other approach, the Gentile one, will not unshackle its captives, either. For to liberate these last we must take the truth of grace into the very place of captivity. No other *exodus* from the contemporary moral and intellectual Egypt is imaginable in the light of the Word of God.'[27] Captives of partial truths, 'spiritual Jews' and 'spiritual Gentiles' live in alienation from each other. The Word made flesh brings them together to discover the treasure of Orthodoxy.

THE HUMANITY OF GOD

The meaning of the Word made flesh may be expressed by the term *bogochelovechestvo*, the divine humanity or humanity of God. In Feodor's theology the term appears now and then without being singled out for special treatment, as when he describes Christ as 'putting his Divine Humanity on the line, so to speak, for the salvation of everything human from falsehood and sin, for all human beings, Jews and Gentiles, for all who are weak and perishing.'[28]

In an important respect Feodor's discussion of the humanity of God foreshadows things to come in Russian theology. Feodor

---

[26] 'O Bozhestvennom zakonodatel'stve chrez sv. proroka i Bogovidtsa Moiseia,' *O pravoslavii*, p. 136.
[27] 'O Bozhestvennom zakonodatel'stve chrez sv. proroka i Bogovidtsa Moiseia,' *O pravoslavii*, p. 137.
[28] 'O Bozhestvennom zakonodatel'stve chrez sv. proroka i Bogovidtsa Moiseia,' *O pravoslavii*, p. 139.

offers the idea of the humanity of God as a basis for dialogue between Orthodoxy and modern philosophy. He writes about a friend of his 'who entered into the dark depths of thought which distorts Christ's truth in modern philosophy; and he was amazed, and amazed me, by the abundance of Christ's light which is disclosed there to the believing mind.' The philosophy in question was German idealism, which Feodor's friend regarded as approximating the truth of the humanity of God in some measure:

> Just as the spirit and power of the self-immolating Lamb of God who takes away the sins of the world proceed 'into all the earth' for all time through the 'sevenfold' gifts of the Holy Spirit (Rev. 5:6), so even philosophers sense the spirit and power of the economy of the God-human. But as children gazing at the horizon or sky embracing the earth on all sides imagine that heaven and earth actually come together somewhere not too far off, so the philosophical mind attributes the mystery of the God-human, which it vaguely senses, to human beings [alone], whence the systems of Fichte, Schelling and Hegel [based on] the deduction of everything from 'the Ego,' the unity of the subjective and the objective, the identity of being and non-being.

Clearly Feodor's friend believed he had discerned rays of 'the light that enlightens every human being who comes into the world' (Jn 1:9) in what some modern philosophers were saying. He also claimed that studying these philosophers enhanced his understanding of the gospel. 'If it were not for the systems of these philosophers,' Feodor's friend concluded,

> or if I had investigated their principles without the help of [your] theory that the Lamb of God takes away even philosophical sins, I would never have acquired such a reverence for what the thought and knowledge of our Savior the God-human during his earthly life meant for the salvation of the human mind. And without investigating the mystery of Christ's grace with regard to the human mind, naturally I would never have been able to appropriate this aspect of Christ's grace in my own thought and mind.'[29]

---

[29] 'Dvanadesiatye tserkovnye prazdniki,' O pravoslavii, pp. 42–5.

This amounts to a defense, on theological grounds, of the value of dialogue with modern, non-Orthodox philosophers.

Feodor does not walk the terrain of philosophical–theological dialogue with confidence despite his obvious interest in the venture. His report relays the results of a friend's experience, not his own; and he expresses the fear that he might not have summarized his friend's report accurately.[30] His account of modern idealist doctrines is sketchy at best. Yet this juncture in his work is interesting because it documents the felt need for a philosophic turn in Orthodox dogmatics. It is also significant Feodor focused the hope of satisfying this need on the idea of the humanity of God. In the work of Soloviev and his successors this idea would bear much of the burden of reconciling Orthodox theology with modern thought.

The most speculative point in Feodor's discussion of the humanity of God in *On Orthodoxy* occurs in a meditation on the icon of Christ's 'Descent to Hades.'[31] In Orthodox iconography the 'Descent to Hades' portrays the risen Christ liberating Adam and Eve, depicted as a very old man and woman, from a black hole representing the realm of non-being, or Hades. Christ the New Adam, the new human being, raises up old mortality to new life. He does the same for all the sons and daughters of Adam and Eve, for he is the one who can say, 'I was dead, and see, I am alive forever and ever; and I have the keys of Death and of Hades' (Rev. 1:18). Feodor appreciates the humanity of Christ was evident before his Passion and death: in his condescension to unconscious life as an embryo in the Virgin's womb, in the learning process of childhood and youth, in the limitations of his human knowledge even as an adult. But it was Christ's pouring out of himself 'unto death ... unto a kind of spiritual *nothing*,' that perfected his humanity. In the God-human '*being* and *non-being* came together spiritually in an unfathomable way, entering into each other in the identity or unity of His "Ego." '[32]

The last proposition was a controversial one. Metropolitan Filaret and others criticized Feodor for ascribing 'non-being' to

---

[30] 'Dvanadesiatye tserkovnye prazdniki,' O *pravoslavii*, p. 42.
[31] 'Dvanadesiatye tserkovnye prazdniki,' O *pravoslavii*, pp. 41–8.
[32] 'Dvanadesiatye tserkovnye prazdniki,' O *pravoslavii*, pp. 44–5.

Christer.[33] Admittedly Feodor reaches a speculative boundary here. Yet his thought is clear enough if we see it in soteriological rather than abstract ontological terms. Christ came down from heaven for the salvation of human beings. But human beings are not ordinary earth-creepers, as the animals are. They live with a strong sense of nothingness on the edge of an abyss. To save human beings Christ the God-human had to embrace not just the earth, but the pit of death. The divine embrace of non-being is a mystery standing close to the heart of Christian faith.

The philosophical needs of modern Orthodox theology could only be met by a gifted speculative thinker, which Archimandrite Feodor was not. Nevertheless, in his dialogue with modern thought Feodor came up with an idea of considerable originality. This was the notion, alluded to above by his philosophical friend, that Christ the Lamb of God who takes away the sins of the world takes away 'the sins of the mind,' intellectual or philosophical sins, along with the others. 'The Lord stands in relation to human thought as He does in relation to other aspects of humanity: He is the Lamb of God who takes away the sins of the world; He took the guilt of all the errors of our thought completely onto Himself.'[34] At first glance the proposition may appear banal: if Christ the Lamb takes away the sins of the whole world he must not omit sins of the mind. But Feodor's interest in this point does not lie in rehearsing the generalities but in bringing dogmatic truths to bear on concrete human problems. The idea of Christ taking away the intellectual sins of the world leads Feodor to envision a fresh and, for Orthodox theology, quite unprecedented approach to modern intellectuality. Rather than seeing non-Orthodox and unbelieving thinkers as enemies of the truth of Christ, Feodor discovers that he can see them as brothers and sisters for whom the Lamb of God sacrificed himself by voluntarily enduring the sins and delusions of their minds. In effect, Feodor can face modern thinkers and say, Not guilty – in Christ. To appreciate the boldness of this approach one has to remember the horror which many of Feodor's Orthodox contemporaries felt toward modern thought. Feodor did not live

[33] Znamenskii, *Pravoslavie i sovremennaia zhizn'*, p. 37; cf. p. 11, note.
[34] 'Dvanadesiatye tserkovnye prazdniki,' *O pravoslavii*, p. 44.

in a liberal society, nor did he serve a church which took its dogmas lightly. In the context of Russian Orthodox integralism Feodor's interpretation of the meaning of the Lamb's sacrifice amounted to nothing less than a call for a more tolerant, more open, less judgmental approach to modern secular thought.

Not that Feodor looked to secular thought for all the answers. On the contrary, he believed by relying exclusively on 'the secular mind' (*dukh mirskoi*) human beings would 'sooner or later bring earthly life itself to the point of total ruin.'[35] But Christ saved the world not by shouting or clubbing it into submission but by taking its nature, even human nature, upon himself. Those who would be followers of the Lamb must engage with, suffer with and be redeemed with their contemporaries. In the Word made flesh God established a dialogue with humankind. A human dialogue in God is a fitting response to the original miracle.

Feodor's tolerance made him critical of the one-sidedness of the Orthodox traditionalists and unbelieving secularists who molded Russian opinion in his day. Feodor compares the situation of Orthodox renewalists to that of the infant Moses in Egypt:

> The state of our moral concerns at present is such that, if something new and refreshing for mind and spirit happens to arise – and if, as is natural, the new thing is also weak and undeveloped, it either falls under the axe of a cruel and murderous zeal for truth or is carried away by a spirit devoid of grace and perishes in embryo. So terribly does the Pharaoh in our minds dispose of newborn spiritual children among us.'[36]

Ever the kind pedagogue, Feodor pleads for patience: 'Take care ... not to demand spiritual maturity this instant, either

---

[35] 'O Bozhestvennom zakonodatel'stve chrez sv. proroka i Bogovidtsa Moiseia,' *O pravoslavii*, pp. 135–6.
[36] 'O Bozhestvennom zakonodatel'stve chrez sv. proroka i Bogovidtsa Moiseia,' *O pravoslavii*, p. 134. Cf. 140: 'But if there should be only a little dewdrop or seed of the true wisdom and disposition of Christ in the spirit of our society, then no matter how the Pharaoh of our minds might devour our newborn thoughts and spiritual promptings, even if the spiritual child of grace should be cast by faith itself into the Nile in a pitch basket, the new Moses will be preserved, handed over to faith for education, enriched by the fruits of secular science itself – this centuries-old Egyptian wisdom – as well as by the unshakable root of Christ's truth and grace

from yourself or, a fortiori, from others. Christ Himself was first a little child for our sake, and as a little child borne in the arms of the Theotokos did Simeon the God-receiver accept him.' Even the stern Elijah, in the great theophany granted him on Mount Horeb, experienced the presence of God not in wind, earthquake or fire but in 'a still, small voice' (1 Kings 19:12). While it is sometimes necessary to discipline 'even the free spiritual child of faith who is Christ's own,' this must be done 'carefully, so as not to offend the Spirit of the Lord, the Spirit of filial freedom, not slavish fear.'[37]

Feodor finds another argument for patience in the fact that many of his contemporaries seemed confused about their basic beliefs. He cites the Samaritans of New Testament times as a biblical paradigm for the phenomenon of value confusion. The Samaritans were neither Gentiles nor orthodox Jews. They represented 'a combination of faith in God's law with pagan license,' not unlike the 'refined paganism' of modern times with its unacknowledged reliance on Christian values. Christ did not reject the Samaritans. Indeed, the latter were sometimes quicker to receive him than his fellow orthodox Jews. Feodor adduces the story of the healing of the ten lepers (Lk 17:11–19). Only the Samaritan among them turned back to thank Jesus. The other nine proceeded to the temple and presented themselves to the priests for purification, too bound to the religion of the letter to acknowledge Christ's love and grace. The Samaritan, by contrast, 'not preoccupied with the false and spiritually calloused zeal of the Jews for the dead letter of God's law surrendered with all his heart to the awareness and consciousness of God's love for him.' Feodor believes the same thing could happen to modern Samaritans. 'The same people and things which have fallen into a spiritually Samaritan schism may still be pervaded more fully and deeply by the all-cleansing and all-ameliorating spirit of

---

in him; and so, with the grafting of all manner of knowledge onto this root, this truly Christian outlook of mind and heart will become aware, and make others aware, of the vocation of liberating New Israel in all its life and learning from intellectual slavery, will survive all the trials of the period of wandering and will reveal at last to the world all the spotless beauty of the bride of Christ, the Orthodox Church, to the joy of the world.'
[37] 'Dvanadesiatye tserkovnye prazdniki,' *O pravoslavii*, pp. 25–6.

Christ than people and things which outwardly appear to stand incomparably closer to Christ.'[38] Feodor is cautioning his Orthodox contemporaries not to underestimate the liveliness of God's love for the 'Samaritans' of the day or the deadening effects of an Orthodoxy practiced with zeal for the letter but not the spirit of Christian faith.

More daunting than value confusion was the problem of outright unbelief, the quintessential intellectual sin. Feodor takes it up in the powerful penultimate chapter of *On Orthodoxy*, 'The Unbelief and Persuasion of the Holy Apostle Thomas.' The chapter is a meditation on the unbelieving apostle, who is remembered in the Orthodox liturgical calendar on the first Sunday after Easter. Feodor takes up the case with a lively sense of paradox. He recalls John the Theologian's vision of the wall of heavenly Jerusalem with 'twelve foundations, and on them are the twelve names of the twelve apostles of the Lamb' (Rev. 21:14). The foundations are the apostles of the church, Thomas among them. Yet 'he who was called to bring the world to faith in the Lord does not himself believe, and moreover his unbelief is of an especially persistent kind.'[39] Feodor examines the Johannine texts on Thomas and finds a consistent pattern of unbelief. En route to the raising of Lazarus Thomas predicts Jesus and the apostles will die at the hands of their enemies (Jn 11:16). At the Last Supper Thomas professes ignorance of Jesus' 'way' (14:5). Confronted with his fellow apostles' reports of the resurrection, Thomas does not believe (20:25). In short, Thomas cannot embrace truth with simple faith; he must have proof. In this he reminds Feodor of the modern age: 'Does not our time in particular stand out for this very attitude, from which the inquisitiveness, distrust and doubts of many people regarding things most holy and precious for human beings arise?'[40] The story of Thomas is a parable for 'a positive age,' as the nineteenth century liked to describe

---

[38] 'Evangelie, chitaemoe na blagodarstvennykh Tsarskikh molebnakh,' *O pravoslavii*, pp. 218–19.
[39] 'Neverie i uverenie sv. Apostola Fomy,' *O pravoslavii*, pp. 318–19.
[40] 'Neverie i uverenie sv. Apostola Fomy,' *O pravoslavii*, p. 320.

itself: an age of concrete, empirical knowledge as distinct from claims accepted on authority.

In what does the good news of the story of Thomas consist? It consists, says Feodor, in the fact the unbeliever is not rejected but redeemed, and not only redeemed but built into the very foundation of the church. Thomas is reckoned one of the Lamb's apostles in order to 'elevate even the most inquisitive mind to the grace and truth of Christ, to confirm in the Lord even hearts which are uninclined to faith.' Moreover, the risen Christ satisfies Thomas' desire for proof: 'Put your finger here and see my hands' (Jn 20:27). This dramatic moment in the story affirms the incarnation. The point is to show that 'the whole earthly and material area [of life] with all its complexity, that area where human beings labor and are heavy laden, should not fall outside Christ's grace and truth.'[41] In other words Thomas was not all wrong; his intellectual stubbornness helped crystallize the meaning of the gospel. Believing that grace can transform unbelief in modern as well as apostolic times, Feodor adopts an irenic approach to the skeptics and unbelievers in his midst:

'Peace be with you,' said the Lord to put them all at ease. By his appearance he confirmed the trustworthiness of the other apostles' witness to His resurrection and at the same time dispelled the darkness of Thomas' unbelief. But that Christ's blessing of 'peace' might be nearer to our heart and mind, let us apply this word of 'peace' to our own time in so far as it is troubled by the spirit of Thomas' unbelief. Let us consider, in fact, what it would mean for us if the Lord were to reveal Himself to our age as the sun of truth in a way convincing to unbelief itself – even in that area of thought which is uninclined to faith, inquisitive to the point of crudity, and which believes only in tangible, earthly things, with the result that it greatly disturbs believers and incurs their pious wrath. Those who now fight each other, the defenders of inquisitive thought and the defenders of simple faith, the zealots of the

---

[41] 'Neverie i uverenie sv. Apostola Fomy,' *O pravoslavii*, pp. 322–3.

heavenly homeland and the zealots of tangible, worldly well-being, would hear the Lord saying, 'Peace be with you.'[42]

THE HUMANITY OF JESUS

The humanity of Jesus is the theme of two of the best essays in *On Orthodoxy*, 'On the Temptation of Our Lord Jesus Christ by the Devil in the Wilderness' and 'The Appearance of Christ to the World (Ivanov's Painting).' Both reflect Feodor's interest in the historical Jesus, one of the central concerns of nineteenth-century theological scholarship.

The temptation narratives in the Gospels (Mt 4:1–11; Lk 4:1–13) have always served Christian theology as evidence of the full humanity of Christ, for they show he was 'like us in all things except sin,' as the Chalcedonian definition puts it.[43] In the nineteenth century, interest in the humanity of Jesus lent new importance to the traditional story. Satan appeared remarkably modern when he offered Jesus bread for the world, signs to authenticate his messiahship and satisfaction of lust for power. What did the positive age yearn for if not bread, proof and power? A decade and a half later Dostoevsky made the temptation story the basis of his celebrated parable, 'The Grand

---

[42] 'Neverie i uverenie sv. Apostola Fomy,' *O pravoslavii*, pp. 321–2. The problem of intellectual sin held Bukharev's interest to the end of his life. Dostoevsky's anatomization of Raskolnikov, the intellectual sinner portrayed in *Crime and Punishment*, inspired one of Bukharev's last essays. Here, as in *On Orthodoxy*, Bukharev insists on dealing with intellectual sinners intellectually, that is to say, by rising to the intellectual challenges posed by such individuals rather than recoiling in zealous rage or imputing dishonorable motives. 'Raskolnikov's crime was of a completely different sort than ordinary crimes; his case called for destroying the spurious principle on the intellectual level – the level of a rigorous and honest mind, a mind that does not deal with life duplicitously or settle for timid half-measures. You may plumb the depths of such a mind with all the power and skill imaginable, but if you give offense by treating it as a case of quixotic pride rather than serious and trenchant honesty, your injustice will cause this mind to withdraw into itself and do nothing but resist you, even if it was not all that disposed against you deep down inside.' 'O romane Dostoevskogo "Prestuplenie i nakazanie" po otnosheniiu k delu mysli i nauki v Rossii,' in Arkhimandrit Feodor (A.M. Bukharev), *O dukhovnykh potrebnostiakh zhizni*, ed. with intro. and notes by Kapitolina Koksheneva (Moscow: Izdatel'stvo 'Stolitsa', 1991), pp. 234–5.
[43] J.N.D. Kelly, *Early Christian Doctrines*, 2nd ed. (New York: Harper & Row, Publishers, 1960), p. 339.

Inquisitor' (*The Brothers Karamazov*, 2:5:5). In 1892 the Orthodox theologian M.M. Tareev inaugurated his theology of kenosis with a book-length analysis of the temptation of Christ.[44] Feodor's essay clearly anticipated the centrality of the story in modern Russian thought.

As a parable for a positive age, the temptation story may be read in different ways. The most conventional reading rests on a dualistic construction: in Jesus the power of spirit overcomes the lures of flesh. The implications are ascetical: the goods of this world must be set aside for things profitable in the next. Feodor rejects this dualism. He observes that when Jesus refused Satan's offer of bread saying, 'One does not live by bread alone, but by every word that comes from the mouth of God' (Mt 4:4), Jesus was quoting a verse from Deuteronomy (8:3) which referred to the actual feeding of the people of Israel in the wilderness through the divine gift of manna. By invoking this precedent Jesus showed he was not rejecting bread but simply putting first things first – the creative word of God ahead of the gift itself. But God, 'who richly provides us with everything for our enjoyment' (1 Tim. 6:17), wants us to have both.[45]

Feodor shows a comparable sympathy for secular values in his reading of the exchange between Satan and Jesus concerning power over the kingdoms of the earth. As Feodor sees it, the issue concerns not just political power but the human desire to master nature and history generally, as seen for example in 'the ambition of modern intellectuality to take everything into account, to explain all the forces of nature and submit them to human control, to exploit all the lessons of the past.' Feodor does not regard this desire as bad in itself.[46] It goes wrong only

---

[44] M.M. Tareev, *Iskusheniia Bogocheloveka, kak edinyi iskupitel'nyi podvig vsei zemnoi zhizni Khrista, v sviazi s istorieiu dokhristianskikh religii i khristianskoi tserkvi* (Moscow: Izdanie Obshchestva liubitelei dukhovnogo prosveshcheniia, 1892). On Tareev, see Paul Richard Valliere, 'M.M. Tareev: A Study in Russian Ethics and Mysticism' (PhD diss., Columbia University, 1974).

[45] 'Ob iskushenii Gospoda nashego Iisusa Khrista,' *O pravoslavii*, pp. 165–6.

[46] Feodor boldly reiterates his appreciation for modern intellectuality in his essay of 1862 on Turgenev's *Fathers and Sons*. He wrote in response to leftist attacks on Turgenev for supposedly ridiculing the progressive movement in the character Bazarov. In Feodor's opinion Bazarov should not be read as a ridiculous or negative character. He is a study in the nobility of a mind which rejects sham and convention in order to seek the positive, all-embracing truth about things. The

when it loses its connection with the divine, for, as Jesus told Satan, 'Worship the Lord your God, and serve only him' (Mt 4:10; cf. Deut. 6:13). Because Christians see this connection with full clarity, they are in a position to help other truth seekers who see it less well. So, Feodor concludes:

> Let us accept with brotherly love and lend the support of our faith to a search which is in fact a search for Christ, albeit still as 'unknown God' (Acts 17:23), in all who conscientiously seek the truth, even if they do not yet contemplate it directly in Christ. If only we did this! Then this terrible, lying temptation would quickly vanish, unto the salvation and perfection of the whole great edifice of knowledge.[47]

Feodor's openness to the secular world is more than an expression of good will. It reflects a reconciling and synthesizing intellectuality. Satan is a dualist. His challenges take the form of either/or propositions: 'If you are the Son of God, command these stones to become loaves of bread' (Mt 4:3); (if, on the other hand, you are a mere mortal, then accept your unmasking.) To Satan Jesus must be either God or a human being; he cannot be both. To Feodor, following Orthodox dogma, Jesus Christ is always both, always the God-human. Taking the incarnation as his foundation, Feodor chooses Christ's both/and over the devil's either/or. The pattern is plain throughout his theology: spirit *and* flesh, word of God *and* bread, Jews *and* Gentiles, Russia *and* the West, Orthodoxy *and* the modern world. Feodor's mind was molded by his incarnational dogmatics.

True, a reconciling mind is not always dialogical; it may be the agent of a monological system. But Feodor had a mission, not a system. His mission, which was to bring Orthodoxy and modernity into a constructive relationship with each other, oriented him to dialogue. The orientation is evident in his interpretation of the temptation narrative. He pauses to

---

pathos of his life is that he does not find what he is looking for. See 'Razbor dvukh romanov, kasaiushchikhsia vazhnykh zatrudnenii i voprosov sovremennoi myslitel'nosti i zhizni: "Chto delat'" g. Chernyshevskogo i "Ottsy i deti" g. Turgeneva,' *O dukhovnykh potrebnostiakh zhizni*, ed. Koksheneva, pp. 148–83.
[47] 'Ob iskushenii Gospoda nashego Iisusa Khrista,' *O pravoslavii*, p. 166.

consider the fact Jesus discourses with Satan and even allows the tempter take him to the mountain top and to the temple when he could just as easily have dismissed him. 'Is not all this long-drawn-out talk [*razglagol'stvie*] with Satan demeaning to the supremely Righteous One?'[48] Feodor does not think so. For a person who is spiritually weak such an extended encounter with temptation is dangerous. But for those who are strong in the Lord, a fortiori for Jesus the God-human, a direct encounter with temptation is sustainable. Furthermore, it is a good thing in that it sets the stage for the effective defeat of the tempter and redeems the weaknesses which the tempter exploits:

> So the power of the Holy Spirit, vesting human weakness with His armor, grants the spirit of malice the freedom to deploy all manner of evil designs against Him, in order to defeat the opponent all the more decisively and triumphantly. Following this prototype, those who are solidly schooled in 'distin-guishing good from evil' will not hesitate to enter the arena of temptations and falsehood in order to reveal the victorious power of justice and truth all the better.[49]

One should not be led by the triumphalist language into mistaking Feodor's point for a piece of traditional moralism. Feodor is marshalling evidence from the temptation narrative to justify the engagement of Orthodoxy with modernity.

Feodor found a promising relationship between Orthodoxy and modern art in the work of a contemporary Russian painter, A. A. Ivanov (1806–58). Feodor's interest in Ivanov was probably sparked by Gogol's discussion of the painter as a model for lay religious vocation in *Selected Passages from Correspondence with Friends*.[50] But Feodor had his own reasons for taking an interest in Ivanov and the painting to which the latter devoted much of his later career, 'The Appearance of Christ to the People' ('The Appearance of Christ to the World,' as Feodor calls it). The subject matter of the work is that

---

[48] 'Ob iskushenii Gospoda nashego Iisusa Khrista,' *O pravoslavii*, p. 160.
[49] 'Ob iskushenii Gospoda nashego Iisusa Khrista,' *O pravoslavii*, pp. 161–2.
[50] Nikolai Gogol, 'The Historical Painter Ivanov,' *Selected Passages from Corre-spondence with Friends*, trans. Jesse Zeldin (Nashville: Vanderbilt University Press, 1969), pp. 146–57.

A.A. Ivanov, 'The Appearance of Christ to the People' (1837–57)

moment in the gospel history when John the Baptist saw Jesus approaching him and said, 'Here is the Lamb of God who takes away the sin of the world!' (Jn 1:29). The idea of the Lamb of God who takes away the sin of the world was, as we have seen, at the core of Feodor's theology. It is not surprising that Ivanov's painting fascinated him.

To Feodor's eye, everything in the painting conspires to impress the viewer with the humanity of God in Christ. One might begin by asking why the artist makes Christ the smallest figure in the painting, placing him at furthest remove from the Baptist who heralds him. The answer, Feodor believes, is that if Christ were placed in the foreground and presented as fully as the other figures:

> He would attract and consume all of [our] attention regardless of the other figures. But in that case *the [essential] idea of the Lord's appearance to the world* would not have been revealed to [us], namely, that He appeared to human beings in our order of things *not for His own sake, but for the sake of us human beings* ... so that our free activity – intellectual, emotional, physical – should not perish but be saved by being brought into the love and favor of God the Father in the very person of our Lord.[51]

The point resonates with the theme of the quietness of God in Feodor's theology. As in the Old Covenant God spoke to Elijah not in earthquake and storm but as 'a still, small voice,' so God sends the Son of the New Covenant into the world as a still, small Christ.

Feodor rightly sees human freedom ('our free activity') is at stake in the way salvation in Christ is understood. In Ivanov's vision Christ does not override freedom but embraces it. Feodor finds one of the most striking features of the painting to be 'the freedom and lack of constraint of the figures and their expressions and positions; neither physical nor spiritual constraint is to be seen in anyone or anything; each person appears to [us] just as he is, just as the Lord found him at His gracious appearing.'[52] Moreover, the artist does not neglect to

---

[51] 'Iavlenie Khrista miru (kartina Ivanova),' O *pravoslavii*, pp. 225–6.
[52] 'Iavlenie Khrista miru (kartina Ivanova),' O *pravoslavii*, p. 226.

represent the diversity of the human condition, depicting both men and women, old and young, learned and simple folk, slaves, Gentile soldiers and others. Ivanov's respect for the freedom and diversity of humankind is the appropriate response to the appearing of 'the One Who will not quench a dimly burning wick or break a bruised reed.'[53]

Feodor shows a particular interest in Ivanov's treatment of women in 'The Appearance of Christ to the People.' The women stand among a group of scribes and Pharisees. The clergymen appear dignified but world-weary. In the women's faces, by contrast, Feodor finds 'a simple, unforced expression exuding peace and purity.' This shows that 'when the grace of the Lamb of God appeared [in the world], it began fashioning the vessels it needed first of all among Israelite women.' In other words, the Jewish religious establishment may have shut itself off from Jesus, but the women of Israel received him. In the church, too, women have a potential for 'bringing the vital and illuminating spirit of Christ to the most calloused souls and offering maternal support and nurture in places where [this spirit] is totally new.'[54] Feodor's interest in women's vocations can be seen as an aspect of his quest for a re-energized modern Orthodoxy.[55]

The baptismal scene in the foreground of 'The Appearance of Christ to the People' allows the artist to present figures in

---

[53] 'Iavlenie Khrista miru (kartina Ivanova),' O pravoslavii, p. 228; cf. Isa. 42:3.

[54] 'Iavlenie Khrista miru (kartina Ivanova),' O pravoslavii, pp. 240–2.

[55] It may be objected that Feodor's reliance on the traditional stereotype of the receptive, nurturing female rules out such an interpretation. However, a comparison of the case at hand with Feodor's discussion of the role of women in society in his article on Fathers and Sons makes it clear we are dealing with a proto-feminist. Feodor regards the female characters in the novel – Anna, Katya, Fenichka – as mediators of the power of reconciliation in a society polarized by conflicts between the males. 'Here is where the Russian poet [Turgenev] appreciates the emancipation of woman, by virtue of which we see that there is truly "neither male nor female" when it comes to the essential task and vocation of humanity, that woman alongside man, and in some circumstances even more than man, can contribute to the enlivening and correction of society and humanity in general. And this can take place, to be sure, in the realm of science and work as well as in the general cause of truth and life.' Feodor goes on to caution against 'distorting this idea of emancipation by one-sidedness or stupidity' of the kind that Turgenev satirizes in his portrait of Kukshina, a caricature of doctrinaire feminism. 'Razbor dvukh romanov,' O dukhovnykh potrebnostiakh zhizni, ed. Koksheneva, p. 179.

various stages of undress, including two nudes. The result is a strong emphasis on the physicality of this presumably spiritual scene. Feodor reports some people were offended by the flesh-liness of the painting, especially the frankly sensuous treatment of the naked, extended body of the youth climbing out of the Jordan after his baptism. The young man is also one of the few figures in the scene who appears to be looking straight in the direction of Christ. In Feodor's opinion, this physicality is essential to the painting not just esthetically and historically, but theologically. He laments the fact that many Orthodox people seem to forget 'that the Lord took our whole nature upon Himself, i.e., not just the soul but the human body, not to destroy but to save human beings even in relation to their own bodies. Think how much of our humanity we treat as hopelessly lost and condemned by forgetting this, when we could so easily elevate it to something saved and spiritual!'[56] Those who object to Ivanov's nudes fail to go beyond a narrow, pharisaical right-eousness. The righteousness of the gospel accommodates everything human.

In the last analysis, of course, the gospel embraces everything human because Jesus Christ, on whom the gospel is founded, is fully human. Feodor's essay on Ivanov ends with the theme of the pan-humanity of Christ. One must note, however, that Feodor presents this theme in a way that caters to the religious and racial prejudices of his Russian Orthodox audience:

> For your comfort I may add that the general appearance of Christ [in Ivanov's painting] is drawn from Orthodox icons of the Savior: an uncovered head with long walnut hair, a beard of the same color, a reddish tunic and sky-blue overgarment. By thus eliminating sharp Jewish features from the face of the Savior, how beautifully [the artist] expresses the fact that the Lord Jesus, belonging to the East and South by virtue of his descent from Abraham and David according to the flesh, belongs to the West and to our North by virtue of his humanity.[57]

If one were to deconstruct Feodor's theology, this passage

---

[56] 'Iavlenie Khrista miru (kartina Ivanova),' O pravoslavii, p. 232.
[57] 'Iavlenie Khrista miru (kartina Ivanova),' O pravoslavii, p. 244.

would be a good place to begin, for one could argue that the universalism which Feodor professes is subverted here by its opposite. On the other hand, if one reads this passage strictly in the context of Feodor's theology, one can see it offers simply another instance of the twofold 'economy' of salvation: Christ comes not to a generic humanity but to Jews and Gentiles. As the glory of the Jews he belongs to East and South; as a light for revelation to the Gentiles he belongs to West and North. As the humanity of God he belongs to everyone.

CHURCH AND SOCIETY

One of Archimandrite Feodor's deepest convictions was that the gospel pertains as much to things on earth as it does to things in heaven. 'The Christian, even when his life and mind are occupied with earthly things, should hold fast to Christ as the head of all things – "things in heaven and things on earth" (Eph. 1:10).'[58] 'In [Christ] all things in heaven and on earth are destined to find their head and reconciliation with God (cf. Eph. 1:10; Col. 1:20).'[59] Piety, as Paul says, 'is valuable in every way, holding promise for both the present life and the life to come' (1 Tim. 4:8).[60] These thoughts led Feodor to take an interest in the secular issues of his day. The Great Reforms era was a period when Russians in many walks of life were seeking better ways of structuring their society. With a theology focused on everyday life, Feodor fit in with the times. He called on his fellow Orthodox to bring the gospel of the Word made flesh to bear on all honest pursuits, 'not just the arts and sciences, but also agriculture, trade and the other earthly interests of our so called positive century.'[61] To these must be added church–state

---

[58] 'Neverie i uverenie sv. Apostola Fomy,' O pravoslavii, p. 322.
[59] 'Pedagogicheskie zametki o prigotovlenii i obrazovanii blagonadezhnykh deiatelei dlia obrashcheniia zabluzhdaiushchikh,' O pravoslavii, p. 298.
[60] 'O printsipakh ili nachalakh v delakh zhiteiskikh ili grazhdanskikh,' O pravoslavii, p. 196.
[61] 'Pedagogicheskie zametki o prigotovlenii i obrazovanii blagonadezhnykh deiatelei dlia obrashcheniia zabluzhdaiushchikh,' O pravoslavii, p. 298; cf. 'Neverie i uverenie sv. Apostola Fomy,' ibid., p. 324, where the list includes law, military affairs, science and technology and the role of women in society.

relations, which Feodor discusses in 'On Principles in Everyday or Civic Affairs,' and international politics, a concern that appears only marginally in *On Orthodoxy* but dominates *Studies on the Apocalypse.*[62]

Of all the Great Reforms none was more important than the abolition of serfdom (1861). In *On Orthodoxy* Feodor comments on it more frequently than on any other contemporary issue. Most of his remarks are designed to persuade a conservative Orthodox readership of the need for change.[63] In a discussion of Mosaic legislation in ancient Israel, for example, he makes a monitory comparison between the ancient Israelite and modern Russian peasantries. In ancient Israel, 'Moses the God-seer organized all the national and civic life of Israel according to the principles and spirit of the promised grace of the Christ to come.' Landholding and agriculture in Israel were handled in the same spirit. This leads Feodor to ask, 'will national and civic life in New Israel, and especially the humble, toiling lot of the tillers of the soil, assume a form that is not subject to Christ's truth and grace? ... It would be a sad and shameful thing if New Israel were to stand lower than Old Israel in this respect.'[64] Elsewhere he speaks of 'putting [the peasants] in a position that corresponds more favorably to their calling in Christ' and 'bringing not just the upper crust but the whole body of Orthodox people to true enlightenment.'[65]

Feodor's discussion of the peasant question is even more pointed in 'The Twelve Feasts of the Church.' The essay takes the form of a letter to a friend who appears to have been a serf owner.[66] Feodor raises the issue of emancipation in a discussion of the feast of Christmas. He observes that Jesus' birth brings together two conditions that are usually viewed as opposites:

---

[62] For *Studies on the Apocalypse* see Ch. 3 below.
[63] For a description of the stance of the Russian Orthodox Church on serfdom in the pre-reform period, see Gregory L. Freeze, 'The Orthodox Church and Serfdom in Prereform Russia,' *Slavic Review* 48 (1989):361–87.
[64] 'O Bozhestvennom zakonodatel'stve chrez sv. proroka i Bogovidtsa Moiseia,' *O pravoslavii*, p. 141.
[65] 'O printsipakh ili nachalakh v delakh zhiteiskikh ili grazhdanskikh,' *O pravoslavii*, p. 203.
[66] See the reference to 'your interests' in 'Dvanadesiatye tserkovnye prazdniki,' *O pravoslavii*, p. 20.

high birth and servitude. As son of David, Jesus was born a prince; as a Jew ruled and taxed by a Gentile state, he was born a kind of slave. Feodor asks his friend to consider that in the peasant issue

> the heart of the matter lies in showing mercy to Christ Himself, the One who for the sake of human beings was born in just such a [subject] state, and in doing Him this good deed in the persons of the least of His brethren. As you share your concerns on this issue with other people of high birth, let all of you use your faith to perceive and spiritually lay hold of that Divine Scion of Kings who for our sake willingly condescended to take on our impoverished nature, and not at the price of a negligible sacrifice on his part. As for the government and Tsar who have proposed the great work of improving the life of the peasants, use your faith to see in them the influence of the grace of the Almighty King who willed to take on the worst part of ourselves in order to give us the best part of Himself, to take on our humanity in order to grant us participation in his Divine Sonship.[67]

Another sign of the times in Feodor's theology was his interest in secular vocations (*zvaniia, poprishcha*). The liberalization of Russian society in the Great Reforms era brought this subject to the fore by shaking up old patterns of social organization. In pre-reform Russia differentiation of spheres and activities existed as it must in any society, but it was greatly limited by tradition. The several walks of life (peasant, landowner, merchant, priest, etc.) were not vocations in the modern sense of the word, i.e. freely chosen professions, but caste-like roles which people inherited and did not have the right to abandon. In the nineteenth century this began to change, especially after the Reforms. Russian society began developing freer and more

---

[67] 'Dvanadesiatye tserkovnye prazdniki,' *O pravoslavii*, p. 21. Bukharev also discusses the peasant issue in 'Chetyre sluchainykh razgovora po 'krest'ianskomu voprosu,' ch. 7 of *O sovremennykh dukhovnykh potrebnostiakh mysli i zhizni, osobenno russkoi* (Moscow: Izdanie knigoprodavtsa Manukhina, 1865), pp. 275–319. Feodor describes his conversations on the issue with four parties: a peasant, a small-time landlord and his family, a group of village clergy and a *starets* (Father Petr Tomanitsky).

specialized forms of labor, and new professions such as law, literature and journalism emerged. Feodor recognized that the illumination of modern Russia by the light of Orthodoxy would increasingly depend on the initiative of Orthodox laity in their secular vocations and avocations. He was greatly encouraged by evidence that lay mobilization was already under way, as in 'the example of Kireevsky in the field of scientific thought [i.e. modern philosophy], the examples of Gogol and Ivanov in the field of art, [and] the example of Speransky in the field of state service.'[68] Feodor regarded the Orthodox laity as 'a royal priesthood' (1 Pet. 2:9) and was genuinely excited by the idea of the priesthood of all believers. He called on his fellow clergy to shun 'the self-exalting spirit typical of the western priesthood, a priesthood concerned above all with protecting and enhancing its privileges vis-à-vis lay people,' and to work instead 'to equip the saints for the work of ministry' (Eph. 4:12).[69]

For all his emphasis on lay ministry, Feodor did not minimize the need for effective clerical ministry in Russian society, especially in a time of change. As he saw it, the attempt to reform Russian society without healing it spiritually could not succeed. Pursuing an analogy with the healing of the ten lepers (Lk 17:11–19) he argued that the work of reform required more than just *glasnost'*, or the public airing of Russia's shortcomings:

> As for the sores and scabs of social and individual life in our own time, the opinion has taken hold of late that we have only to expose these defects mercilessly in print, to publicize them [*obnazhat' ikh v knigakh, ili glasnostiu*], and they will be healed. But the Savior does not at all mandate a cure of this kind to those who suffer from sores and scabs. 'Go,' he tells them, 'and show yourselves to the priests.'[70]

Feodor knew not all of his contemporaries found it easy to walk the path to the church and suggested the clergy was partly

---

[68] 'O sovremennosti v otnoshenii k pravoslaviiu,' *O pravoslavii*, p. 309.
[69] 'Evangelie, chitaemoe na blagodarstvennykh Tsarskikh molebnakh,' *O pravoslavii*, p. 214.
[70] 'Evangelie, chitaemoe na blagodarstvennykh Tsarskikh molebnakh,' *O pravoslavii*, p. 212.

to blame. 'Do the spiritual or worldly defects, real or imagined, that one sees in us, the servants of God's church, hold you back from the path to the realm [of God's love]?'[71] In other words, are the priests and other clergy of the Orthodox Church effective agents of Christ's high priesthood, or are they part of the problem?

Feodor arrived at a fresh idea about the clergy's role in society by taking a look at the high priesthood of Christ. The high priesthood of Christ is not a platonic form or generic priesthood. It is the priesthood of the Word made flesh, of the Lamb that was slain to take away the sins of the world. To Feodor this implied

> we [priests] must awaken and cultivate in ourselves the most solicitous attention to the sores and diseases of human life, to the needs and hardships of our fellow human beings on all of life's paths ... We must take to heart the diseases and failures of the rest of our brethren as if they were our own diseases and failures. If we actually do this it may be that the healing of these diseases will not be far off, for it is only through gracious communion in the love of the all-healing Lamb of God who takes away the sins of the world that we come to accept other people's diseases, even grave ones, as our own.[72]

To put it another way, priests must be pastors, good shepherds who identify with their flock. Engagement with the world is a professional imperative for them. In the Russian Orthodox context this view implied criticism of the ritualism and isolation which characterized many of the activities of the clergy. It also implied criticism of monastically inspired perfectionism. Priests do not have to be perfect to perform the role Feodor would assign them. Their ministry is to imperfect beings whose lot they are called to share. A priest does not fail because he manifests human weaknesses or because he cannot solve all the problems with which he wrestles. A priest fails by paying no

---

[71] 'Evangelie, chitaemoe na blagodarstvennykh Tsarskikh molebnakh,' *O pravoslavii*, p. 212.
[72] 'Evangelie, chitaemoe na blagodarstvennykh Tsarskikh molebnakh,' *O pravoslavii*, pp. 213–14.

attention to the world, by refusing to deal with human beings as they are, by not standing side by side with them.

Another matter which the reform era stimulated Feodor to think about was the relationship of the Orthodox community to non-Orthodox communities in the Russian empire and abroad. While for the most part Feodor addressed his theological critique to 'spiritual Jews' and 'spiritual Gentiles' within the Orthodox community, he occasionally commented on relations with real Jews and real Gentiles. At these moments we see a Russian churchman struggling to live up to the humane implications of the theology of the humanity of God:

> [Christ] became a human being for every human being, taking away the sins of every person as well as of the whole world. With His radiant truth, goodness and beauty 'He enlightens every human being who comes into the world' (Jn 1:9). Thus even when you encounter an infidel, a pagan, a Jew or a Muslim, let your spirit contemplate the One Who, though He was God, put on our humanity for our sake, for the sake of human beings of every time and place, and Who secretly enlightens even this infidel or pagan with the spiritual reflection of His truth and goodness. Unlike the pagan Diogenes, the Christian does not need a lantern to find a human being in the crowd in broad daylight.[73]

A good test of the practical significance of Feodor's view is his attitude toward the Jews, the quintessential outsiders of the Russian empire. Orthodox Russia in Feodor's time was untouched by anything resembling genuine interfaith dialogue with the Jews. Feodor himself shared many popular misconceptions about Jews and Judaism, e.g. the Jews were uniquely responsible for spilling the blood of Christ, the Jews 'forced' the Roman government to crucify Christ; Judaism is bound by 'a dead and slavish spirit consisting of zeal for only the letter of God's truth divorced from its power and spirit,' and so on.[74] At the same time a more humane attitude struggled against this burdensome negativism. 'It would be a calamitous and sorry thing,' Feodor writes, 'if in our zealous insistence on the

---

[73] 'Dvanadesiatye tserkovnye prazdniki,' O pravoslavii, p. 23.
[74] O pravoslavii, pp. 55, 216; cf. pp. 153–4.

responsibility of the Jews for the shedding of our Savior's blood our cries should blot from our hearing and that of others the quiet voice of that same blood of Christ which "speaks a better word than the blood of Abel" (Heb. 12:24) and cries not for vengeance but for mercy and forgiveness of enemies: "Father, forgive them; for they do not know what they are doing" (Lk 23:34).' The key to the thought lies in the comparison of Christ's blood to Abel's. In patristic tradition Abel is the prototype of Christ the Lamb of God, the innocent one who dies at the hands of his brother. But while Abel's blood called down a divine curse on Cain (Gen. 4:10–12), Christ's blood brings mercy and forgiveness. As followers of the Lamb, Orthodox people should conduct themselves in such a way that they, too, 'speak graciously' to one and all. When they act in cruel and bigoted ways, believers incur 'alienation from Christ's truth and grace.' Their misguided zeal 'gives grounds only for various hostile criticisms of Orthodox Christianity' and so ironically fulfills God's word: 'On your account my Name is forever despised among the nations' (Isa. 52:5).[75]

Feodor's struggle to bring his view of the Jews into line with the love of the Lamb can be seen in his comments on the issue of the admission of Jews to the British Parliament. There were Russian liberals in his day who saw such a reform in a positive light. Feodor quotes one who believed that 'the interests of Christianity will be advanced as a consequence of the ever greater separation between that which belongs to Caesar and that which belongs to God.' Most Russian Orthodox at the time believed otherwise. If they thought about such a far-flung issue as the admission of Jews to the British Parliament at all, they viewed it with incomprehension or pious dread. Feodor rejects both the secularizing liberal position and the anti-Semitic one in favor of evangelical non-judgment and humanity:

> Let our readers not suppose that we wish to inveigh against the admission of Jews to the English Parliament. No, our struggle is not with mortal human beings, whoever they might be, Jews or Englishmen. We will do better to see that Jewish and Gentile principles hostile to Christ do not take their seat

---

[75] 'O sovremennosti v otnoshenii k pravoslaviiu,' *O pravoslavii*, pp. 55–6.

on the throne of our own minds. 'For what have I to do with judging those outside? God will judge those outside' (1 Cor. 5:12–13). Let us drive falsehood and evil from ourselves. For then we will be all the quicker and more forthright about taking the side of the human being for whom Christ died, no matter who that person happens to be. And so we will fix our concern not just on that person's external rights, but on his essential, truly human rights as well.[76]

It is characteristic of Feodor to seek a standpoint beyond the polarized positions of his contemporaries, the secularist liberals and Orthodox conservatives. He finds higher ground in a christological humanism. His standpoint is not yet ecumenical or oriented to interfaith dialogue, for he deems both Jews and Englishmen to be outsiders to the true church. At the same time, Feodor's appreciation for the humanity of God and his call for a more humane Orthodoxy, if not yet ecumenical, may be seen as preconditions for the emergence of ecumenical and interfaith dialogue in Russia. Closer to home, Feodor's call for a gentler approach to Russian Old Believers may be appreciated in the same light.[77]

SOME OBJECTIONS

The general lines of Feodor's response to his cultural and ecclesiastical situation are clear enough by now, but a word should be said about the tone of his work. *On Orthodoxy* is a book which conveys a strong sense of urgency, even crisis, about the challenges facing Orthodox Russia in the modern world. Feodor communicates this forcefully in the concluding pages of 'On the Modern World in Relation to Orthodoxy,' where he anticipates and attempts to answer some of the objections he expects to hear from Orthodox conservatives.

The first objection is that worldly people are too sunk in sin

[76] 'O printsipakh ili nachalakh v delakh zhiteiskikh ili grazhdanskikh,' *O pravoslavii*, p. 197.
[77] See 'Pedagogicheskie zametki o prigotovlenii i obrazovanii blagonadezhnykh deiatelei dlia obrashcheniia zabluzhdaiushchikh' and 'Vrazumlenie raskol'nikam iz Evangeliia,' *O pravoslavii*, pp. 265–302.

to appreciate the fullness of the Christian message, hence the engagement with the world advocated by Feodor is naive. 'Are we to be merciful towards people mired in the vortex of this world? Can the word and spirit of [Christian] meekness really have an effect on hard-baked minds and souls?'[78] The pessimism of these questions reminds Feodor of the words of the psalmist: 'The faithful have disappeared [Slav. *oskude*, become few] from humankind' (Ps. 12:1). But Feodor wants to know why the pious should isolate themselves from the world even if their number is few, an allegation which he refuses to concede in any case. Does Christian isolationism express the spirit of the gospel? Feodor adduces the parable of the dishonest steward (Lk 16:1–9) as evidence to the contrary. A steward was squandering his master's estate. When the master demanded an accounting, the steward realized he would soon be out of a job. So he summoned his master's debtors, rewrote their debts and thereby made new friends who would offer him shelter after his ejection from the master's estate. Jesus did not tell this story to condemn the dishonest steward. On the contrary, he commended the thief as an example to the faithful with the observation 'the children of this age are more shrewd in dealing with their own generation than are the children of light' (Lk 16:8). So in his own day Feodor advises that 'true piety can and should "make friends for itself by means of unrighteous mammon" and so find or open up spacious "habitations" for itself in case the number of pious should "become few."'[79] Christians should not doubt the power of the gospel or the reach of divine providence.

The second objection to Feodor's project is that a simple and unsophisticated faith, as long as it is sincere, bears sufficient witness to Orthodoxy in the world. 'What need do we have for lofty and clever philosophizing? Let us treasure and find salvation in the simple faith of the Russian past.'[80] To this Feodor replies that simplicity is not always an expression of

---

[78] 'O sovremennosti v otnoshenii k pravoslaviiu,' *O pravoslavii*, p. 311.
[79] 'O sovremennosti v otnoshenii k pravoslaviiu,' *O pravoslavii*, p. 312.
[80] This was in fact one of Askochensky's complaints about *On Orthodoxy* in an April, 1861 review: 'For faithfulness to Christ we do not need science but simple faith, for the mysteries of Christ are revealed not to the wise and reasonable of this world, but to babes.' Quoted by Znamenskii, *Pravoslavie i sovremennaia zhizn'*, p. 46.

'purity and goodness of heart.' It is actually a form of robbery if it keeps people from recognizing the vast treasures of the gospel. As for the Russian past, Feodor believes it was not all that simple and the Orthodox Church played an active role in it in any case. To assume a comparable role in modern times the church has to come to terms with a Russia which has grown into a huge and complex modern state. Spiritual simplicity is a Christian virtue, but it 'should not be used as a mask for ignorance or apathy toward our neighbors.'[81]

'But surely we don't need western education and progress? Couldn't we become enlightened even without western civilization?' Feodor parries this objection with the argument it would be spiritually dangerous for Russian Orthodox people to 'renounce our brotherhood with the western peoples to such an extent as to be unwilling to profit in any way from them.' Trying to isolate themselves from their 'Gentile' neighbors, Russians commit the sin of 'pharisaic smugness.' Even worse, they abandon the missionary responsibility to share the gospel with the whole world. Feodor pleads with his community to recognize 'that it is high time for us to stop doing harm to ourselves and others by paying little or no attention to the universal light of Orthodoxy.'[82] The universality of Orthodoxy demands a cosmopolitan and activist approach to the church's mission:

> Childish self-sufficiency and careless laziness amount to throwing ourselves down from the height of the Jerusalem temple on the one hand and trusting the angels to catch us on the other. Russian, 'Do not put the Lord to the test.' It is time for you to recognize and utilize the treasure of Orthodoxy as something given to and needed by the whole world.[83]

---

[81] 'O sovremennosti v otnoshenii k pravoslaviiu,' O *pravoslavii*, pp. 313–16.
[82] 'O sovremennosti v otnoshenii k pravoslaviiu,' O *pravoslavii*, pp. 316–17.
[83] 'Ob iskushenii Gospoda nashego Iisusa Khrista,' O *pravoslavii*, p. 167.

3

The Church on the Horizon

A Wedding

While distressed by the attacks on *On Orthodoxy*, Feodor pushed ahead with an ambitious program of publications. In swift succession he brought out *Three Letters to N.V. Gogol* (1860), *Essays on the Apostle Paul* (1860), *The New Testament of Our Lord Jesus Christ* (1861) and a number of shorter works.[1] He also found a publisher for his cherished Apocalypse commentary. The work was in press in 1861, but the Holy Synod delayed publication and confiscated the manuscript for inspection. The following year the Synod officially banned publication of the commentary and deposited the manuscript in a closed archive.

By this time Feodor had been removed from his post on the censorship committee because of the controversy over *On Orthodoxy* and had been sent to a monastery in Pereslavl-Zalessky, Vladimir Province. From there, following the final rejection of the Apocalypse commentary, he petitioned the Synod for release from holy orders. As he explained to friends, his decision to leave the clergy was motivated 'by the impossibility of remaining in a relationship of unquestioning obedience (by virtue of monastic vows) to ecclesiastical authority when this [relationship] is contrary to conscience.' He was also

---

[1] Arkhimandrit Feodor, *Neskol'ko statei o sviatom apostole Pavle* (St Petersburg: V tipografii Koroleva i komp., 1860); *O novom zavete gospoda nashego Iisusa Khrista* (St Petersburg: V tipografii Iosafata Ogrizko, 1861). For *Three Letters to N.V. Gogol* see Ch. 1, n. 7 above. Znamensky tells us that some of Feodor's essays on Paul, written while he was still at Moscow Theological Academy, were slated for publication in the inaugural volume of *Pravoslavnyi sobesednik*, an organ of Kazan Theological Academy which began publication in 1855. For some reason Feodor's contribution did not appear. See Znamenskii, *Istoriia kazanskoi dukhovnoi akademii*, 2:219, 536.

inspired by the idea of working for the sanctification of all things from inside the secular world, in conformity with the kenosis of the Only-Begotten Son.[2]

Granting Feodor's petition, the Synod defrocked him and stripped him of his academic rank. In July 1863 he became Aleksandr Matveevich Bukharev again.

Two weeks later he took another irrevocable step when he married Anna Sergeevna Rodyshevskaia (b. 1840), daughter of a Pereslavl landowner. Coming so soon after his laicization, the marriage appeared to confirm the suspicions of Feodor's critics that he had been a closet worldling all along. Askochensky quipped that by abandoning monasticism and taking a wife Bukharev 'completed the reconciliation of Orthodoxy with the modern world in the most seductive manner.'[3]

In all likelihood Bukharev did not abandon the clerical vocation in order to marry but viewed marriage as a natural consequence of his decision to abandon the monastic life.[4] In this connection it may be helpful to think of the comparable, albeit fictional, drama of Alyosha Karamazov in Dostoevsky's *The Brothers Karamazov*. 'As soon as God sees fit that I should pass away – leave the monastery,' Father Zosima commands the novice Alyosha. 'Leave it forever ... This is not the place for you. I give you my blessing to go out into the world in humility and obedience. You still have a long pilgrimage before you. And you must marry, you must.'[5] Dostoevsky's vision of a monk who gives himself to the service of the world and accepts marriage as an indispensable part of that vocation corresponds exactly with Bukharev's self-understanding a decade and a half earlier.[6]

---

[2] Znamenskii, 'Vmesto vvedeniia,' pp. xx–xxi.

[3] Quoted in Znamenskii, *Pravoslavie i sovremennaia zhizn'*, p. 76.

[4] See the discussion in Behr-Sigel, *Alexandre Boukharev*, pp. 72–9 and Bukharev's letter of July 1862 to his friend A.A. Lebedev, quoted in Znamenskii, *Pravoslavie i sovremennaia zhizn'*, p. 74.

[5] Fyodor Dostoevsky, *The Karamazov Brothers*, trans. with intro. and notes by Ignat Avsey (Oxford and New York: Oxford University Press, 1998), 1:2:7, pp. 96–7.

[6] Znamensky recalls that Archimandrite Feodor 'regarded monasticism itself as a condition that pledged him to selfless service to the cause of Christ, particularly to social service and not just the concern for personal salvation alone. "The monastic state," he used to say, "is called 'angelic' because monks, like the ministering spirits of heaven, are 'sent to serve for the sake of those who are to inherit salvation' (Heb.

It is also likely Bukharev viewed his marriage in terms of the mystical ideas at the heart of his theology. In Orthodoxy as in all classical Christianity marriage is thought to symbolize the union of Christ and his church. This idea had special poignancy for Bukharev because of its prominence in the Apocalypse, which culminates in a vision of the marriage feast of the Lamb (Rev. 19–22). The theme of Bukharev's Apocalypse commentary is the readying of the Orthodox Church to be the bride of the Lamb through her liberation from external and internal bondage. It is difficult to resist the thought that Bukharev regarded his own marriage as a foretaste of the free and glorious life of the church at the end of the age.

Aleksandr and Anna Bukharev's marriage seems to have been a happy one despite misfortunes which might have demoralized weaker couples. Aleksandr's marginal social status and chronic poor health, the couple's lack of means and the death of their only child, Aleksandra, who died in infancy on Easter day, 1869, were heavy burdens for the Bukharevs to bear. Nevertheless, an aura of joy and gratitude pervades the accounts of their relationship. In a memoir and letter describing the last weeks of her husband's life, Anna describes how the two of them marveled over their ability to live a pleasant life for years without a steady income, how Aleksandr begged her to keep the doctor and visitors away so as not to disturb their 'paradisiacal days' together (Aleksandr's words), and how her husband twice whispered 'Thank you' to her as he dozed in a pre-comatose state.[7] When Pavel Florensky visited Anna Bukhareva more than forty years later (1913), he was impressed by the spiritual freshness he sensed in her, calling it 'the ray of a grace-filled marriage, of the fully assimilated grace of marriage.' He also admired Anna's intellectual independence. In her discussions with Florensky she frequently mentioned issues about which she and Aleksandr had disagreed. While she was imbued with the ideas of her late husband, Anna was not just a keeper of the

---

1:14). The specifically ascetical side of monasticism is itself a service, ancillary to the first and main form of service, though it, too, is necessary.'" *Pravoslavie i sovremennaia zhizn'*, p. 10.

[7] See Anna's memoir and the related letter to A.A. Israilev in *Arkhimandrit Feodor: pro et contra*, pp. 380–90, 394–400.

flame and certainly not a slavish disciple. The Christian freedom preached by Bukharev flourished in Anna, a fact which caused Florensky to feel all the more admiration for both of them. Aleksandr and Anna had indeed entered into 'a mystical, Christian wedlock reflecting the apocalyptic marriage of the Lamb with the Church.'[8]

In professional terms Bukharev's first couple of years as a layman were very productive. He published a series of monographs on prophetic literature and on the Book of Job.[9] He continued writing on the theme of Orthodoxy and modernity in articles for *Syn otechestva* (*Son of the Fatherland*). These formed the core of a collection of essays *On the Spiritual Needs of Modern Thought and Life, Especially in Russia.*[10] This large work (633 pages) illustrates the wide range of contemporary issues which Bukharev sought to evaluate theologically. Judicial reform, military reform, the peasant question, the secular and theological periodical press, theological education, contemporary novels (Chernyshevsky's *What Is To Be Done* and Turgenev's *Fathers and Sons*) and the Polish Rebellion of 1863 are among the topics to which the author devotes one or more of the seventeen dialogues (*razgovory*) that make up the volume. The use of the dialogue form rather than the discursive essay lends the book the qualities of openness and informality. Bukharev's tone is not magisterial or even homiletical, but conversational. He invites Orthodox readers to join him in assessing the issues of the age from a theological perspective.

The two dialogues devoted to the Polish question along with

---

[8] *Arkhimandrit Feodor: pro et contra*, pp. 595–7. As one of the exceptional women of nineteenth-century Russian Orthodoxy, Anna Sergeevna Bukhareva deserves a monograph in her own right. Florensky rightly notes 'the insufficiency of discussions of Bukharev's marriage that focus on him alone and not on Anna Sergeevna along with him' (ibid., p. 594).

[9] A. Bukharev, *Sv. Iov mnogostradal'nyi: obozrenie ego vremeni i iskusheniia, po ego knige* (Moscow: Izdanie knigoprodavtsa A.I. Manukhina, 1864); *Sv. prorok Daniil: ocherk ego veka, prorocheskogo sluzheniia i sviashchennoi knigi* (Moscow: Izdanie knigoprodavtsa A. I. Manukhina, 1864). Monographs on Isaiah, Jeremiah, Ezekiel, 3 Esdras (2 Esdras in the Apocrypha), the Song of Songs and other topics in biblical literature came out in 1864–5. For a complete bibliography see *Arkhimandrit Feodor: pro et contra*, pp. 766–71.

[10] A.M. Bukharev, *O sovremennykh dukhovnykh potrebnostiakh mysli i zhizni, osobenno russkoi* (Moscow: Izdanie knigoprodavtsa Manukhina, 1865).

a related essay on Father I.V. Vasiliev, a Paris-based Orthodox priest and pioneer of theological dialogue with Roman Catholicism and Anglicanism, are noteworthy evidence of Bukharev's proto-ecumenical concerns. Bukharev saw that the Polish-Russian conflict, to the extent it stemmed from the religious quarrel between Roman Catholicism and Orthodoxy, could not be solved without efforts on the dogmatic-theological level. Progress on this front was slow, however, because secular thinkers viewed dogmatics as hopelessly esoteric while theologians confirmed their critics' suspicions by focusing on the letter as opposed to the spirit of dogma. Bukharev saw the Russian–Polish conflict of the 1860s as a moment of divine judgment upon Orthodox apathy, an occasion for Orthodoxy to wake up to its inner truth and its responsibility for promoting Christian unity and human community. While

> the power of Orthodoxy lies in the dogmas of faith, the power of the dogmas consists in life and spirit, not the dead letter ... The dogmas of Christ's truth are spirit and life. Thus the fact that the cause of Orthodoxy vis-à-vis non-Orthodoxy is moving out of the sphere of dogmatic controversies into life itself, into the spiritual realm of events that are taking place in the world, is something which I see as the direct result of the grace of Him Who, being Himself truth and life ... wishes to teach the world His truth by means of present-day reality [*zhivoiu zhe deistvitel'nostiu*] and to bring this truth into the very life of the world.'[11]

There is no evidence that Bukharev's enthusiasm for theological assessment of contemporary issues ever abated. However, he was not able to reverse the narrowing of his professional options. The theological journals of the Orthodox Church, the natural forum for his work, were closed to him. He failed to find steady employment and was forced to live in provincial towns on the charity of family and friends. He never succeeded in finding a patron in the secular publishing world. The eminent Moscow Slavophile Mikhail Pogodin (1800–75)

---

[11] *O sovremennykh dukhovnykh potrebnostiakh*, pp. 196–8; cf. p. 214: 'It is high time for the Orthodox-Russian spirit, which in many of us has been fast asleep for such a long time and doing nothing except raving in its slumber, to wake up.'

took an interest in him, but Bukharev was not able to solidify a productive relationship with him. In the late 1860s his health, which had never been good, deteriorated. He died on the Friday after Easter, April 2, 1871.

SEARCHING FOR TRUTH IN THE
REVELATION OF JOHN

Studies on the Apocalypse[12] occupies a special place among Feodor's works for a number of reasons. The author saw it as his magnum opus. The ecclesiastical authorities saw it as a dangerously speculative work which disturbed the peace of church and state. As we have seen, the ban on its publication triggered the crisis that led Feodor to abandon the professional service of the church. The work also stands out because of its subject matter. No book of the Bible is more mysterious than the Revelation of John, and no theological task more challenging than envisioning last things.

Despite these peculiarities, however, *Studies on the Apocalypse* is consistent with the thematics and problematics of Feodor's theology. It also represents the culmination of his work as a teacher and scholar of the Bible.

Feodor begins *Studies on the Apocalypse* with a plea for freedom of inquiry in the Orthodox Church, offering his Apocalypse project as a case in point. He observes that Orthodox people typically respond to the Revelation of John in one of two ways. The pious eschew investigation altogether for fear of intellectual pride. In their view Christ's command to 'search the scriptures' (Jn 5:39) is better left unfulfilled in connection with this book. More critical minds, on the other hand, find the imagery of the Revelation of John strange to the point of embarrassment and wonder whether the book deserves reverence at all. Feodor claims the middle ground, proposing to fulfill the Lord's command regarding scripture by investigating the Apocalypse while at the same

---

[12] A.M. Bukharev (Arkhimandrit Feodor), *Issledovaniia Apokalipsisa*, with two portraits and three autographs of A.M. Bukharev, Izdanie redaktsii 'Bogoslovskogo Vestnika' (Sergiev Posad: Tipografiia Sviato-Troitskoi Sergievoi Lavry, 1916).

time bringing critics to 'a fitting reverence for the divine
knowledge and wisdom contained in this divinely inspired
book.' He argues that failure to work seriously on the Revelation of John simply abandons the subject to parties who
cannot be trusted to seek Orthodox truth. Old Believers,
Roman Catholics and Protestants use the book to support
their own 'one-sided' doctrines, while 'the [secular] world
fusses and philosophizes about worldly success and all
conceivable sorts of improvements with hardly a thought
about God's purposes.' In other words, heterodox apocalypses and the anti-apocalypse of modern materialism crowd
out Orthodox truth. There is, therefore, a vital need for an
Orthodox commentary, as long as it contains 'a glimmer of
the light of God's truth,' as Metropolitan Filaret said about
Feodor's book in its early stages.[13]

Toward the end of the introduction to *Studies on the Apocalypse* Feodor again affirms the importance of biblical studies.
Charting a middle way between loose speculation and conservative fear of interpretation he reminds his readers of the
grandeur of all scripture, hence of the inherent limits of
interpretation:

> It goes without saying that we can scarcely undertake to
> reveal the whole depth of meaning of this mysterious book in
> all the details and particularities of its contents. This would be
> an act of irrational daring and an unrealizable dream, for in
> the Revelation of John from beginning to end a grand, myste-
> rious and divine spectacle is presented, a spectacle in which
> the heavenly, the earthly and sometimes even the infernal are
> revealed to a single spiritual eye, and the reality of the present
> life is viewed in its inner connection to the future life of eternal
> glory.

Hence the full meaning of the book will not be plain until the
life of the age to come. In the meantime the interpreter must be
content with 'explaining this book "only in part" (1 Cor. 13:9),
that is, in so far as one can understand it on the basis of
ordinary, simple, exact and therefore firm hermeneutical

---

[13] *Issledovaniia Apokalipsisa*, pp. 1–3.

principles.' The resources at the interpreter's disposal are the book itself, the other books of the Bible that shed light on it, patristic commentary and the actual course of events in human and church history, this last forming the particular subject matter of the Apocalypse.[14]

Replying to ecclesiastical conservatives who believed that he was 'undertaking an investigation of something totally inaccessible and reaching for the tree of knowledge which for now is forbidden to us,' Feodor adduces the words of Christ himself in the Revelation of John: 'Do not seal up the words of the prophecy of this book, for the time is near' (Rev. 22:10). Feodor does not see how one can fulfill this command without engaging in acts of interpretation:

> For, 'the words of the prophecy of this book' by themselves, without interpretation, would obviously remain sealed. That is, the revelation was given to the Seer precisely so that Christians would investigate and elucidate it along with the other divine scriptures in obedience to the words of Christ, 'Search the scriptures' (Jn 5:39). Or in another place, 'Blessed is the one who reads aloud the words of the prophecy, and blessed are those who hear and who keep what is written in it; for the time is near' (Rev. 1:3). But obviously there is no blessedness to be had from reading or hearing 'the words of the prophecy' in the Revelation of John if one does not understand them; and if one does not understand them, how is one to 'keep the words of prophecy?'[15]

Feodor's chief aim in *Studies on the Apocalypse* was to respond to a prophetic imperative. But he was honest enough to see that a prophetic imperative, whatever else it requires, entails a hermeneutical imperative.

Studies on the Apocalypse is a well-organized book. The tensions and contradictions with which it is replete arise not from its form, but from its content.

The book begins with a prefatory essay, 'On the Purpose and Meaning of *Studies on the Apocalypse*,' which summarizes the

---

[14] *Issledovaniia Apokalipsisa*, pp. 65–6.
[15] *Issledovaniia Apokalipsisa*, p. 66.

whole work in about twenty pages.[16] While a handy outline, the preface does not convey the richness of the book it introduces. For the sake of brevity Feodor reduces his interpretation of the Apocalypse to its historiosophical skeleton, i.e. to the outline of world history which he believes he has discovered in the Revelation of John. But the value of *Studies on the Apocalypse* lies not in the skeleton, which is the construct of a pre-critical mind, but in the flesh with which Feodor clothes it, the insights of a mature theological mind.

The commentary follows the order of the biblical book, beginning with Revelation 1–3.[17] These chapters, relating to the destiny of seven Asia Minor churches of John the Theologian's day, stand outside the apocalyptic narrative which begins at Revelation 4. Appropriately enough Feodor treats these chapters as a separate unit. Starting with Revelation 4, however, he alters his approach in an important way. While still following the order of the text, he molds its contents by correlating the chapters with a periodization of world history. The procedure is arbitrary and totally dependent on allegorical interpretation. In fairness to Feodor, of course, one must concede that the Apocalypse is a book which invites allegorization.

The historical outline which Feodor imposes on the Revelation of John is a product of eastern Christian and Slavophile mythology. The scheme places the Orthodox Church at the center of world history by merging history with Christian revelation. As Feodor puts it, 'revelation and history are nothing but expositions of one and the same subject matter in different languages: revelation prefigures history, and the latter verifies the former.'[18] This principle covers the whole of human history, although the Revelation of John deals only with the era of the New Covenant. Revelation 4–6 describes the establishment of the New Covenant, the supplanting of old Judaism and the destruction of the Jerusalem temple. Revelation 7–9 describes the spread of Christianity in the Roman empire and the overthrow of paganism. Revelation 10 envisions the dawn of

---

[16] 'O naznachenii i znachenii "Issledovanii Apokalipsisa,"' *Issledovaniia Apokalipsisa*, pp. 1–22.
[17] *Issledovaniia Apokalipsisa*, pp. 70–157.
[18] *Issledovaniia Apokalipsisa*, p. 22.

established Orthodoxy under Emperor Constantine; Revelation 11, the age of the ecumenical councils; Revelation 12, the papal apostasy in the West, but also (thanks to Orthodox missions) the divine election and protection of the Orthodox Slavs. Revelation 13–14 prophesies the anti-Christian rationalist revolt in the West culminating in the wars of Napoleon, but also signs of the renewal to come, such as the preaching of Bossuet, the rise of the Bible societies and Empress Catherine's Greek Project for the liberation of the Orthodox East from the Turks.

Revelation 15–20:3 prophesies events which Feodor believes are beginning to unfold in his own time. Because this phase of the historical drama is still in process the scriptures pertaining to it are necessarily less clear, the commentary necessarily more elliptical. Still, Feodor believes he can positively identify the whore of Babylon (Rev. 17–18) with the Turkish empire which the Slavic East, united by Russia, will destroy so the 'New Israel' of enslaved Orthodoxy may go free. Revelation 20:4–15 describes the seventh period of the New Covenant featuring the final showdown between the forces of good and evil in history. Revelation 21–22:5 envisions the end of history and the revelation of a new heaven, a new earth and New Jerusalem.[19]

Given the artificiality of Feodor's scheme it is not difficult to see why his book has provoked strong complaints.[20] Yet religious faith is never the most sober or rational way of looking at things, and prophetic religion in particular is fraught with tension. If *Studies on the Apocalypse* fails as a modern critical commentary on scripture, as it surely does, it does not fail to shed light on modern Russian religious experience or to contribute something of value to the Orthodox theological tradition. The patient student will discover *Studies on the Apocalypse* possesses some very real virtues. To see them,

---

[19] Feodor follows this scheme with minor inconsistencies throughout the commentary. For summary outlines see *Issledovaniia Apokalipsisa*, pp. 5–22 and 152–7.

[20] '[Feodor] was simply not a historian, he had a poor knowledge of history and traced the historical process by means of textbooks that happened to come his way. In the words of Giliarov [N.P. Giliarov-Platonov], "Feodor interprets the destiny of the world with the Apocalypse in one hand and Lorents in the other."' Florovskii, *Puti russkogo bogosloviia*, p. 346. Fridrikh Karlovich Lorents (1803–61) was a history professor at a pedagogical institute in St Petersburg.

however, one must read the book not as an isolated work but in the context of Feodor's theology and the predicament of modern Russian Orthodoxy. The themes of Feodor's theology furthered by *Studies on the Apocalypse* are the humanity and accessibility of God, the renewal of the church through theologically informed self-criticism, and the universal mission of Orthodoxy.

HISTORY AND THE HUMANITY OF GOD

Feodor begins his commentary by considering the epigraph of the Apocalypse: 'The revelation of Jesus Christ, which God gave him to show his servants what must soon take place' (Rev. 1:1). What revelation is spoken of here? Feodor does not think it can be 'the eternal revelation of all the Father's secrets which is given to the Only-begotten Son in the council and unity of the Godhead.' Jesus Christ is the name that 'belongs to the Son of God in His being-made-human.' Moreover, the revelation which Jesus Christ receives from the Father is one which he shares with human beings 'to show to his servants what must soon take place.' Before the glorification of his human nature in the resurrection and ascension, Feodor believes, the human Jesus did not possess such a revelation. Concerning the end of history Jesus admonished his disciples 'about that day and hour no one knows, neither the angels of heaven, nor the Son, but only the Father' (Mt 24:36; cf. Mk 13:32). But in the Revelation of John, the Son not only knows the days and hours but shares this knowledge with the church.[21]

Feodor's point is that the revelation given to John concerns the course of human history and is therefore comprehensible to human beings. Feodor's preoccupation with fixing the historical referentiality of the Apocalypse, pre-critical as it was, expressed a basic insight. Feodor was one of the first Russian Orthodox theologians to take seriously the historical dimension of the humanity of God. Feodor saw that when Christ put on human nature he took on human history. This means the humanity of God should not be conceived in static terms as a fixed quantity or epitome of humanity in general, but as a dynamic, continuing

---

[21] *Issledovaniia Apokalipsisa*, pp. 70–2.

historical incarnation. The Revelation of John, as Feodor reads it, opens the curtains on this grand process. John's prophecy does not so much elevate human seeing to a vision of divine things as it contextualizes the vision of divine things in historical time. The Apocalypse throws history open to theologizing.

The humanity of God in history is centered on the history of the church. Historical theology is ecclesiocentric theology – not in antagonism with christocentric theology, to be sure, but as sequential to it. The humanity of God in Christ spills over into the world in the form of the church, and this gracious emanation continues to the end of time. The Apocalypse is one of the great books of the church in the New Testament. The 'servants' of Revelation 1:1 are the early church. The seven epistles of Revelation 2–3 are not just letters to the seven Asia Minor congregations but address the whole church by virtue of their incorporation in the New Testament canon. The sweeping historical scenario of Revelation 4–20 focuses on the 'saints,' that is to say, the church. The Revelation of John comforts and fortifies the church by means of hopeful prophecies.

By 'church' Feodor did not mean a generic association or abstract idea. He meant the Orthodox Church. Recognizing this one can read *Studies on the Apocalypse* as a meditation on the historical destiny of Orthodoxy and its role in world civilization. In this sense *Studies on the Apocalypse* continues and clarifies the central theme of *On Orthodoxy in Relation to the Modern World*. We have already observed that modernity had little specific content for Feodor; it was mainly a category of challenge and expectation. The historical scenario of the Revelation of John brings this dimension of modernity into even sharper focus. The key question is where Feodor locates his own time in the historical-apocalyptic process.

Feodor sees his own time as the eve of the fall of Babylon described in Revelation 17.[22] He takes Babylon to mean the Ottoman Empire which was holding 'New Israel,' i.e. the Orthodox East, in bondage. Babylon would soon fall, and with it all spirits hostile to Christ (Rev. 18), through the intervention of the Russians and other Slavs called by divine providence to

---

[22] See *Issledovaniia Apokalipsisa*, pp. 16–21.

84

liberate New Israel and 'shepherd the Gentiles with a rod of iron' (Rev. 12:5) – not just Muslim 'Gentiles' but those of the secularist West as well. 'This is our [Orthodox Russia's] gracious calling and world-historical task: to cleanse thought and knowledge, literature, the whole civilization of the Christian world from the terribly false outlook and spirit of apostasy from Christ.' Feodor is vague about how this will happen. The rod of iron would seem to suggest some sort of military intervention, although Feodor insists 'we can conquer all that is Babylonian only in the company of the Lamb and with His spirit of love for humankind.' In any case the great work was not yet accomplished. Yet the Revelation of John declares that even now, in Babylonian captivity, 'a mind that has wisdom' (Rev. 17:9) sees what is to come.[23] We have noted that Feodor identified Father Petr Tomanitsky as the mind with wisdom. One must suppose Feodor saw himself as possessing it, too, at least derivatively. The mind with wisdom sees the course of history in the light of its apocalyptic destiny.

All this shows Feodor construed modernity as an unprecedented historical turning point, a moment on the eve. On the eve of what? Not secularism. Feodor recognized that secularism was shaping the world civilization of his day. But tomorrow? Feodor expected a dramatic new manifestation of Christian truth and Christian civilization. To borrow a term from Paul Tillich, Feodor experienced modernity as a *kairos*, an epochal moment or moment of spiritual challenge and decision.[24] Modernity was a religious category for Feodor; it contributed an existential dimension to his theology. It also colored his borrowing from other thinkers, notably the early Slavophiles. They, too, looked to Russia to give the world a shining example of an integral, Christian civilization. But the early Slavophiles were romantic conservatives. Their vision was inspired by the Russian past. Feodor was a prophet. His vision was proleptic. He saw the modern world falling into God's future, into the promised kingdom of the Lamb.

---

[23] *Issledovaniia Apokalipsisa*, pp. 20–1.
[24] Paul Tillich, 'Kairos,' in *The Protestant Era*, abridged ed., trans. James Luther Adams (Chicago: The University of Chicago Press, 1957), pp. 32–51.

The Accessibility of God

Meditation on destiny is a paradoxical undertaking, for it means contemplating that which is not yet. How is this possible?

For the Christian it is possible on the basis of a revelation which gives some sort of insight into the end of things in the mind of God. All revelation implies the accessibility of God to some extent, but John's revelation has a special power in this respect because it comes last. Its ultimacy in the canon implies an ultimacy of access to divine things.[25]

The point comes out clearly in Feodor's observations on the instrumentality or 'angel' of the revelation (Rev. 1:1). The appearance of the angel at first perplexes Feodor. In the Old Covenant God communicated to this servants by means of angelic intermediaries, but in the New Covenant he spoke through his Son, who called his disciples 'my friends' (Jn 15:14). Does the revelation to John represent a step backward towards the Old Covenant? Feodor adduces two reasons why this is not the case. First, before the angel appeared to him John tells us he was 'in the Spirit on the Lord's day' (Rev. 1:10). Thus he was already in Christ, and Christ himself 'placed his right hand on [him], saying, "Do not be afraid"' (Rev. 1:17). Second, the Old Testament prophets who were visited by angels were reduced to fear and trembling by the experience. Daniel, for example, 'was overcome and lay sick for some days' (Dan. 8:27). But John was lifted up to a kind of equality with the angel despite his initial reaction, which was one of fear. More than once, Feodor observes, John 'fell down at [the angel's] feet to worship him,' only to be told, '"You must not do that! I am a fellow servant with you and your comrades who hold the testimony of Jesus. Worship God!"' (Rev. 19:10; cf. 22:8–9). 'Thus,' Feodor concludes, 'the angel's role in revelation, far from contradicting the new testamental character of the revelations, is itself an

---

[25] Martha Himmelfarb has called attention to the accessibility of God as one of the characteristic concerns of apocalyptic literature. See 'The Apocalyptic Vision,' *The Oxford Study Bible: Revised English Bible with the Apocrypha*, ed. by M. Jack Suggs, Katharine Doob Sakenfeld and James R. Mueller (New York: Oxford University Press, 1992), Articles, pp. 188–9.

appurtenance and reflection of the grace of the New Covenant.'[26]

Feodor develops the theme of the accessibility of God even more eloquently in his exegesis of the vision of Revelation 4–5. The opening verse of the text suggests this theme in a powerful image: 'After this I looked, and there in heaven a door stood open!' (Rev. 4:1). More images of aperture and insight follow. Through the door John saw a rainbow throne and 'one seated on the throne . . . [who] looks like jasper and carnelian' (4:2–3). Around the great throne twenty-four elders on thrones of their own and four living creatures 'full of eyes in front and behind' (Rev. 4:6) sang unending praises to the enthroned one, who held a sealed book in his right hand. An angel asked, 'Who is worthy to open the scroll and break its seals?' When John heard this question he 'began to weep bitterly because no one was found worthy to open the scroll or to look into it.' But one of the elders counseled the seer, 'Do not weep. See, the Lion of the tribe of Judah, the Root of David, has conquered, so that he can open the scroll and its seven seals.' The seer looked again and saw between the throne and the living creatures a Lamb 'standing as if it had been slaughtered.' The Lamb received the scroll from the one on the great throne as the elders and living creatures fell down in worship and praise (Rev. 5:2–8).

As Feodor interprets the vision, the one on the great throne is God the Father, the Lamb is Christ, the twenty-four elders are the twenty-four books of the New Testament,[27] and the four living creatures are the four Gospels. The ensemble presents a picture of the Universal Church as a heavenly, yet accessible, reality. At the same time, accessibility does not mean closure: the precise historical destiny of the struggling church on earth is indeterminate enough to cause even the seer to weep.[28] The picture epitomizes the prophetic vocation: to see but also to weep. Was this not Feodor's fate?

But the Lamb, the sacrificial love of God in Christ, is the antidote to tears. The Father is presented as seated 'on a throne,

---

[26] *Issledovaniia Apokalipsisa*, pp. 73–5.
[27] Feodor counts the four Gospels (*Chetvero-Evangelie*) as one book. See *Issledovaniia Apokalipsisa*, p. 180.
[28] *Issledovaniia Apokalipsisa*, pp. 159–60.

high and lofty,' as Isaiah described it (Isa. 6:1), for the love of God is as high 'as the heavens are high above the earth' (Ps. 103:11). 'But at the same time,' Feodor observes, '[God's love] in Christ is already revealed to faith and inculcated in the Church so that, high though it is, it forms a divine throne that is always available to the pilgrim Church and accessible to faith, just as the Seer contemplated it.'[29]

The accessibility of God is not just an inference of the pious imagination, but the result of God's real condescension to the human measure. Human beings can contemplate divinity because of the humanity of God. Feodor employs this central idea of his theology in a meditation on Revelation 4:3: 'And the one seated there looks like jasper and carnelian.' The verse reminds Feodor of Ezekiel's vision of a sapphire throne on which 'something that seemed like a human form' was seated (Ezek. 1:26). The enthroned one of Revelation 4–5, too, is revealed in human form, for he holds a scroll in his right hand (Rev. 5:1). Both visions testify to the humanity of God:

> When Divinity condescends to an open and gracious appearance to humankind in this life, appearance in human form is totally appropriate, first because this form is closest and most akin to human beings, but especially because the heavenly Father Himself was disposed to make Himself visible to people in His Own Son who became a human being: 'Whoever has seen Me,' says the Lord Jesus, 'has seen the Father' (Jn 14:9). Similarly, the Holy Spirit openly rested upon [the Son], as John the Baptist saw when he baptized Him (Lk 3:22). Also, when Divinity appeared in this way it did not shine with the light of the sun when it shines in all its strength, something that the Apostles on Mount Tabor could not bear, nor, at the beginning of his mysterious visions, St John the Theologian. Rather, it shone with the beautiful yet approachable and beckoning brilliance of precious stones. This very fact signifies how marvelous and approachable Divine Grace is for us even though it reveals the very 'fullness' of the Triune God. Truly, we cannot do otherwise than 'with boldness,' a most reverent boldness, 'approach the throne of

---

[29] *Issledovaniia Apokalipsisa*, p. 161; cf. p. 188.

Grace,' as the Apostle Paul exhorts us (Heb. 4:16). For that [Grace] stretches out its arms to us and is ready to embrace us, to introduce us to the inner mysteries of Divinity, the mystery of God's relations with the world and especially the mystery of the salvation of sinful humanity; all this so that we might be 'filled with all the fullness of God' (Eph. 3:19) to the extent that we can accommodate it.[30]

Human beings are not the measure of divinity, for God is God. The measure of divinity is Trinity, a measure surpassing human thought. Yet when human beings are enlightened by revelation to contemplate God in Trinity, they discover a human being there. Divinity incorporates the human measure even as it transcends it. This is what makes the contemplation of Trinity not only relevant to human beings but possible and endurable. It is what makes contemplation of the triune God 'salvation.' It also clarifies the nature of the church. The church is the community of the humanity of God.

WORTHY AND UNWORTHY CHURCHES

Biblical prophecy is never so oriented to the future that it loses its connection with the present. On the contrary, one of the chief functions of prophetic visions is to provide a basis for criticizing the present or, as the case may be, consoling those who suffer in it. Feodor's vocation of promoting a more self-critical Orthodoxy in his day finds support in the prophecies of John the Theologian.

The seven epistles which John delivers to the churches of Asia Minor (Rev. 2–3) are an especially rich source in this respect. Feodor sees these churches as representing 'the whole Universal Church in its various conditions.' He takes the 'angels' of the seven churches to be priestly hierarchs who collectively represent 'the sacred hierarchy of the whole Holy Universal and Apostolic Church to the end of the age.' The one 'who holds the seven stars in his right hand' (Rev. 2:1) and dictates the letters is Christ. The seven stars symbolize the seven hierarchs; by

---

[30] *Issledovaniia Apokalipsisa*, p. 164.

holding them in his hand Christ 'expresses [his] special favor towards the sacred ecclesiastical hierarchy.' But the Lord's interest in the hierarchs extends to their faults as well as their virtues. The epistles show 'the Lord's special, probing attention to these guardians of the Church, to their virtues and short-comings, their merits and weaknesses.' With this observation Feodor opens the way to using Revelation 2–3 as a critical instrument for commenting on the state of the church and its hierarchy not just in ancient times but in any era, including his own. The Universal Church stands at all times under the gaze of the Son of Man. His eyes are 'like a flame of fire' (Rev. 1:14; 2:18), and he 'searches [the] minds and hearts' of all the churches (Rev. 2:23).[31]

Turning to the seven communities addressed in Revelation 2–3, Feodor divides them into three groups: worthy, unworthy and middling churches. The churches of Smyrna and Philadelphia receive only praise from the Lord; Sardis and Laodicea, only blame; Ephesus, Pergamum and Thyatira, a mixed report.

The church of Smyrna suffered 'affliction and poverty' yet the Lord calls them 'rich' (Rev. 2:9). The Philadelphians had 'little power' (Rev. 3:8) but not 'little hearts' (*malosil'nye Filadelfiitsy ne malodushestvovali*).[32] Christ promises to make these congregations pillars in the church of God and bearers of God's name (Rev. 3:12), that is, the name of Christ. For Christ, too, knew weakness and humiliation but subsequently received 'the name that is above every name' (Phil. 2:9). In a humble church the grace of God operates all the more powerfully, for God's power 'is made perfect in weakness' (2 Cor. 12:9). Feodor's references to these two classic texts of kenotic christology demonstrate the close link between his critical program and his dogmatic concerns. The first principle of his ecclesiastical criticism is: better for a church to be 'weak but faithful' than outwardly grand but lacking in 'active faith.'[33]

In the letters to the unworthy and middling churches Feodor finds an anatomy of the faults to which churches at all times are

---

[31] *Issledovaniia Apokalipsisa*, pp. 91–5; cf. pp. 97, 101–3.
[32] *Issledovaniia Apokalipsisa*, pp. 103–4.
[33] *Issledovaniia Apokalipsisa*, pp. 107–10, 115; cf. pp. 151–2.

susceptible. The problem at Sardis was dead faith. Unlike the Philadelphian church, the church at Sardis was large and prosperous. But 'the living power of Christianity which manifests itself in active faith was not to be found ... The Christians there were for the most part false or merely nominal Christians.'[34] The Laodicean church was not as dead as its sister in Sardis, but it lacked 'spiritual zeal.' The Lord brands it as 'lukewarm' (Rev. 3:16), which Feodor takes to mean smug and self-satisfied.[35] Among the three middling churches those of Pergamum and Thyatira were spiritually alive but abused Christian freedom. They practiced immorality, ate food sacrificed to idols and, in Thyatira, tolerated the heresy of 'Jezebel' (Rev. 2:20), which Feodor takes to be 'gnosticism – a blend of Christianity and principles of pagan philosophy.'[36] The Ephesian church, by contrast, erred by carrying a rigorous piety too far. The Ephesian Christians rightly spurned the heretics whom the Pergaminians and Thyatirans accepted, but 'they had a weakness that seems to have found a hiding place in their strictness of faith and morals: the Ephesians grew weak in Christian love.'[37] In Feodor's anatomy of the faults of the three middling churches one sees a characteristic pattern of his theology: the critique of 'spiritually Gentile' and 'spiritually Jewish' extremes.

Feodor believed he could read the results of the prophecies in Revelation 2–3 in the historical fate of the Asian churches. His confidence shows how literally he accepted the Revelation of John as a guide to historical events. By his day, Feodor observes, Sardis and Laodicea had ceased to exist as settled communities. 'Nowadays beasts and reptiles make their home in the ruins of Laodicea,' and Sardis presents a similar picture.[38] The churches of Pergamum, Thyatira and Ephesus still preserved a modest existence (in the case of the Ephesian church, in a new location). The churches of Smyrna and Philadelphia, on the other hand, continued to be vital centers of Orthodoxy. Smyrna survived

---

[34] *Issledovaniia Apokalipsisa*, p. 115.
[35] *Issledovaniia Apokalipsisa*, pp. 120–8.
[36] *Issledovaniia Apokalipsisa*, p. 138.
[37] *Issledovaniia Apokalipsisa*, p. 135.
[38] *Issledovaniia Apokalipsisa*, pp. 128–9.

martyrdoms, earthquakes, invasions and other disasters to become 'one of the most flourishing commercial cities of the Ottoman empire.' Despite Islamic domination the city supported seven Orthodox churches and an Orthodox population of 40,000.[39] The Philadelphian Christians also flourished in spite of geographical isolation and relative poverty. They numbered 1200 families, all of them proud of their Orthodox faith. The mothers of Philadelphia taught their children to recite John the Theologian's Philadelphian prophecy 'as soon as they begin to talk, right along with the Lord's Prayer.' Nor could Feodor fail to be impressed by the following incident reported by more than one recent visitor to the city:

> [In 1836] Protestant missionaries [biblisty] arrived in Philadelphia and offered the Greek priests there a considerable sum of money – considerable in view of their poverty – if [the priests] would refrain from warning the Philadelphians against them. The money was refused, and the disseminators of Protestantism failed to make a single convert in Philadelphia. Our Russian traveler Norov concludes his report on this incident with these words: 'You have but little power, and yet you have kept my word and have not denied my name' (Rev. 3:8).[40]

Feodor's interest in the Asian Christians of his day, in addition to its connection with his research on the Apocalypse, links him to the growing attention which nineteenth-century Orthodox Russians were giving to their co-religionists in the Balkans and the Near East. Their attention was engaged by national liberation movements in those regions but also by religious and ecclesiastical challenges, such as the threat posed by Protestant missionary activity in the Orthodox world. Feodor's commentary illustrates very clearly how an interest in the oppressed Christians of the East contributed to the development of a self-critical attitude in Russian Orthodoxy. When Russian Orthodox people contemplated the poverty and oppression in which Balkan and near-eastern Orthodox were forced to live, they became more acutely aware of their own

---

[39] *Issledovaniia Apokalipsisa*, pp. 110–11.
[40] *Issledovaniia Apokalipsisa*, p. 114.

power and independence as subjects of a great Orthodox empire. At the same time the endurance and heroism of their 'lesser' brothers and sisters stood in marked contrast to the relative apathy of many Russian Orthodox toward their faith. Were Russian Orthodox guilty of living at ease in Zion? Were they living up to their great responsibilities? Did they appreciate the treasure of Orthodoxy, or did they take it for granted? Questions such as these, which stood in the foreground of Feodor's theology in any case, acquired even greater urgency when examined in the light of the circumstances of Orthodoxy in other parts of the world.

Feodor's exegesis of Revelation 2–3 was not an academic exercise but a way of getting his church to think about itself in critical and prophetic terms. Feodor challenged his readers to wonder: Was the church of Russia, for all its size, wealth and power, a worthy or an unworthy church?

THE PROMISE OF ORTHODOXY

The Revelation of John closes the New Testament with an ecclesiocentric rather than christocentric story. Christ the Lamb that was slain presides over the apocalyptic scenario from his place in heaven but does not enter the apocalyptic drama in person until the end. His Passion is over, his victory won. The drama revealed to the seer of Patmos is the Passion of the church, beginning with the toils of the Asia Minor congregations in Revelation 1–3, continuing through the travails of the radiant but persecuted woman of Revelation 12 and culminating in the marriage feast of Christ and his church in Revelation 19–22. In *Studies on the Apocalypse* Archimandrite Feodor honors the ecclesiocentrism of the biblical text by reading its scenarios as allegories of the historical struggles of Orthodoxy.

Feodor's allegories are very specific. The 'mighty angel' of Revelation 10 is Constantine, the first Christian emperor; his rainbow aureole signifies the peace between church and empire achieved during his reign. The 'two witnesses' of Revelation 11 are the civil and ecclesiastical authorities of the Christian empire of the fourth through seventh centuries, whose collaboration, like that of the Davidic prince Zerubbabel and the high priest

93

Joshua in post-exilic Jerusalem (Zech. 4), realized a perfect symphony of church and state in the cause of Christ. 'Neither quarrels nor conflicts nor rivalry with respect to the common cause of being "Christ's witnesses" marked the relations between the Orthodox authorities in church and state; rather, each acted with the independence proper to it without encroaching on the independence of the other,' as Feodor puts it in an idyllic flight of fancy.[41] The woes foreseen in Revelation 11 refer to the external and internal assaults on the Christian empire by Islam and iconoclasm, respectively. The revelation of the heavenly temple and ark at Revelation 11:19, which Feodor takes to mean the Orthodox Church and its corpus of dogma, refers to Orthodoxy's victory over iconoclasm at the seventh ecumenical council in 787. The 'woman clothed with the sun' of Revelation 12 is 'the Church revealed in the full light of triumphant Orthodoxy' in 843, when the veneration of icons was definitively restored in Byzantium under the imperial regent Theodora.[42]

The triumph of Orthodoxy in 843, commemorated on the First Sunday of Lent in the Orthodox liturgical calendar, serves as a paradigm of the renewal toward which Feodor saw history moving. The church as Feodor knew it was not the embodiment of triumphant Orthodoxy, for it was oppressed by the Turks in the East and perplexed by the forces of modernity in Russia. But Feodor was emboldened by John the Theologian's prophecy to preach a new and grander triumph of Orthodoxy in the future.

The victory of 843 was short-lived on the world-historical stage, for Orthodoxy was soon checked by the rise of the papal monarchy in the West. Feodor takes the dragon of Revelation 12 to signify papalism. As the dragon swept a third of the stars from heaven with its great tail, so papal power carried off a 'third' of the church into bondage and heresy. The war between the dragon and the heavenly angels refers to the polemics between papalists and the rightly guided hierarchs of Orthodoxy. The beast of Revelation 13, spiritual offspring of the dragon, is the unbelieving mind of the modern West,

---

[41] *Issledovaniia Apokalipsisa*, pp. 371–2. For Zerubbabel and Joshua see pp. 343–4.
[42] *Issledovaniia Apokalipsisa*, pp. 393–6.

an intellectual and spiritual monster which Feodor sees as 'vengeance for the mercilessness with which [the papal church] deprived the children of God of freedom of spirit by subjecting them to [the authority of] a mere human being.'[43] The second beast of Revelation 13 is the 'free thinking literature of the West' that propagandizes for the cause of godless rationalism. Its 'two horns like a lamb' are secular ideals which outwardly resemble Christian values but in fact serve a different master. The whore of Babylon, ally of the dragon and the beast in Revelation 14–18, is the mighty Ottoman empire which enjoyed the support of the western powers even though it held Orthodox peoples in captivity. The forces arrayed against Orthodoxy – papalism, rationalism and Ottoman Turkey – will be overcome by the child born to the radiant woman of Revelation 12, which Feodor takes to mean a mighty Orthodox people exercising imperial power in the service of Christ and his church. This of course is Russia, a late-comer to Orthodoxy who was at first sequestered from the outside world but later 'guided by Providence into a constant and close relationship with the western world as well as the East' for the sake of the 'great and universal vocation' of renewing Orthodoxy for all the world to see.[44]

The anticipated triumph of Orthodoxy is cause for rejoicing among the saints of heaven, who sing 'a new song' before the divine throne, 'the song of Moses, the servant of God, and the song of the Lamb' (Rev. 14:3, 15:3). As Feodor glosses it the song of the Lamb celebrates the verities of the Orthodox faith, 'the inexplicable mystery of the Incarnation [*Bogochelovecheniia*], the dwelling of Very God in flesh on earth, His divine deeds and circumstances of life, His persecution at the hands of human malice, His death on behalf of sinners, and the resurrection and glorious ascension of His Divine Humanity [*Ego Bogochelovechestva*].' However, the song celebrates these truths in a new key. While the essence of Christian truth is

---

[43] *Issledovaniia Apokalipsisa*, pp. 515–16. The beast exercises authority for forty-two months (Rev. 13:5), i.e. three and a half years, which Feodor glosses as the three and a half centuries from the rise of Protestantism in the sixteenth century to his own day. The chronology allows him to claim 'the end of this period is in our time' (p. 543).

[44] *Issledovaniia Apokalipsisa*, pp. 433–4; cf. pp. 412–14.

always the same, the melody of theology 'has been altered in a certain way, albeit only in mode of expression, in response to new circumstances and needs of faith' (*tol'ko nekotorym obrazom vidoizmenilas' kak by v svoem vyrazhenii sootvet-stvenno novym obstoiatel'stvam i nuzhdam very*). The renewed and radiant Orthodoxy of the future will

> keep away from all false knowledge yet still have a *forehead* that shines with living and charitable rationality and a love of learning that heeds the all-embracing Spirit of the Almighty Father, so as to maintain every jot and tittle of Orthodoxy against spiritual Gentilism, but, in contrast to spiritual Judaism, accomplishing this in a power and spirit that can be intellectually assimilated and introduced into every conceivable sphere of life: this is the spiritual song in its new and distinctive mode of expression.'[45]

In other words, Orthodoxy will do more than verbally proclaim and commemorate the incarnation; it will embody this truth in its mind and ministry. Feodor recognized that the church and society of his day were far from having achieved such a thing. 'How little skilled we are in the "new song" stands out especially in the fact that up to now people who are zealous for spiritual things for the most part spurn and even condemn earthly and worldly things, while those who are occupied with the latter neglect and even totally cast aside spiritual things.'[46] Yet, emboldened by the Revelation of John, Feodor believed the time of abstract and merely nominal Orthodoxy was already starting to pass away.

Feodor's gloss on the song of the Lamb in the spirit of incarnational theology is consistent with his analogy between the triumph of Orthodoxy in 843 and the world-historical renewal of Orthodoxy which he held to be the promise of modern times. The victory of 843, re-establishing the veneration of icons, was indeed a triumph for faith in the incarnation. 'For behold, the Church is clothed in a beauty that surpasses all things earthly, through the ikon of the incarnate Christ,' as the Great Vespers

---

[45] *Issledovaniia Apokalipsisa*, pp. 550–1. For the 'forehead' of the saints, see Rev. 14:1.
[46] *Issledovaniia Apokalipsisa*, pp. 555–6.

for the eve of the Sunday of Orthodoxy put it.[47] Feodor looked forward to a new historical concretization of the superhistorical beauty of Orthodoxy, when Orthodox truth would be embodied in science, art, letters and everyday life in the modern world, a time when 'Christ's truth [would] be revealed in all its vital power as the one rational principle for all spheres of knowledge and life.'[48]

Feodor's ecclesiocentrism was exuberant but not self-congratulatory. He took pains to distance himself from 'unreasonable zealots [who] have a sad and inhumane tendency to tar with the name of "apostate" everyone who disagrees or merely appears to disagree with what is in fact non-essential and superficial in Orthodox Christianity, never mind what is really essential.' The Revelation of John 'leaves no room for the unreasonable and inhuman zeal of inquisitors.'[49] Inquisitors look for heresy and apostasy everywhere, while the church should look for the incarnation everywhere. Orthodox Christians should approach the world with an open and charitable mind, or as Feodor phrases it, 'a fundamentally inquiring and unslavish cast of mind inspired by Christ's philosophic [liubomudrogo] and profoundly free spirit.'[50]

Feodor's exuberance is also checked by his anxiety over the concept of remnant in the Revelation of John. The apocalyptic seer fixes the number of the Lamb's companions at 144,000 (Rev. 14:1). Feodor allegorizes the number in such a way as to enlarge considerably the sum of the saved. Still, he recognizes

[47] *The Lenten Triodion*, trans. Mother Mary and Archimandrite Kallistos Ware (London and Boston: Faber and Faber, 1984), p. 300.

[48] *Issledovaniia Apokalipsisa*, p. 635.

[49] *Issledovaniia Apokalipsisa*, pp. 530–1. Feodor takes the number of the beast, 666 (Rev. 13:18), to mean 'apostate' by analyzing the numerical values of the letters of the word in Greek. But rather than taking this as a sanction for seeking out apostasy wherever it might be suspected, he asks his readers to ponder the fact that 'divine revelation did not directly and openly affix the fateful name of "apostate" but deeply concealed it' in the mysterious number of the beast. Feodor recommends a comparable reticence to the church, going so far as to claim that 'no one except Christ Himself is capable of ... truly and accurately discerning the extent to which someone turns away from the spirit of Christ's incarnation [*ot dukha vochelovecheniia Khristova*]' (ibid.).

[50] *Issledovaniia Apokalipsisa*, p. 542. Cf. p. 544, where Feodor excoriates the journals *Russkoe slovo* and *Domashniaia beseda* for destructive zeal, secular-minded in the first case, ecclesiastically motivated in the second.

the sum represents a remnant and not the whole company of Israel or the church. This leads him to some critical observations about his own people and church. When discussing relations between eastern and western Christianity, for example, he observes that 'the *eternal* Gospel has not ceased to be proclaimed even amid western error and unbelief; while, on the other hand, *on Zion Mount*, i.e. in the Orthodox Church, the number of the chosen has shrunk to a remnant equivalent to the chosen or believing Jews at the beginning of Christianity.'[51] When he elaborates the Slavophile myth of Russia's mission to the modern world he concedes God alone knows whether the sacred task will be invested 'in the national body as a whole or in a chosen remnant thereof.'[52] This issue would emerge again in the Russian school. In his own apocalypse, composed a generation later, Vladimir Soloviev portrayed the great corporate bodies of church and state as deeply vulnerable to apostasy and prophesied the vindication of Christian faith in an ecumenical remnant.[53]

Feodor's zeal was also tempered by the reverence for Christ the Lamb which sets the tone for all of his theology. He cautions prophets against erring as Jonah did when the latter complained to God about the sparing of Nineveh. The only militancy worthy of emulation is that which imitates the God 'who invests His glory rather in sparing people than in strictly and exactly executing His terrible verdicts.'[54] Feodor ends *Studies on the Apocalypse* on this note, asking his readers to remember

> that even a zealous piety, if it is contrary to the disposition and impulses of the love of the Lamb of God for human beings, will not find a place in that beloved city which the Seer calls *the bride, the wife of the Lamb* ... Only *the one who conquers* in the spirit of the Lamb of God who conquered the evil of the world by taking it upon Himself even unto death on the cross, only such a one *will inherit all*.'[55]

---

[51] *Issledovaniia Apokalipsisa*, p. 588.
[52] *Issledovaniia Apokalipsisa*, p. 633.
[53] See Ch. 9 below.
[54] *Issledovaniia Apokalipsisa*, p. 544.
[55] *Issledovaniia Apokalipsisa*, p. 648.

4

Bukharev's Legacy

After the crisis of 1863 Bukharev's theological writings for the most part were forgotten in the church except among a few of the theologian's friends and former students. Since the ex-monk also failed to attract a secular audience, it appeared his work would be consigned to oblivion.

And so it was for almost thirty years. At the turn of the twentieth century, however, there was a revival of interest in Bukharev. It began at Kazan Theological Academy, an institution with a reformist tradition where the memory of the gentle *inspektor* Feodor had not died out. Professor P.V. Znamensky drew a sympathetic portrait of Bukharev in his *History of Kazan Theological Academy* (1891–2).[1] He also wrote two well-researched articles on the Bukharev Affair, resolutely defending Feodor's renewalism and exposing the intellectual crudity of his detractors, especially Askochensky.[2] By the time Znamensky's second article appeared (1902) a new reform era was beginning in Russia. The atmosphere was congenial to a fresh debate about the relation of Orthodoxy to the modern world. Znamensky hailed Bukharev as 'the first pioneer in the elaboration of this issue' and recommended his works to the theologians of the day.[3]

One of the first to heed the call was V.V. Rozanov, a well-known publicist of the new religious consciousness in the intelligentsia. Rozanov was engaged in the investigation of issues of sexuality and marriage from an Orthodox Christian point of view and found the case of Aleksandr and Anna

---

[1] *Istoriia kazanskoi dukhovnoi akademii*, 1:124–36, 176–80; 2:205–21.
[2] 'Pechal'noe dvadtsatipiatiletie' and 'Bogoslovskaia polemika 1860-kh godov ob otnoshenii pravoslaviia k sovremennoi zhizni,' *Pravoslavnyi sobesednik*, 1896 and 1902, respectively. See Ch. 1, n. 1 and Ch. 2, n. 6 above.
[3] 'Vmesto vvedeniia,' p. xxviii.

Bukharev fascinating in this regard.[4] Academic theologians, especially at Moscow Theological Academy, Bukharev's alma mater, were not slow to respond to the intelligentsia's interest in one of their own. An extensive memoir on Bukharev by V.V. Lavrsky, a cathedral dean who had been one of Feodor's students in Kazan, was published in the scholarly journal of the Moscow Academy.[5] M.M. Tareev, professor of moral theology at the Academy, devoted a substantial essay to Bukharev in a survey of modern Russian religious thinkers.[6] The publication of a new edition of *On Orthodoxy in Relation to the Modern World* by the Synodal Press in 1906 and the free distribution of the book to subscribers of *Tserkovnyi golos* (*The Voice of the Church*) completed Bukharev's rehabilitation.

Publication of the Apocalypse commentary was a more complicated task, as the manuscript had to be retrieved from the archives and edited. The project was taken up in the following decade by Father Pavel Florensky, the most brilliant young theologian at Moscow Theological Academy, and came to fruition in 1916.[7] Florensky promoted the Bukharev revival in other ways as well. The scholarly journal of the Academy, which Florensky edited from 1913 to 1917, published three collections of Bukharev's correspondence.[8] The most detailed study of Bukharev to appear in the imperial period was prepared as a Masters' dissertation supervised by Florensky.[9] Florensky's

---

[4] For selected commentary on the Bukharev Affair by Rozanov including four letters to Rozanov from Anna Sergeevna Bukhareva see *Arkhimandrit Feodor: pro et contra*, pp. 526–52.

[5] V.V. Lavrskii, 'Moi vospominaniia ob arkhimandrite Feodore (A.M. Bukhareve),' *Bogoslovskii vestnik*, 1905, nos 7–8; 1906, nos 5, 7–8, 9, 11.

[6] M.M. Tareev, *Osnovy khristianstva*, 4 vols (Sergiev Posad: Tipografiia Sv.-Tr. Sergievoi Lavry, 1908), 4:314–35.

[7] See Ch. 3, n. 12 above.

[8] [Arkhimandrit Feodor,] 'Pis'ma k A.A. Lebedevu,' *Bogoslovskii vestnik*, 1915, nos 10–12; 'Pis'ma arkhimandrita Feodora (A.M. Bukhareva) k Varvare Vasil'evne Liubimovoi i Antonine Ivanovne Dubrovinoi,' 1917, nos 2–3; and 'Pis'ma arkhimandrita Feodora k o. protoiereiu Valerianu Viktorovichu Lavrskomu i supruge ego Aleksandre Ivanovne,' 1917, nos 4–5. In the last two cases Florensky himself did the annotations. The letters to Valerian and Aleksandra Lavrsky have been translated into French by Elisabeth Behr-Sigel, *Alexandre Boukharev*, pp. 99–164.

[9] A.M. Belorukov, 'Vnutrennii perelom v zhizni A.M. Bukhareva,' *Bogoslovskii vestnik*, 1915, nos 10–12.

personal acquaintance with Anna Sergeevna Bukhareva has already been mentioned.[10]

Thus, at the end of the imperial period Bukharev's voice was heard again in the Russian Orthodox Church. Unfortunately the revival was short-lived. The communist society which emerged from five years of revolution and civil war was a hostile environment for the cause of dialogue between Orthodoxy and the modern world. The only work by Bukharev to appear in Soviet Russia before the *glasnost'* reforms of 1985–91 was a previously unpublished series of exegetical essays on the catholic epistles, a minor piece.[11] Bukharev's thought was ignored in the Russian Orthodox diaspora as well. Florovsky's negative assessment in *The Paths of Russian Theology* discouraged interest, as did the fact Bukharev could not be claimed as a forerunner of the Neopatristic tendency which came to dominate Orthodox theology in the West. The most important exceptions to this habit of neglect came from the pens of Orthodox laywomen. Nadejda Gorodetzky discussed Bukharev in her widely admired *The Humiliated Christ in Modern Russian Thought*, and Elisabeth Behr-Sigel published a major monograph on him along with a collection of his letters.[12]

Florovsky would have us believe the Bukharev Affair 'was not a theological quarrel ... but a psychological conflict first of all, and a very personal one at that,' between Askochensky and Archimandrite Feodor.[13] The denial of theological substance to

---

[10] See Ch. 3, 'A Wedding' above. For more details on Florensky's interest in Bukharev, see *Arkhimandrit Feodor: pro et contra*, pp. 750–2.

[11] A.M. Bukharev, 'O sobornykh apostol'skikh poslaniiakh,' *Bogoslovskie trudy* 9 (1972):149–225. The manuscript was prepared for publication by a docent of Moscow Theological Academy, Archimandrite Anatoly (Kuznetsov), who was subsequently elected to the episcopate.

[12] Nadejda Gorodetzky, *The Humiliated Christ in Modern Russian Thought* (London: Society for Promoting Christian Knowledge; New York: The Macmillan Company, 1938), pp. 115–26. For Behr-Sigel see Ch. 1, n. 1 above. Zenkovsky devotes a few pages to Bukharev in *A History of Russian Philosophy* (1:315–19), claiming 'the most important tendencies of subsequent Russian religious thought (Vladimir Solovyov, in a part of his theoretical constructions, and especially Fr Sergius Bulgakov) – even in those who, like Rozanov, remained "outside the walls of the Church" – are a direct continuation of Bukharev's "theology of culture."' The present study demonstrates the validity of Zenkovsky's observation.

[13] Florovsky's discussion of Bukharev is found in *Puti russkogo bogosloviia*, pp. 344–9.

his opponents is standard operating procedure with Florovsky, of course, and must be rejected in Bukharev's case. The dogmatic seriousness of Bukharev's thought has been amply documented above and was implicitly conceded by Florovsky himself when he noted the extent to which Archimandrite Feodor was indebted to Metropolitan Filaret's dogmatic theology.[14] Moreover, Florovsky's chief criticism of Bukharev's thought clearly turns on a point of theology, not personality. Florovsky complains that Feodor's 'unrestrained optimism and joy in reconciliation,' which sprang from 'a very vivid experience of salvation as something that has already been completed,' blinded him to the sinfulness and perversity of the world. The plain fact is Archimandrite Feodor's theology does not fit the procrustean bed into which Florovsky would tuck modern Russian theology. Florovsky believed that, except for a few lonely geniuses who grasped 'the mind of the fathers' (e.g. Metropolitan Filaret), modern Russian Orthodox theologians propounded either a scholasticism patterned on Roman Catholic theology or a pietism borrowed from Protestant sources. Archimandrite Feodor's thought clearly transcends these alternatives. It is too dogmatic to be termed pietistic, too experiential to be called scholastic, too humanistic to be construed in Neopatristic terms.

Florovsky's verdict on Archimandrite Feodor was severe. 'Bukharev lacked creative power, he did not possess ascetical fortitude. He did not bear his own cross. Hence his collapse. His example is touching but in no way prophetic or heroic.' The issue of course is what one means by prophetic or heroic. If these words are merely synonyms for ascetically motivated suspicion or rejection of the secular world, then Florovsky's conclusion might be justified. But should prophetic faith be reduced to world-renouncing asceticism?

A comparison between Metropolitan Filaret and Archimandrite Feodor is suggestive in this regard.[15] The great metropolitan was famed for his ascetical outlook. Strictness,

---

[14] See Ch. 1, n. 5 above.
[15] Florovsky, too, was drawn to this comparison: 'One might call Filaret a *tragic prudentialist* [*tragicheskim ekonomistom*]. Bukharev was a maximalist [*akrivist*] – a *utopian of maximalism*.' *Puti russkogo bogosloviia*, p. 348.

suspicion and a nearly pathological caution toward everything secular were hallmarks of his ministry. Yet at the heart of Filaret's dogmatics stood the Lamb of God who gives himself for the life of the world. Filaret resolved the apparent contradiction between his dogmatic vision and his practical attitude by homiletic means. By virtue of his exceptional eloquence in the Russian language he brought dogma to life in the elegant theological poetry of his sermons. The excitement, indeed charisma, of Filaret's dogmatic vision enchanted his protégés in the younger generation, Archimandrite Feodor included. But what were the students supposed to do with the master's dogmatics other than simply repeat his words less eloquently? Florovsky does not allow for an extra-homiletic, extra-liturgical activation of Filaret's dogmatics, nor did Filaret. Archimandrite Feodor's dogmatic vision was very close to Filaret's, but he brought it to life not rhetorically but in a call to action, in a program for ministry and mission to the modern world. Filaret could not condone the application of his dogmatics to a world which he viewed in profoundly negative terms. 'It seems we are already living on the outskirts of Babylon, if not actually in it,' he once said.[16] Archimandrite Feodor, as we have seen, had a different view of the impure city: 'Fallen, fallen is Babylon the great' (Rev. 14:8). This, too, was a judgment upon worldly powers, but a judgment which opened the world to the activism of the saints, a prophetic faith that declared the world safe for Orthodoxy, so to speak. Florovsky excoriated such faith as 'utopian.' But are utopianism and custodialism the only options for the gospel in the modern world?

Elisabeth Behr-Sigel sees Bukharev as the prophet of a better way, an 'Orthodox prophetism' that does not seek 'a crusade against the modern world, nor flight, nor genuflection before it, but a way through the walls of division to that Light "which, by coming into the world, enlightens every person."'[17] At the same time she cautions against viewing Bukharev as 'an anarchising

---

[16] Quoted by Florovsky, *Puti russkogo bogosloviia*, p. 184.
[17] *Alexandre Boukharev*, pp. 96-7. Note that Behr-Sigel translates John 1:9 a bit differently than Bukharev, who always rendered it 'the light that enlightens every human being who comes into the world.'

modernist' or as a reformer in the Protestant sense of the word, i.e. one who rejects the historic church in the name of a pristine and putatively original Christianity.[18] Bukharev's thought was shaped by classical dogma, and his prophetism served historic Orthodoxy.

With her intellectual generosity and sense of moderation Behr-Sigel is much fairer to Bukharev than Florovsky. She rightly criticizes Neopatristic scholars for diminishing modern Orthodox theology by disregarding Bukharev and other creative Russian Orthodox theologians whose work does not fit the Neopatristic mold. One might ask, however, whether Behr-Sigel fully appreciates the impact which a fresh look at Bukharev and other reconstructionist theologians would have on modern Orthodox theology. In the conclusion of her study she calls for 'the integration of the best intuitions and aspirations of [modern] creative thought into the grand patristic, palamite and philokalic tradition which has now been rediscovered and reassimilated.'[19] The integralism of this proposal, while well-intentioned, will inevitably deflect the humanizing thrust of Bukharev's theology unless it is paired with a simultaneous recasting of patristic, palamite and philokalic categories. But such a recasting is not something which contemporary Neopatristic theologians are likely to accept. In other words Bukharev's legacy is probably better served by calling for a frank and open dialogue between different approaches to Orthodox theology than by pressing for a premature synthesis which would satisfy no one.

The appropriation of Bukharev's theology is also affected by the complications of the theological scene in post-Soviet Russia. An anthology of some of Bukharev's writings appeared in Russia in 1991, and a large sourcebook with detailed bibliographies came out in 1998.[20] But the central theological institutions of Russian Orthodoxy have not yet shown an interest in Bukharev comparable to that of the period 1900–17. The

---

[18] *Alexandre Boukharev*, pp. 67, 89.
[19] *Alexandre Boukharev*, p. 92.
[20] *O dukhovnykh potrebnostiakh zhizni*, ed. Koksheneva, 316 pp.; *Arkhimandrit Feodor: pro et contra*, 831 pp.

unhappy denouement of Archimandrite Feodor's monastic vocation is one reason for this reticence, but probably not the crucial one. A weightier factor is the perfectly natural desire on the part of post-Soviet Russian theologians to assimilate the Neopatristic legacy of the Orthodox diaspora from which they were forcibly cut off by decades of Soviet repression. This *neo*-Neopatristic tendency, paralleling the neo-traditionalism of much church life in post-communist Russia, discourages attention to reconstructionist and philosophic Orthodox theologians. But the relevance of the latter is guaranteed by a huge and obvious fact of life to which Russian Orthodox theology will eventually have to turn its attention in a systematic way: the emergence of a free and profoundly secularized modern civilization in Russia.

To modern western Christians who take the involvement of the church in contemporary affairs for granted, Bukharev's call for an engaged church might seem unexceptionable. In its time, however, his witness was a bold break with the tradition of social, cultural and political passivity on the part of the Orthodox Church in Russia. The tradition was deeply ingrained in Russian custom and law and enforced by the highest authorities in church and state. A critique of passivity and isolation, carried on deep within established church institutions and in terms of Orthodox dogmatic theology, was an impressive accomplishment.

At the same time Bukharev's renewalism should not be equated with the secularizing type of Christian activism that became common in the West beginning in the nineteenth century. Bukharev did not preach engagement with the world without reference to dogmatic faith or as some sort of alternative to it; on the contrary, the dogma of the Word made flesh was his bridge to the world. The dogmatic content of his thought kept his renewalism theologically serious. Bukharev was as concerned with Orthodox tradition as he was with the brave new world of modernity. A dialogical both/and governed his mentality. For a comparable phenomenon in the West one might look to some of the reform-minded catholics of nineteenth and twentieth century Anglicanism, such as F.D. Maurice and Charles Gore. But comparisons are ultimately beside the point. Bukharev belongs first and foremost to the history of Orthodox theology. In that context his thought represented a new development, a home-grown theology of dialogue, different from what came before it and prophetic of the opportunities and challenges that lay ahead. He was Russia's, and Orthodoxy's, first modern theologian.

PART II

SOLOVIEV: THE CRITICAL TURN

5

Young Soloviev: Mystic and Critic

Vladimir Sergeevich Soloviev was born in Moscow in 1853.[1] On
the paternal side he came from a long line of Orthodox priests,
although his father, Sergei Mikhailovich, had received a secular
education and was a professor of history at Moscow University.
Vladimir's mother, Poliksena Vladimirovna, grew up in a
military family.

[1] The most nuanced biography of Soloviev is K. Mochul'skii, *Vladimir Solov'ev:
zhizn' i uchenie*, 2nd ed. (Paris: YMCA-Press, 1951). A more detailed study is S.M.
Solov'ev, *Zhizn' i tvorcheskaia evoliutsiia Vladimira Solov'eva* (Brussels:
Izdatel'stvo Zhizn' s Bogom, 1977). The portrait by Maxime Herman, *Vie et
oeuvre de Vladimir Soloviev*, Collection Prémices (Éditions Universitaires Fribourg
Suisse, 1995), originally published in 1947, remains an excellent introduction.
Soloviev's religious activism is described in detail by D. Strémooukhoff, *Vladimir
Soloviev et son oeuvre messianique*, Publications de la Faculté des Lettres de l'Uni-
versité de Strasbourg, fasc. 69 (Paris: Société d'Édition, Les Belles Lettres, 1935);
English version: *Vladimir Soloviev and His Messianic Work*, ed. Philip Guilbeau
and Heather Elise MacGregor, trans. Elizabeth Meyendorff (Belmont, Mass.:
Nordland, 1980). A good recent survey of Soloviev's thought focusing on his
religious ideas is Jonathan Sutton, *The Religious Philosophy of Vladimir Solovyov:
Towards a Reassessment* (New York: St Martin's Press, 1988). Essays on Soloviev
by the distinguished philosopher A.F. Losev (1893–1988) have been published in
Russia: 'Tvorcheskii put' Vladimira Solov'eva,' in Vladimir Sergeevich Solov'ev,
Sochineniia v dvukh tomakh, ed. with intros by A.F. Losev and A.V. Gulyga,
Filosofskoe nasledie 104–5, 2 vols (Moscow: Akademiia nauk SSSR, Institut
filosofii, Izdatel'stvo 'Mysl'', 1988), 1:3–32; and A. Losev, *Vladimir Solov'ev i ego
vremia*, ed. L.V. Blinnikov (Moscow: Izdatel'stvo 'Progress', 1990). Soloviev's
correspondence is collected in *Pis'ma Vladimira Sergeevicha Solov'eva*, ed. E.L.
Radlov, 3 vols (St Petersburg: Tipografiia t-va 'Obshchestvennaia Pol'za',
1908–11); supplementary vol. (St Petersburg: Izdatel'stvo 'Vremia', 1923). For a
select bibliography of works about Soloviev including English and other translations of his writings, see Sutton, *The Religious Philosophy of Vladimir Solovyov*,
pp. 228–39.

Soloviev's father was the dominant personality in the family.[2] Already well-known by the time Vladimir was born, Sergei Mikhailovich was the leading Russian historian of his generation. An admirer of the Enlightenment and a moderate liberal, Sergei was also an observant Orthodox Christian who kept his household on a strict ecclesiastical regimen.

Several features of Vladimir's outlook can be traced to his father's influence: political liberalism, Europeanism and a basic, though not uncritical, loyalty to church and state. In taste and temperament, however, the son differed markedly from his father. Sergei was methodical, prosaic, a family man and punctilious churchman. His scholarship was concrete and historical. Vladimir was a visionary, a poet, a lifelong bachelor. His Orthodox faith was oriented to mysticism and prophecy. His mind thrived on theoretical philosophy.

Soloviev received his secondary education in a classical gymnasium and entered Moscow University in 1869. He took most of his work in the Physical-Mathematical Faculty but passed the candidate's examination in the Historical-Philological Faculty in 1873. The switch was prompted by academic reverses as well as by the clarification of his own deepest interests. As he later put it:

> In the natural sciences, to which I intended to devote myself, I was not interested in the specific details but in the general results, the philosophical side of natural science. I made a serious study of only two sciences: plant morphology and comparative anatomy. Since it was philosophy that I was seeking in the natural sciences it was natural for me to turn to philosophy itself.[3]

Soloviev needed little prompting by teachers. The only professor to whom he was close in his student years was

---

[2] For a sketch of the Soloviev family see S.M. Solov'ev, *Zhizn' i tvorcheskaia evoliutsiia*, pp. 31–49.

[3] Quoted in S.M. Solov'ev, *Zhizn' i tvorcheskaia evoliutsiia*, p. 59.

P.D. Yurkevich (1827–74).[4] A product of Orthodox theological schools, Yurkevich began his career on the faculty of Kiev Theological Academy, moving to Moscow University in 1861 to take a chair in philosophy. Like F.A. Golubinsky, Bukharev's teacher at Moscow Theological Academy, Yurkevich was an important link between Orthodox theology and modern philosophy in Russia. He obviously succeeded in imparting a sense of the importance of this connection to his star pupil, for upon graduation from the university Soloviev decided to spend a year as an auditor at Moscow Theological Academy.

It was unusual for a university graduate to proceed to the theological academy. Soloviev's family and friends feared he was contemplating a monastic vocation. However, this was not the case. Disavowing ascetical ambitions in a letter to a girlfriend, he expressed the opinion that 'monasticism at one time had a high destiny, but now the time has come not to flee the world but to enter it and transform it.'[5] Moreover, while Soloviev enjoyed his year at the theological academy, it was not because the atmosphere was otherworldly. 'The academy ... is not the absolute vacuity that the university is,' he wrote. 'For all their coarseness the students strike me as a practical lot, besides which they are happy, good-natured, and great masters of the bottle – in short, healthy people. Nevertheless, I won't be mixing with them – there'll be no time for that.'[6]

There was no time because Soloviev's purpose was to read, think and write. By the end of the year he had completed his first book, *The Crisis of Western Philosophy (Against the*

---

[4] Mochul'skii, *Vladimir Solov'ev*, p. 41. On Yurkevich see V. V. Zenkovsky, *A History of Russian Philosophy*, 1:313–15; and Soloviev's memorial essay of 1874: 'O filosofskikh trudakh P.D. Iurkevicha,' *Sobranie sochinenii Vladimira Sergeevicha Solov'eva*, eds S.M. Solov'ev and E.L. Radlov, 2nd ed., 10 vols (St Petersburg, 1911–14; photographic reprint, Brussels: Foyer Oriental Chrétien, 1966), 1:171–96. The Solov'ev and Radlov edition of Soloviev's works, including supplementary vols 11–12 (Brussels: Izdatel'stvo Zhizn' s Bogom, Foyer Oriental Chrétien, 1969–70), is hereafter abbreviated *SSVSS*. A collection of Yurkevich's works appeared in Russia at the end of the Soviet period: P.D. Iurkevich, *Filosofskie proizvedeniia*, ed V.S. Stepin *et al.* (Moscow: Izdatel'stvo 'Pravda', 1990).

[5] Quoted in S.M. Solov'ev, *Zhizn' i tvorcheskaia evoliutsiia*, p. 88.

[6] Quoted in S.M. Solov'ev, *Zhizn' i tvorcheskaia evoliutsiia*, p. 90.

Positivists). He defended it as a Masters' thesis in philosophy at St Petersburg University in 1874.[7] Early in 1875 he began teaching philosophy at Moscow University, taking over from Yurkevich, who had died a few months earlier.

In the summer of 1875 Soloviev went abroad for the first time. The university awarded him a year-long travel grant to do research on gnosticism and mystical philosophy in the British Museum. Shortly before his departure he proposed marriage to one of his students, the young aristocrat Elizaveta Mikhailovna Polivanova, who rejected him. Far from being depressed by her refusal, Soloviev set out for London in an exalted mood, vowing to discover 'a new, eternal day' beyond the shadowy and insubstantial realm of 'earthly sleep.'[8]

In London Soloviev looked for soul-mates in the flourishing spiritualist community but came away from the séances unimpressed, concluding 'the spiritualism there (and consequently spiritualism in general, since London is its center) is an utterly paltry thing.'[9] In the British Museum, on the other hand, Soloviev found what he was looking for. After some weeks of research on the gnostic and mystical notion of Sophia, the Wisdom of God, while sitting in the main reading room of the museum, Soloviev had a vision of the Lady. Many years later he described the apparition in his poem 'Three Encounters' (1898):

> It was towards autumn when once
> I said to her: 'O bloom of divinity!
> You are here, I feel it; why have you not shown
> Yourself to me since my childhood years?'

---

[7] *Krizis zapadnoi filosofii (Protiv pozitivistov)*, SSVSS, 1:27–170; and Solov'ev, *Sochineniia v dvukh tomakh*, eds Losev and Gulyga, 2:3–138. English trans.: Vladimir Solovyov, *The Crisis of Western Philosophy (Against the Positivists)*, trans. Boris Jakim (Hudson, New York: Lindisfarne Press, 1996). The thesis received a fair amount of attention in the press. The radical publicist N.K. Mikhailovsky and the philosopher K.D. Kavelin were critical. The Slavophile M.P. Pogodin and the eminent literary critic N.N. Strakhov were sympathetic. See Mochul'skii, *Vladimir Solov'ev*, pp. 56–8, and S.M. Solov'ev, *Zhizn' i tvorcheskaia evoliutsiia*, pp. 99–100.

[8] Poem to Polivanova, quoted in S.M. Solov'ev, *Zhizn' i tvorcheskaia evoliutsiia*, p. 111.

[9] Quoted in Mochul'skii, *Vladimir Solov'ev*, p. 65.

The moment these words came to me,
Suddenly all was golden-azure,
She shone before me again,
But only her face – that alone.

Entreating the Lady to reveal herself more fully, Soloviev heard a voice say, 'To Egypt!' Taking this to be a promise of further revelations he packed his bags and headed for the Channel. Before long he was on the banks of the Nile, whence he departed for the most famous forcing-house of visions in eastern Christendom, the Thebaid desert. The outing came close to costing Soloviev his life as he fell into the hands of hostile bedouins and then nearly perished from exposure. Yet once again he found what he was looking for:

Somnolent, in fear, I lay there.
But then a breeze whispered, 'Sleep, poor friend!'
And I slept. When I woke up
The earth and heavenly vault breathed roses.

And in the violet splendor of the heavens,
With eyes of azure flame
You gazed at me, like the first rays
Of the universal day of creation.[10]

Soloviev remained in Egypt for four months. Before returning home he visited Italy and France. In Italy he conceived a brief but powerful attachment to a young married woman, an affair which showed Soloviev's mystical preoccupations had not eradicated his susceptibility to earthly love.[11] Not long after his return to Russia he fell in love with another married woman, Sofia Petrovna Khitrovo. He directed his affections to her for many years, composing love poetry for her to the end of his life.[12]

---

[10] 'Tri svidaniia,' in Vladimir Soloviev, *'Nepodvizhno lish' solntse liubvi ...': stikhotvoreniia, proza, pis'ma, vospominaniia sovremennikov*, ed. with intro. by Aleksandr Nosov (Moscow: Moskovskii Rabochii, 1990), pp. 118–24.
[11] Mochul'skii, *Vladimir Solov'ev*, p. 75; S.M. Solov'ev, *Zhizn' i tvorcheskaia evoliutsiia*, p. 147.
[12] On Soloviev's friendship with S.P. Khitrovo, see S.M. Solov'ev, *Zhizn' i tvorcheskaia evoliutsiia*, pp. 203–13; and Losev, *Vladimir Solov'ev i ego vremia*, pp. 656–63.

In the academic year 1876–7 Soloviev returned to teaching and worked on a second book, *The Philosophical Principles of Integral Knowledge*.[13] Before the year was over, however, he resigned his academic post and moved to St Petersburg. At the time he attributed his decision to quarrels with the faculty at Moscow University, but in the light of his later career Soloviev's move can be seen as a step toward the lifestyle which suited him best, that of an independent scholar and publicist.

Soloviev picked a good time to begin his publicistic career. Early in 1877 Russia declared war on the Ottoman empire in response to Turkish violence against Orthodox Christians in the Balkans. For the first time since the end of the Crimean War (1856), the Eastern Question returned to the center stage of European politics and lent new urgency to the issue of Russia's historical mission. Gripped by Panslav and Orthodox enthusiasm, many Russians hoped the war would result in the restoration of a Christian empire in Constantinople.

Like Archimandrite Feodor during the Crimean conflict, Soloviev fell in with the prophets. Hitching religious philosophy to Russian messianism, he delivered a rousing lecture, 'Three Forces,' to the Society of Amateurs of Russian Literature in April 1877.[14] His thesis was as simple as it was bold. The world is dominated by two opposed, but equally flawed, religious principles: the Islamic or oriental principle of 'the inhuman God,' a formula justifying universal servitude, and the modern European principle of 'the godless human individual,' a formula validating 'universal egoism and anarchy.' The conflict between these principles can only end in a vicious circle. Fortunately for humanity there is a country, Russia, where East and West meet and transcend their spiritual division in a higher religious principle: *bogochelovechestvo*, the humanity of God. As history's 'third force,' Russia is destined to blaze the path not just to Constantinople but to the universal, divine-human cultural synthesis of the future.

Soloviev heeded his own call to arms. He set out for the

---

[13] *Filosofskie nachala tsel'nogo znaniia*, SSVSS, 1:250–407; and Solov'ev, *Sochineniia v dvukh tomakh*, eds Losev and Gulyga, 2:139–288.
[14] 'Tri sily,' SSVSS, 1:227–39. See also the summary by Mochul'skii, *Vladimir Soloviev*, pp. 80–3.

Balkans with thoughts of soldiering or serving as a war correspondent. He never reached the front, but his enthusiasm for the visionary scheme of 'Three Forces' was undiminished. It found a more compatible outlet in a series of public lectures delivered in St Petersburg in 1878–81 and published under the title, *Lectures on the Humanity of God*.[15]

A work of philosophical and theological speculation, *Lectures on the Humanity of God* surely flew over the heads of most of the Petersburg intelligentsia who attended them. But the audience would have had no trouble understanding the dedication: 'for the Red Cross, but also in part for the restoration of St Sophia's in Constantinople.'[16] The unstable juxtaposition of humanitarianism and imperialism evident here was typical of Soloviev's thinking at the time. It would be a few years before the first commitment displaced the second in his vocation.

Soloviev's publicism did not keep him from applying himself to the more rigorous tasks of theoretical and academic philosophy. In 1880 he defended a brilliant doctoral dissertation, *The Critique of Abstract Principles*, at St Petersburg University.[17] It was his fourth book in six years. He was twenty-seven years old.

The Critique of Abstract Principles and *Lectures on the Humanity of God*, written concurrently, have a direct bearing on each other. The relationship is one of complementarity, not similarity, for the books are very different. In the *Critique* Soloviev proposes a critical method for evaluating truth claims and applies it to the dominant systems of thought in his day. His conclusion is that all of the systems fall short because they lack a connection with 'positive religion.' In *Lectures* he draws on mythology, world religions and Christian theology to clarify the principles of positive religion. In the next two chapters I offer a systematic reading of these two works.

[15] See Ch. 7, n. 1 below.
[16] Letter to D. Tsertelev quoted in Mochul'skii, *Vladimir Solov'ev*, p. 91; cf. S.M. Solov'ev, *Zhizn' i tvorcheskaia evoliutsiia*, p. 164.
[17] See Ch. 6, n. 1 below.

6

The Critique of Abstract Principles

The Critique of Abstract Principles is the masterpiece of Soloviev's early career.[1] In it he defines the terms of his philosophy and outlines a critical program for ethics and epistemology. In the preface he tells us he intends to extend the program to esthetics in a work on 'the principles of creativity.'[2] He never wrote this book, although he contributed many seminal essays on more restricted topics in esthetics later in his career. As for religion, Soloviev considered it to be an integral dimension of all spheres of human experience. Critical reflection on religion therefore occurs throughout the *Critique*.

In *The Critique of Abstract Principles* criticism has both a general and a specialized meaning. Criticism in the general sense means the study of criteria, something which all philosophers do. Criticism in the specialized sense refers to Soloviev's project, which he calls 'the critique of abstract principles.'

Let us begin with criticism as the study of criteria. A criterion is a first principle or other measure by which human beings evaluate the data of experience as good, true, beautiful or the opposite. Whether they realize it or not, people are always making judgments about goodness, truth and beauty, for otherwise they would experience the world as totally chaotic. Much of the time, of course, people find it possible to live their lives without voicing, much less defining, their criteria. However, two facts of life occasionally disrupt this intellectual

---

[1] *Kritika otvlechennykh nachal, SSVSS,* 2:v–xvi, 1–397. A portion of the work (preface, chs 25–46, conclusion and notes) is included in Solov'ev, *Sochineniia v dvukh tomakh,* eds Losev and Gulyga, 1:581–756. All references to *Kritika* in the present study are to the Solov'ev and Radlov edition (*SSVSS*).

[2] *Kritika,* p. vii.

apathy. First, actual human experience is full of tensions and contradictions. Second, individuals and communities often disagree about what is good, true or beautiful. Conflicts of this sort, when sufficiently grave, force people to attempt to clarify their principles. In a word, they begin to philosophize.

Certain historical periods are marked by deeper conflicts over first principles than others. They may be called critical ages. At such times philosophizing becomes a matter of considerable practical importance. When, for example, 'there are scholars who regard the brilliant ideas of Plato or Kant as idle inventions or simply absurdities; when there are artists and critics who despise Shakespeare and Raphael; when, finally, so many moralists see Indian or Christian ascetics as nothing but blind fanatics or even crude beasts, then one must ask: to what end have these best efforts of humankind been made?'[3] That is, those who prize Plato, Kant, Shakespeare and so on are forced to say why they prize them. Are their predilections merely arbitrary, or are they justified by objective criteria?

To be sure, people can turn away from intellectual challenges, at least for a while. But when they do so they become 'like the rich man who possesses very real treasures, but on the basis of contested or even legally invalid documents, with the result that he cannot use his property as it should be used; and so it becomes a thing of little value to him'; or they come to resemble the unwitting heir to a hidden treasure 'who neither knows nor wishes to know anything about it because he deems it a fairy tale and considers those who tell him about it to be superstitious people or charlatans.'[4]

With good reason Soloviev judged his age to be 'a critical epoch.'[5] The materialists and positivists of nineteenth-century Europe did in fact reject the ideas of Plato and Kant, radical literary critics rejected classical standards in letters, anticlericals and atheists rejected traditional religious beliefs and even religion as such. The time was ripe for philosophy.

---

[3] *Kritika*, p. 6.
[4] *Kritika*, p. 6.
[5] *Kritika*, p. v. The phrase appears in the opening paragraph of *Kritika* and helps establish the theme of the work.

THE CRITICAL PROGRAM

The critique of abstract principles rests on a basic distinction. According to Soloviev there are two kinds of principles for determining the goodness, truth or beauty of anything – 'positive or substantive,' and 'abstract or negative' principles:

> The first sort are those principles which present themselves to the mind as ready-made, already given and essentially independent of reason; principles, therefore, which are accepted by *faith* and not on the basis of rational investigation ... Principles of the *second type* do not present themselves to the mind as already given and beyond all doubt; on the contrary, they arise when the individual mind, relating *negatively* to all that is immediately given, especially to the aforementioned positive principles, frees itself from the power of the latter, loses faith in them and strives by means of rational investigation of all worldly relations to arrive at certain general propositions or norms which necessarily have an *abstract* quality.

The relationship of the mind to the first sort of principles is primarily, though not exclusively, passive; to the second, primarily, but not exclusively, active.[6]

Soloviev follows up this primary distinction with two secondary ones. Positive principles are either 'traditional' or 'mystical' in origin. Abstract principles are 'empirical or material,' i.e. constructed from sense data, or else 'formal or pure-rational' principles based on the mind's own forms and categories.[7]

The secondary distinctions make it plain Soloviev's primary distinction between positive and abstract principles has to do with the difference between making judgments on the basis of received models or personal inspiration and making judgments by means of rational discourse. For example, one could evaluate an action by consulting the moral example of Jesus or, alternatively, by assessing the action in terms of its universal

---

[6] *Kritika*, pp. 8–9.
[7] *Kritika*, pp. 13–14.

application, i.e. by asking whether the maxim of the action could be taken as a universal law. Jesus' moral example and Kant's categorical imperative both speak to the need for ethical criteria, and both provide powerful guides to action. But as principles they rest on very different grounds and have different strengths and weaknesses as a result. The example of Jesus will be a powerful ethical criterion only where some sort of faith in Jesus is present, whereas Kant's imperative addresses all rational beings. On the other hand, where the requisite faith is present the example of Jesus has immense practical force as well as the virtue of simplicity, whereas Kant's categorical imperative, even if it is accepted (and there are always reasons to prolong the discussion), stands at a remove from concrete human experience. Moreover, Kant's imperative could never move an irrational being, but the example of Jesus could, if faith were present. In short, positive principles are 'religious and close to life,' while abstract principles are 'scientific and academic.'[8]

Soloviev recognizes the distinction between abstract and positive principles is not as clear-cut in practice as it may appear in theory. Moreover, as we shall see later on, it is important to Soloviev that the distinction between the two types of principles not be absolutized. At the beginning of the discussion, therefore, Soloviev takes pains to observe there is no positive principle which is so completely grounded in faith (traditional or mystical) as to lack a rational component, nor any abstract principle so purely rational as to lack an element of faith: 'Just as positive principles, for all their actuality and connection with religious and mystical doctrines, cannot be totally devoid of an abstract philosophical element, so, too, abstract principles as they exist in philosophical systems and scientific theories can never free themselves entirely from a dogmatic element.'[9] As an example of the latter case Soloviev cites philosophical materialism, an abstract principle claiming to rest on sense data but in fact requiring dogmatic faith in the exclusive reality of 'matter' (whatever that might be). Admittedly materialism is an extreme

[8] *Kritika*, p. 10.
[9] *Kritika*, p. 10; cf. p. 8, n. 2.

case. But Soloviev maintains all rational systems, philosophic or scientific, 'necessarily demand a certain faith – faith in reason, at least.'[10]

With Soloviev's distinctions in mind we are in a position to consider his critical program. The critique of abstract principles is essentially a critique of critiques which operates by assessing abstract principles in the light of what Soloviev calls 'the whole of things' (*vseedinstvo*):

> By abstract principles I mean those particular ideas (particular aspects and elements of the idea of the whole of things) which, when they are abstracted from the whole and affirmed in their exclusivity, lose their true character and, through mutual contradiction and conflict, plunge the human world into the condition of intellectual discord in which it has existed up to now. The critique of these abstract and (in their abstractness) false principles must consist in defining their particularity and demonstrating the internal contradiction into which they necessarily fall when they try to take the place of the whole. By removing the claims of principles to signify the whole this critique takes its stand on a certain positive concept of what the authentic whole of things is, and in this way it becomes a positive critique. First, the critique presupposes the idea of the whole of things in its general and still undefined aspect as a certain unconditional criterion without which no criticism is possible. Second, by defining the true meaning of particular principles as isolated elements of the whole of things, the critique ends by lending a certain positive content to this last and so elaborates for us the idea of the whole of things.[11]

The critique of abstract principles is designed to apply to all spheres of human activity: morality, scientific and theoretical knowledge, artistic creativity. The Solovievian critic does not have to import abstract principles into these spheres; he finds them there already in the form of various one-sided or 'exclusive' theories of goodness, truth or beauty. Examining

---

[10] *Kritika*, pp. 11–12.
[11] *Kritika*, pp. v–vi.

these theories, he discovers they all suffer from abstraction, either of the empiricist or of the rationalist type.

In ethics, for example, empirically based theories of the good (e.g. eudemonism, hedonism, utilitarianism) vie with rationalist theories (e.g. Kant's categorical imperative). These conflicts complicate the search for the good. Yet the critic must not think he can simply banish abstract principles from morality, as this would mean abolishing the ethical quest as such. Abstract principles are unavoidable, and only by formulating them rigorously and carrying them to their logical extreme can one evaluate them properly. However, the Solovievian critic points out that the conflicting extremes of abstraction cannot be the terminus of the ethical quest. Empiricist theories of ethics, for example, fail to account for human freedom; yet without assuming the freedom of human beings one cannot account for the phenomenon of an ethical quest in the first place, never mind arrive at a substantive moral vision. Pure rationalism falls short for the opposite reason. While it posits a free, rational will, it does so by abstracting the ethical subject from the world in which moral action is to take place and from the objective ethical good, which must be something greater than the individual ethical subject.

The same sort of extremes arise in the search for the ground of scientific and theoretical truth. 'The essential marks of truth' for Soloviev are 'unconditional reality and unconditional rationality.'[12] Pure rational theories of truth satisfy the demand for rationality but not for reality; the opposite is the case with thorough-going empiricist theories. In both cases the search for the ground of truth aborts; or to be more precise, it aborts if the search is seen as terminating with the clarification of abstract principles. But the Solovievian critic does not see abstraction as an end in itself but as the starting point for a new round of critical reflection, namely, a critique of critiques in the light of the whole of things.

The diagnostic proposition of this new critique is that the fault of every abstract principle lies not in the principle itself in so far as it makes a positive statement about the world, but in the tendency to regard the principle as the whole of things in the

[12] *Kritika*, p. ix.

sphere of experience to which it pertains. That is to say, the intellectual sin of abstraction is one-sidedness, exclusivity. So, for example, the empiricist is not wrong to insist moral activity be construed with reference to the flesh-and-blood world; he is right about this. But he is wrong to enthrone empiricism as the final arbiter of ethics. The Kantian rationalist is not wrong to insist actions should conform with the demands of the categorical imperative, but he is wrong to suppose that conformity with the categorical imperative alone or above all else makes an action moral. Likewise in other spheres of experience where conflicts over criteria arise, the Solovievian critic finds the origin of error to lie in the substitution of one or another abstraction for the living whole of things.

One can see now why the critique of abstract principles involves the assumption of the whole of things to which all criticism ultimately refers. The assumption has both a formal and a material side. The formal side concerns the idea of first principles. A principle is 'first' when it accounts for the whole of that for which it is the principle. An ethical first principle will account for the whole of moral experience; an esthetic first principle, for the experience of beauty in all its forms, and so on. Moreover, as human experience is one, the principles of its several spheres must be assumed to be compatible with each other.

The material side of Soloviev's assumption is the belief that, by clarifying what abstract principles positively affirm about the world, the critic discovers part of the contents of the whole of things. So, for example, by the concrete results issuing from the assumption of a material world order, the physical sciences show that the whole of things, whatever else it might be, must comprise a material world order. By the results issuing from the assumption of the rules of rationality, pure reason shows that the whole of things must comprise rationality, and so on. Formally and materially, then, the critique of abstract principles, which begins by relativizing abstractions, ends by arousing curiosity about the whole of things. Negative criticism transforms itself into a positive quest.

To many a critical mind Soloviev's assumption of the whole of things may appear problematic. Indeed, the whole of things may appear to be nothing more than an abstraction in its own right – an ironic outcome for a critique of abstractions. Our appreciation of Soloviev's whole of things will be enhanced, however, if we consider it in connection with the wider currents of thought which inspired his critique.

The first of these was critical idealism, the dramatic outcome of Kantian criticism in continental philosophy. Soloviev was well-schooled in the thought of all the modern idealists, although he stood closest to F.W.J. Schelling (1775–1854).[13] Like all the idealists Soloviev regarded human consciousness as the mysterious fact with which philosophy must begin. Human consciousness is mysterious because it cannot be understood as the sum of its functions; on the contrary, it enjoys a measure of sovereignty (freedom) over them. Seeking the ground of consciousness, the philosopher recognizes it cannot lie in nature, for spirit or mind, being free, transcends nature. Yet spirit or mind cannot be its own ground because it does not exist apart from that upon which it reflects, i.e. nature. The idealist responds to this problem with the theory that the ground of consciousness must lie in a transcendent 'absolute,' the source of nature and spirit alike. Soloviev's program for transcending the conflicts between empiricism and rationalism in a vision of the whole of things is a version of this theory.

Soloviev also resembles the idealists in his all-embracing humanism. For him as for them, philosophizing meant seeking a unified vision of the human good, 'a harmonious synthesis of religious, philosophical and experimental-scientific knowledge.'[14] He believed all creative human activities – ethics,

---

[13] Schelling's influence on Soloviev has always been recognized, but how extensive it was is only beginning to be appreciated. See Arsenii Gulyga, *Shelling* (Moscow: Izdatel'stvo 'Molodaia Gvardiia', 1984), pp. 289–309; V.V. Lazarev, 'Filosofiia Vl. Solov'eva i Shelling,' in *Filosofiia Shellinga v Rossii*, ed. V.F. Pustarnakova (St Petersburg: Izdatel'stvo Russkogo Khristianskogo gumanitarnogo instituta, 1998), pp. 477–99; and Paul Valliere, 'Solov'ev and Schelling's Philosophy of Revelation,' *Vladimir Solov'ev, Reconciler and Polemicist*, eds Wil van den Bercken, Manon de Courten and Evert van der Zweerde, Selected Papers of the International Conference on Vladimir Solov'ev 15–18 Sept. 1998, vol. 2 of Eastern Christian Studies (Leuven: Peeters, in press). See also the discussion of Soloviev's first published work, 'The Mythological Process in Ancient Paganism' (1873), in Sutton, *The Religious Philosophy of Vladimir Solovyov*, pp. 102–5.

[14] *Kritika*, p. 13.

politics, economics, science, art, piety – were or could be shown to be mutually relevant.

The idealist theory of the absolute does not exhaust the meaning of the whole of things for Soloviev. Religious interests also play a role. For Soloviev the whole of things is not just a theoretical postulate but a living divine reality, or God. That he regards the absolute in this way is clear from his use of religious language to describe ultimate reality.[15]

The religious character of Soloviev's thought is also clear from the outcome of the critique of abstract principles. Once Soloviev has exposed the one-sidedness of abstract principles and turns to the business of drafting more adequate principles, the latter all turn out to involve the divine ground of being. The critique of abstract principles in social and political philosophy generates the ideal of 'free theocracy'; in theoretical philosophy, 'free theosophy'; in esthetics, 'free theurgy.' What these three terms mean will occupy us in a moment. Here the point is simply that the knowledge resulting from the critique of abstraction in its several spheres invariably involves *theos*: the integration of goodness with God, scientific truth with God, artistic creativity with God. This infusion of theological content into the philosophical absolute was not original with Soloviev, to be sure. One finds it in some other idealist thinkers, above all in the later Schelling.[16] But in contrast to Schelling, who grew more

---

[15] See, for example, *Kritika*, p. 190, where Soloviev writes that 'each and every [human being] is inwardly and essentially in solidarity with all others in the absolute or whole of things (in God); this is the foundation of religion.' Later on the same page he addresses the question 'of the real existence of the being comprising the whole of things, or God.'

[16] On Schelling's later thought, see Frederick Copleston, *Fichte to Hegel*, vol. 7, pt 1 of *A History of Philosophy* (Garden City, New York: Doubleday & Company, Inc., Image Books, 1965), pp. 157–82. Copleston observes that 'Schelling is perhaps most notable for his transformation of the impersonal Absolute of metaphysical idealism into the personal God who reveals himself to the religious consciousness' (p. 182). The centrality of theological concerns in the later Schelling is also apparent to Andrew Bowie, *Schelling and Modern European Philosophy: An Introduction* (London and New York: Routledge, 1993). While Bowie himself regards Schelling's theology as a dead letter, he concedes that it 'still lives on in the theology of the kind developed by Rosenzweig, Paul Tillich and others' (p. 165). Soloviev's name should be added to this list. See also Robert Brown, 'Resources in Schelling for New Directions in Theology,' *Idealistic Studies* 20 (1990):1–17.

theological toward the end of his long career, Soloviev was God-intoxicated from the beginning.

The idea of the whole of things also acquires content through Soloviev's anthropology. Critical idealism and theological doctrines aside, Soloviev believes the idea of the whole of things is prompted by ordinary human experience. Human experience is a vast matrix. Nowhere in the world do human beings find anything which they do not feel themselves to be part of or aspire to be part of. To be sure, a human person is first of all a free, rational being:

> [Yet] it is a fact beyond doubt – however we explain it, a fact beyond doubt – that along with the rational consciousness that makes a person human there exists also physical attractions in the human being that make him a being of the natural world and mystical attractions that make him a divine or demonic being. A human being does not wish to be, and cannot be, *only* a human being, and this is but an instance of the law common to every concrete or living being:
>
> > Denn Alles sich mit göttlichem Erkühnen
> > Zu übertreffen strebt.
> > (For everything strives with divine temerity
> > to surpass itself.)[17]

This striving makes human beings religious in Soloviev's sense of the word: 'the human being possesses a religious striving, that is, the striving to affirm himself not as a conditional phenomenon only, but as an unconditional being; he strives to affirm himself in God and God in himself.'[18]

The wide dimensions of Soloviev's anthropology appear when he tries his hand at a formal definition of a human being. 'A human being, or humanity, is *a being containing in itself* (in the absolute order) *a divine idea*, that is, *the whole of things* or unconditional fullness of being, *and realizing* this idea (in the order of nature) *by means of rational freedom in material nature*.'[19] In other words, human beings are seekers of the

---

[17] *Kritika*, p. 159. The verses are from Goethe's 'West-östlicher Divan.'
[18] *Kritika*, p. 190.
[19] *Kritika*, p. 174.

whole. To disenfranchise them of this ambition is to violate their humanity.

Soloviev's idea of the whole of things has content, then, even if a system of the whole is not to be found in the *Critique*. Indeed, it would be surprising if such a system were found there. A system of the whole would necessarily be positive philosophy, which begins only after the critique of abstract principles has finished its work. The most that Soloviev promises in the *Critique* is 'a certain grounding of positive principles, but an insufficient and only preliminary one.'[20] As a matter of fact, a system of the whole is not to be found anywhere in Soloviev's works. Solovievian criticism is not a system but a project.

To get a better idea of the project we must see what it means in practical terms. Soloviev's critique of social and political principles, a major concern in *The Critique of Abstract Principles*, offers a good example.

THEOCRACY AND FREEDOM

The critique of social and political principles seeks to clarify a satisfactory social and political ideal. Now no one looks for anything without some idea of what he is looking for, and the philosopher is no exception. In the social and political sphere Soloviev wants an ideal that will meet the needs of free individuals on the one hand and the need for community on the other, hence 'the ideal of a free communality' (*svobodnaia obshchinnost'*).[21] In the modern critical age the effort to clarify the form which such an ideal might take gives rise to antagonistic abstractions paralleling the split between empiricist and rationalist principles in theoretical ethics. Empirically minded critics advance the principle of socialism; rationalists propound legalism, or the rule of law.[22] Both principles are valid up to a point, but each suffers from the defect of absolutizing one element of the social and political whole to the detriment of the others.

---

[20] *Kritika*, p. vi.
[21] *Kritika*, p. 166.
[22] For the discussion of socialism see *Kritika*, chs 14–17; for legalism, chs 18–20; for a concise summary of the results of both discussions, ch. 23:166–8.

Soloviev takes socialism to be the highest form of empiricist social ethics. It locates the social ideal in the creation and distribution of material well-being for all people, and for all people equally. In so far as a satisfactory social ideal should secure the economic well-being of all people, socialism makes a positive contribution. But socialism alone is not a satisfactory social ideal. Its preoccupation with material production and distribution is one-sided and hence abstract. Moreover, socialism fails to account for its own ideal:

> The material incentives and interests that hold sway over [the economy] by their very nature fail to provide any sort of basis for true unity, since material interest by itself is egoistic and exclusive. Nor [do material interests provide] for freedom, since a human being appears here as nothing more than one of a number of natural forces. Given the natural inequality of these forces and the struggle between them, the subjection of some to others is inevitable, and consequently the freedom of the individual person is by no means guaranteed.'[23]

Socialists sometimes try to answer these criticisms by appealing to human sympathy or to a primordial 'social instinct.' But these forces, even if their existence is conceded, do not provide a firm foundation for the social ideal. For one thing, the conscious, purposive motives of human beings interfere with the operation of instinct. Furthermore, the feeling of sympathy, if regarded as an empirical datum rather than as the expression of a transcendental principle, appears to be a more or less accidental phenomenon. To the extent that it can be predicted at all, its 'intensity stands in reverse proportion to its extension.'[24] That is to say, people feel greater sympathy for family members, friends and ethnic fellows than for people at further remove. As a basis for ethics, then, natural sympathy is limited in scope and notoriously unstable.

The rational legalist has solutions to some of the problems which socialism ignores. First, the legalist assumes from the start that human beings are to be treated as free, rational agents, for this assumption is essential to the concept of rationally derived

[23] *Kritika*, p. 166.
[24] *Kritika*, p. 167.

norms of behavior such as rights and duties. Second, the legalist vindicates human equality in the notion of equality before the law. This sort of equality is, indeed, the whole point of law. Free, rational beings devise law in order to guarantee the freedom and rights of all. 'Law is freedom conditioned by equality,' as Soloviev puts it.[25] Moreover, legal institutions lend rational norms of behavior a practical realization which is every bit as concrete as the economic order propounded by the socialists.

How, then, does legalism fall into abstraction? Soloviev's answer is that legalist justice, when taken as the sole or ultimate basis of the social and political ideal, has no place for love; and without love the sense of community which should pervade every society lacks a ground. Rational legalism achieves an admirable balance between social and individual principles in the juridical concept of equality:

> But this balance is purely outward and negative. To say that all people are equal before the law is to say that all are equally *restricted* by the law, or that all people restrict each other in equal measure; here, then, we have no inward and positive unity among people but only the proper division and demarcation between them.'[26]

That is to say, the most a legal system can ever command is, 'Respect your neighbor,' i.e. do not violate your neighbor's rights. The law can never command, 'Love your neighbor.' Indeed, it would not be law if it did so. Sympathy, as we have seen, is too accidental a thing to be the ground of law, while the formal concept of a free rational being, the proper subject of law, does not entail the idea of a loving being. In fact, the formal concept does not dictate any positive moral object:

> Law defines the normative character of the means or method of action ... but not the ends or objects of action. From the viewpoint of law all ends are indifferent, it leaves them completely undetermined. For law there is no *normative* end, no normative will or intention. Heroic self-denial and self-

[25] *Kritika*, p. 153.
[26] *Kritika*, p. 167.

interested calculation present no difference from the viewpoint of law: it does not require the first and does not forbid the second.[27]

But the general social and political ideal must contain a normative end; moreover, that end must be one which all people can love and which nurtures their love for each other. On this point the socialists with their 'social instinct' are on the right track even though they misconstrue the ontological ground of sympathy.

Where should the search for this ground be directed? Soloviev believes it should be directed to religion. Religious or mystical insight transforms natural sympathy into universal love; it replaces an accident with a divine energy. The proposition may be formulated in the terms of Soloviev's anthropology: if socialist well-being fulfills human beings as creatures of nature, and if legal justice fulfills them as free, rational agents, then love fulfills them as 'gods,' i.e. whole-seekers, God-seekers. Of course an isolated individual cannot be the ground of love. That ground can only be the living divine reality or whole of things that envelops human life. The ultimate basis of ethics is 'the solidarity of all things,' the living divine whole.[28] The expression of this solidarity in the social and political community is what Soloviev means by 'theocracy,' i.e. the connecting of all the functions and institutions of society to the love of God. The economy and the state play crucial roles in realizing this solidarity, but a third institutional order is also required: 'a mystical or religious association, that is, a *church*.'[29]

Readers of the *Critique*, knowing Soloviev is a religious thinker, might suppose that with the introduction of the concepts of theocracy and church the search for the social and political ideal comes to an end. That this is not the case demonstrates the power and originality of Soloviev's thought. While the two concepts bring Soloviev closer to his end, he recognizes that they, too, must be subjected to criticism. That is to say, Soloviev recognizes that, however sweet the words theocracy

[27] *Kritika*, p. 156.
[28] *Kritika*, pp. 168–9.
[29] *Kritika*, p. 160.

and church might sound to pious ears, particularly in Orthodox Russia, they too can become abstract principles and do the same kind of damage that other abstractions do:

> Even though it is obvious that the divine principle in its true form, that is, as actually unconditional, embraces everything and cannot exclude any principle or element of being, the abstract mind nevertheless may affirm this principle as something *particular* and exclusive, apart from the others – that is, apart from the human and natural principles or even in direct opposition to them. Such an abstract understanding and affirmation of the divine principle as applied to the social ideal, that is, to the ideal of the church, gives rise to abstract clericalism and false theocracy.'[30]

False theocracy results from the domination of nature or reason by religion, or of the economy or state by the church. Its classic form for Soloviev, as for most Russian Orthodox, was Roman Catholic clericalism.[31] But Soloviev saw false theocracy as a threat arising in other social systems, too, including his own (as we shall see). The critic of abstract principles must reject false theocracy. Yet he must not reject the theocratic principle itself, for this would mean surrendering the values served by positing this principle in the first place. What, then, is the proper (critical) form of the theocratic ideal? Soloviev's answer is 'free theocracy,' that is to say, theocracy qualified by the freedom of the other spheres of the social whole.[32]

Since abstract clericalism proceeds by stifling natural desires or oppressing conscience, a right-minded theocracy will grant freedom to these forces and to all the activities connected with them, such as commerce, government, science, the arts and so on. Merely to say this, however, is not to show how the goal can be reached. The critic must be vigilant with regard to the means proposed.

One means of combatting clericalism is 'the complete separation of the spiritual sphere from the secular, or the principle of

---

[30] *Kritika*, pp. 160–1.
[31] See, for example, *Kritika*, pp. x and 161.
[32] *Kritika*, p. 166.

"a free church in a free state." '[33] Many European liberals subscribed to this solution in one form or another. Soloviev did not. To him it represented 'an unqualified dualism,' an abstraction not unlike clericalism. Indeed, Soloviev viewed this dualism as the result of the extreme to which Roman Catholic clericalism was carried in the West. Western clericalism aimed at the domination of society by the church; but as this was impossible, the western church ended up making all sorts of deals with secular forces to the detriment of its religious mission. Arbitrarily and unnaturally joined together, secular and religious forces struggled against each other. Dualism emerged as an attempt to resolve this antagonism by a precise demarcation of spheres. What dualists fail to see, however, is that church and state legislate norms in overlapping and sometimes identical spheres of activity. When these norms conflict human beings must find some way to mediate between them. Abstract dualism contains no mediating principle and thus fails as the criterion for free theocracy.[34]

For example, how is an individual to act when conflict arises between the claims of justice as defined by the state and the claims of love as defined by the church? Soloviev offers the case of capital punishment – a poignant one for him because, as we shall see, he staked his career on it in 1881. He insists that 'we simply cannot concede that I could *actually* show Christian love to a neighbor whom I send to the gallows in my capacity as a judge.'[35] The 'free church in a free state' formula cannot solve this dilemma in a principled way. It may salve the conscience of the Christian judge, but in no sense does it reconcile justice and love.

In place of dualism Soloviev argues for a hierarchy of values, formulating the hierarchy in such a way as to preserve the integrity of the several spheres and the creative tensions between them. The supreme good in Soloviev's value hierarchy is the living, divine whole of things. The love which springs from the divine whole and aspires to return to it comes next; it finds institutional expression in the church. Next comes justice, or

[33] *Kritika*, p. 163.
[34] *Kritika*, pp. 163–5.
[35] *Kritika*, p. 164.

respect for the freedom and rationality of human beings; it finds expression in a state based on the rule of law. Last comes material welfare, which is promoted by economic initiative and commerce. The supreme social and political ideal is one in which all these values operate together in proper order: 'Love by means of justice is to be realized in welfare. [Ethical] activity issues from love, takes the form of justice and puts on flesh in material welfare.'[36] The terms are not interchangeable. That is, Soloviev would not allow us to say 'justice by means of love' or '[ethical] activity issues from justice and takes the form of love.' The hierarchy must be respected. If one were to ask why, Soloviev would appeal to his metaphysics. The whole of things, as the inclusive reality, is greater than its components; free, rational beings are greater than non-rational organisms, and so on.

The integrity of each component of the hierarchy must be respected, too. Soloviev is very clear about this. For him a hierarchy of values is not a mask for authoritarianism but a dynamic expression of relatedness. The guiding principles are relative autonomy and relative dependence:

> So, in a society embodying the norm of free theocracy all the various elements of society, all the aspects and spheres of social relations are preserved, and they exist not as isolated, introverted, mutually irrelevant fields, or as fields that compete for exclusive dominance, but as necessary parts of one and the same complex entity ... Here we cannot have contradiction and exclusivity between the elements, for if all are necessary to each other, then all are autonomous and also dependent on one another at the same time.[37]

For example, even though love is greater than justice, as the church is greater than the state, the greater may not take the place of the smaller. Law may not be swallowed up by grace; on the contrary, when it comes to showing love for human beings,

---

[36] *Kritika*, p. 182. 'Welfare' translates *pol'za*, literally 'use' or 'profit.' Soloviev makes it clear that he uses the word in the broadest possible sense when, earlier on the same page, he writes of 'pleasure, or *pol'za* in the sense of the aggregate of [all] pleasures.' *Pol'za* thus means all the material goods affirmed by utilitarian, hedonist and eudemonist ethics.

[37] *Kritika*, p. 185.

'*justice is the necessary form of love.*'[38] Why? Because human beings are free, rational beings, which is to say beings with certain inalienable rights. Loving human beings without regard for their rights means not loving them for who and what they are, hence in the strict sense not loving them. The same principle applies to the integration of human beings in a theocracy. Theocracy is the social and political reflection of the whole of things. But a free, rational being must participate in the whole of things *as* a free, rational being; otherwise he or she strictly speaking does not participate in it. Thus, in a world peopled by free, rational beings, freedom and rationality must be accepted as the 'formal means' for realizing the ideal of theocracy, a point which is clearly stated in Soloviev's terminology: *free* theocracy.[39] Soloviev makes an analogous argument for the incorporation of nature into the theocratic ideal. Nature and economy (the molding of nature by human beings) are the material means for realizing theocracy. The material realm must not be excluded from the ideal, for precisely because of its material (non-ideal) status it is '*the source of real force for the idea.*' Without material embodiment theocracy hangs in the air. A theocracy that adequately represents the whole of things, by contrast, will achieve 'the mutual spiritualization of matter and materialization of spirit, or the inner agreement and balance of both principles.'[40] This does not mean that economy should be so free from subordination to reason and God that one could formulate the social ideal as a free economy in a free state in a free church. It does mean, however, that 'that sphere of society which has material interest or welfare as its special task must be considered a necessary component in the whole organism of a model society, and in this sense society as an economic union or *zemstvo* has a fixed and independent significance and cannot be eliminated or swallowed up by any other social sphere.'[41] The relative autonomy of the economy and all other spheres of society must be respected.

---

[38] *Kritika*, p. 180.
[39] On freedom and rationality as the 'formal means' for realizing theocracy see *Kritika*, pp. 172–3.
[40] *Kritika*, p. 174.
[41] *Kritika*, pp. 182–3.

An interesting implication of the relative autonomy of the lower levels of the value hierarchy is the relative dependence of the higher levels on the lower. This dependence does not reverse the hierarchy of values but simply articulates it from a different perspective, namely, the perspective of practice as distinct from pure theory. In theory, under the eye of eternity as it were, the sovereignty of love over justice and of justice over material benefit is perfectly clear by Soloviev's criteria. But in the actual struggle to realize this sovereignty in concrete historical relationships the priorities appear to be reversed. Loving people requires treating them justly; just treatment requires respecting people's material needs. Disregard for these requirements reduces the expression of love and justice to a series of unsystematic episodes.[42]

Soloviev's point shows considerable insight into how human beings actually experience social institutions. In everyday life the church appears to be a rather weak thing compared with the state, and the state a rather weak thing compared with the whole matrix of economic relations in society. Beyond this psychological insight, Soloviev's acceptance of the practical dependence of higher on lower values keeps his hierarchy from degenerating into an abstract principle. By stressing the relativities and perspectival complexities of the hierarchy Soloviev also distinguishes it from absolutist forms of theocracy.

The practical implications of Soloviev's hierarchical distinctions require investigation in their own right. This is not the task of *The Critique of Abstract Principles*. Yet Soloviev does give some indication of the kind of social and political arrangements he had in mind. The case of capital punishment has already been mentioned. In 1881, following the assassination of Tsar Alexander II, Soloviev argued that the Christian monarch of a Christian society must not practice capital punishment, not even for regicides. Soloviev was witnessing to his hierarchy of values in this case. As Andrzej Walicki observes, 'in Soloviev's theory, in contradistinction to Hegelianism, the highest manifestation of the institutionalized, objective ethic was not the state but the church.'[43] Thus, while Soloviev's political ideal assigns a very

---

[42] *Kritika*, pp. 185–6.
[43] Andrzej Walicki, *Legal Philosophies of Russian Liberalism* (Oxford: Clarendon Press, 1987), p. 187.

positive role to the state, the ideal is not statist. Ultimately the state must be judged by the prophetic and evangelical conscience of the church, as in the case of capital punishment. Even so, Soloviev did not regard the church by itself to be a sufficient limit on the power of the state. His free theocracy requires a political order based on the rule of law, in other words some form of constitutionalism.

In the economic sphere Soloviev's ideal suggests a middle course between egalitarian socialism and laissez-faire capitalism. Soloviev does not believe love and justice require 'the greatest possible economic well-being' or 'equality of material wealth' in society because such demands, taken literally, imply maximizing material well-being is an absolute value, which it is not. Soloviev accepts the division of labor, competition and the dichotomy of labor and capital as 'civilized forms of production and economic activity.' At the same time:

> Owing to the fact that all economic activity and the wealth resulting from it are not ends in themselves but only the means or material base for a fuller realization of the supreme religious ideal, all these forms [of economic activity] lose their sharply exclusive character and cease to serve the egoism of the few while being the source of distress for the many. For here, in a society directed by the religious principle, in a free theocracy, all people find solidarity in a single common purpose, and that which benefits the few serves the good of all.[44]

Later in his career, in *The Justification of the Good* (1897), Soloviev worked out his concept of economic justice in greater detail. While still rejecting radical egalitarianism he defended the right of all people to the material minimum required for 'a dignified existence.'[45] One already sees the kernel of this idea in the theme of social and economic 'solidarity' in the *Critique*.

---

[44] *Kritika*, pp. 183-5.
[45] For a discussion of Soloviev's social philosophy at the end of his career see Walicki, *Legal Philosophies of Russian Liberalism*, pp. 190-206. Walicki rightly emphasizes the role of Soloviev's religious views in the shaping of his socio-economic ideal: 'The peculiarly modern element in this definition of "the right to a dignified existence" – the stress on "positive freedom", on providing everyone with the material means for spiritual development – derives not from Kantianism but

Soloviev's social and political ideal has been described as a form of Russian 'liberalism.'[46] While the word is not Soloviev's, it fits. To be sure, the fact Soloviev pursued 'theocracy' throws many readers off the track, since to most people this word suggests the very opposite of liberalism. But as we have seen, Soloviev's free theocracy contains prominent liberal elements. It mandates the relative freedom of economy, state and society from the church. It summons the church to break with absolutist theocracy and abstract clericalism. It steers clear of extreme doctrines and holds to the center. In the end, though, free theocracy is a religious ideal. Soloviev's liberalism is full of theological content and so must be distinguished from secularist forms of liberalism.

Additional evidence of Soloviev's liberalism is found in the second part of *The Critique of Abstract Principles*. Here Soloviev is concerned with epistemology, or the critique of theoretical and scientific knowledge. While this part of the *Critique* need not occupy us at length, its results in the area of theology are important for our theme and demand attention at this point.

THEOLOGY AND CRITICISM

Soloviev construes human knowledge as a synthesis of three elements: the natural (or empirical), the mystical and the rational. For a great many people this synthesis is

---

from Soloviev's own religious philosophy. He freely acknowledges Kant's merit in defending human dignity while still accusing him of formalism and, consequently, of clinging to a narrowly negative conception of justice. This formalistic one-sidedness was absent in the conception of man as potentially divine. Such a conception assumed that each human being had an inherent capacity for self-perfectibility, and this view could be used as an argument for "positive freedom". Extreme poverty and other social handicaps, argued Soloviev, could clearly create insurmountable obstacles to the actualization of human capacities. Therefore these obstacles should be removed by providing each person not only with formal freedom but also with the necessary aid in the worthy fulfillment of man's destiny' (pp. 195–6).

[46] Walicki entitles chapter 3 of *Legal Philosophies of Russian Liberalism*, 'Vladimir Soloviev: Religious Philosophy and the Emergence of the "New Liberalism." ' Greg Gaut has made another helpful terminological proposal by speaking of a 'social gospel' in Soloviev. See Gaut, 'Christian Politics: Vladimir Solovyov's Social Gospel Theology,' *Modern Greek Studies Yearbook* 10/11 (1994/95): 653–74.

unselfconscious. It becomes a subject for reflection only with the rise of critical thought. Even then, 'the synthesis of mystical and natural elements with the mediation of the rational element, the synthesis which is necessary for true knowledge, is not a *datum of consciousness* but a *task* for the *mind*; and for this task consciousness presents only uncoordinated and, in part, enigmatic data.' Modern thought fails to heed the many demands of this synthesis. The mystical element of knowledge in particular tends to be neglected. One-sided methods of thinking produce the extremes of abstract rationalism and abstract empiricism, such as Hegelianism ('a system of concepts without any reality') and postivism ('a system of facts without any inner connection'). As the failures of these positions become obvious many modern thinkers resign themselves to 'the emptiness and nullity of a fruitless skepticism.'[47]

Meanwhile, conservative thinkers reassert traditional religious systems of thought. Pope Leo XIII would have the modern world return to Thomas Aquinas. 'Certain Russian writers' would have it return to the fathers of the eastern church. Soloviev appreciates both proposals:

> Without a doubt the theological systems of the eastern and western fathers of the church, by virtue of the perfection of their logical form, constitute a spiritual monument which the human mind can only take pride in; doubtless, too, by virtue of its actual content this theology is much closer to the truth than any of the abstract philosophical systems.

But if this is so, why does the modern mind not accept these masters? Unlike the neo-traditionalists Soloviev does not believe 'willful error' or 'a second Fall' explains the case.[48] Alert to the positive side of every philosophical position, Soloviev sees good spiritual and intellectual reasons for the modern bias against traditional theology.

First, theology as traditionally practiced 'excludes the free relationship of reason to the content of religion, the free appropriation and development of this content by reason; second, it does not implement the content [of religion] on the

[47] *Kritika*, pp. 347–9.
[48] *Kritika*, p. 349.

empirical plane.' These limitations undermine the truth of theology, 'for if reason and experience without mystical knowledge lack truth, truth without reason and experience lacks fullness and reality.' Only a synthesis of empirical, rational and mystical elements is finally 'true.' Theology which presses its claims on the basis of mystical or traditional grounds alone ends up in 'abstract dogmatism,' the theoretical equivalent of abstract clericalism in ethics. Moreover, abstract dogmatism is objectionable not only on rational and empirical grounds but on religious grounds as well. 'In the field of theology we know the truth as absolute or divine, but absolute or divine truth by definition cannot be one-sided, exclusive; it must be the whole truth, it must be all in all.'[49] For all its magnificent architecture, traditional theology is one-sided and exclusive, and thereby falls short of the truth about the whole of things. Reason and science are right to turn away from it.

How, then, is theology to proceed in the critical age? The task is 'not to restore traditional theology in its exclusivity but, on the contrary, to free it from abstract dogmatism, to put religious truth into the form of free-rational thought and implement it with the data of experimental science, to link theology internally to philosophy and science and so to organize the whole field of true knowledge into a full system of free and scientific theosophy.'[50]

This ambitious proposal clearly makes unprecedented demands on theology, which may be the reason why Soloviev gave it the untraditional name of theosophy. Certainly the demands of Solovievian theosophy upon theoretical philosophy are as great as those which theocracy makes in the realm of social and political philosophy. Both theocracy and theosophy demand a new and more dynamic relationship between religious and secular pursuits: between church, economy and state in the case of theocracy; in the case of theosophy, between theology, philosophy and science. Second, Soloviev calls his theosophy 'free' as a way of denying traditional theology hegemonic status among the theoretical disciplines, just as free theocracy rejects the pretensions of abstract clericalism. Third, both theocracy and theosophy demand a new level of concreteness in religion

---

[49] *Kritika*, pp. 349–50.
[50] *Kritika*, p. 350.

and theology. Free theosophy draws upon the natural sciences, while free theocracy seeks realization in the material and economic order of society.

In his concern for concreteness Soloviev invites comparison with modern positivists such as Comte and Chernyshevsky, thinkers with whom he felt a kinship despite their negative attitude toward religion.[51] Like them, Soloviev saw modern times as a positive age in which truth claims have to be validated in the material world. But unlike the positivists, he believed religion could pass this test The positivists saw humankind as advancing through a series of negations: theology is negated by metaphysics, which in turn is negated by modern science. For Soloviev knowledge advances through ever more inclusive forms of insight. Thus the critique of traditional theology ('abstract dogmatism') does not lead to the negation of theology but to its assimilation in a richer synthesis of divine truth, or free theosophy.

To avoid misunderstanding, three additional points need to be made about free theosophy. First, Soloviev's enterprise has little to do with the type of speculation generally associated with the term. While it may not be true to say, as Losev does, that Soloviev had nothing in common with the modern theosophists (Madame Blavatsky and others), the differences far outweigh the few similarities.[52] Methodologically rigorous and profoundly

---

[51] Soloviev's appreciation for the positivists is indicative of his intellectual generosity. For Soloviev's sympathetic appraisal of Chernyshevsky see his seminal essay on esthetics, 'Pervyi shag k polozhitel'noi estetike,' *SSVSS*, 7:69–77. For Soloviev's appreciation of the Comtian idea of humanity, which he saw as adumbrating his own concept of Sophia, see 'Ideia chelovechestva u Avgusta Konta,' 9:172–93. Both essays are reprinted in Solov'ev, *Sochineniia v dvukh tomakh*, eds Losev and Gulyga, 2:548–55 and 562–81.

[52] Losev writes: 'What [Soloviev] means by "free theosophy" has absolutely nothing in common with the theosophical teachings which were widespread in Europe throughout the nineteenth century and which have not died out even now. He needed the term "theosophy" in order to keep his distance from the traditional sort of theology which he always viewed as too rationalistic, too dead, too unfree.' 'Tvorcheskii put' Vladimira Solov'eva,' in Solov'ev, *Sochineniia v dvukh tomakh*, eds Losev and Gulyga, 1:9. While Losev is right as far as the essentials are concerned, Soloviev's life-long interest in theosophic and kabbalistic ideas cannot be denied. See Judith Deutsch Kornblatt, 'Solov'ev's Androgynous Sophia and the Jewish Kabbalah,' *Slavic Review* 50 (1991):487–96; and Maria Carlson, 'Gnostic Elements in the Cosmogony of Vladimir Soloviev,' *Russian Religious Thought*, eds Judith Deutsch Kornblatt and Richard F. Gustafson (Madison and London: The University of Wisconsin Press, 1996), pp. 49–67.

learned in the history of philosophy, Soloviev made no claims to esoteric knowledge and recognized that theosophy, like everything else, would have to pass before the bar of philosophical and scientific criticism.

Second, one should not assume Soloviev envisioned creating a finished system when he called for the construction of a free theosophy. Everything Soloviev says about the whole of things (*vseedinstvo*) makes it clear he regarded it as a vast divine reality exceeding the boundaries of every conceivable intellectual system. No system claiming finality can survive the critique of abstract principles. In other words, the rational criticism of theology and the empirical realization of theological truth are parts of an ongoing project. The problem with traditional theology is not that it fails to complete the rational criticism and empirical realization of religion but that it scarcely begins. These important tasks are neglected or actively suppressed out of deference to traditional authorities.

Finally, Soloviev's theosophy is a positive religious synthesis. That is to say, the religious or mystical element is not reducible to the empirical and rational elements. Free theosophy requires all three. The *theos* of free theosophy is not an abstract principle but God, the living divine reality.

The last point raises the question of how Soloviev's theosophical project relates to actual religious life and ecclesiastical institutions. What is left of positive religion once philosophical criticism has done its work? To shed light on this question we turn to *Lectures on the Humanity of God*.

7

The Critique of Positive Religion (1): *Lectures on the Humanity of God*

MODERN FAITHS AND THE HUMANITY OF GOD

Soloviev does not discuss positive religion in its own right in *The Critique of Abstract Principles*. Religious principles, whether traditional or mystical, are positive principles, whereas the *Critique* is devoted to the investigation of abstract principles. Still, Soloviev does not restrict his attention entirely to the latter, as is evident from his criticism of clericalism and dogmatism, both of which arise from positive religion. That Soloviev applies his critique to these phenomena, if only in passing, suggests the possibility of a general critique of positive religion.

Soloviev's critique of positive religion is not concentrated in a grand systematic work, but is found in essays and monographs written at various times throughout his career. The subject matter of these works is as diverse as positive religion itself. Christian dogma, church history, ecumenical and theocratic topics, ecclesiastical politics, religious conditions in Russia and the assessment of other religions, such as Judaism and Islam, all captured Soloviev's attention at one time or another. Exposition of a representative sample of these works in this and the following chapter will serve to delineate the main lines of Soloviev's critique of positive religion.

The first work which Soloviev devoted to positive religion was *Lectures on the Humanity of God* (1877–81).[1] As the

---

[1] *Chteniia o bogochelovechestve*, *SSVSS*, 3:1–181. English trans.: Vladimir Solovyov, *Lectures on Divine Humanity*, trans. Boris Jakim (Hudson, NY: Lindisfarne Press, 1995). All references to *Chteniia o bogochelovechestve* in the present study are to the Solov'ev and Radlov edition (*SSVSS*).

title indicates, the work focuses on *bogochelovechestvo*. While this concept appears occasionally in Russian theology before Soloviev's time, in Bukharev's works for example, *Lectures* played the decisive role in establishing *bogochelovechestvo* as the central theological idea of philosophic Orthodoxy. The appeal of *Lectures* lay in Soloviev's ability to articulate the dogma of the humanity of God in such a way that it measured up to the demands of modern critical thought as well as to the existential situation of Orthodoxy in the modern world.

For all its influence, however, *Lectures* is something of an anomaly in the Solovievian corpus. The book lacks the strong architecture and methodological consistency of Soloviev's other theoretical works. Moreover, the subject matter is extremely variegated. Besides offering an interpretation of the humanity of God and related dogmas Soloviev sketches a philosophy of religion and outlines a history of religions. He devotes many pages to topics in metaphysics, such as the problem of the one and the many and the nature of atoms, monads, ideas and persons. The book also contains cosmological speculation, ideas for a philosophy of nature, a theory of the 'world soul' and a rudimentary doctrine of divine Wisdom (Sophia). Strictly speaking, *Lectures* is not a monograph but a colorful philosophical and theological sketchbook. This may have been the key to its influence. *Lectures* tantalized religiously inclined intellectuals; there was something in it for everyone. Yet one suspects Soloviev was unclear about the kind of book he was trying to write in *Lectures*. The fact the work grew out of a series of public lectures may have contributed to its looseness. But one should also consider the possibility Soloviev was not sure how to approach positive religion in a systematic way when he composed *Lectures*. His later works on the subject were more focused and specialized.

Soloviev begins *Lectures* by pleading for seriousness about religion in the modern world while admitting most of his contemporaries have other things on their mind. 'I shall be speaking about the truths of positive religion,' he writes in the opening sentence of the book, 'about matters which are far removed from and alien to the modern mind, to the interests of modern civilization.' Modern civilization is concerned above all with molding the material world for the sake of human well-being without reference to religious illumination. Inspired by socialism, positivism or some other form of secularist humanism, modern activists and ideologists adopt a negative attitude toward religion. Are they wrong in this? In the first instance Soloviev thinks not. 'I will not engage in polemics with those who at the present time have a negative attitude toward the religious principle, I will not argue with the modern opponents of religion – because they are right.' They are right because religion in the modern world is a paltry thing compared to what it could and should be. Religion, 'the connection of human beings and the world with the unconditional principle and focal point of all that is,' should be a comprehensive, all-embracing thing. It should enter into all human activities and concerns. But what does one see when one inspects contemporary religion? One sees anything but an all-embracing concern. 'Instead of being all in all, [religion] steals away into a very small and very distant corner of our inner world, it is but one of a number of interests which share our attention.' In other words one sees 'religiosity' rather than religion, a specialized taste which some people have and others do not. Such a thing by definition cannot provide a powerful spiritual center for modern people. On the contrary, it merely compounds the general 'anarchy' (*beznachalie*, lit. principle-less-ness) from which modern civilization suffers.[2]

With religion sidelined, modern civilization advances as best it can by its own lights, sometimes pursuing socialism, at other times inclining to positivism. Both of these ideologies address human beings without reference to God or a transcendent order of things. Socialism preaches human rights, notably those which the French Revolution sought to realize: freedom, equality and community. Positivism preaches 'the rights of human reason,' which it seeks to vindicate through science. Both ideologies are profoundly right in what they affirm, namely the dignity of human beings. They are also right in seeking not just a symbolic attestation of human

[2] *Chteniia*, pp. 3–4.

dignity but social and political actualization. For these reasons Soloviev forswears all interest in trying to refute socialism or positivism. He observes that 'the people who try to refute socialism are most often those who fear its truth,' such as the 'plutocrats' of his day.[3] As for the positivist interest in material facts, Soloviev regards this as a healthy antidote to the abstract dogmatism of traditional theology.[4] In short, to the extent both socialism and positivism affirm the dignity of human beings, Soloviev has no desire to attack them.

The problem of course is that socialism and positivism are also systems of denial. Both assert a mechanistic and material-istic worldview which, though it may seem to be a means of saying what the universe is, is actually a means of saying what the world is not: not morally constituted, not spiritual, not divinely grounded. Soloviev rejects these negations, citing Leibniz's famous dictum that philosophical doctrines tend to be right about what they affirm but wrong about what they exclude or deny.[5]

Soloviev recognizes his philosophical qualms might seem to be beside the point if socialists and positivists actually succeeded in accomplishing their goals. In fact both parties fail to achieve what they set out to do for reasons which Soloviev believes are directly attributable to their mechanistic and materialistic worldview. Socialists seek to institute freedom, equality and community through the struggle of the masses for material welfare. But how do socialists propose to deal with the selfishness and egoism which undermine freedom, equality and community? Will material welfare or class consciousness overcome selfish impulses? On the contrary, materialism and class struggle, when raised to the status of moral imperatives, nurture egoism:

> Proclaiming the restoration of the rights of matter as a moral principle amounts to proclaiming the restoration of the rights of egoism, as the founder of a certain socio-religious sect in America did when he replaced the Ten

[3] *Chteniia*, p. 5; cf. p. 7.
[4] *Chteniia*, p. 11.
[5] *Chteniia*, p. 22.

Commandments of Moses with twelve of his own beginning with 'Love thyself' – a perfectly legitimate demand, but quite superfluous.'[6]

Socialists might reply to this criticism by saying that by rights they mean not just material rights but other kinds as well, such as intellectual and spiritual rights. But as soon as one begins talking about intellectual and spiritual rights one clearly violates the mechanistic and materialistic worldview. In short, socialism asserts the unconditional rights of human beings but does not grasp the implications of this assertion. Something cannot be unconditional and material at the same time.

Positivism runs into similar trouble. The positivist believes only material facts are real, but human experience seems to contradict this view. 'A human being *does not wish* to be only a fact, only a phenomenon, and this not-wishing already hints that he is actually not just a fact, not just a phenomenon, but something more. For what is a fact that does not wish to be a fact, or a phenomenon that does not wish to be a phenomenon?'[7] True, this objection could be parried by denying that human beings enjoy a privileged status among the facts of the world. But then what becomes of the humanist pathos of positivism, the 'rights of human reason?' Rights imply some sort of sovereignty or autonomy, yet the positivist worldview offers no grounds for such claims.

For Soloviev the solution to these dilemmas is to think more deeply about the basic assumption of all modern humanisms, namely, the absolute value of human beings. As soon as one takes this proposition seriously one discovers a point of convergence between the modern mind and religion, especially the Christian religion, for Christianity, too, sees human personality as having unconditional significance. 'Human personality – and not human personality in general, not the abstract concept, but the actual, living person, every living human being – has

---

[6] *Chteniia*, p. 8.
[7] *Chteniia*, p. 21.

unconditional, divine significance. Christianity and modern secular civilization are in agreement on this affirmation.[8]

Soloviev believes Christianity as traditionally practiced has not actualized this affirmation in a sufficiently concrete way. Nevertheless, he thinks Christians still have an enormous resource to offer modern humanism. As adherents of a positive religion, Christians have *faith*, that is to say, they believe in the positive or divine content of their affirmations, which is precisely what modern humanism cannot do because of its mechanistic and materialistic worldview:

> The modern mind ascribes divine rights to human personality but does not give it divine powers or divine content because the modern person, in life and in knowledge, accepts only limited, conditioned reality, the reality of particular facts and phenomena, and from this point of view a human being is only one of these particular facts.[9]

Socialism, positivism and other forms of non-religious humanism cannot elude the demon of negation because they do not recognize a positive reality for which they would freely and faithfully 'deny themselves.' That is to say, they remain trapped in forms of exclusivity: socialism in natural egoism despite its best intentions, positivism in a meaningless continuum of facts. Positive religions, by contrast, know that besides being 'negatively unconditional,' i.e. dissatisfied with the conditions of existence, human personality

> can also attain positive unconditionality, i.e. that it can possess all-inclusive content, fullness of being, and therefore that this unconditional content, this fullness of being, is not a fantasy or subjective apparition but a true reality full of power. At this point faith in oneself, faith in human person-ality, is also faith in God.'[10]

This analysis brings Soloviev to the central proposition of *Lectures on the Humanity of God*, namely, modern humanism

[8] *Chteniia*, p. 19.
[9] *Chteniia*, p. 20.
[10] *Chteniia*, p. 25.

and positive religion, when pushed further than the apologists for either have heretofore allowed, will converge upon the common project of discerning and actualizing the humanity of God:

> The old, traditional form of religion proceeds from faith in God but does not follow it to the end. Modern extra-religious civilization proceeds from faith in human beings but it, too, is inconsistent; it does not follow its faith to the end. Both these faiths, faith in God and faith in human beings, when they are pursued consistently and finally realized, come together in the one, full and all-inclusive truth of the Humanity of God.[11]

This bold proposition earned Soloviev the unique place he occupies in the Russian intellectual tradition. With a passionate inclusiveness Soloviev managed both to affirm and challenge all positions on the Russian intellectual spectrum. He affirmed radical humanism but asked the radicals to take religion seriously. He affirmed Orthodox Christianity but asked Orthodox Christians to develop a more positive approach to modern humanism. He asked East and West to take each other seriously while prophesying to both a common, pan-human future. No Russian thinker had ever brought such a rich offering to the altar of thought. Soloviev was 'the Pushkin of Russian philosophy: all the others are more fragmentary, he dealt with the Whole [VseTseloe].'[12]

RELIGIOUS EVOLUTION

One might have supposed Soloviev would begin his exposition of the humanity of God with Christian dogma, since there can be no doubt the idea originated there. He begins instead with the history of religion, attempting to show that the idea of the humanity of God is the logical outcome of religious evolution. Always the universalist, Soloviev seeks to situate the humanity

---

[11] *Chteniia*, p. 26.
[12] Georgii Gachev, *Russkaia duma: portrety russkikh myslitelei* (Moscow: Novosti, 1991), p. 54.

of God in the context of world history in order to demonstrate the scope of the idea.

In the body of *Lectures on the Humanity of God* (lectures 3–8) Soloviev traces religious evolution to its culmination in Christ the God-human. At this point, however, rather than wrapping up his presentation, he starts over again. Questions about freedom and evil upset the smooth evolutionary picture which he has drawn. To deal with these questions he feels obliged to consider even grander topics than religious evolution. In lectures 9 and 10 he presents a theory of cosmic evolution and the emergence of the world-process from the being of God. In lectures 11 and 12 he turns again to Christ the God-human and also offers some observations about the church.

The vast scope of Soloviev's discussion of the humanity of God affects the idea from the start. If, as Soloviev would have it, the humanity of God should be regarded as the culmination of cosmic evolution, then the whole evolutionary process must have a divine-human character from the beginning. Believing this, Soloviev cannot accept certain things that are commonly believed about the incarnation or humanity of God in Christ, such as: it was an unprecedented miracle, or it happened 'all at once in a single act of divine creativity.'[13] Soloviev insists 'the incarnation of Divinity is not something miraculous in the strict sense, i.e. it is not something *alien* to the general order of being, but on the contrary it is essentially connected with the whole history of the world and of humanity, it is something prepared for by and logically following from this history.'[14]

Historical logic does not mean, however, the embodiment of God incarnate or the succession of events leading to it could have been predicted in advance by a finite mind. Religious knowledge is ex posteriori. It is not fully known until it is concretely embodied. Nevertheless, revealed truth is not a stone thrown through the window of the world but the result of the operation of God in human experience, including human thought. The contents of revelation accumulate gradually and grow richer as the meaning of the humanity of God is revealed.

---

[13] *Chteniia*, p. 146.
[14] *Chteniia*, p. 165. 'Miraculous' (*chudesnyi*) and 'alien' (*chuzhdyi*) are cognates in Russian.

In other words, 'religious consciousness is not something finished, ready-made, but something emerging and in process, and thus the revelation of the divine principle in this consciousness is necessarily gradual.' While unfinished, however, religious consciousness at all times enjoys actual, undeferred experience of God: 'Since the divine principle is the actual object of religious consciousness, i.e. the object that acts upon this consciousness and reveals its content in it, religious development is a positive and objective process, a real inter-action between God and human beings – a divine-human process.'[15]

If the evolution of religion is a divine-human process, every stage must embody the humanity of God to some extent. Does this mean that all religions are in some sense true? Soloviev says yes. 'It is clear from the objective and positive character of religious development that not one of its stages, not one of the moments of the religious process, can be in itself a lie or delusion. "A false religion" is a contradictio in adjecto.'[16] Of course, saying no religion is false does not necessarily mean all religions are equally true. Still, the working assumption of Soloviev's theory of religious evolution is that every positive religious claim contains a measure of divine truth.

Soloviev's outline of religious evolution is easily summarized, since the point lies in the general scheme rather than the partic-ulars. The first stage was nature religion. Here divinity lay concealed behind the forces and objects of the natural world with the result religious consciousness attached itself to the latter. Revelation at this stage was '*natural* or *immediate* revel-ation.'[17] This has validity because nature really is grounded in God. However, ascribing divine significance to the objects and forces of nature lends them a significance which they do not merit. The practical outcome of nature religion was the subjection of human beings to elemental forces. This slavery of the higher to the lower eventually precipitated a revolt.

The revolt began in India with the discovery of the religious significance of personhood. The early Indian ascetics were

[15] *Chteniia*, p. 36.
[16] *Chteniia*, pp. 36–7.
[17] *Chteniia*, p. 40.

'intoxicated by freedom, by the awareness of their unity and unconditionality.'[18] The religion of acosmic freedom reached its apogee in the Buddhist renunciation of the phenomenal world and the quest for nirvana, or extinction. This, too, was a moment of revelation, albeit 'negative revelation.' Its validity lies in the perception of divinity as radically free with respect to the phenomenal world.[19] It is even true to say divinity is 'nothing' in the sense that God is not 'some sort of determinate, limited being or entity alongside other entities.'[20]

Yet Buddhism errs by not distinguishing between 'freedom from all being' and 'privation of all being,' i.e. between negative and positive freedom. Soloviev argues it is a greater thing to be free from all beings and still have power over them than not to have being at all. Thus the next stage of religious consciousness was oriented to 'positive freedom,' to the search for God as the 'positive all' which transcends yet still contains the world. It was the ancient Greeks, and Plato in particular, who achieved this insight in the theory of divine ideas as the ground of the phenomenal world. In the 'ideal cosmos' of the ancient Greeks the concept of divinity again became cosmic, as it had been in nature religion; but cosmism now incorporated the awareness of free, transcendent being.[21]

Among the several religions discussed in *Lectures* Soloviev pays attention to the particulars of only one. Interestingly this is not Judaism or Christianity but Platonism. While Soloviev believes Platonism does not provide an adequate conception of God without the aid of biblical religion, the reader of *Lectures* cannot fail to sense his enchantment with the ideal cosmos of Hellenism. Simply noting the number of pages devoted to Hellenism (21) as compared with the Old Testament (7) reveals the degree of Soloviev's interest. Nor is this the only point in *Lectures* where Soloviev expounds a Platonist conceptuality. Disregarding the danger of appearing less than Orthodox in his theology, Soloviev forthrightly defends hellenic idealism:

[18] *Chteniia*, p. 155.
[19] For the discussion of nature religion and the revolt against it culminating in Buddhism see *Chteniia*, pp. 40–7.
[20] *Chteniia*, p. 48.
[21] For Soloviev's discussion of Greek religion, Platonism and the theory of ideas see *Chteniia*, pp. 48–69.

If the ancient Greek knew the divine principle only as harmony and beauty, then surely he did not know the *whole* truth about it, for it is *more* than harmony and beauty. But this idealism, while it did not embrace the *whole* truth of the divine principle, clearly represented a certain aspect or side of Divinity, it contained something positively divine. To maintain the opposite, to see this idealism as pagan delusion pure and simple, is to maintain that the truly divine does not need harmony and beauty of form, that it can just as well not be realized in an ideal cosmos. But if beauty and harmony constitute a necessary and essential element of Divinity, as they obviously do, then without a doubt we must see Greek *idealism* as the first positive phase of religious revelation.[22]

The next phase of positive religion is the revelation of the great 'I am,' the living God of Israel. For all its truth Platonism does not have a sufficiently centered or personal concept of God. This deficiency leads to the relative passivity of Platonism as a religion. The active, personal God of the Old Testament enriches the concept of divinity and especially the ethical content of religion, which finds expression in the religious law of the Jews.

One must ask a question about the Old Testament idea of God, however. Is the active, personal God of Israel only 'a devouring fire' (Ex. 24:17) or also a God of connectedness and relationship? If only the former, then one can scarcely speak of 'religion,' which in its very etymology refers to a link between human beings and the divine. In point of fact the evolution of biblical religion favors the concept of linkage, which in turn has an impact on how the will and law of God are understood. The divine law comes to be seen 'as the law and norm of human will not in the sense of a *fiat which we accept* but of a *good which we consciously recognize*. In this inward relationship a new covenant between God and humankind comes into being, a new divine-human order of things which takes the place of that preparatory and transitional religion based on the outward law.'[23] Anticipated by the prophets of Israel, the new covenant is

[22] *Chteniia*, p. 68.
[23] *Chteniia*, p. 77.

revealed in Christ, a unique individual who is both fully human and fully divine, the humanity of God in person.[24]

Given his theory of religious evolution it is obvious why Soloviev can say, as he turns to the discussion of Christianity, that 'all phases of religious consciousness are included in Christianity [and] form part of its make-up.'[25] Christianity is not one religion among many, nor is it an exclusive religion. Viewed in terms of its contents, Christianity is the epitome and fulfillment of all religions. The fullness of God in Christ is reflected in the fullness of Christianity as a religion. This does not mean Christianity is merely the sum of the other religions. 'Christianity has its own proper content which is independent of all the elements which enter into it, and this proper content is solely and exclusively Christ. In Christianity we find Christ and only Christ: this is a truth which has been proclaimed often but poorly understood.'[26]

What does it mean to say that in Christianity we find Christ and Christ alone? Soloviev proceeds by means of a contrast. In the Protestant world, he observes, 'we often encounter people who call themselves Christians but believe that the essence of Christianity lies not in the person of Christ but in His teaching.'[27] The same view would soon be propounded in Russia by Tolstoy and his followers. Soloviev considers this view profoundly wrong because it fails to recognize that which is most distinctive in Christianity. The latter cannot be Christ's moral teachings, for example, because there was nothing new about them compared with earlier biblical precepts. Nor was there anything 'specifically Christian' in Jesus' idea of God as loving Father and highest good. Many religions teach the same. What was special about Jesus was the claim which he and his followers made concerning himself. Christianity is not just the religion of the humanity of God as an idea but recognition of the humanity of God in person, faith in the God-human 'as living incarnate truth.'[28]

[24] *Chteniia*, pp. 70–8; cf. pp. 161–2.
[25] *Chteniia*, p. 111.
[26] *Chteniia*, p. 112.
[27] *Chteniia*, p. 112.
[28] *Chteniia*, p. 113.

Soloviev devotes most of the second half of *Lectures* to exploring the divinity of Christ. Significantly, he does not proceed by means of a speculative scheme but by following a traditional outline of Christian dogmatic theology, offering a doctrine of Trinity, a christology and finally, if briefly, an ecclesiology. Even in the cosmological and theosophical digression of lectures 9 and 10 Soloviev takes christology as his point of departure and returns to christological and ecclesiological themes to conclude the book.

If Soloviev follows a traditional dogmatic outline, however, he does not confine himself to defending purely traditional positions. He approaches dogmatics with the same intellectual freedom he shows in other areas of inquiry. Yet he does not run to the opposite extreme, either, by going out of his way to offend Orthodox sensibilities. Soloviev would not have devoted so much intellectual energy to expounding Orthodox dogmas if he had thought they were misguided or had been superseded. The whole point of *Lectures on the Humanity of God* is to justify the contents of positive religion, the dogmas of Orthodoxy included. Whether and to what extent Soloviev's interpretation of dogma agrees with the mind of Orthodoxy is an issue to which we will return.

TRINITY, CHRIST, SOPHIA AND CHURCH

Soloviev's trinitarianism relies on two assumptions about the doctrine of the Trinity which, while common enough in the nineteenth century, would be rejected by most historians of dogma today. The first is the assumption that the idea of the triunity of God arose in pre-Christian, hellenistic Judaism and represents a synthesis of biblical and Platonist religious ideas. As Soloviev construes the history, the later prophets of Israel preached a mature religious universalism; but, being primarily ethical teachers and activists rather than theologians, they were unable to come up with a doctrine of God adequate to their vision. In hellenistic Judaism, however, thinkers schooled in Greek philosophy, such as Philo of Alexandria, worked out the essentials of trinitarian doctrine to satisfy the demands of Greek thought and biblical faith alike. Thus the early Christians found a ready-made doctrine. Their contribution to it was practical and existential rather than theoretical. They experienced the triunity of God 'as a fact, as a historical reality – in the living individuality of a historical person.'[29]

The second assumption takes the doctrine of the Trinity to be 'the crown of pre-Christian religious wisdom and the fundamental speculative principle of Christianity,' a philosophical doctrine of God which reason can grasp. Soloviev promises to 'derive this truth [the Trinity] in the form which I take to be the most logical, the most responsive to the demands of speculative reason,' assuring his reader that trinitarian doctrine 'is not only totally comprehensible in its logical aspect but is also based on the general logical form which defines every actual being.'[30]

Soloviev tries to make this case by arguing 'if in general we accept that the divine principle exists with unconditional content, then we must accept that it contains three consubstantial and undivided subjects, each of which relates *in its own way* to one and the same unconditional essence and in its own way possesses one and the same unconditional content.' To spell it out: positive divinity exists in itself, as its own ultimate source; for itself, as its own self-expression; and with itself, as the interaction of the self-existent with its self-expression. In itself divinity is absolute will; for itself it is absolute representation or idea; with itself it is absolute sensitivity or feeling. These terms reveal the contents of divinity. The object of divine will is absolute good. The substance of the divine idea is absolute truth. Divine feeling is directed to absolute beauty. God wills the good, knows the true, loves the beautiful. Soloviev's final and most concise formulation of the doctrine is even more integrative:

> *The absolute realizes the good through truth in beauty.* These three ideas or three general unities, being but different aspects or states of one and the same thing, together and through interpenetration form a new, concrete unity which represents the full realization of the divine content, the wholeness of

[29] *Chteniia*, pp. 80–2.
[30] *Chteniia*, pp. 83, 100.

absolute essence, the realization of God as *the whole of things* 'in which all the fullness of Divinity dwells bodily.'[31]

The platonized contents of Soloviev's trinitarianism make it easier to appreciate why he does not consider the Trinity to be a daunting mystery for the human mind. This is not to say Soloviev finds speculating about the nature of God an easy thing to do. God is ultimate reality, not 'an ordinary object of our thought.' But the fact human nature is made in the image of God supports the mind's quest for God. Soloviev approves of Leibniz's view that self-consciousness itself is triune in the sense that subject, object and the relationship between them can be logically distinguished even though the three are unbreakably united in every conscious act. He also commends Augustine's trinitarianism in the *Confessions*, where the great Latin father argued that each of the three distinguishable acts of the human soul – being, knowing and willing – contains and fulfills the other two, showing the human soul to be a triune whole.[32]

The abstractness of Soloviev's trinitarianism makes it something less than a forceful proclamation of Christ as the humanity of God in person. A more practical concern for salvation and sanctification comes out in the christological portion of *Lectures*, although even here Soloviev's speculative concerns continue to play the dominant role.

As one would expect, Soloviev's concept of Christ is closely linked to his idea of God. For Soloviev God is the whole of things, 'the universal organism.' At the same time God is the supremely individual organism because individuality grows in proportion to the differentiation of parts in a whole. 'The universal organism expressing the unconditional content of the divine principle is a particular, individual being par excellence. This individual being or realized expression of the unconditional being of God is Christ'[33]

The divine organism, or Christ, may be viewed in two ways: in terms of the animating principle which produces its unity, or in terms of the unity that is produced. Soloviev calls the first the

---

[31] *Chteniia*, pp. 103–11.
[32] *Chteniia*, pp. 101–2. However, Soloviev rejects Augustine's view that 'vestiges' of the Trinity can be found in the natural world.
[33] *Chteniia*, pp. 113–14.

Logos or Word of God; the second, Sophia or the Wisdom of God. In metaphorical terms Logos is Christ's 'soul' while Sophia is Christ's 'body.'[34] Together they constitute the divine organism: Christ the Word and Wisdom of God.

Because Soloviev's terms are abstract, metaphorical and to some extent esoteric, they do not immediately convey the point of his christology. Sophia in particular presents an obstacle because of the theosophical associations of the term. However, close attention to the theoretical context in which Soloviev uses christological and sophiological terms makes it clear he is looking for a way to speak about the relationship between God and the world, or more particularly, between God and humanity. The case may be construed as follows.

The aim of *Lectures on the Humanity of God* is to make a contribution to positive theology, i.e. a theology adequate to the witness of positive religion. 'Positive' means brimming with content. The outcome of much traditional theology is anything but positive in this sense. For fear of introducing the multiplicity of nature into divinity and thus (supposedly) compromising God's absoluteness, many theologians take pains to purify the idea of God of all actual determinations and so reduce divinity to 'pure abstraction.' Now the concern to safeguard divine transcendence is praiseworthy, but as a general program abstract theology fails because it leaves us with a God who, though acknowledged as real, is less interesting than the living, pulsating, endlessly productive world which we actually experience. Abstract theology is, indeed, the first step in the direction of atheism, for people will naturally pay more attention to living nature than to abstract deity. Moreover, as they enjoy and study nature, they will not look for God in it because they have been taught by abstract theology not to do so. Nature thus becomes 'this world,' godless by definition, although still supremely interesting. Eventually the God-abstraction is discarded altogether.

Soloviev believes the way to avoid this outcome is to take a positive approach right from the start by assuming that 'God, as the integral being, comprises not just unity but also multiplicity – a multiplicity of substantial ideas, i.e. of potentialities and

[34] *Chteniia*, pp. 114–15, 121.

powers with definite and particular content.'[35] To put it another way, one must assume God possesses a 'world' of his own. This is the idea at the heart of Soloviev's christology and sophiology: Christ/Sophia is the 'world' which God experiences from all eternity, the world which he begets for himself.

How do human beings gain insight into the divine world? They do so first through contemplation, or the exercise of pure reason. The forms of goodness, truth and beauty given to reason are reflections of the divine world. They are the criteria by which reason judges 'the given natural world, our reality, to be something conditional, abnormal and transient.' True, pure reason sees these forms as ideals, not actualities, for reason cannot establish the actual existence of anything. Yet reason does more than hover in the void, for it is exercised by an actual being, namely the human being. The human being is the link between the divine and phenomenal worlds. Through humanity, pure or contemplative reason is actualized in the abnormal world of conditioned being. This can happen only because humanity is actualized already in the divine world, which brings us to Sophia: 'Sophia is the ideal and perfect humanity which is eternally comprised in the integral divine being, or Christ.' Christ as Logos is the self-manifestation of God; but '[this] manifestation presupposes an other for which and in relation to which God manifests himself, i.e. it presupposes a human being.'[36] Christ as Sophia is the humanity which God sees and loves from all eternity.

This passage in *Lectures* is the inaugural moment of modern Russian sophiology.[37] One should note that sophiology is a branch of christology and thus connected with the concern for the salvation of human beings. Soloviev's sophiology is not in the first instance esoteric speculation on the inner life of God.

---

[35] *Chteniia*, pp. 115–16.

[36] *Chteniia*, pp. 120–2.

[37] Soloviev wrote a dialogue and treatise on Sophia during his travels in Egypt, Italy and France in 1876, but these materials lay unpublished for a century. Interestingly, these and many of his later sophiological essays were originally composed in French. An excellent edition of Soloviev's French writings, including the previously unpublished sophiological material, is available: Vladimir Soloviev, *'La Sophia' et les autres écrits français*, ed. François Rouleau (Lausanne: La Cité – L'Age d'Homme, 1978).

The soteriological dimension is evident in the promise which the humanity of God holds for actual human beings. The absolute divine-human being, 'in order to be real, must be one and many. Consequently, it is not only a general, universal essence abstracted from human individuals; it is at the same time an individual being which actually contains all these individuals in itself. Every one of us, every human being, is essentially and actually rooted in the universal or absolute human being and participates in it.' In other words, Christ is not just an individual human being but the 'pan-human organism.'[38] As members of this organism human beings have a share in divine freedom and immortality. In a word, they are divinizable.

A question may be raised at this point about Soloviev's motive in introducing the name Sophia. If his point was to articulate the traditional Orthodox doctrine of theosis (deification), why was 'Sophia' necessary? 'God-human' and 'second Adam' would have sufficed. Puzzling over this question, Copleston offers the explanation that Soloviev 'doubtless thought that the Wisdom literature in the Bible and the reflections of Greek Fathers and theologians required a place for Sophia, a conviction which was reinforced by his "visions", some of which he interpreted as visions of Sophia.' But this explanation overlooks the fact Soloviev's sophiology is one of the least traditional features of his thought.[39] Far from being something which Soloviev found in patristic sources or in the Bible for that matter, sophiology as he and his continuators practiced it became a major stumbling block preventing many Orthodox from appreciating their thought.

To make sense of Sophia one needs to view Soloviev's concept of theosis in connection with the critique of abstract principles

---

[38] *Chteniia*, pp. 126–7.
[39] Frederick C. Copleston, *Philosophy in Russia: From Herzen to Lenin and Berdyaev* (Notre Dame, Indiana: Search Press, University of Notre Dame, 1986), p. 225. However, Copleston shows he appreciates the systematic function of Sophia in Soloviev's thought when he assimilates Sophia to the concept of *vseedinstvo* (the whole of things, total-unity). 'The central idea of Solovyev's thought was not so much that of Sophia as of total-unity. If this idea is taken seriously, it demands that the world should be somehow included within the divine life, that it should be conceived as the self-manifestation of the Absolute' (ibid.). This is not an idea that can be found in patristic theology, at least not in patristic theology as the latter has usually been understood in the Orthodox Church.

and the project of Orthodox engagement with modern civilization. While Soloviev affirms the Orthodox doctrine of theosis, he also broadens it. The traditional doctrine, formulated almost exclusively by monks, is an ascetical theory which envisions the image of God stripping itself bare of worldly attachments so that the Tabor light may irradiate it fully. The danger in this approach is what one might call abstract theosis, that is to say, deification of the ontological shell or template of the human being. For Soloviev human beings are divinizable not just as primordial image but as creative agents engaged in the pursuits that fulfill humanity in the flesh, such as politics, science, education, the arts, technology and so on. To put it another way, Christ as the humanity of God has the power to divinize human 'wisdom,' i.e. culture, and in this capacity is appropriately called Sophia. The name fits the function. The function supports the project of Orthodox engagement with modern civilization.[40]

Soloviev completes his christology by discussing the negativities from which Christ redeems human beings, namely, sin and death. Soloviev has a rather elaborate theory of the pre-cosmic origin of evil and the consequent struggle between good and evil in cosmic evolution. The theory is of some interest for the discussion of Soloviev's metaphysics. But for purposes of the critique of positive religion one may focus on the practical question: How, according to Soloviev, do human beings land themselves in the state of sin and death in the first place?

His answer is, they isolate themselves. Sin is exclusivity, the rebellion of the part against the whole. Sin leads to death by

---

[40] For a clear description of Soloviev's concept of salvation see Richard F. Gustafson, 'Soloviev's Doctrine of Salvation,' *Russian Religious Thought*, eds Kornblatt and Gustafson, pp. 31-48. While stressing Soloviev's debt to patristic tradition, Gustafson also observes 'what distinguishes Soloviev's doctrine of salvation from the patristic tradition of Eastern Christianity is his application of the idea of deification not to the individual monk contemplating in the monastery but to all human beings living in the world community' (p. 40). My reading of the matter figures Soloviev's sophiology into Gustafson's account, thereby clarifying the soteriological character of Soloviev's theology of culture. On the connection between Russian sophiology and the project of Orthodox engagement with modern civilization see the discussion of Bulgakov's sophiology in pt 3, ch. 11 below; and Paul Valliere, 'Sophiology as the Dialogue of Orthodoxy with Modern Civilization,' *Russian Religious Thought*, eds Kornblatt and Gustafson, pp. 176-92.

diminishing fullness of being, which is attainable only through communion with the whole of things. Sin and death are overcome by renouncing exclusive being for integral being in the community of the whole. Renunciation transforms 'the natural human being,' inclined to selfish exclusivity, into 'the spiritual human being.' Christ is the model of renunciation, the perfectly spiritual human being. More than that, by virtue of his incarnation he renounces even divine exclusivity and so actualizes the perfect humanity of God. In Christ 'we have an actual divine-human personality capable of executing the twofold challenge of divine-human self-denial.'[41]

For a portrait of the self-denying humanity of God Soloviev turns to the biblical account of the temptation of Christ Soloviev's use of the story provides additional evidence of how deeply the temptation narrative appealed to modern Orthodox thinkers. His discussion is also noteworthy as the one and only substantive reference to the life of Jesus in *Lectures on the Humanity of God*, a point to which we shall return below.

Soloviev interprets the temptation story allegorically. The three temptations – bread, miracle, dominion – correspond to the temptations of flesh, mind and will, respectively. The most powerful of the three is the last, seduction by lust for power, because it disguises itself as a moral claim:

> In the name of his moral grandeur a human being may desire domination over the world in order to bring it to perfection; but the world is full of evil and does not willingly submit to moral excellence. Thus it seems necessary to force the world into submission, to apply one's divine power in the form of violence to bring the world to submission. But this use of violence, i.e. of evil in the service of good ends, would be an admission that the good in itself does not have power, that evil is stronger – and this is tantamount to *worshiping* the *evil principle* which holds sway in the world: 'and [Satan] showed him all the kingdoms of the world and their splendor; and he said to him, "All these I will give you, if you will fall down and worship me" '(Mt. 4:8–9).[42]

---

[41] *Chteniia*, pp. 166–7.
[42] *Chteniia*, p. 170.

But Jesus renounces violence, lust for power and all other pseudo-divine prerogatives, and Satan departs from him.

The ethic of renunciation, perfected in the mutual self-limitation of God and humanity in the humanity of God, solves the problem which Soloviev sets forth at the beginning of *Lectures*. Socialism, positivism and other one-sided humanist ideologies subvert the humane values which they claim to serve. The way out of the dilemma lies in renouncing all abstract 'isms' for a positive ideal. Every positive ideal is a religious ideal in the last analysis because it links human beings to the living whole of things, the divine ground of being. Through this link all values are resurrected from the dead, so to speak, and transfigured. Human values become divine-human values.

The transfiguration of humanity does not come to an end with the work of Christ, though he plays the central role in the establishment of the new, divine-human covenant. The process continues for the rest of time, acquiring ever richer content. The church serves the divine-human process as the community of the humanity of God. It seeks 'the full installation of the free, divine-human bond in all of humanity and in all spheres of human life and activity; all these spheres are to be brought to a harmonious, divine-human unity and become part of a free theocracy in which the Universal Church will attain the full measure of the stature of Christ'.[43]

The way of the church and the way of Christ are of course consistent with each other. But unfortunately the church as a human institution is vulnerable to the same temptations Christ endured in the wilderness. In the western church the trouble began when Rome fell prey to lust for power, or lack of faith in the power of truth, and suppressed human freedom in the name of the gospel. Protestantism vindicated human freedom but surrendered to the intellectual temptation when it subordinated scripture and tradition to the individual mind. The ensuing rationalism grew ever more extreme in the period of the Enlightenment until it precipitated the positivist-materialist revolt. But materialism cannot resist the temptation of bread, the selfish absolutization of material well-being, and brings modern

---

[43] *Chteniia*, p. 172; cf. p. 171: 'Humanity reunited with its divine principle through the mediation of Jesus Christ is the *Church*.'

western civilization to a spiritual dead end. Even so, Soloviev is not pessimistic about the West. He believes 'western humanity, having come to know by experience the falsehood of the three wide roads, the deceptiveness of the three great temptations, sooner or later must return to the truth of the humanity of God [k bogochelovecheskoi istine].'[44]

Where, concretely, is this truth to be found? Up to a point Soloviev agrees with the Slavophile view that it is to be found in the Orthodox East. The East, unlike the West, 'did not give in to the three temptations of the evil principle – it preserved Christ's truth.' Yet Soloviev is not willing to say Christ's truth is to be found exclusively in the East because 'the Eastern Church, while she preserved [Christ's truth] in the *soul* of her peoples, failed to give it real expression, failed to create *a Christian culture* while the West created an anti-Christian culture.' Moreover, the problem was not just that the eastern church did not try hard enough to concretize Christ's truth. Orthodox people could not have achieved this end in earlier times because the secular spheres of life had not undergone the degree of free and independent development in the Christian East as they had in the West. In the absence of a vigorous secular culture the Orthodox Church ended up dominating the secular spheres in absolutist fashion if it engaged with them at all; or else it rejected them altogether and made an ascetical exit from the world. 'Thus Christian truth, distorted and later rejected by western humanity, remained unperfected in eastern humanity.'[45]

The religious program suggested by Soloviev's reading of history is clear enough. Eastern and western humanity should work together to realize a new divine-human cultural synthesis. 'If the overshadowing of the human Mother by the active power of God brought forth the human incarnation of Divinity, then the impregnation of the divine Mother (the Church) by the active, human principle must bring forth the free deification of humanity.' In other words, the historical division of labor by which the West explored the meaning of humanity while the East preserved divine truth needs to be overcome. The history of

[44] *Chteniia*, p. 178.
[45] *Chteniia*, pp. 178–9.

both church and humanity from now on will be the story of the rebirth of faith in the free, active but unbelieving West and the energization and renewal of the backward but believing East. East and West together will build the divine-human community of the future, which Soloviev calls 'pan-humanity [*vseche-lovechestvo*] or the Universal Church.'[46]

EVALUATION

How well does Soloviev succeed in reconciling the claims of modern thought and Christian dogma in *Lectures on the Humanity of God*? The answer depends in part on how adequately one thinks he represents each side in its own right, since no proposal for reconciliation will be convincing if it misrepresents or diminishes either group of the inter-locutors.

The modernity of *Lectures* is apparent to any careful reader. The religious universalism, the call for the free development of the secular spheres, the critique of Orthodox particularism and the appreciation of modern humanism contribute to a distinc-tively contemporary philosophic vision. This vision is religious, not agnostic or atheist. Doctrinaire secularist liberals might find it baffling for this reason, but their perplexity says more about their own limitations than about Soloviev's. To them as to the conservative Orthodox dogmatists of his day Soloviev issues the same challenge: broaden your minds!

But what about the claims of dogmatic faith and historic Orthodoxy? Does Soloviev do justice to them in *Lectures on the Humanity of God*? The case is not so clear because of several features of Soloviev's position which appear to place it at a remove from classical Orthodoxy. The first and most striking of these is the neglect of the person of Jesus in *Lectures*. As Florovsky observes, 'Soloviev speaks much more about the humanity of God than about the God-human, and the image of the Savior is a pale shadow in his system.'[47] One might even argue that Soloviev reduces the humanity of God to an 'abstract principle' in *Lectures* by ignoring the concrete historical

---

[46] *Chteniia*, p. 180.
[47] *Puti russkogo bogosloviia*, p. 317.

embodiment of the idea. Moreover, lack of attention to Jesus means lack of attention to the Gospels and to the New Testament as a whole. The Christian canon, or for that matter the Hebrew Bible, does not seem to have been a particularly important source for *Lectures*. The word 'gospel' scarcely occurs in the work. Of course it is possible for someone to expound the biblical faith without being a biblical theologian. Still, the relative absence of biblical theology from *Lectures* forces an Orthodox Christian to regard Soloviev's work with a certain amount of suspicion.

One finds additional evidence of Soloviev's rather free relationship to historic Orthodoxy in his handling of traditional dogma. His trinitarianism is highly platonized and in this sense rationalistic. The extent to which the Trinity is a mystery of faith for Soloviev, as it must finally be for an Orthodox believer, is moot. Soloviev's approval of Augustinian and Leibnizian analogies between the Trinity and human consciousness must also disturb the Orthodox mind, which is schooled to view creaturely analogies of the Trinity as a characteristic error of western theology. In christology Soloviev's theory of the humanity of God as the product of religious evolution calls into question the Orthodox view that the incarnation was a unique miracle. Finally, in ecclesiology, Soloviev's apparent equation of the Universal Church with pan-humanity (*vsechelovechestvo*) appears to compromise the distinctiveness of the church as a sacramental community.

To say that *Lectures* raises questions about Soloviev's Orthodoxy is not to imply he or an apologist could not come up with satisfactory answers. While the vindication of Soloviev's Orthodoxy is not the purpose of the present study, we may nevertheless explore a couple of important contextual questions which must to be taken into account in any evaluation. The first is why Soloviev adopted the free approach to dogmatics which one finds in *Lectures*. The second question concerns the direction which Soloviev's career took in the decade after *Lectures*.

The motive underlying Soloviev's free approach to dogma is not immediately obvious. The case would be clearer if Soloviev were a moralizing theologian whose project was to rescue the supposedly authentic, historical Jesus from the alleged distortions of later church dogma. But Soloviev was not this kind of theologian. A second possibility is that Soloviev was trying to liberalize the practice of dogmatic theology in Orthodoxy. But this observation, true as far as it goes, does not tell us why Soloviev was interested in dogma in the first place, nor does it take into account the essentially religious character of Soloviev's thought.

A clue to what Soloviev was up to in *Lectures* can be found in an important distinction which he draws but does not elaborate in *The Critique of Abstract Principles*. It will be recalled that in the *Critique* Soloviev distinguishes between abstract and positive principles, which he breaks down further into rational and empirical, and mystical and traditional principles. Since the *Critique* deals with abstract rather than positive principles, the distinction between mystical and traditional principles does not come up for discussion in its own right in the book. *Lectures on the Humanity of God*, on the other hand, deals with positive principles; hence one assumes the distinction between mystical and traditional principles is pertinent. Here is the distinction as Soloviev formulates it in the *Critique*:

> Positive or religious principles are either based on direct, personal perception and contemplation of divine things, or they presuppose the mediation of historical tradition, faith in authority. Religious principles of the first sort I call *mystical*; of the second, *traditional*. Now since positive or religious principles by themselves do not constitute the subject of the present essay, I will not pause over this distinction. I will only observe that, despite the factual inseparability of the mystical element from the traditional, the very existence of the latter is a temporary phenomenon and not an unconditional necessity, for it has only a historical foundation. I mean that there is no essential reason why we cannot imagine a state of universal human consciousness in which the traditional foundation of religion would be swallowed up by the mystical, i.e. the religion of all people would be based on the immediate perception of divine things, and everyone would view historical tradition merely as the idea of an outlived past.[48]

---

[48] *Kritika*, pp. 13–14.

Applied to *Lectures* this passage suggests the following line of reasoning. Dogmas are historical traditions, handed down by churches rather than independent thinkers. Yet dogmas also encapsulate religious experience, they have a mystical dimension. Traditional and mystical religion, while historically connected and sharing the same ultimate concern (the humanity of God), are not equivalent. Tradition is a relative, time-bound phenomenon; mysticism offers contemplation of divine things and in this sense enjoys a certain pre-eminence in religious life. This pre-eminence will appear in dogmatic theology as elsewhere and will lead the theologian to prize the mystical content of dogma more than the historical shell. This, in effect, is what Soloviev does in *Lectures*. The freedom with which he handles historic dogmas in this work is not that of the free thinker or moralizer, but of the mystic.

This interpretation has the virtue of explaining most of the particulars of Soloviev's approach to dogma in *Lectures*. It explains his detachment from the historical Jesus, for example, since the events of Jesus' life are even more time-bound than the dogmas that express the meaning of those events in general terms. It explains Soloviev's platonized trinitarianism, for this can be seen as a way of construing the Trinity in experiential terms. An absolute, unfathomable mystery cannot be experienced, while the good, the true and the beautiful can be. As for the theory of Christ as the perfect, spiritual human being and the theory of the church as pan-humanity, both may be seen as ways of opening dogmatics to mystical univeralism. At the same time, the mystical content of Soloviev's concept of the humanity of God keeps it firmly within the bounds of positive religion and rules out a secularizing interpretation. Finally, the fact that Soloviev preserves a positive attitude toward dogma even as he seeks to transform it fits in with the irenic, if visionary, suggestion in the *Critique* that dogmatic religion will ultimately be absorbed into mystical religion.

If this interpretation of Soloviev's approach to dogmatics is correct, it follows that the distance separating him from stricter Orthodox dogmatists does not result in the first instance from the particular dogmatic positions which he defends but from his general view of tradition. Theory of tradition is a fundamental part of the critique of positive religion. The fact that Soloviev does not address the subject in *Lectures* suggests he had an attenuated appreciation for tradition. In this he resembled many nineteenth-century theologians of liberal or reformist views.[49]

If Soloviev's theoretical grasp of tradition fell short, however, his practical engagement with it did not. This point stands out clearly when one examines the course of his career following *Lectures on the Humanity of God*. Given the privileging of mysticism over tradition in this work, one might have supposed Soloviev would stray even further from traditional Orthodoxy in subsequent years. In fact the opposite was the case. Instead of distancing himself from Orthodoxy after *Lectures*, Soloviev took a livelier interest in it. For a period of about a decade Soloviev shifted his attention from theoretical to practical religious issues, becoming much more intimately involved with the ideas and institutions of traditional religion than one would have expected on the basis of *Lectures*.

The change may be noted by comparing the first and second decades of Soloviev's work. The first decade, roughly the 1870s, saw an enormous output of theoretical philosophy: *The Crisis of Western Philosophy*, *The Philosophical Principles of Integral Knowledge*, *Lectures on the Humanity of God* and *The Critique of Abstract Principles*. The next decade witnessed a large output of historical and publicistic works, such as *The National Question in Russia*, *The History and Future of Theocracy*, 'The Jews and the Christian Question,' *La Russie et l'Église universelle* and other writings on social, political and ecclesiastical topics. While these essays were informed by the grand vision of the earlier theoretical works, they were also necessarily shaped by the demands of advocacy and activism. An effective advocate or activist must engage in a concrete dialogue with those to whom he preaches. When the issues are religious this means, among other things, listening carefully to those who represent specific religious traditions. This relationship has as

---

[49] For a definition of tradition in religion see Paul Valliere, 'Tradition,' *The Encyclopedia of Religion*, ed. Mircea Eliade (New York: Macmillan Publishing Company, 1987), 15:1–16. On the impact of critical-historical method on the concept of an unchanging Christian tradition in nineteenth-century theology, see Jaroslav Pelikan, *Christian Doctrine and Modern Culture (since 1700)*, vol. 5 of *The Christian Tradition: A History of the Development of Doctrine* (Chicago and London: The University of Chicago Press, 1989), pp. 253–65.

much of an effect on the advocates and activists as it does on those whom they would persuade. As a theoretical thinker Soloviev could afford to treat tradition as a secondary category; as an engaged preacher he was forced to accept it as a vitally important fact.

Perhaps one should not say 'forced,' which implies a grudging assent. Soloviev's rapprochement with tradition was freely chosen and served the grand imperative of his theoretical works. The whole burden of the latter was the critique of abstract principles, the justification of concreteness and 'positive' reality. Was not Soloviev's engagement with historic traditions a move in the direction of concreteness? Religious traditions are living things, the forms which positive religion takes in the world of flesh and blood. On the level of pure theory mysticism may appear to contain and exceed tradition, as the whole exceeds the part. In actual religious life the opposite is the case. Tradition comprises mysticism and exceeds it. Without a traditional framework mystics cannot talk to anybody, not even to each other, indeed not even to themselves. As soon as communication begins, however, so does engagement with the mediating structures of tradition.

In matters involving dogmatic theology Soloviev's engagement with tradition took two forms. First, he began to pay attention to historical scholarship on dogma, an interest which bore fruit in his important essay of 1886, 'The Development of Dogma in the Church in Connection with the Question of Church Union.' Second, he devoted himself to ecumenical and theocratic activism. Ecumenism and theocratism, whatever else they might be, are instances of applied dogmatics, for an idea lacking dogmatic content cannot be either ecumenical or theocratic. Stripped of dogma, a theocratic proposal is just one more social or political manifesto. The case of ecumenism is even clearer. A vision of unity in which all churches or even all religions are seen as mystically one and the same is not an ecumenical proposal. An ecumenical proposal addresses churches and religions that make specific dogmatic claims and suggests a course of dialogue or action designed to reconcile these claims. At least some claims on all sides must be regarded as legitimate, otherwise there would be no basis for dialogue. In other words, an ecumenical proposal is always a dogmatic statement even if the dogmatic element may not exhaust the content of the proposal.

The course of Soloviev's career shows one cannot clarify the issue of modern thought and dogma in his work on the basis of *Lectures on the Humanity of God* alone. The problem must be examined in the light of his practical theological works of the 1880s. These amount to nothing less than a second critique of positive religion.

8

The Critique of Positive Religion (2): Ecumenical and Theocratic Themes

SOLOVIEV'S RELIGIOUS ACTIVISM

Moving to St Petersburg in 1877 Soloviev made his living working for the Ministry of Public Education. After completing the doctorate he also began teaching at the university. In the spring of 1881, however, he resigned both positions following a clash with the highest authorities in the state.

On 1 March 1881, to the horror of the vast majority of Russian people including Soloviev, Tsar Alexander II was assassinated by populist revolutionaries. In a speech later in the month Soloviev called on the martyred tsar's son and heir to demonstrate a spirit of Christian forgiveness by sparing the regicides from the death penalty. Alexander III and his government were not impressed. The new tsar wondered how such a 'psychopath of the purest water' could be the son of 'dear old' Sergei Mikhailovich Soloviev (who had died in 1879). Pobedonostsev, Procurator of the Holy Synod, called Soloviev 'idiotic.' No punishment was imposed, but Soloviev resigned his posts anyway.[1]

---

[1] Losev, 'Tvorcheskii put' Vladimira Solov'eva,' p. 6. The text of Soloviev's speech on the regicides has not survived. Soloviev remained a foe of capital punishment. The position he articulates in the introduction to *La Russie et l'Église universelle* (1889) is typical: 'It follows that three things are absolutely inadmissible in a Christian state: first, wars inspired by national egoism, conquests that raise up one nation on the ruins of another, because the dominant interest for the Christian state is universal solidarity or Christian peace; next, civil and economic slavery which

The crisis of 1881 was a turning point in Soloviev's career, launching him on the path to a more humanitarian interpretation of his Slavophile faith. During the 1880s he worked out his new orientation in essays, speeches and monographs on a wide range of political and ecclesiastical topics.

The first notable work of the new phase of Soloviev's career was 'Three Speeches in Memory of Dostoevsky' (1881–3).[2] Soloviev and Dostoevsky (1821–81) became friends in the 1870s. Dostoevsky admired *Lectures on the Humanity of God* and echoed some of its ideas in *The Brothers Karamazov* (1878–80) and his celebrated Pushkin speech.[3] In his memorial lectures Soloviev stressed the univeralism of Dostoevsky's Slavophilism, the preaching of pan-humanity (*vsechelovechestvo*) and world community, while criticizing the nationalistic and particularistic elements. In the third lecture he made some sympathetic observations on the Roman Catholic Church, *bête noire* of the Slavophiles, and advocated the reunion of the eastern and western churches. In 'The Great Schism and Christian Politics'

---

makes one class the passive instrument of another; and finally, vindictive penalties (especially the death penalty) which society applies to the guilty individual, using him as a means of public safety. By committing a crime the individual shows that he regards society merely as a means and the neighbor as the instrument of his egoism. One must not respond to this injustice by committing another, by abasing human dignity in the criminal himself, reducing him to the level of a passive instrument by a penalty which excludes his improvement and regeneration.' Vladimir Soloviev, *La Russie et l'Église universelle*, 4th ed. (Paris: Librairie Stock, 1922), p. xxiii.

[2] 'Tri rechi v pamiat' Dostoevskogo,' *SSVSS*, 3:185–223; and Solov'ev, *Sochineniia v dvukh tomakh*, eds Losev and Gulyga, 2:289–323. On the relationship between Soloviev and Dostoevsky see Mochul'skii, *Vladimir Soloviev*, pp. 79–83 and 130–3; and Marina Kostalevsky, *Dostoevsky and Soloviev: The Art of Integral Vision* (New Haven and London: Yale University Press, 1997).

[3] In June, 1880 Dostoevsky took part in a series of festivities in Moscow connected with the dedication of a monument to the Russian poet Alexander Pushkin (1799–1837). In a speech before the Society of Amateurs of Russian Literature he called on the Russian intelligentsia to transcend the bitter division between Slavophilism and Westernism in modern Russian culture by emulating Pushkin's ability to appreciate the many sides of human experience. Dostoevsky maintained that 'to become a real Russian, to become completely Russian, can only mean (in the last analysis, to be sure) to become a brother of all people, *a pan-human* individual [*vsechelovek*], if you will.' F.M. Dostoevskii, *Sobranie sochinenii*, eds L.P. Grossman *et al.*, 10 vols (Moscow: Gosudarstvennoe izdatel'stvo khudozhestvennoi literatury, 1958), 10:457.

(1883) he expressed his ecumenical ideas in greater detail.[4] His Slavophile colleagues were appalled and soon closed their journals to him. Important friends in the Orthodox clergy supported Soloviev, however, notably Archimandrite Antony (Vadkovsky), an administrator at St Petersburg Theological Academy and later metropolitan of the city, and Father P.A. Preobrazhensky, editor of *Pravoslavnoe obozrenie* (*The Orthodox Review*).[5]

In 1884 Soloviev expanded his irenic vision to include the Jews. In a long article in *Pravoslavnoe obozrenie*, 'The Jews and the Christian Question,' Soloviev attacked anti-Semitism, arguing that peace between Israel and the nations was the sine qua non of genuine theocracy. In the same year he began studying Hebrew with a young Talmudic scholar, F.B. Gets, who became a close friend.[6]

In the mid-1880s Soloviev began writing *The History and Future of Theocracy*, a historical and prophetic work advocating Orthodox–Roman Catholic ecumenism as the way to a general renewal of Christendom and all humanity.[7] Defining theocracy in biblical terms as a commonwealth based

---

[4] 'Velikii spor i khristianskaia politika,' *SSVSS*, 4:3–114.

[5] While Soloviev became the best-known ecumenist in nineteenth-century Russian Orthodoxy, the idea of mending the division of Christendom had long been discussed in the Orthodox East. For a detailed account, see Georges Florovsky, 'The Orthodox Churches and the Ecumenical Movement Prior to 1910,' *The Collected Works of Georges Florovsky*, 2:161–231.

[6] Soloviev also promoted an irenic approach to other religious and ethnic minorities in the Russian empire. See Greg Gaut, 'Can a Christian Be a Nationalist? Vladimir Solov'ev's Critique of Nationalism,' *Slavic Review* 57 (1998): 77–94.

[7] *Istoriia i budushchnost' teokratii. (Issledovanie vsemirno-istoricheskogo puti k istinnoi zhizni.),* *SSVSS*, 4:241–633. Portions of the book came out as separate articles in *Pravoslavnoe obozrenie* in 1885–6. The whole volume was published in Zagreb in 1887 shortly after Soloviev's return to Russia. In a notice written en route to Zagreb in 1886 Soloviev described *The History and Future of Theocracy* as 'a complete philosophy of history from the religious point of view or – what is the same thing – a history of theocracy.' He envisioned a three-part study, dealing with theocracy in the biblical world, in the history of the church and in his own time, respectively. The published volume contains the first (biblical) part, to which Soloviev attached a preface and a related article, 'The Development of Dogma in the Church in Connection with the Question of Church Union' (see n. 15 below). The second and third parts were never written. The notice of 1886 is reproduced with related material in *SSVSS*, 11:68–83. The same volume contains a collection of Soloviev's letters on ecumenical and theocratic themes, pp. 349–456.

upon the harmonious union of prophecy, priesthood and monarchy, Soloviev envisioned a renewed Christendom brought about by the joint activism of the Roman pontiff, the Russian emperor and a prophetic agent whose identity was less fixed.[8] Completing the first volume in 1886, Soloviev went abroad to arrange for publication of the book in the West. He also wanted to discuss his ideas with Roman Catholic leaders. His destination was Zagreb, then part of the Austro-Hungarian empire, where he was hosted by two ecumenically minded Croatian clergymen, Canon Franko Rački, president of the South Slav Academy, and Bishop Josip Juraj Strossmayer of Bosnia. Soloviev's stay in Croatia lasted more than three months, giving rise to rumors of his conversion to Roman Catholicism. In fact, he confessed and communicated in an Orthodox church while in Zagreb and left the city 'as Orthodox as ever.'[9]

The Russian authorities were suspicious, however. Returning home to a chilly reception, Soloviev saw there was little hope of publishing *The History and Future of Theocracy* in Russia. He described his predicament in a letter to Gets:

> You probably know I am now enduring outright persecution. All my writings, not just the new ones but reprints of the old, are unconditionally banned. The Chief Procurator of the Synod, Pobedonostsev, told one of my friends that all my activities are harmful to Russia and Orthodoxy and consequently cannot be allowed. And to justify such a verdict, all sorts of falsehoods about me are being fabricated and circulated. Today I am a Jesuit, tomorrow perhaps I will accept circumcision; right now I am in the service of the Pope and Bishop Strossmayer, but tomorrow I'll probably be serving the Alliance Israélite and the Rothschilds. Our political,

[8] The prophet may be seen as Soloviev himself; thus Strémooukhoff, *Vladimir Soloviev et son oeuvre messianique*, pp. 142, 163–4. In 'The Jews and the Christian Question' Soloviev assigns the prophetic role to the Jews. In *La Russie et l'Église universelle*, pp. 320–9, he seems to regard modern humanism, interpreted sophiologically as presaging 'l'idéal parfait de l'Humanité divinisée,' as the prophetic force, a view reflected also in his positive appraisal of Auguste Comte (see Ch. 6, n. 51 above and Ch. 10, n. 23 below).

[9] S.M. Solov'ev, *Zhizn' i tvorcheskaia evoliutsiia*, pp. 256–7. Soloviev's dealings with Strossmayer, Rački and other Roman Catholic leaders are described by Strémooukhoff in *Vladimir Soloviev et son oeuvre messianique*, pp. 188–211.

ecclesiastical and literary scoundrels are so brazen, and our public so stupid, that anything might happen. Of course I am not depressed, and I stick to my motto: God won't let the pig go hungry. Nevertheless I need to be as careful as possible.[10]

Caution did not mean passive acceptance of his lot, however. Although Soloviev abandoned *The History and Future of Theocracy* as he had originally outlined it, he composed an abridged version in French, again with the intention of publishing it abroad. In the spring of 1888 he traveled to Paris for a stay lasting most of the rest of the year. Anatole Leroy-Beaulieu, a pioneer of Russian studies in the West, and the philosopher of religion Eugène Tavernier were his primary hosts. The Roman Catholic newspaper *L'Univers* opened its pages to 'Saint Vladimir et l'État chrétien,' an essay commemorating the nine-hundredth anniversary of the baptism of Kievan Rus'. The monograph on theocracy, *La Russie et l'Église universelle*, was published in 1889. In the introduction Soloviev expressed the hope that he would 'see the day when my country will possess the good which it needs first of all – religious liberty.'[11]

In spite of successes and friendships in the West, however, Soloviev's ecumenical activism was reaching its limits. In Russia most of the Slavophiles and conservative Orthodox remained opposed to his work, and even in Europe Soloviev's admirers never numbered more than a few like-minded Christian idealists. Pope Leo XIII, to whom Strossmayer had sent a copy

---

[10] Quoted in S.M. Solov'ev, *Zhizn' i tvorcheskaia evoliutsiia*, p. 258. The letter was written in December, 1886.
[11] Vladimir Soloviev, *La Russie et l'Église universelle*, 4th ed. (Paris: Librairie Stock, 1922), p. lxi. The first French edition (1889) was published in Paris by Albert Savine. A Russian translation lacking the third and final part of the work came out in Cracow in 1904 (2nd ed., 1908). This translation was subsequently published in Russia proper: Vladimir Solov'ev, *Rossiia i vselenskaia tserkov'*, trans. G.A. Rachinskii (Moscow: Tovarishchestvo tipografii A.I. Mamontova, 1911). The Rachinskii translation (still lacking the third part) is included in Vladimir Solov'ev, *O khristianskom edinstve* (Moscow: Rudomino, 1994), pp. 181–265. The French text in its entirety is reproduced in Vladimir Soloviev, *La Sophia*, ed. François Rouleau, pp. 123–297. A complete English translation is available: Vladimir Soloviev, *Russia and the Universal Church*, trans. Herbert Rees (London: Geoffrey Bles – The Centenary Press, 1948). For Soloviev's visit to France see Mochul'skii, *Vladimir Solov'ev*, pp. 181–6.

of *La Russie et l'Église Universelle*, sympathized with Soloviev's vision of a reunited Christendom but did not regard it as a practical proposition. 'Bella idea!,' Leo reportedly said, 'ma fuor d'un miràcolo è cosa impossibile.'[12] In a letter to Rački Soloviev lamented that 'people from two quarters disapprove of my French book: the liberals because of its clericalism and the clericals because of its liberalism. The reverend Jesuits have written me off and are trying to "muzzle" me.'[13] While Soloviev preserved his ecumenical convictions to the end of his days – 'A Brief Tale of the Anti-Christ' (1900) is a masterpiece of ecumenism[14] – he had little interest in becoming an ecclesiastical Don Quixote. In the 1890s he turned to other concerns.

DOGMA AND CHURCH UNION

'The Development of Dogma in the Church in Connection with the Question of Church Union' brings together several of the concerns of Soloviev's critique of positive religion in the activist stage of his career.[15] The essay evinces a greater interest in the history of Christian dogma than one finds in *Lectures on the Humanity of God*. It is also one of the best statements of Soloviev's ecumenism. The investigation of dogma has ecumenical implications because it sheds light on the divisions between churches. A theocratic point is at stake, too, because Soloviev did not believe theocracy was realizable apart from the reunion of Christendom. Finally, 'The Development of Dogma' is a masterful essay of philosophic Orthodoxy in which critical method, free thought, liberal humanism and positive Christian

---

[12] Mochul'skii, *Vladimir Solov'ev*, p. 185. 'A fine idea, but short of a miracle it's an impossibility.'

[13] Quoted in S.M. Solov'ev, *Zhizn' i tvorcheskaia evoliutsiia*, p. 289.

[14] See Ch. 9 below for my reasons for rejecting the received view of the 'Brief Tale' as a repudiation of ecumenism.

[15] 'Dogmaticheskoe razvitie tserkvi v sviazi s voprosom o soedinenii tserkvei,' *Sobranie sochinenii Vladimira Sergeevicha Solov'eva*, supplementary vol. 11 (Brussels: Izdatel'stvo Zhizn' s Bogom, Foyer Oriental Chrétien, 1969), pp. 1–67; and Solov'ev, *O khristianskom edinstve*, pp. 85–126. Soloviev wrote the essay in the fall of 1885. It was first published in *Pravoslavnoe obozrenie* and also came out as a separate brochure (Moscow: Universitetskaia tipografiia [M. Katkov], 1886). All references to 'Dogmaticheskoe razvitie' in the present work are to *SSVSS*.

faith all work together in a balanced and mutually enriching way.

The debate over the development of dogma arose in nineteenth-century theology from the application of the critical historical method to dogmatic theology.[16] The issue was whether and to what extent dogmas are the product of historical evolution and subject to its laws. On the most general level the question was whether dogmas could be regarded as absolute and unchanging truths. In more practical terms the debate focused on doctrinal differences between churches. The Orthodox churches accepted the dogmas of the first seven ecumenical councils. The Roman Catholic Church claimed twenty ecumenical councils, the most recent being Vatican I (1870). Protestant churches accepted a few ancient councils, or fewer or none, depending on the denomination. But all churches affirmed some sort of dogma and for that reason had a stake in the debate over development.

Soloviev's ecumenical project strained his relations with Slavophile and conservative Orthodox. On one level he shared much with these people, for they, too, believed that Russia was called to bring the truth of Christianity to the whole world, including the secularized West. But the Slavophiles identified universal Christian truth with historic Orthodoxy and viewed the western forms of Christianity negatively, while Soloviev saw negativism toward western Christianity as an irrational and unchristian prejudice. He also recognized that Russia's mission to the world presented a mighty challenge to Russia itself. Soloviev's theocratism, in other words, walked hand in hand with criticism of existing conditions in Russia:

> The project of uniting the churches is for Russia a task of greatest difficulty demanding an inner self-denial even more profound than that which was required two centuries ago for the rapprochement of Russia with the secular civilization of the West. That civilization, too, offended the national feeling of our forebears. And today as in the past the distaste for foreign elements is more than a mere fact of life; it can be said

---

[16] For a comprehensive yet concise exposition of the impact of the idea of 'historical mediation' on Christian doctrine in nineteenth-century theology, see Pelikan, *Christian Doctrine and Modern Culture*, pp. 227–81.

to be justified, at least to the extent that the distaste which a
sick person feels toward bitter medicine is justified.'[17]

The metaphor could hardly have soothed Slavophile anxieties,
as it implied Orthodox Russia was somehow ailing.

The Slavophile opponents of ecumenism replied that 'the
union of the churches is impossible and even unnecessary.'[18]
Soloviev dispatches the latter objection first. Adopting an
offensive rather than defensive line of criticism, he takes the
Slavophiles to task not in terms of his own ecumenical project,
which they rejected, but in terms of something dear to their own
hearts: the mobilization of Slavdom. Soloviev wants to know
how preachers of Slavic solidarity can regard the reunion of the
churches as unnecessary when the Slavic world itself is divided
along religious lines. Soloviev observes that the reunification of
the churches is 'a pressing demand, an urgent necessity without
which Slavdom as *a whole* cannot exist at all.' To be sure,
Slavophiles could reply by proposing a union of the Slavs on a
non-religious basis, e.g. material interests. But Soloviev wants to
know where in the Slavic world one could imagine such calcula-
tions outweighing the 'national egoism' of the Slavic nations.
Even among Slavic peoples who share an ecclesiastical bond,
such as Serbs and Bulgarians, contemporary history presents the
sorry spectacle of competing nationalisms. If 'the church,
paralyzed by its own division, cannot exert its unifying influence
even over its own peoples,' how can one expect 'religious indifferentism' to do better, even if all Slavs embraced it? 'The
decline of religion has never held individuals and nations back
from hating and destroying each other.' In any case, Orthodox
idealists could scarcely approve of a Slavdom united on the basis
of indifference to religion. In short, the reunion of the churches
is as necessary to the Slavophile program as to Soloviev's own.[19]

But perhaps church union is impossible. Soloviev takes this
challenge more seriously than the first, for he does not doubt the
difficulty of mending the unity of Christendom. Deep-seated
prejudices and real doctrinal differences present serious
obstacles. Yet the existence of obstacles does not prove the

[17] 'Dogmaticheskoe razvitie,' p. 4.
[18] 'Dogmaticheskoe razvitie,' p. 3.
[19] 'Dogmaticheskoe razvitie,' pp. 6–8.

impossibility of a project. There must be some other reason why conservative Orthodox and Slavophiles doubted the possibility of church union.

The reason was not far to seek: Orthodox critics of ecumenism viewed the western churches as heretical and refused to make common cause with heresy. Soloviev asks how his critics have determined that western Christianity is heretical. Have they made a careful study of the matter, or have they simply condemned western Christians *'in advance*, without investigation or trial?'[20] The question prompts Soloviev to launch his own investigation of the doctrinal differences separating eastern and western churches.

'The Development of Dogma' focuses chiefly on the doctrinal differences between Orthodoxy and Roman Catholicism. Protestants present a more difficult case, since they 'were excommunicated or, to say it better, excommunicated themselves from the Universal Church in that they not only rebelled against certain conciliar dogmas but rejected the whole idea of the authority of ecumenical councils.'[21]

Soloviev begins by examining two Roman Catholic dogmas which Orthodox apologists typically condemn as heretical: the *filioque* and papal infallibility. He admits neither dogma is Orthodox but wants to know whether either one actually contradicts Orthodox doctrine. Many usages of the Roman Church, while not found in Orthodoxy, are not for that reason heretical.

On the surface the *filioque* appears to be a grave problem, since it is an intrusion in the Creed. Soloviev calls for a careful examination of the case. His own review of the documents in the light of the scholarship of his day leads him to conclude that the early medieval Spanish church, where the *filioque* first appeared, accepted it as a means of protecting Nicene Orthodoxy against a powerful local Arianism; furthermore, the *filioque* circulated in Spain not as an innovation but as part of what the churches there took to be the integral text of the Creed. Since the evolution of the text of the Creed was a complicated process even apart from the Spanish developments, and in any

---

[20] 'Dogmaticheskoe razvitie,' pp. 9–10.
[21] 'Dogmaticheskoe razvitie,' p. 10.

case took place at a time when texts and translations were not easily standardized, Soloviev sees no grounds for accusing the Spanish Christians of malevolence against the Orthodox faith. Thus he rejects the standard Slavophile view that the addition of the *filioque* to the Creed was 'a fratricidal act.' Moreover, he points out that none of the ecumenical councils recognized by Orthodoxy explicitly rejected the *filioque*.[22]

The ecumenical councils do not explicitly reject papal infallibility, either, although this does not prove much because the doctrine is so recent (officialized at Vatican I in 1870). More to the point, one may ask whether the ecumenical councils or any other authority in Orthodoxy ever propounded 'an *indisputable* and absolutely *definite* dogma concerning the nature and form of ecclesiastical administration and the organs of the ecumenical teaching ministry.'[23] Soloviev denies that any such dogma exists in Orthodoxy, which means Orthodox Christians are not so strictly bound in these matters that any departure from traditional views necessarily involves heresy.

These and other particular dogmatic issues do not exhaust the conservative Orthodox brief against Rome, however. A different sort of objection concerns not the letter but the spirit of Roman Catholic and Orthodox dogmatics. The conservatives argue 'the Roman Church permits itself to *develop* the dogmatic truth of Christianity, while the Eastern Church only *safeguards* that which was originally and once for all given in Christian revelation.'[24] That is to say, while not all the teachings promulgated by Rome after the seventh ecumenical council are heretical in and of themselves, the fact the Roman Church added to the original revelation is a violation of that revelation and an insurmountable barrier to reunion. The strongest form of this view 'considers each of the dogmas of Orthodoxy to be a *particular datum* of the original Revelation, a datum which was always *manifest*, obligatory and beyond dispute for all Orthodox

---

[22] 'Dogmaticheskoe razvitie,' pp. 11–15. The de-escalation of the *filioque* issue is now widely accepted by ecumenists. For a sampling of Roman Catholic and Orthodox opinion, see Yves Congar, *Diversity and Communion*, trans. John Bowden (Mystic, Connecticut: Twenty-Third Publications, 1985), pp. 97–104.
[23] 'Dogmaticheskoe razvitie,' p. 16.
[24] 'Dogmaticheskoe razvitie,' p. 18.

people.'[25] The historical evidence against such a view is, in
Soloviev's opinion, so overwhelming that Orthodox who hold it
could be accused of 'closet Old Belief.' They might as well
maintain 'that the two-fingered [Old Believer] sign of the cross
was handed down to the apostles by Christ Himself.'[26]

In softer versions of their position conservative Orthodox
apologists do not deny that certain changes in Christian dogma
occurred during the first eight centuries of church history. But,
while conceding the fact of change, these apologists deny the
changes constituted development. They argue the alterations
represented merely 'subjective' adjustments, not new 'objective'
truths. Or they argue the additions introduced by the Orthodox
were qualitatively different from those made by the Romans. So,
for example, T. Stoianov, one of Soloviev's critics, maintained
that Orthodox dogmatic theologians merely added restrictive
expressions such as 'only' or 'solely' to the traditional dogmatic
formulas, while the Romans allowed themselves to say 'but also'
or 'on the other hand.' In the matter of the procession of the
Holy Spirit, for example, the Romans said *filioque* (and from
the Son), forcing the Orthodox to reply 'from the Father *alone*.'
'Thus the *essential* difference between our new dogmatic propositions (we allow ourselves to use this inaccurate expression)
and the new Latin dogmas lies in the fact that the former are
conservative in nature, the latter are *progressive*.'[27] The apolo-
getic stereotype is thus maintained: the West develops dogma,
the East preserves it.

Soloviev denies the validity of the arguments on which this
stereotype rests. To say, for example, that the dogmatic adjustments approved by the ecumenical councils were of a purely
subjective character overlooks two objective facts. First, as a
result of the councils certain dogmas became more explicit than
they had ever been before; second, all Orthodox people were
required to accept them. Prior to the confession of the
homoousion by the Council of Nicaea, for example, loyal
Orthodox could and did hold various views concerning the

---

[25] 'Dogmaticheskoe razvitie,' p. 42.
[26] 'Dogmaticheskoe razvitie,' p. 48.
[27] Quoted in 'Dogmaticheskoe razvitie,' p. 50. Stoianov's article appeared in *Vera
i razum*, 1885.

relationship of the Son to the Father. Eminent theologians such as Justin Martyr and Origen could teach a subordinationist christology without separating themselves from Orthodoxy. After Nicaea, the *homoousion* became an absolute criterion of Orthodoxy. Does this not show that truth in the objective sense was at stake at Nicaea?[28] To insist that all Orthodox additions to dogma were conservative rather than progressive also overlooks obvious facts, such as the novelty of some of the key terms on which the great dogmatic debates turned, e.g. *homoousion* and Theotokos, neither of which is to be found in the Bible or the earliest fathers.[29]

The conservative view of dogma also makes it difficult if not impossible to express the coherence of Christian dogma to anyone outside the circle of like-minded believers. How, for example, would Stoianov justify the dogma of the Trinity to a Jew? Would he not have to admit the possibility of dogmatic development? Soloviev imagines such a dialogue:

JEW: You agree, don't you, that the truth of the unity of God is the most indubitable and original truth entrusted to our fathers by God Himself?

STOIANOV: Without a doubt.

JEW: And we are obliged to treasure this truth?

STOIANOV: Of course.

JEW: And therefore to protect it, too?

STOIANOV: Yes.

JEW: Well, then, in view of the fact that various *goim* (Gentiles) encroach on the purity of this truth we have the right and even the obligation to insist on this truth strenuously and to say over and over again that God is one, only one, exclusively one.

STOIANOV: But divine revelation also attests to God in three persons.

JEW: Now this, as far as we are concerned, is a great novelty. Our fathers never heard this from God and did not hand it down to us. From the beginning we have all known only that God is one.

---

[28] 'Dogmaticheskoe razvitie,' pp. 20–1, 31–3, 45–6.
[29] 'Dogmaticheskoe razvitie,' pp. 37, 53.

STOIANOV: But the unity of God does not exclude trinity. Like you, we affirm that God is one in His essence *but* at the same time is in three persons.

JEW: Perhaps! Perhaps what you affirm does not contradict monotheism, perhaps it is even true. Let us accept it for the moment. Nevertheless, these 'buts' of yours, these 'at the same times,' affirm something which is not contained in the simple and original truth of monotheism, they introduce new content, new evidence, a new idea.[30]

With characteristic boldness Soloviev makes a crucial point here: the history of Christian dogma did not begin with Christianity. It was underway already in the Old Covenant. Just as there is no New Covenant without the Old, so there is no Christian dogma without the dogmas received from Judaism. If so, then the Christian gospel turns out to be an instance of the development of dogma, a point which acquires its full force when one considers the gospel from a Jewish perspective. In view of this essential property of the gospel, do Christian dogmatists have the right to deny development in principle?

A conservative dogmatist might reply that Soloviev's analogy is false because the gospel of Jesus Christ is the final revelation, the development to end all development, so to speak. Thus, even though the gospel was new, the church's vocation remains conservative: to preserve the gospel without additions or subtractions. But to Soloviev's mind this way of construing the dogmatic witness of the church has already subtracted something of utmost importance, namely, the Holy Spirit:

If in the decisions of the Universal Church the pastors were merely witnesses to the faith that existed as a matter of fact among the flock, there would have been no need for any special action of the Holy Spirit; for purposes of bearing witness to a known fact, common human honesty would have sufficed.'[31]

But the pastors of the ancient church viewed the decisions of the ecumenical councils as works of the Holy Spirit. What does this

---

[30] 'Dogmaticheskoe razvitie,' p. 51.
[31] 'Dogmaticheskoe razvitie,' p. 56.

view mean if not that the dogmas of the councils were in some sense new gifts to the church, not just rote repetitions of earlier testimonies or the bright ideas of theologians about how best to adjust the gospel to the 'subjective' limits of the human mind? True, the councils were not as great a gift as the gift of Christ himself; yet all gifts are instances of God-with-us, actual interventions of God in the life of humankind.

A conservative dogmatist might think such an open-ended theory of dogma threatens the essence of Christian revelation by implying it changes over time. Soloviev rejects this inference. The development of dogma no more destroys the essence of Christianity than growth destroys the essence of a seed. Soloviev does not doubt the existence of a kernel or essence of Christian revelation, and he is anything but agnostic about its contents:

> The truth of revelation is one and indivisible. From the first chapters of Genesis to the last chapters of the Apocalypse, from Eden in the East to New Jerusalem coming down from heaven, this truth consists of one and the same thing and to it belongs one and the same name – *the humanity of God, the union of God with creation*. This one and unchangeable truth, deposited in humankind first as a *hope* (for the Gentiles) and as a *promise* (for the people of God), becomes an *event* through the incarnation of the real God-human Jesus Christ, the personal focal point of the universal humanity of God.[32]

The essence of Christianity is the humanity of God. This is 'the unique dogma, the one truth that contains all others – the truth of the God-human who came in the flesh, rose again, ascended and poured out the Holy Spirit on His disciples.' This is '*the unique dogmatic criterion* for distinguishing true Christians from false, right belief from heresy, children of God from children of the Adversary,' as John the Theologian made clear when he wrote in his first epistle: 'By this you know the Spirit of God: every spirit that confesses that Jesus Christ has come in the flesh is from God, and every spirit that does not confess Jesus is not from God' (1 Jn 4:2–3).[33] If conservative dogmatists wish to

---

[32] 'Dogmaticheskoe razvitie,' pp. 21–2.
[33] 'Dogmaticheskoe razvitie,' pp. 23–5.

construe subsequent developments as 'elucidations' of this original deposit, Soloviev has no objection as long as they concede that the number of original dogmas 'is not very large, to wit, that it comes down basically to one *original dogma of the perfect humanity of God* in which the whole fullness of truth is logically contained.'[34]

But conservative dogmatists usually fail to understand that the debate about the development of dogma is not only a debate about essences but also a debate about actualities. The church, which is the community of dogma, is not an essence but a living reality. The dogmas which the church teaches also manifest the logic of actuality in that their primary function is not to express abstract truths but to bear witness to living realities. In the early church, for example,

> the evangelical baptismal formula, 'in the name of the Father and of the Son and of the Holy Spirit,' was originally connected not with some sort of abstract theological doctrine concerning the three divine hypostases, but with the living event of the revelation or theophany of those [divine] persons through the incarnation of Christ, in whom the whole fullness of God dwells bodily.'[35]

Because dogma develops in response to living realities, its specific contents cannot be predicted in advance even though the logical connection of that which comes later with that which comes before can be appreciated ex post facto. Thus Soloviev would not claim to know what the contents of Christian dogma will be at some point in the future; but he would firmly maintain that, whatever those contents turn out to be, they will corroborate the truth of the humanity of God. This combination of firm conviction with prophetic openness is characteristic of all genuinely existential religious reflection.

Dogma, then, turns out to be inspired reflection on the humanity of God in the context of actual religious life. It is neither an immutable divine thing, as conservatives would have it, nor a mutable human thing, as skeptics would have it. Like

---

[34] 'Dogmaticheskoe razvitie,' p. 47.
[35] 'Dogmaticheskoe razvitie,' p. 23.

the humanity of God which it proclaims, it is a divine-human thing:

> In all [dogmatic] decisions of the Universal Church when it works through its legitimate representatives, neither the divine nor the human power operates independently. Rather, the divine-human being of the Universal Church operates. In it the divine principle combines with the human principle without division or confusion. By virtue of the divine principle these determinations express unalterable truth; by virtue of the human principle they express this truth in less than all its fullness and so admit of further development through similar decisions of the Universal Church revealing different aspects of the same truth.[36]

Soloviev adduces testimony from patristic sources to support his theory of development. The tradition of Christian Hellenism represented by the Apologists, Origen, the Cappadocians and others provides congenial material for him, as it did a generation earlier for Bukharev. The concept of revelation as divine *paideia* (education) unfolding gradually, but logically, from the beginning to the end of time naturally encourages tolerance in dogmatic matters.[37] Soloviev cites the example of Gregory Nazianzus, who with the other Cappadocians promoted the doctrine of the divinity of the Holy Spirit. Soloviev admires Gregory for recognizing this doctrine was just beginning to be clarified in his day and for showing tolerance toward Christians who did not accept it, provided of course they did not question the divinity of the Son, an issue settled at Nicaea two generations earlier.[38]

Gregory's stance toward his dogmatic opponents was based on the view of revelation which he spelled out in the Fifth Theological Oration. There Gregory observes that in the history of the world there have been two great transitions, from paganism to the Old Covenant, and from the Old Covenant to the New. Although both of these changes were 'earthquakes' in the history of the human race, God introduced them with care,

[36] 'Dogmaticheskoe razvitie,' p. 62.
[37] See Ch. 1, n. 22 above.
[38] 'Dogmaticheskoe razvitie,' pp. 33–5.

making allowances for human weakness. In the Old Covenant God forbade idols but tolerated sacrifices; in the New Covenant God forbade sacrifices but tolerated circumcision. In the transition still to come, namely, the transformation of this world into the next, an even greater degree of perfection will be achieved. Why does God act 'by means of gradual changes?' He does so, says Gregory,

> that no violence might be done to us, but that we might be moved by persuasion. For nothing that is involuntary is durable; like streams or trees which are kept back by force. But that which is voluntary is more durable and safe. The former is due to one who uses force, the latter is ours; the one is due to the gentleness of God, the other to a tyrannical authority. Wherefore God did not think it behooved him to benefit the unwilling but to do good to the willing. And therefore, like a tutor or physician, he partly removes and partly condones ancestral habits, conceding some little of what tended to pleasure, just as medical men do with their patients, that their medicine may be taken, being artfully blended with what is nice.

Theology educates the human race in the same spirit but employs the opposite method. In the giving of the covenants God worked by means of subtraction. In theology, however, Gregory continues,

> perfection is reached by additions. For the matter stands thus: The Old Testament proclaimed the Father openly, and the Son more obscurely. The New manifested the Son, and suggested the deity of the Spirit. Now the Spirit himself dwells among us, and supplies us with a clearer demonstration of himself. For it was not safe, when the Godhead of the Father was not yet acknowledged, plainly to proclaim the Son; nor when that of the Son was not yet received, to burden us further (if I may use so bold an expression) with the Holy Spirit; lest perhaps people might, like men loaded with food beyond their strength, and presenting eyes as yet too weak to bear it to the sun's light, risk the loss even of that which was within the reach of their powers; but that by gradual additions, and, as David says, goings up, and advances and

progress from glory to glory, the light of the Trinity might shine upon the more illuminated.[39]

Soloviev defends the development of dogma, then, not just on historical grounds but on religious and theological grounds. Dogmatics reflects the dynamics of the church as a Spirit-filled community. 'Orthodoxy is upheld not by antiquity alone but by the eternally living Spirit of God. The dogmatic definitions of the ecumenical councils were accepted by the church not because they were old – on the contrary, in a certain sense they were new – but because they were *true*.'[40] Or again:

> The experience of church history forces us resolutely to maintain that the only means of safeguarding Orthodox truth lies in the faithful, progressive explication of this truth in ever newer and fuller definitions – definitions articulated by the church in her teaching function with the good will and aid of the indwelling Holy Spirit as well as on her own authority, as in the apostolic formula: *it seemed good to the Holy Spirit and to us*.[41]

Soloviev's conservative critics might have replied that they, too, believed in the Holy Spirit; and so they did. But did they recognize the implications of this belief for the practice of theology? A spiritual as distinct from merely literal belief in the 'life-giving' Holy Spirit means regarding the church as a living thing, as '*a real, living being* growing continuously in spiritual power and understanding.' Indeed, 'the living church, organically united, enjoying inner solidarity and bound together by an indissoluble hierarchical bond, is a totally real and independent being.'[42] Now if the church is a living thing, it is a growing, developing, expanding thing. Dogma expresses the unity of church tradition, but that unity derives not from the letter of tradition but from the Spirit-filled organic community in which tradition itself is rooted.

---

[39] Quoted in Solov'ev, 'Dogmaticheskoe razvitie,' pp. 35–6; English trans. from *Christology of the Later Fathers*, ed. Edward Rochie Hardy in collaboration with Cyril C. Richardson, *The Library of Christian Classics*, vol. 3 (Philadelphia: The Westminster Press, 1954), pp. 209–10.
[40] 'Dogmaticheskoe razvitie,' p. 48.
[41] 'Dogmaticheskoe razvitie,' p. 53.
[42] 'Dogmaticheskoe razvitie,' pp. 53, 56.

Conservative dogmatism, relying on the letter of doctrine, can at best authenticate the 'moral unity' of the church, a unity based on history and human intention. It cannot authenticate 'the being of the church as something metaphysically real.'[43] Only living experience can do that. The rejection of dogmatic development leads to traditionalism, an abstract principle.

Soloviev's conception of dogmatic development strongly supports ecumenism. If dogma develops, then the ecumenist has grounds for hope that the dogmatic basis for the reunion of the churches will be clarified at some point, even if it cannot be seen at the present time. In the traditionalist view the church as a community of dogma is a finished work. It may abide unchanged or change as a result of defections, but it cannot grow, at least not dogmatically. In Soloviev's view the Spirit has yet more to reveal to the church, and it is not unreasonable to expect that the gifts to come will propel the church toward new unions. Moreover, because of the positive character of revelation one need not construe the Spirit's guidance in purely negative terms as protection from error. One may think of it also as guidance toward a new synthesis to which all parts of Christendom will make a positive contribution. On this view the divisions of the present age, far from being simply negated, may actually be utilized, transformed and justified. Here again one sees the concreteness of Soloviev's faith. He is not interested in what might be called abstract ecumenism, a brittle and exclusive unity that ignores the positive claims of the several churches.[44]

Soloviev concludes 'The Development of Dogma' with a plea for freedom as well as faith. Once again one sees the happy marriage of Christian belief and critical inquiry which is the hallmark of his thought:

> The *solution* of the great ecclesiastical quarrel can only belong to the Universal Church herself. But until her mind is

---

[43] 'Dogmaticheskoe razvitie,' pp. 54–5.
[44] The word 'ecumenism' in its present meaning did not exist in Soloviev's day. The lack of a term probably helped Soloviev keep the emphasis where he wanted it, namely, on the positive contents of church union. Once something is named it becomes easier to reduce it to an abstract principle. The 'ism' of ecumenism represents the permanent threat of abstraction (in Soloviev's sense) in the movement to which the word refers.

finally revealed in the sight of all, every living member, being linked to the Spirit of truth in and through the church, may and sometimes must submit this greatest of contemporary questions to free investigation. The positive benefit of such investigation directly depends on the extent to which the practitioners manage to free themselves from every sort of personal and national exclusivity, the extent to which they are guided by the spirit of ecumenical unity [*rukovodimy dukhom vselenskoi tselosti*], which is also the Spirit of God.[45]

THE JEWS AND THE CHRISTIAN QUESTION

For an example of Soloviev's theocratic vision in the middle period of his career we turn to 'The Jews and the Christian Question' (1884).[46] The essay brings together a number of the concerns of Soloviev's theology. It presents his theocratic proposal clearly and concisely. It exemplifies the heightened appreciation for dogmatic religion which characterizes his middle and late works. And of course it presents his view of the Jews and Judaism.

Judaism is a matter of cardinal significance for Soloviev's theocratism in more ways than one. The roots of Christian theocracy lie in the theocratic faith of Israel, a connection which must be explored by any serious advocate of Christian theocracy. At the same time, it must be admitted that most attempts to implement Christian theocracy have depended on a social and political integralism which abuses minorities in general and the Jews in particular. In 'The Jews and the Christian Question' Soloviev seeks to distance theocracy from the egoistic integralism of the past and to combine it with a very positive attitude toward the Jews.

Soloviev begins his essay with a critical observation about Jewish–Christian relations through the centuries:

---

[45] 'Dogmaticheskoe razvitie,' p. 64.
[46] 'Evreistvo i khristianskii vopros,' *SSVSS*, 4:135–85.

The Jews have always related to us in a Jewish way; we Christians, on the other hand, up to now have not learned how to relate to the Jews in a Christian way. In their relations with us the Jews have never broken their religious law, but we have broken and still break the commandments of the Christian religion in our relations with them.[47]

Soloviev is referring to Jewish separateness on the one hand and Christian persecution of the Jews on the other. By keeping their distance from Christians, showing no particular love for them and protecting the integrity of the Jewish community, the Jews prove themselves loyal to the religious law of Judaism. Christians, however, violate the charitable commandments of their religion when they persecute Jews, as they have so often done. Such behavior is not Christian but 'pagan.'

In modern times, Soloviev believes, traditional bigotry toward the Jews is giving way to toleration, at least in the advanced countries of Europe. This new tolerance, however, has come about not as a result of lively Christian faith but because of indifference toward religion. Thus once again, albeit in a different way, Christians fail to observe their religion.

The consequences of this failure are deleterious for modern European civilization. 'The chief concern of modern Europe is money,' Soloviev observes. 'After centuries of antagonism, the Christian world and the Jews have finally come together in a single common interest, a single common passion for money.' Jews, however, use their prosperity to enhance the welfare of the chosen people as a whole and so advance God's cause on earth, while 'enlightened Europe has fallen in love with money not as a means to a *common* high end, but solely for the sake of those material benefits which money affords to each person *individually*.' It is wrong, therefore, to speak of a 'Jewish question' in Europe. The so-called Jewish question is 'a question not about the Jews but about the Christian world.'[48] So it was in the past when Christians persecuted the Jews; so it remains in a tolerant but religiously indifferent Europe. Accordingly Soloviev entitles his essay 'The Jews and the Christian Question.'

---

[47] 'Evreistvo i khristianskii vopros,' p. 135.
[48] 'Evreistvo i khristianskii vopros,' pp. 136–7.

Rejecting both fanatical zeal and religious indifferentism as a basis for relating to the Jews, Soloviev proposes a relationship founded 'on the real ground of spiritual and natural kinship and positive religious interests.' More specifically, he looks forward to 'the coming union of the house of Israel with Orthodox and Roman Catholic Christianity on the *theocratic* ground which is common to all of them.'[49] The 'Christian question' thus turns out to be a question of free theocracy. The theocratic beliefs of Judaism, Orthodoxy and Roman Catholicism are the positive religious contents of the theocratic idea. By taking these beliefs seriously Soloviev steers away from abstraction.

Theocratic beliefs are beliefs concerning the sovereignty of God in history. Examining the historical experience of the Jews, Soloviev notes three facts which he believes must be taken into account in any theory of theocracy. They concern, respectively, the past, present and future of historic Israel. The first fact is the divine election of Israel as the nation through which the salvation of the human race was to come in the incarnation of God in Christ The second fact is the rejection of Christ by a large segment of historic Israel and the alienation between Jews and Christians. The mysterious fact pertaining to the future is the settlement of the large majority of the world's Jews 'in the land of the Slavs, among peoples who have not yet spoken their word to the world,' i.e. among Poles and Russians. These three historical facts are directly connected with the humanity of God. The Israel of the past bore the promise of the humanity of God into the world. The Israel of the present stands apart from the first fruits of the humanity of God. 'The Israel to come will live life abundantly when in a renewed Christianity it will find and recognize the image of the *perfect* humanity of God.'[50] Thus Paul's vision in Romans 9–11, the normative theological statement of the destiny of Israel in the Christian dispensation, will be fulfilled: 'all Israel will be saved' (Rom. 11:26).[51]

Israel will not be saved by Christianity as it exists at the present time, however. Christianity must first be renewed. This point is integral to Soloviev's theocratic proposal, for it is the

---

[49] 'Evreistvo i khristianskii vopros,' p. 138.
[50] 'Evreistvo i khristianskii vopros,' pp. 139–40.
[51] 'Evreistvo i khristianskii vopros,' p. 140; cf. p. 138.

basis of his hope that Christians will eventually overcome their false notions about the Jews. For example, some Christians justify hostility toward the Jews by citing the words of the Jewish crowd calling for the crucifixion of Jesus, 'His blood be on us and on our children!' (Mt 27:25). Soloviev points out that these Christians forget something: namely, that the blood of Christ 'is *the blood of redemption.*' They also forget that the crowd of 3,000 who heard Peter preach and were baptized on Pentecost Day was a Jewish crowd, as were the 5,000 added to the church shortly thereafter (Acts 2–3). They forget the apostles and early leaders of the church were Jews. Most of all, they forget Jesus Christ, the humanity of God in person, 'was body and soul a purest Jew.' Christian anti-Semites thus contradict the founding facts of their own faith and church. In the meantime they overlook the real source of the anti-Christian movement in their time. The luminaries of modern anti-Christianity are for the most part not Jews at all but lapsed Christians. 'Better Spinoza than Voltaire, better Joseph Salvador than Ernest Renan,' sums up Soloviev's attitude.[52]

In the light of these considerations, Soloviev concludes 'to scorn the Jews is insane, to fight with the Jews is unprofitable. The better course is to understand the Jews, though it is also the more difficult.'[53] Seeking understanding Soloviev returns to the three facts of Jewish historical existence mentioned earlier: the divine election of Israel, the rejection of Jesus Christ by most of historic Israel, and the destiny of Israel among the nations, especially the nations of eastern Europe where most Jews lived in Soloviev's day.

Why did God choose Israel as the nation from which the Messiah would spring? Ultimately this is a question about divine freedom, and purely human explanations must fall short. Nevertheless, the freedom of God, unlike human caprice, does not exclude reason but contains it; thus it is reasonable to assume that divine election conforms not only to the will of the Elector but also in some way to the qualities of the elect, that is

---

[52] 'Evreistvo i khristianskii vopros,' pp. 140–1. Joseph Salvador (1796–1873) was a Franco-Jewish historian of religion who envisioned a universal, progressivist religion combining features of Judaism, Christianity and other faiths.

[53] 'Evreistvo i khristianskii vopros,' p. 141.

to say (in the tradition of nineteenth-century Romanticism) to the 'national character' of Israel. What are the essential components of the Israelite national character? Soloviev believes they are a deep religiosity, a highly developed sense of 'self-esteem, self-consciousness and initiative,' and finally an 'extreme materialism (in the broad sense of this word).' None of these traits is unprecedented when considered in isolation, but taken together they add up to a rare, even unique combination. Deep religiosity, for example, tends to attenuate self-assertion and attachment to the material world. A hearty materialism, on the other hand, weakens deep religious attachments, though it may nourish a strong ego. What is it that holds '*Jewish* religion, *Jewish* humanism and *Jewish* materialism' together in the powerful synthesis which is Judaism?[54]

It is first of all the highly personal nature of the Jewish religion and the Jewish view of God. For Israel, God is 'not the infinite void of a universal substrate, but the infinite fullness of a being that has life in itself and gives life to others.' Jewish religion accordingly takes the form of 'a union or covenant between God and the human being, two beings who, while not equal in power, are *morally akin*.' To put it another way, Judaism, like Christianity after it, is neither a human nor a divine religion but '*a divine-human religion*.'[55] As such it nurtures a high sense of self-worth in human beings even as it directs them to the service of the one God. As for materialism, the Jewish variety must be distinguished from two other kinds: the 'practical' materialism of those who devote their lives to satisfying their physical needs and appetites, and 'scientific-philosophical' materialism, which is a theoretical worldview assigning ultimate reality to material particles or forces. Neither of these materialisms finds a place in Judaism. What does have a place, and a central one, is the 'religious materialism' which 'compels Jews to give a great deal of attention to material nature, not in order to serve it, but to serve God Most High in it and through it.' The essential idea is 'the idea of *holy corporeality*.' This sacred materialism, far from undermining religiosity or human energy, enriches both. It also equipped the historic

---

[54] 'Evreistvo i khristianskii vopros,' pp. 142–3.
[55] 'Evreistvo i khristianskii vopros,' pp. 144–5.

people of Israel to serve as the vessel for the fullest conceivable realization of the humanity of God in the world: the incarnation of God in an individual human life.[56] Thus far, at least, Soloviev believes we can understand why God became incarnate in a Jew. The Judaism of Jesus was in any case not an accidental characteristic but an essential ingredient of the humanity of God.

But if Judaism and the humanity of God are so closely connected, why did a large faction of historic Israel reject Jesus Christ, and why does Israel persist in this rejection to the present day? Soloviev rejects the traditional explanation based on alleged moral and spiritual deficiencies of the Jews. While he agrees the rejection of Christ resulted from moral and spiritual deficiencies, he observes 'in the *immediate* opponents of Jesus Christ we see vices and errors of the common human sort, not of a specifically Jewish sort.'[57]

A second explanation levels a more specific accusation against Judaism, namely, that Judaism past and present has an egoistic and nationalistic view of the kingdom of God. The Jews, so this argument goes, see the kingdom of God as the political and material triumph of Israel over other nations, while Jesus preached a spiritual kingdom of God. The Jews could not accept this message and rejected the one who proclaimed it. Soloviev finds this explanation to be 'extremely shaky' (*khromaet na obe storony*) for two reasons. First, it falsifies the Old Testament record, for an honest reading of the prophets of Israel proves beyond the shadow of a doubt that the best minds of Israel understood the kingdom of God in spiritual and universal terms. The Jewish theocracy was 'not exclusively political but *religiously* political.'[58] Second, the idea of a purely spiritual kingdom falsifies the gospel. The gospel preaches the incarnation of God in Christ. But if God became *incarnate* in Christ, then the kingdom of Christ cannot be seen as purely spiritual; nor did Christ present it as such when he prophesied, 'Blessed are the meek, for they shall inherit the earth,' and other such things. In short, 'Christians, just as much as the Jews (in the prophets), seek not just the renewal of the human spirit but hope

---

[56] 'Evreistvo i khristianskii vopros' pp. 147–50.
[57] 'Evreistvo i khristianskii vopros,' p. 151.
[58] 'Evreistvo i khristianskii vopros,' pp. 152–5.

for a new heaven and a new *earth* according to [Christ's] promise ... The kingdom of God is not just an inner kingdom, in the spirit, but an external kingdom, in power: it is a real *theocracy.*' Thus 'the ultimate goal for Christians and for Jews is one and the same – universal theocracy, the realization of divine law in the human world, the incarnation of the heavenly in the earthly.'[59] This goal distinguishes Judaism and Christianity from most other world religions.

The crucial difference between Christianity and Judaism concerns the means for advancing toward the goal. Judaism has a covenant and a hope but no clear idea of how to get from promise to fulfillment. It does not comprehend the long, complex and extremely uneven process of realizing the kingdom of God. Christianity, by contrast, sees a path through the process. 'This path is the *cross.*' The way of the cross is the distinguishing feature of Christianity. The cross teaches those who are destined to inherit the earth must first renounce it; those who would rule the world, must first serve it; those who would be citizens of the kingdom of heaven, must first be citizens of earth. The history of Christianity is a history of martyrs, ascetics and other followers of the cross. 'But this remarkable path, which leads to its destination by steering away from it, was totally incomprehensible to the majority of the Jews.'[60] The Jewish virtues of realism and self-esteem proved to be obstacles to appreciating the way of cross. Hence most Jews rejected Jesus, and Judaism and Christianity became estranged.

As they work to overcome the schism with Judaism, Christians must recognize that the question of appropriate means is all important. Because the issue dividing Christianity from Judaism does not involve the fundamental message or goal of either religion but rather the path which is to be followed, it is pointless for Christians to try to convince the Jews of the truth of the cross by means of abstract arguments. Christians must validate their distinctive path by actually following it:

> Only *by facts* can we prove to the Jews that they are mistaken, only by actually realizing the Christian idea, by consistently

---

[59] 'Evreistvo i khristianskii vopros,' p. 156.
[60] 'Evreistvo i khristianskii vopros,' pp. 156–8.

introducing it into real life. The more fully the Christian world expresses the Christian idea of a spiritual and universal theocracy, the more powerfully Christian principles influence the individual lives of Christians, the social life of Christian nations and the political relations of Christian humanity, the more obvious the refutation of the Jewish view of Christianity will be, and the nearer and more possible the conversion of the Jews will be. Thus, *the Jewish question is a Christian question.*[61]

By calling the Jewish question a Christian question, Soloviev does not mean to imply Christians must build theocracy all by themselves. The Jews still have a crucial role to play. To clarify it Soloviev takes a closer look at the biblical precedents.

From the start theocracy consisted of three institutions: prophecy, priesthood and kingship. Prophecy came first and provided the basis for the other two. The prophet Moses established the Israelite priesthood; the prophet Samuel authorized kings. Prophecy was the firm foundation of Israelite religion and remains the most lasting feature of the Jewish heritage. Israelite kingship and the Jewish priesthood passed away, but the prophetic word lives on in the Bible.[62]

Prophets cannot create theocracy by themselves, however; they need the help of priests and kings. The post-biblical pursuit of theocracy for a long time focused on these two offices.

---

[61] 'Evreistvo i khristianskii vopros,' p. 159. Soloviev reiterated his position two years later in another important essay on Jewish-Christian relations, 'The Talmud and the Recent Polemical Literature on it in Austria and Germany' (1886). The trenchant last paragraph of this article reads as follows: 'The Jews, who thanks to the Talmud have preserved their particular religious-national way of life, have not lost the meaning of their existence. They are to this day a living reproach to the Christian world. They do not quarrel with us about abstract propositions but address us with a demand for justice and truth: either renounce Christianity or really put it to work in life. Our misfortune is not the excessive influence of the Talmud but the insufficient influence of the gospel. The longed for solution of the Jewish question depends on us, not on the Jews. We cannot force the Jews to abandon the laws of the Talmud, but it is always in our power to apply the commandments of the gospel in our dealings with the Jews. One or the other, then: either the Jews are not our enemies, in which case the Jewish question does not exist; or they are our enemies, in which case the sole Christian solution of the Jewish question is to relate to them in the spirit of love and peace.' 'Talmud i noveishaia polemicheskaia literatura o nem v Avstrii i Germanii,' *SSVSS*, 6:32.
[62] 'Evreistvo i khristianskii vopros,' pp. 161–3.

Christianity contributed a priesthood which proved to be superior to its Jewish antecedent because it did not depend on inheritance through the flesh. Christianity also drew upon Greco-Roman political institutions to build a Christian empire. Yet the history of ancient and medieval Christendom shows that Christians did not succeed in achieving a just and balanced synthesis of the three theocratic offices. In Byzantium the emperors dominated the church and discouraged spiritual initiative. Lively spirits fled to the monasteries, causing the rest of society to grow even more passive. In the medieval West the church dominated the state and usurped powers and functions that do not belong to the priestly institution. Various revolts ensued, of which Protestantism was the most important theologically because it recovered the prophetic element of Christian faith. Compared with Judaism, however, Protestantism is an inferior form of prophetism. Protestantism rejects kings and priests, preaches justification by faith without works and submits the Bible to criticism without the check of tradition. So doing it deracinates prophecy, undermines the theocratic ideal and opens the door to secularism of the type that triumphed in western Europe during the Enlightenment. But 'universal secularization' is no substitute for free theocracy.[63] The theocratic mission must continue. But where, and how?

Soloviev pins his hopes on eastern Europe. Here three great peoples who have not abandoned the theocratic faith live side by side: Russians, Poles and Jews. If they worked together, Russians, Poles and Jews could strengthen each other's faith, for the virtues of their traditions are complementary. The Russians have 'the great advantage of sacred and autocratic imperial authority' embodied in the Orthodox tsar, but they 'make poor use of this blessing' because of the chronic underdevelopment of civil society in Russia and the excessive dependence of the Russian Orthodox Church on the state. The Poles lack a clear idea of state authority and chase after political chimeras, but they are redeemed by faith in the primacy of the Roman pontiff

---

[63] The phrase 'universal secularization' (*vseobshchaia sekuliarizatsia*), referring to the Latin and Germanic societies of modern Europe, occurs on p. 171. Not yet part of the Russian vocabulary in Archimandrite Feodor's time, 'secularization' here makes its debut in modern Orthodox theology.

and in 'the *unconditional* independence of ecclesiastical authority vis-à-vis state and society.' The Jews lack both a state and a priesthood; but as heirs to the prophets of Israel they manifest the virtues of 'the free, active personality' and have a deep understanding of the proper use of creation. It is no accident they have become the dominant urban-industrial class of eastern Europe in spite of oppression and persecution. As true theocracy depends on the co-operation of prophet, priest and king, so in Europe the cause of theocracy depends on the collaboration of Jews, Poles and Russians.[64]

'The Jews and the Christian Question' was one of the first essays in the Russian Orthodox tradition to call for the improvement of Jewish–Christian relations. The essay is remarkable for its relative fairness toward the Jews and its critical appraisal of Orthodox Christian attitudes. While it is not free of ethnic stereotypes and to some extent even depends on them, Soloviev invariably makes humane applications of his material. So, for example, the Jews remain for Soloviev the masters of money in modern Europe, a skill which he traces to the 'materialism' of their religion. Anti-Semites believed the same. But while the latter drew conclusions prejudicial to the Jews from the phenomenon of Jewish economic activity, Soloviev saw the matter differently:

> The problem is not the Jews or money, but the domination, the *omnipotence of money*, and this omnipotence has not been brought about by the Jews. It was not the Jews who made gain and enrichment the end of all economic activity, not the Jews who separated the economic sphere from religion and morality. Enlightened Europe established these godless and inhuman principles in our social economy and now blames the Jews for following these principles.

Gentile Europe blames the Jews 'simply for remaining Jews, for keeping themselves apart.' But Soloviev does not see Jewish particularity as a bad thing. Bearers of the promise of salvation, the Jews are destined to help Christian humanity realize the theocracy of the future. Even if economic activity is oriented to selfish gain in the present age, it will not always be so:

[64] 'Evreistvo i khristianskii vopros,' pp. 178–85.

In theocracy the end of economic activity is the *humanization* of material life and nature . . . And just as the flower of Israel once served as a receptive environment for the incarnation of Divinity, so the Israel to come will serve as active mediator for the humanization of material life and nature, for the creation of a new earth where justice abides.[65]

Soloviev's irenic vision of a commonwealth of Russians, Poles and Jews contrasts so starkly with the desolation of eastern Europe in the twentieth century that contemporary readers may have difficulty taking it seriously. A century of emigration, war, revolution, anti-Semitism and genocide obliterated the world which Soloviev summoned to a peaceful, religious future. However, our difficulty in appreciating Soloviev's prophetism says more about the failures of the twentieth century than about the faults of his scheme. Russians, Poles and Jews did in fact inhabit a common Russian empire in Soloviev's time. Moreover, the large majority of all three communities remained deeply committed to their faith tradition despite the in-roads of secularism. It was not idle speculation to propose a faith-based ideal which all three groups might come to share. Soloviev's essay can also be seen as an early effort at Jewish–Christian dialogue. However unfavorable the religious conditions of nineteenth-century Russia might have been for such a dialogue, they were far from the abyss into which Jewish–Christian relations were hurled in twentieth-century Europe.

Soloviev was a highly original thinker. He was also a very Russian thinker. In the theocratic essays his debt to the Slavophiles in particular is evident. The Slavophile connection was, in fact, essential to Soloviev's appreciation of Judaism, however paradoxical it might sound to put it this way. One legacy of Slavophilism was Russian nationalism, and Russian nationalism has often posed a threat to Jewish identity in Russia by abetting anti-Semitism or promoting assimilation. But the Slavophiles were also Christian idealists who believed in theocracy. Soloviev took up the theocratic theme while suppressing the proto-nationalist elements.

Thus, when he confronted the so-called Jewish question,

---

[65] 'Evreistvo i khristianskii vopros,' pp. 183–5.

Soloviev found himself in an unusual position. As a philosophical universalist and opponent of nationalism he cultivated a tolerant and humane attitude toward the Jews. As a Christian theocrat he could not overlook the faith of the Jews or the significance of the Jews for Christian theocratic hopes. On the contrary, he embraced these dogmatic realities with a passion. As a result, he was able to preach fairness and civility toward Jews without denaturing Judaism in the process. For Soloviev the Jews were exactly who they claimed to be: God's chosen people. Moreover, he held Christian destiny to be unbreakably linked to the destiny of Israel. Precisely because of these dogmatic convictions, he rejected nineteenth-century liberal theories which evacuated Judaism of spiritual significance by portraying it as a legalistic, particularistic or merely political religion. The same theories, after all, also robbed Christianity of much of its content by relegating it to the purely spiritual realm. Soloviev's devotion to theocracy kept him loyal to both the Jewishness of Judaism and the messianism of Christianity. He sympathized with Jewish theocrats because he was a Christian theocrat. He also understood that the true theocrat looks not to the past but to the future. There, on the brightening horizon, he saw signs of a grand reconciliation between Israel and the nations.

Soloviev's theocratic vision provides yet another illustration of his intellectual breadth. Soloviev believed in Israel and also in Orthodoxy. He was a liberal and also a theocrat; a humanist and also a dogmatist. These unusual linkages account for the enormous power of his thought.

9

Soloviev's Apocalypse

Toward the end of a survey of Schelling's thought Frederick Copleston observes 'the philosophy of Schelling is a philosophizing rather than a finished system or succession of finished systems.'[1] Saying this Copleston does not mean to belittle Schelling's systematic talent, which was prodigious, but to call attention to the self-revising character of his thought. Schelling spent his life trying to envision human and cosmic reality in a comprehensive philosophical system, but he was never satisfied with the results. All along the way, even at the end, he was ready to start over again, to try a new path, to reconsider basic issues.

Soloviev was this kind of thinker. The repeated breaks and new beginnings in his career issued from a philosophic eros which refused to rest in abstractions. Soloviev was also inspired by love of God, the living God who goes always ahead of those who seek him.

The most obvious shift in Soloviev's career in the 1890s was his return to large-scale projects in academic philosophy. This renewed commitment to the passion of his youth was stimulated in part by an important initiative launched by the Russian philosophical community in 1889. In that year Nikolai Grot, professor of philosophy at Moscow University and president of the Moscow Psychological Society, founded Russia's first professional philosophical journal, *Voprosy filosofii i psikhologii* (*Questions of Philosophy and Psychology*). The journal provided Russia's philosophers with a forum of their own for the first time. A brilliant pléiade of thinkers gathered around it. Soloviev was one of the original collaborators and remained closely associated with *Voprosy* until his death. The

---

[1] Copleston, *Fichte to Hegel*, p. 126. The existential character of Schelling's philosophizing is described by Alan White, *Schelling: An Introduction to the System of Freedom* (New Haven and London: Yale University Press, 1983).

outpouring of original philosophy from his pen in the 1890s owed much to the collegial atmosphere of the journal and the Moscow Psychological Society.

Another project to which Soloviev devoted himself in this period was the translation of the dialogues of Plato in collaboration with his brother, Mikhail. Soloviev dedicated the project to the memory of a life-long friend, the poet A.A. Fet (1820–92), who 'seventeen years ago already, while he himself was absorbed in the translation of the Latin poets, tried to convince me that it was my patriotic duty "to give Plato to Russian literature." '[2]

There were also new developments in Soloviev's personal life. In 1891 he fell in love with Sofia Mikhailovna Martynova, an aristocratic matron known as 'Sappho' to her salon companions. Soloviev followed her around, tarried on the outskirts of her family nest, wrote love poetry for her and tried to make sense of his experience in 'The Meaning of Love.'[3] As on other occasions, the poetic and philosophic aspects of his love were more fruitful than the relationship itself.[4] Soloviev's ardor for Martynova cooled in less than a year, but not his renewed dedication to poetry. Much of his best verse dates from the last decade of his life.

Despite the collapse of his ecumenical project, Soloviev had not lost interest in political and ecclesiastical affairs. The watershed event of the period in Russia, the terrible famine of 1891, made a profound impression on him. Appalled by the enormity of his people's sufferings and the ineptitude of the

---

[2] Quoted in S.M. Solov'ev, *Zhizn' i tvorcheskaia evoliutsiia*, p. 371. Only one volume of the Plato translation was completed. The project lapsed after Vladimir's death in 1900. Soloviev's important essay, 'The Drama of Plato's Life' (1898), dates from this period: 'Zhiznennaia drama Platona,' *SSVSS*, 9:194–241; and *Sochineniia v dvukh tomakh*, eds Losev and Gulyga, 2:582–625.

[3] 'Smysl liubvi,' *SSVSS*, 7:3–60; and *Sochineniia v dvukh tomakh*, eds Losev and Gulyga, 2:493–547.

[4] As Mochulsky observes, 'Soloviev believed that transformation through love was not a poetic dream but something vital and real. Love here on earth must seek to transform Aldonza into Dulcinea. But he was able to transform his beloved only in the mirror of art. He possessed the magic of words, but not the magic of deeds, and his magic circle broke down in real life.' *Vladimir Solov'ev*, p. 202. On Soloviev and Martynova see also S.M. Solov'ev, *Zhizn' i tvorcheskaia evoliutsiia*, pp. 307–14; and Losev, *Vladimir Solov'ev i ego vremia*, pp. 89–92.

imperial state, he began to recast some of his social, political and ethical principles. The shift has been described as the 'de-utopianization' of Soloviev's thought.[5] Backing away from his vision of a worldwide theocratic order, Soloviev focused instead on the more concrete needs of Russian society, especially the need for basic social justice. In *The Justification of the Good* (1897) he presented a general theory of economic and social welfare based on the idea that all human beings have a 'right to a dignified existence.'[6] Lending impetus to the liberal political movement in Russia at the turn of the century, Soloviev's book also anticipated twentieth-century theories of social and economic rights.

The new realism of Soloviev's social and political thought in the 1890s led him to an increasingly pessimistic appraisal of the existing political regime in Russia. While his ideal remained constitutional monarchy, not democracy, Soloviev was distressed by the institutional and attitudinal gap between his liberal monarchism and contemporary tsarism. Even the nobler gestures of the regime no longer impressed him. When the government of Tsar Nicholas II issued its famous circular of 1898 calling for an international conference on peace and disarmament (the first Hague Conference took place the following year), Soloviev poured cold water on a friend's enthusiasm for the initiative by reminding her that

> at the same time as the circular of August 12, two other administrative actions were taken: the forced russification of Finland was decided upon and decrees of the Holy Synod were published by which some 400,000 Russian Uniates who consider themselves Roman Catholics were once and for all declared 'Orthodox' by virtue of an administrative order of 1875. You will agree, Princess, that these two measures cast a very peculiar light on the peacemaking scheme of the same period.[7]

Yet Soloviev felt little kinship with the most radical critics of the tsarist regime, such as the socialists and Tolstoyans. In the

---

[5] Walicki, *Legal Philosophies of Russian Liberalism*, pp. 190–206.
[6] *Opravdanie dobra: nravstvennaia filosofiia*, *SSVSS*, 8:3–516; and Solov'ev, *Sochineniia v dvukh tomakh*, eds Losev and Gulyga, 1:47–580.
[7] Quoted in S.M. Solov'ev, *Zhizn' i tvorcheskaia evoliutsiia*, p. 387.

spring of 1899, while vacationing on the French Riviera, he began work on his last book, *Three Dialogues on War, Progress and the End of World History, with a Brief Tale of the Anti-Christ*, which mercilessly criticizes Tolstoyan pacifism, secularized Christianity and secularism in general.[8]

Three Dialogues is actually a single dialogue distributed over three days. The conversations take place in the garden of a villa on the French Riviera. Five Russian tourists take part: a retired general, a state councilor (called the statesman), a young Tolstoyan prince, an affable middle-aged lady and a mysterious 'gentleman of indeterminate age and social standing' called Mr Z.[9] The narrator claims to have been present also, although he does not have a speaking part and his presence goes unnoticed by the interlocutors.

The subject of the dialogue is the struggle against moral evil and how this struggle bears on the meaning of history. This unlikely topic of conversation among the leisured denizens of a mediterranean resort arises from a quarrel. A newspaper article attacking the military profession from a pacifist point of view has come to the attention of the group. The statesman, when questioned by the lady, replies that he regards the international pacifist movement as a useful development. The general vehemently objects, and the debate begins.

The three days of the dialogue correspond to the topics enumerated in the title. The opening day is given over to a debate about the uses of war, with the general as the protagonist. On the second day the statesman takes center stage to speak for 'progress,' by which he means the enlightened and pacific values of modern European civilization. The third day belongs to Mr Z, who first explicates the concept of the end of history and then edifies the company with 'A Brief Tale of the

---

[8] *Tri razgovora o voine, progresse i kontse vsemirnoi istorii, so vkliucheniem kratkoi povesti ob antikhriste i s prilozheniiami*, SSVSS, 10:81–221; and Solov'ev, *Sochineniia v dvukh tomakh*, eds Losev and Gulyga, 2:635–762. English trans.: *War, Progress, and the End of History: Three Conversations. Including a Short Story of the Anti-Christ*, trans. Thomas R. Beyer, Jr (Hudson, New York: Lindisfarne Press, 1990). All references to *Tri razgovora* in the present study are to SSVSS.

[9] *Tri razgovora*, p. 92.

Anti-Christ,' a fiction supposedly composed by an Orthodox cleric and friend of his named Father Pansofy.

In the preface Soloviev tells us the three protagonists represent, respectively, the 'conventional-religious' (*religiozno-bytovaia*) viewpoint of the past; the 'cultured-progressive' view of modern times; and the 'unconditional-religious' view of the future.[10] In other words, the general speaks for tradition, the statesman for modernity, Mr Z for prophecy and philosophy.

The conflict between tradition and modernity is evident in the opening lines of the dialogue. The general unleashes his assault on the pacifist movement by asking the assembled, 'Just tell me one thing: does the *Christ-loving and glorious host of the Russian state* still exist in our day, or not?' The statesman replies, 'You mean, does the Russian army exist? Evidently it does. Have you heard that it has been abolished?'[11] The semantic clash between the general's religious language ('Christ-loving and glorious host') and the statesman's matter-of-fact phraseology ('Russian army') betokens the substance of the dispute. The general's words, echoing the fifth petition of the Great Litany of the Liturgy of St John Chrysostom in which the church prays for the state and the armed forces, affirm the Russian military as a holy establishment serving a divine end. The statesman is a positivist. He accepts the military establishment as a fact of life but does not glorify it. Like the pacifist prince he regards war as a species of barbarism, but as a realist and man of the world he recognizes that a war machine is likely to remain a necessary evil, and occasionally a useful tool, for some time to come. Such a grudging acceptance of the military does not satisfy the general, however. For him war is a personal vocation, not just a tool. He complains that the statesman's utilitarian attitude toward the armed forces is bound to sap the devotion which soldiers need to execute their arduous task. War takes courage, and courage demands 'absolute confidence that war is a holy cause.'[12]

The climax of the first day of the dialogue comes when the general describes an encounter between a cossack unit under his

[10] *Tri razgovora*, p. 87.
[11] *Tri razgovora*, p. 93.
[12] *Tri razgovora*, p. 95.

command and a band of Turkish irregulars who had been massacring defenseless Armenian villagers in eastern Anatolia during the Russo-Turkish War of 1877–8. Intercepting the marauders as they were about to fall upon another settlement, the cossacks mercilessly wiped them out. That day, the general declares, was a moment of spiritual illumination and moral certitude for him: 'it was Easter in my heart.'[13] The link between human means and absolute ends was indubitable.

The second day belongs to the statesman. His outlook is summed up in his words to Mr Z toward the end of the day, 'Of course everything is relative.'[14] The rejection of absolutes, in morality and religion as well as politics, is the thread that runs through his view of things. The statesman is astonished that modern philosophers discourse about war without paying attention to the historical context. 'Does war have meaning? C'est selon [It depends].'[15] The statesman is willing to concede war was an indispensable means of advancing civilization in the past and it might still be appropriate 'somewhere in Africa or Central Asia.' But he agrees with the pacifists that war is doomed to extinction in the long run because it is inconsistent with civilized values, that is to say (avoiding absolutes), inconsistent with the '*minimum* of rationality and morality' necessary for civilized existence. 'Peaceful politics is a criterion and a symptom of cultural progress.'[16] The more civilized and polished human beings become, the less they will resort to war.

The statesman's reference to peace as a symptom of progress gives Mr Z the opening he needs to suggest a different approach to the subject. He cites a passage in Turgenev's novel *Smoke* where one of the characters calls progress itself 'a symptom.'[17] Now if peace is a symptom of progress, and progress a symptom of something else, then peace is 'a symptom of a symptom.' But this view does not offer a very strong foundation for peace. Framing his objection in terms reminiscent of Socrates' Allegory of the Cave in the *Republic*, Mr Z asks, 'If the politics of peace

[13] *Tri razgovora*, p. 113.
[14] *Tri razgovora*, p. 157.
[15] *Tri razgovora*, p. 131.
[16] *Tri razgovora*, pp. 155–6.
[17] The passage to which Mr Z refers is in chapter 10 of *Smoke*.

is only the shadow of a shadow, is it worth our time talking so much about it, or for that matter about the rest of this shadowy progress [of yours]?'[18] The statesman's intentions are humane, but his relativism consigns humanity to an insubstantial existence.

On the third day of the dialogue Mr Z draws the issue of teleology or ultimate purpose out of the idea of progress. He proposes 'palpable, accelerated progress is always a *symptom of the end.*'[19] Faith in progress makes sense only if one has some idea of where progress is headed. In the absence of such knowledge one's faith will be vulnerable to the contingencies and non sequiturs of existence, and one will begin to suspect progress is little more than a floating cloud, if not an illusion. The statesman's remark that Lucretius is his favorite poet is revealing in this regard.[20]

But what is the end toward which the world-historical process is moving? Mr Z answers 'actual resurrection' (*deistvitel'noe voskresenie*), a reply which is as much a Christian prophecy as it is a philosophical doctrine.[21] To clarify his position Mr Z takes pains to distinguish it from the kind of Christianity preached by the prince. As Mr Z sees it, the error of Tolstoyanism is to suppose Christian moral teachings can be separated from the ontological affirmations enshrined in Christian doctrine, such as the living God, the incarnate God-human and the resurrection of the dead. Dismissing these fundamentals as obscurantism, Tolstoyanism effectively disconnects Christianity from its ground in reality. Mr Z is seconded on this point by the statesman, who, while personally sceptical of religion, knows the difference between the real article and the counterfeit. The statesman derides the prince's pseudo-evangelical notion that human beings are 'sent' (*poslany*) into the world by a master in whose service they will find true happiness. When he served as an envoy (*poslannik*) of the Russian government, the statesman reminisces, he never once doubted his status, for he possessed documents of unquestionable authenticity, he had received his

[18] *Tri razgovora*, p. 157.
[19] *Tri razgovora*, p. 159.
[20] *Tri razgovora*, p. 161.
[21] *Tri razgovora*, p. 184.

instructions in a personal audience with Tsar Alexander II, and he received 10,000 rubles in gold three times a year to support his work. The statesman wants to know what sort of credentials the prince possesses to validate the status which he claims for himself and enjoins upon others. Getting no reply, the statesman begs the prince to stop telling him his life belongs to someone other than himself.[22]

Mr Z is quick to point out the prince's credentials are unconvincing because he has turned his back on the realities which Christian dogma affirms, such as the divinity of Christ and the authority of the church. The same point applies to the kingdom of God. Preaching 'the kingdom of God is within you,' as the Tolstoyans never tire of doing, is just an exercise in moralistic rhetoric if it is not backed up by faith in an actual kingdom of God, a kingdom in which eternal life or the deification of the world is being or is to be effected. 'The kingdom of God is the kingdom of life that triumphs through resurrection; here is where the actual, realizable and final good is to be found.'[23] Here Mr Z finds an end of history which is strong enough to empower the struggle against moral evil and metaphysical doubt.

Mr Z's theory of the end of history is genuinely dialectical in that it emerges through the critique of discordant preliminary positions. The higher truth transcends the earlier positions while affirming the partial truths encapsulated in them.[24] Thus Mr Z's vision of resurrection vindicates the general's crude but honest faith in the divine reward awaiting his fallen cossack soldiers, while it also clarifies the statesman's faith in human progress by supplying that faith with an ontological foundation. At the same time Mr Z's view escapes the limitations which impair the other positions. The general's faith in God is disfigured by his callousness toward human beings outside the Orthodox

---

[22] *Tri razgovora*, pp. 174–5.
[23] *Tri razgovora*, p. 184.
[24] The dialectical movement in *Three Dialogues* is a deliberate design. In the preface Soloviev tells us: 'While I myself subscribe to [Mr Z's] point of the view, I recognize the relative truth of the first two and thus could dispassionately report the opposing arguments and declarations of the *statesman* and the *general*. The higher, unconditional truth does not exclude and does not negate the prior conditions of its appearance, but justifies, clarifies and sanctifies them.' *Tri razgovora*, p. 87.

Christian fold. The statesman's regard for humanity, while more generous than the general's, is undercut by his lack of sympathy for uncivilized or semi-civilized people, especially when these appear to stand in the way of 'progress.' He accepts the English war against the Boers in South Africa, for example, which prompts the lady to observe 'once upon a time there was God and war, but now in place of God there's culture and peace.'[25] The point is that the statesman is not the utter relativist he claims to be. Civilization of the modern European type is his absolute. For Mr Z, by contrast, the only valid absolute is the living God.

The idea of the humanity of God figures centrally in *Three Dialogues*. While the word appears only once, the concept is implicit in the dialectic which has just been described.[26] The general has faith in God, but his faith in humanity is underdeveloped. The statesman has faith in humanity, but his awareness of the divine is weak. Mr Z believes in both God and humanity and sees the integral connection between the two. He stands for the humanity of God.

The concept of the humanity of God also helps explain why the Tolstoyan prince fares so badly in *Three Dialogues*. The prince has nothing to contribute to the dialectic because he believes in neither God nor humanity. His contempt for historic Christianity causes him to reject divine things while his doctrine of non-resistance to evil and other unnatural teachings fatally alienate him from humanity. Soloviev seems to be saying either traditional faith in God or modern faith in humanity suffices to keep a person somewhere on the road to reality, but to reject both leads nowhere. He compares Tolstoyanism to a sect of Siberian peasants whose object of worship is a hole they scoop out for themselves in the wall of their hut.[27] Tolstoyans reduce the kingdom of God to an idiosyncratic utopia.

---

[25] *Tri razgovora*, p. 154.
[26] The term occurs in Mr Z's criticism of the prince's misuse of the Gospel parable of the wicked tenants (Mt 21:33–41): 'No, but you arbitrarily see in [the parable] the supreme norm of the relations between humanity and Divinity while arbitrarily throwing out the very essence of the Gospel text – the reference to the son and heir, in whom the true norm of the divine-human relationship [*bogochelovecheskogo otnosheniia*] lives.' *Tri razgovora*, p. 188; cf. p. 174.
[27] *Tri razgovora*, pp. 83–5.

With the theory of resurrection as the end of history the dialectical progression of *Three Dialogues* comes to an end. But Mr Z's discourse continues with 'A Brief Tale of the Anti-Christ.' By appending such a fantastic story to a carefully constructed philosophical dialogue Soloviev implicitly concedes the limits of a teleological theory of history. An idea of the end of things is needed to orient human action, yet no theory of the end – Mr Z's or anyone else's – can be verified on the basis of present-day realities because the end by definition is not yet given. A teleology of history cannot be consummated *in medias res* except in visions, intimations, presentiments or parables of some kind. Accordingly Mr Z's contribution to *Three Dialogues* ends not in reasoned dialectic but with a prophetic parable.

The 'Brief Tale' is a literary apocalypse, the product of Soloviev's imagination, although it draws on the canonical apocalypse to some extent. The story is set in twenty-first century Europe, where a fledgling United States of Europe has emerged from a century of internecine war and Asiatic invasions. In this promising but still shaky new world order there arises an extraordinary leader, called simply *Griadushchii chelovek*, 'He that cometh,' or 'the Man of the future.'[28] Endowed with remarkable talents, well-connected with the military and the financial elites of his day and pledged to a platform of peace and prosperity, the Man is elected president for life of the European union and soon acclaimed emperor. From this supreme office he consolidates the political integration of Europe, settles the social question through a bold program of distributive justice and implements measures to enhance reverence for life, for he is a vegetarian and a great lover of animals.

Yet these accomplishments are not all the emperor has in mind. He also plans to straighten out the religious life of Europe by effecting the reunion of the churches. He transfers his capital from Rome to Jerusalem, convenes an ecumenical council and

---

[28] 'Man of the future' is Bethea's translation; see David M. Bethea, *The Shape of Apocalypse in Modern Russian Fiction* (Princeton, New Jersey: Princeton University Press, 1989), p. 113. The Russian echoes the messianic proclamation which seals the Trisagion in the eucharistic liturgy, *Blagosloven griadyi vo imia Gospodne* ('Blessed is he that cometh in the name of the Lord').

asks the delegates to tell him what is dearest to them in Christianity so he can award it to them. When the delegates fail to agree among themselves the emperor takes the initiative and gives each group of Christians that which he takes to be its *pium desideratum*. To the Catholics he promises the restoration of the papacy to Rome (from which it was expelled in the twentieth century) and imperial recognition of papal primacy. To the Orthodox he promises a splendid museum of Christian antiquities to be built in Constantinople; to the Protestants, an equally splendid institute for biblical research. These donations win over a large majority of the council, although there are some holdouts, including the most venerable members of the Catholic, Protestant and Orthodox delegations, respectively: Pope Peter II, Dr Ernst Pauli and the Orthodox monk Ioann. The last-named unleashes the denouement of the story. When the emperor, in a fresh attempt to win over the intransigents, asks again about what is dearest to them in Christianity, Ioann replies:

> Great Sovereign! That which is dearest to us in Christianity is Christ himself ... As to the question of what you can do for us, this is our clear response: here and now in our presence confess Jesus Christ, the Son of God, who came in the flesh, who was resurrected and who is coming again – confess Him, and we will lovingly accept you as the true forerunner of His second and glorious coming.

The answer takes the emperor by surprise. Speechless, he makes a superhuman effort to suppress his rage at the old monk; but the contortions that grip his ashen face and the sparks that fly from his eyes give him away. 'Little children,' the monk cries out, 'the Anti-Christ!'[29]

There follows a quasi-biblical conflict of Gog and Magog as the forces of the Anti-Christ do battle with the saints. At first the laurels fall to the emperor and the pliable churchmen in his train. But their victory is short-lived. The three legitimate leaders of Christendom, now refugees in the Judean desert, seal an authentic church union on the basis of mutual respect and their common love for Christ Thereupon a woman clothed with the sun, with the moon at her feet and a crown of twelve stars on her

[29] *Tri razgovora*, pp. 212–13.

head, the figure of the mystical church in the canonical Apocalypse (Rev. 12:1), appears in the sky and guides the refugees to Sinai. There they are joined by an ever-growing number of Christians disenchanted with the imperial church. But the decisive blow to the evil empire comes from another quarter. The Jews of Palestine, angered to discover the master of Jerusalem is not circumcised, rise up and inflict a defeat on his forces. The emperor flees, there is a huge earthquake, Christ descends from the heavens to the city of David, the Christian faithful return from Sinai to hail him, and the saints – Christians and Jews together – rule with Christ for a thousand years.

The interpretation of *Three Dialogues*, particularly the 'Brief Tale,' is a vexed issue in Soloviev studies for a number of reasons. The composition is so unlike the rest of Soloviev's writings that analogies with other works are not easily drawn. Moreover, the fact Soloviev died shortly after finishing *Three Dialogues* removed the possibility of authorial clarification and made it all but inevitable that some would read the work as a last will and testament of some kind. The Anti-Christ's ecumenical project was an especially tantalizing feature in this regard, for it could be taken to signify that Soloviev repudiated his earlier ecumenism. Evgeny Trubetskoi, whose massive exposition of Soloviev's thought set the course for Soloviev studies for years to come, maintained the synthesis which Soloviev sought throughout his career shifted in his late works from a historical synthesis to be accomplished within the world to the resurrection of the dead in an eschatological realm beyond the world.[30] Lev Shestov went further and read *Three Dialogues* as a rejection of the whole project of idealist religious philosophy.[31] Florovsky had a more

---

[30] Evgenii Trubetskoi, *Mirosozertsanie Vl. S. Solov'eva*, 2 vols (Moscow: Izdanie avtora, 1913), 2:303.

[31] Lev Shestov, 'Speculation and Apocalypse: The Religious Philosophy of Vladimir Solovyov,' in *Speculation and Revelation*, trans. Bernard Martin (Athens, Chicago, London: Ohio University Press, 1982), pp. 18–88. Shestov's argument depends in part on the assumption that in the extremely negative portrait of the prince in *Three Dialogues* Soloviev was attacking not just Tolstoyanism but all forms of rationalized Christianity, including the philosophy of Schelling which had inspired him earlier in his career. Shestov's position is extreme, but its roots can be found in Trubetskoi, who saw the late Soloviev as outgrowing 'the pantheistic tendencies of Russo-Schellingian gnosticism' and 'the half-Schellingian forms of *Lectures on the Humanity of God*.' See *Mirosozertsanie Vl. S. Solov'eva*, 2:392–7.

nuanced view than Shestov but still maintained 'in "A Tale of the Anti-Christ" Soloviev renounced the illusions and temptations of his entire life, he condemned them with full force.'[32] Andrzej Walicki, one of the foremost historians of Russian philosophy, also reads the 'Brief Tale' as a repudiation of many of Soloviev's earlier ideals, although he concedes that lack of evidence outside the text leaves the question open.[33]

More recently critics have begun to question the received view. Their point of departure is the literary form of *Three Dialogues*. Judith Kornblatt proposes 'Soloviev experimented in his dialogues and in the short story not with new ideas, but with new genres.' Assessing the allegedly negative presentation of some of Soloviev's own cherished ideals, such as ecumenism, Kornblatt suggests Soloviev was engaging in 'self-parody, not self-negation.'[34]

The revisionist approach has much to recommend it. Soloviev's *Three Dialogues*, whatever else it is, is clearly a literary experiment; and unless we wish to embrace the dubious proposition that literary inventions should always be taken literally, the appropriateness of figurative, parodic, ironic and other readings needs to be explored. Moreover, non-literary arguments can be adduced in support of the view that *Three Dialogues* is not discontinuous with Soloviev's earlier thought. I have already shown that the idea of the humanity of God is one of the organizing principles of the work. Soloviev's continuing devotion to ecumenism can be sensed in the touching portrait of an authentic church union being consummated at Sinai by the most venerable leaders of Catholicism, Orthodoxy and Protestantism.[35] The fraternal collaboration of Christians and Jews in

---

[32] *Puti russkogo bogosloviia*, p. 466.

[33] *A History of Russian Thought: From the Enlightenment to Marxism*, trans. Hilda Andrews-Rusiecka (Stanford, California: Stanford University Press, 1979), pp. 390–1.

[34] 'Soloviev on Salvation: The Story of the "Short Story of the Antichrist," ' *Russian Religious Thought*, eds Kornblatt and Gustafson, pp. 70–1.

[35] Trubetskoi, who was sympathetic to ecumenism, saw very clearly that Soloviev's last work bears eloquent testimony to the ecumenical ideal. 'In *Three Dialogues* there is not a trace of the [Slavophile] "God-bearing nation"; instead we see the three branches of the single Christian trunk, which essentially complement each other and *in equal measure* prepare for the coming of the genuine Messiah. There is *Petrine Christianity* or Roman Catholicism, *Pauline Christianity* or Protestantism, and the

the messianic kingdom attests yet another Solovievian ideal. Finally, as Kornblatt has shown, the morality of *Three Dialogues* is activist, not quietist or contemplative.[36]

A matter which the revisionists have not sufficiently addressed is the nature of the connection between the two genres (dialogue and parable) of *Three Dialogues*. The dialogue form has been traced to Soloviev's work on Plato in the last years of his life.[37] The parable has been regarded as inspired by Dostoevsky's 'Legend of the Grand Inquisitor' in *The Brothers Karamazov*.[38] But what did Soloviev have in mind when he linked these two forms together in a single composition? I suggest that the literary procedure of linking a philosophical dialogue with a parable came to Soloviev from the same source as the dialogue form, namely Plato. Both of the great Platonic dialogues on good and evil, *Gorgias* and *Republic*, are compositions in which dialectical argument in the end passes over to an eschatological parable of divine judgment.[39] Moreover, the

---

Orthodox and Russian *Johannine Christianity*; but no one of these by itself exhausts the Truth; rather all three taken together in their totality as a single ecumenical [*vselenskoe*] Christianity possess [the Truth] in all its fullness.' *Mirosozertsanie Vl. S. Solov'eva*, 2:326. Soloviev's threefold scheme derives partly from the end of Schelling's *Philosophy of Revelation*, where Schelling envisions an ecumenical church of the future incorporating Petrine, Pauline and Johannine principles. Schelling does not figure Orthodoxy into the equation, however. His Johannine church is pure futurity, the ideal synthesis of Roman Catholic, Protestant and philosophic principles. See F.W.J. Schelling, *Philosophie der Offenbarung 1841/42*, Paulus Nachschrift, ed. Manfred Frank (Frankfurt am Main: Suhrkamp Verlag, 1977), pp. 314–25.

[36] 'Soloviev on Salvation,' *Russian Religious Thought*, eds Kornblatt and Gustafson, pp. 82–4. It would indeed be strange if Soloviev renounced an activist concept of morality after devoting so much of *Three Dialogues* to criticizing Tolstoyan passivism in the face of evil. One of the reasons the general and the statesman fare so much better than the prince in *Three Dialogues* is that they actually do something to combat evil in the world. The general uses the crude but tested instrument of war. The statesman uses the superior if slippery tool of persuasion. The prince, on the other hand, writes articles and brochures telling people not to resist evil. See also the discussion of 'The Drama of Plato's Life' below.

[37] Kornblatt, 'Soloviev on Salvation,' *Russian Religious Thought*, eds Kornblatt and Gustafson, pp. 71–3.

[38] Bethea, *The Shape of Apocalypse in Modern Russian Fiction*, p. 113; Kornblatt, 'Soloviev on Salvation,' pp. 77–9.

[39] *Gorgias* (523a–27e) ends with the Myth of Judgment, *Republic* (614a–21d) with the Myth of Er. The subject of both parables is the divine vindication of the good and punishment of the wicked in the world to come.

dialectical positions presented in *Three Dialogues* parallel those of the two Platonic dialogues. In all three cases the opening position is articulated by an honorable older man who accepts traditional morality but is incapable of defending it intellectually (Gorgias/Cephalus/general). The second position belongs to a sophisticated skeptic who believes the human is the measure of all things and for that reason doubts or even rejects traditional morality and religion (Callicles/Thrasymachus/statesman). The third position is articulated by an untraditional intellectual (Socrates/Mr Z) who defends divinely grounded morality and religion by means of a higher philosophical principle. In the end, however, the philosopher must resort to an eschatological parable to cap his justification of the good.

This analysis is not meant to imply *Three Dialogues* should be read as an exercise in Platonism. As a Christian intellectual Soloviev was very much aware of the distance separating him from Plato on issues of morality and religion. In 'The Drama of Plato's Life' (1898) Soloviev criticized Plato for adopting a purely contemplative view of the love of God and neighbor:

> The true task of love is actually to eternalize the beloved, actually to save him from death and decay, to regenerate him once and for all in beauty ... Forgetting his own idea that Eros 'begets in beauty,' i.e. in the *tangible* realization of the ideal, Plato left him to beget only in contemplation.

The task of vindicating divine love in the world of flesh and blood fell not to Socrates but to the God-human, 'the one who has the power of resurrection unto eternal life.'[40] Mr Z's vision of resurrection obviously fits in with this line of reasoning, for what is resurrection if not the actual eternalization of the beloved?

Soloviev also parts company with Plato in his assessment of humanism. Radical humanism in all its forms is based on the idea of the human as the measure of all things. In the Platonic dialogues the radical humanists (sophists) are never reconciled with Socrates, and there is no reason to suppose they will ever make peace with him. When Socrates finally takes command of the conversation they listen in contemptuous silence or exit the

[40] 'Zhiznennaia drama Platona,' *SSVSS*, 9:231, 241.

scene. The statesman's relationship to Mr Z in *Three Dialogues* is more promising. When Mr Z offers to treat his interlocutors to a discourse on the Anti-Christ on the third day of dialogue the prince exits in disgust, but the statesman not only stays to listen but takes an interest in Mr Z's theological views.[41] Soloviev could regard humanism more optimistically than Plato because of his Christian faith in the humanity of God. Since God became human in Christ, the human is actually a path to the divine, albeit one which demands amendment of life and transfiguration. 'Mere' humanity is abolished forever.

Soloviev's reliance on the incarnation is part of a general pattern of respect for the dogmatic core of Christian faith in *Three Dialogues*. Mr Z's preaching of resurrection is another example. Still another is Mr Z's defense of historic Christianity in his debate with the prince, who regards the church as a perversion of the gospel.[42] Mr Z also shows himself to be well-informed about the growing respect among the biblical scholars of the day for the antiquity of the dogmatically rich Gospel of John, a view at odds with the skepticism of earlier generations of critics.[43] The supreme gesture on behalf of Christian dogma comes when the monk Ioann pointedly asks the emperor to confess 'Jesus Christ, the Son of God, who came in the flesh, who was resurrected and who is coming again,' in effect to confess the Nicene faith.

Three Dialogues can thus be read as an affirmation of classical Christian dogma. At the same time the work vindicates less traditional ideals which, while partly inspired by dogma, bear the stamp of Soloviev's prophetic, philosophic and activist Orthodoxy. The ecumenical ideal and the ideal of Christian–Jewish solidarity are cases in point. The extent to which both are affirmed in the 'Brief Tale' has been underappreciated because of the tendency to take Soloviev's portrait of the Anti-Christ's ecumenism out of context. Soloviev's point is

---

[41] For the statesman's curiosity about religion see *Tri razgovora*, pp. 161, 164.
[42] *Tri razgovora*, pp. 182–3.
[43] *Tri razgovora*, p. 180. The rehabilitation of the dogmatic character of earliest Christianity by continental scholars around the turn of the twentieth century had a significant impact on the understanding of the gospel in the generation of Russian religious thinkers immediately following Soloviev. See the discussion of Bulgakov's 1908 essay 'On Early Christianity' in Ch. 11, below.

not to invalidate ecumenism but to show the father of lies can pervert any ideal, even the most sublime. This is a crucial point in the polemic against Tolstoyanism and an ironic reminder of the limits of Christian activism. Yet the fact remains that ecumenism, far from being an effective tool in the Anti-Christ's hands, leads to his demise. Soloviev's Anti-Christ solves the political and social questions of his day without difficulty or dissent, but he falters on the religious question thanks to the dogmatism of unassimilated Jews and a new spirit of unity among Christians. The gates of hell do not prevail against the Universal Church.

A comparison of Soloviev's apocalypse with Bukharev's reveals both similarities and differences. The latter are more readily apparent. Bukharev's apocalypse is a commentary on the New Testament book; Soloviev's, an original literary composition. Bukharev reads the Revelation of John as a historical allegory; Soloviev's deliberately fantastic 'Brief Tale' is a parable. Bukharev draws heavily on Slavophile mythology; Soloviev is a thoroughgoing universalist.

Still, on the level of substantive religious values the two apocalypses have much in common. First and foremost, both Bukharev and Soloviev construe the vocation of Orthodoxy in prophetic terms, a view inspired by the traditional view of Orthodoxy as the church of John the Theologian, prophetic seer among the apostles. The whole of Bukharev's commentary is a gloss on John's prophecies, but the Johannine testament has a central place in Soloviev's apocalypse, too. The monk Ioann, 'the actual but unofficial leader of the Orthodox,' is consistently depicted as a prophet. He occupies no ecclesiastical office, not even in the monastic estate to which he titularly belongs, for 'he did not reside in any monastery but continually wandered through all parts.' His radiant white habit, betokening the paradisiacal reality of the church beyond the vale of tears and penance, is another prophetically inspired irregularity. Rumors concerning his identity abounded among the folk. Some, inspired by a piece of theological folklore popular in the Christian East, believed him to be John the Theologian in person. John, so the legend goes, did not taste death as the other apostles did but was appointed to live on as an unseen minister to the historical church with a special role to play in the preparation for apocalyptic times.[44] In every detail the portrait of Ioann seems designed to conjure the genius of prophetic Orthodoxy out of the flask in which the priestly, episcopal and state-bureaucratic establishments would contain it. In the fictional monk Ioann, Soloviev celebrates the same values which Bukharev cultivated through his relationship with Petr Tomanitsky.

Bukharev and Soloviev also share a faith in the special role Orthodoxy has to play in the coming of the radiant church of the future. This theme naturally receives more emphasis in Bukharev's commentary than in the ecumenically oriented 'Brief Tale,' yet it is not absent from the latter. Ioann, not Pope Peter II or Professor Pauli, is the first to recognize the Anti-Christ. He is also the one who initiates the authentic reunion of the churches.

Bukharev's and Soloviev's commitment to the renewal of Orthodoxy goes far toward explaining why they took an interest in apocalyptic literature. Renewalism demands a prophetic approach to the affairs of church and world, something which the apocalyptic tradition surely provides. Nevertheless, renewalism alone is probably not a sufficient explanation for Bukharev and Soloviev's interest in apocalyptic. The sources that nourish prophetic religion are numerous, and most are easier to handle than apocalyptic literature. Moreover, apocalyptic interests placed Bukharev and Soloviev outside the theological mainstream of their day. Nineteenth-century theology for the most part cultivated a 'realized' eschatology, an approach which stressed the perfecting of spiritual life here and now as distinct from future-oriented eschatology. The categories of crisis and catastrophe, so essential to apocalyptic, were politely set aside. Among the theological virtues love came first, faith second, hope a distant third. Not until Albert Schweitzer rehabilitated apocalyptic in *The Quest of the Historical Jesus* (1906) did the subject begin to be taken seriously by a wide spectrum of modern theologians.

Bukharev's and Soloviev's interest in apocalyptic was therefore something of an anomaly. In Soloviev's case, *fin de*

---

[44] *Tri razgovora*, pp. 208–9.

siècle foreboding, popular in Russian intellectual circles around 1900, may have played a role. But the example of Bukharev as well as Soloviev's own visionary projects dating back to the 1870s show the future-oriented eschatology of *Three Dialogues* was something more than the reflection of a passing cultural mood. Perhaps apocalyptic appealed to Orthodox renewalists because of the anomalousness of their situation. Nineteenth-century Russian Orthodoxy was still in the main a conservative, priestly and bureaucratic establishment. While renewalism attracted
a following among educated clergy and laity, it remained a minority position. Perhaps the radical prophetic sensibility of apocalyptic lent renewalists the spiritual boldness and emotional gratification needed to sustain their campaign against the odds. Perhaps it was also a way of expressing their hope that Orthodoxy had a fresh, prophetic word to speak to a modern European civilization which still viewed Russians and Orthodox as outsiders.

However we wish to explain it, Bukharev's and Soloviev's apocalypticism enriched modern Orthodox theology. Admittedly the riches were not unproblematic. The flawed methodology of *Studies on the Apocalypse* harmed Bukharev's reputation as an academic theologian, while *Three Dialogues* complicated Soloviev's legacy in ways he almost certainly did not intend. In the last analysis, however, apocalypticism sanctified and safe-guarded an enormously attractive characteristic of both thinkers. Call it the prophetic spirit, or theological eros, or simply faith in the God who makes all things new, Bukharev and Soloviev were men on the move, *podvizhniki* in the truest sense of the word. They were not at ease in Zion.

PART III

BULGAKOV: DOGMATICS OF THE HUMANITY OF GOD

10

The Religion of Humanity and the Humanity of God

FAITH IN PROGRESS

Sergei Nikolaevich Bulgakov came from a long line of Russian Orthodox priests.[1] His father, Nikolai Vasilievich, served for 47 years as priest of a non-parochial cemetery church in Livny, Orel Province. His mother, Aleksandra Kosminichna Azbukina, also came from a family with priestly blood, although Sergei's

---

[1] The best overall treatment of Bulgakov's life and work is Catherine Evtuhov, *The Cross and the Sickle: Sergei Bulgakov and the Fate of Russian Religious Philosophy* (Ithaca and London: Cornell University Press, 1997). The book deals mainly with Bulgakov's career up to his exile from the Soviet Union in 1922; his dogmatic theology is not discussed. Another detailed study is L.A. Zander, *Bog i mir (Mirosozertsanie ottsa Sergiia Bulgakova)*, 2 vols (Paris: YMCA-Press, 1948). A recent anthology of Bulgakov's writings in English translation with explanatory articles and notes is an excellent source with which to begin the study of Bulgakov, especially in theological perspective: *Sergii Bulgakov: Towards a Political Theology*, ed. Rowan Williams (Edinburgh: T&T Clark, 1999). For a concise and philosophically nuanced sketch of Bulgakov's *oeuvre*, see S.S. Khoruzhii, 'Sofiia – Kosmos – Materiia: ustoi filosofskoi mysli ottsa Sergiia Bulgakova,' *Posle pereryva: puti russkoi filosofii* (St Petersburg: Izdatel'stvo 'Aleteiia', 1994), pp. 67–99. Bulgakov's autobiographical memoirs are a sketchy but colorful source of information: Sergii Bulgakov, *Avtobiograficheskie zametki*, posth. ed., preface and notes by L.A. Zander (Paris: YMCA-Press, 1946). A biographical essay with a large bibliography of Bulgakov's works appeared in a publication of the Moscow Patriarchate late in the Soviet period: Monakhinia Elena, 'Professor Protoierei Sergii Bulgakov (1871–1944),' *Bogoslovskie trudy* 27 (1986): 107–94. See also Winston F. Crum, 'Sergius N. Bulgakov: From Marxism to Sophiology,' *St Vladimir's Theological Quarterly* 27 (1983): 3–25. The most complete bibliography is Kliment Naumov, *Bibliographie des oeuvres de Serge Boulgakov*, preface by Constantin Andronikof (Paris: Institut d'études slaves, 1984). See also Sergius Bulgakov, *Orthodoxy and Modern Society*, with a bibliography of Bulgakov's works in English, ed. Robert Bird (New Haven, Conn.: The Variable Press, 1995).

maternal grandfather was a layman. The Bulgakov family's daily life revolved around the rituals of Orthodoxy. The seasonal fasts and feasts had the force of a 'law of nature,' as Bulgakov later put it, for nature itself appeared to observe them. Bulgakov described the religiosity of his early years as 'a child's Christian "pantheism," ' a view of things to which he would remain remarkably faithful. The sense of the wholeness of things in God extended even to the realm of death for which Sergei's father was, so to speak, vocationally responsible. 'Funerals were well done in Livny,' Bulgakov recalled. 'The place was a kind of [ancient] Egypt. Above all there was no fear of death.'[2]

In later years Bulgakov made much of his priestly roots. 'I am a levite, and I recognize and cherish my levitism more and more; I am prepared to say I take pride in it.' His friend Evgeny Trubetskoi told him he was 'born in a stole.'[3] Yet the boy who was born in a stole in 1871 would not enter the ranks of the priesthood until a few days before his forty-eighth birthday in 1918. He began conventionally enough, entering Orel Theological Seminary at the age of thirteen. But in 1888, after three years of the prescribed four, he transferred to a secular gymnasium to prepare for the university. The problem was spiritual: Sergei had lost his faith in God and decided to commit himself instead to the struggle for social and economic justice. His decision soon led him to embrace Marxism, the rising star in the Russian ideological firmament. Marxism was the up-to-date choice for a young radical of the day. Vladimir Ulianov (Lenin) made the same choice at about the same time, as did many other men and women who went on to play leading roles the Russian revolutions of 1905 and 1917.[4]

---

[2] *Avtobiograficheskie zametki*, pp. 16–18.

[3] *Avtobiograficheskie zametki*, pp. 25, 37.

[4] Marxism made its appearance on the Russian scene in 1883 with the formation of the Liberation of Labor group in Geneva by G.V. Plekhanov and other expatriate radicals. Lenin (1870–1924) became a Marxist in 1887–8. Parallels may be drawn between the early careers of Lenin and Bulgakov. Both men matriculated in law faculties, specialized in political economy, married in 1898 and devoted their first substantive scholarly work to the history of capitalism. Lenin's *The Development of Capitalism in Russia* came out in 1899, Bulgakov's *Capitalism and Agriculture* in 1900. In other ways the two careers were very different. Lenin was a man of the revolutionary underground; he knew expulsions, prison, exile. Bulgakov was an academic or 'legal' Marxist.

Entering Moscow University's faculty of law in 1890 Bulgakov devoted himself to political economy. Taking his first degree in 1894 he continued his studies on the graduate level while teaching in a Moscow polytechnical school and publishing his first articles. A fellowship from the university allowed him to spend two years in western Europe completing his dissertation and enhancing his language skills. He returned to Russia in 1900. His dissertation, *Capitalism and Agriculture*, was published later the same year.[5]

In *Capitalism and Agriculture* Bulgakov investigated the applicability of the Marxist critique of capitalism to the agrarian sector of modern European economies. The topic was an appropriate choice for a number of reasons. Bulgakov was a Marxist in a country where 85 per cent of the populace took their living from agriculture. The famine of 1891 had recently demonstrated the inadequacies of the rural economy. As an Orel man, Bulgakov hailed from one of Russia's rich black-earth zones and brought a provincial's sense of local patriotism to his work. Also, the agrarian question was receiving attention from Marxist scholars throughout Europe at the time. Lenin, Kautsky and others wrote on the subject. Thus Bulgakov appeared to be on a normal career path for a budding Marxist academic. There was just one problem: by 1900 Bulgakov had concluded that Marx's critique of capitalism was flawed.

Bulgakov reached this conclusion in the course of his research for *Capitalism and Agriculture*. The project required him to read deeply in the specialized literature on European agriculture. (Russian agriculture per se is not treated in the book.) The more Bulgakov read, the more he came to believe the agricultural sector of the economy differed in important ways from the industrial sector. The continuing relevance of natural forces, the conservatism of agricultural products, the productivity of privately tended plots compared with fields worked by wage labor and the increased productivity of land made possible by technical improvements in farming led Bulgakov to doubt whether the agricultural economy was as much in the grip of centralizing tendencies as the industrial

---

[5] Sergei Bulgakov, *Kapitalizm i zemledelenie*, 2 vols (St Petersburg: Tipografiia V.A. Tikhanova, 1900).

sector. This in turn forced him to question the Marxist theory of capitalism. Marx viewed the centralization of resources in the hands of the few and the proletarianization of the many to be the inevitable result of capitalism in all sectors. Precisely for this reason Marx regarded capitalism as a self-destructive system, the engine of social revolution, since such a polarization of society would prove intolerable in the long run. Bulgakov's findings relativized this scheme:

> In agriculture not only is concentration not going on, but decentralizing tendencies are coming forward with extraordinary force ... But once agriculture and industry (and trade as well) are characterized at least by a different, if not by an opposite course of development, can one define the development of the capitalist economy in terms of any one dominant tendency, as Marx attempted to do? *Clearly one cannot.*[6]

The relation between a theory and its applications is always complex. The incongruity between Marxist doctrine and aspects of modern agricultural development did not cause most Marxists to question their theoretical assumptions. But

---

[6] *Kapitalizm i zemledelenie*, 2:456. Bulgakov's findings bore implications for the Russian case in that they questioned the inevitability of rural pauperization under capitalism and so suggested the prospect of a prosperous and relatively autonomous peasantry emerging in the countryside. Bulgakov anticipated the conclusions of the leading agricultural economist of the early Soviet period, Aleksandr Chaianov, as well as recent western scholarship on the Russian peasant economy. See Irina Rodnianskaia, 'Sergei Nikolaevich Bulgakov,' *Literaturnaia gazeta*, 27 Sept. 1989, no. 39, p. 6; and Teodor Shanin, *The Awkward Class: Political Sociology of Peasantry in a Developing Society: Russia 1910–1925* (Oxford: The Clarendon Press, 1972). Among late Soviet intellectuals, well aware of the catastrophes of collectivized agriculture in Stalin's time and the stagnation of the Russian countryside in their own, Bulgakov's prescience as an agricultural economist contributed mightily to his reputation. 'Already some seventeen years before the October Revolution and thirty years before the beginning of collectivization Bulgakov was proving that "the specific advantages of the concentration of labor or cooperation" which Marx declared for industrial production do not manifest themselves in agriculture, that agricultural production cannot be the object of [centrally] planned cooperation. Meanwhile we "reap the fruits" of a new round of agrarian "centralization" – the elimination of "unpromising" villages.' V.N. Akulin, 'S.N. Bulgakov: vekhi zhizni i tvorchestva,' in S.N. Bulgakov, *Khristianskii sotsializm*, ed. V.N. Akulin (Novosibirsk: 'Nauka', Sibirskoe otdelenie, 1991), p. 8.

Bulgakov had the born philosopher's curiosity about the reasons for things, including the intellectual things we call theories. The gap between theory and life always bothered him, and it particularly bothered him as a Marxist. Marxists distinguished themselves from other nineteenth-century radicals precisely by claiming their theories were scientific as opposed to romantic or utopian. But a scientific theory must have predictive value; otherwise its scientific status is moot. Moreover, the breakdown of a scientific theory in one of the arenas in which it is supposed to apply is a sufficient reason to question it in other arenas as well.

Bulgakov's questions led him to seek a new theoretical position. He found it in idealism, a word which he used in both a general and a more specialized sense. In 'Ivan Karamazov as a Philosophical Type,' a lecture Bulgakov gave in 1901 shortly after taking up a teaching position in political economy at Kiev Polytechnical Institute, idealism means taking a passionate interest in metaphysical questions – God, immortality, good and evil, and the like.[7] The following year Bulgakov's most important theoretical essay of the period, 'Fundamental Problems of the Theory of Progress,' appeared as the lead article in a collection of essays by many hands entitled *Problems of Idealism*.[8] The collaborators included professional philosophers associated with the Moscow Psychological Society and ex-Marxists including Nikolai Berdiaev and Petr Struve along with Bulgakov. For this group idealism meant the trenchant and principled rejection of all forms of positivism and philosophical materialism. *Problems of Idealism* was designed to overturn the worldview of the Russian radical intelligentsia.

The neo-idealist Bulgakov had not yet returned to active

[7] 'Ivan Karamazov (v romane Dostoevskogo "Brat'ia Karamazovy") kak filosofskii tip,' in Sergei Bulgakov, *Ot marksizma k idealizmu: sbornik statei (1896-1903)* (St Petersburg: Tovarishchestvo 'Obshchestvennaia Pol'za', 1903; reprint, Frankfurt am Main: Posev, 1968), pp. 83–112.

[8] 'Osnovnye problemy teorii progressa,' *Problemy idealizma: sbornik statei*, ed. P.I. Novgorodtsev (Moscow: Moskovskoe Psikhologicheskoe Obshchestvo, 1902), pp. 1–47. Bulgakov republished the essay the following year in *Ot marksizma k idealizmu*, pp. 113–60. I cite the essay from the latter source. The best treatment of the *Problemy idealizma* group and Russian Neo-idealism in general is Randall Allen Poole, 'The Moscow Psychological Society and the Neo-Idealist Development of Russian Liberalism' (PhD diss., University of Notre Dame, 1995).

involvement in the Orthodox Church, much less decided to dedicate himself to priestly service. Yet a religious pathos was becoming obvious in his work. 'Fundamental Problems of the Theory of Progress' is case in point. On the surface the essay is an analysis of the nature of sociological concepts, but it may also be read as an existentially motivated critique of the faith that inspired Bulgakov's youthful radicalism.

Bulgakov takes Auguste Comte's doctrine of progress as the paradigm of the type. Comte envisioned humanity as progressing from an initial religious-mythological stage of consciousness through a metaphysical-philosophical stage to the modern scientific stage based on 'positive' knowledge, by which Comte meant knowledge derived from the observation and measurement of material entities. Positive knowledge empowers human beings to organize the world for their purposes. Marx followed much the same scheme as Comte, only he elaborated it in more dynamic ('dialectical') terms and with special stress on the economic basis of society. Humanity passes from an initial feudal stage of production marked by dependence on irrational natural and social forces through a bourgeois stage based on individual self-consciousness to a socialist stage that reconciles collectivity and individuality, and also nature and humanity, in a grand synthesis. The synthesis is absolute in the sense of realizing the stage of human development beyond which no other can be conceived on the basis of positive science. Both Comte and Marx were humanists in that they envisioned human beings gradually taking control of the forces that shape their lives. As Bulgakov sums it up:

> The victory of reason over the irrational principle is accomplished not all at once but gradually as the collective reason of human beings who have come together in society extends its conquest of lifeless nature and learns to use [nature] for its own purposes; thus dead mechanism gradually gives way to its absolute opposite, rational purposiveness.[9]

Bulgakov sees fundamental flaws in this theory. The first is the contradiction between the concepts of mechanism and teleology. Comtian and Marxist visions of progress are

[9] 'Osnovnye problemy teorii progressa,' p. 120.

predicated on a materialist worldview; only empirical facts are deemed real. But Comte and Marx also maintained the world-process embodies rational purposiveness, that it has an intelligible end, indeed a satisfying human end. But where in a continuum of material forces, the origin of which is unknown and unknowable, lies the evidence for the existence of ends, especially ends which are satisfying to human beings? The same sort of question may be asked about human freedom. Progressivists imagine modern humanity to be making a world-historical leap from the realm of necessity to the realm of freedom. But how can human beings be said to be free in a world-process which is 'really' a field of materially determined forces? Or, if human freedom is assumed to be self-evident, how can the world-process be said to be materially determined if human beings are free to refashion it for their own ends?

Progressivism runs into methodological difficulties, too. Both Comte and Marx claimed to practice a science which allowed them to predict the general course of human development. Indeed, all theorists of progress advance this claim in one form or another, although some tone it down by claiming to discern only certain 'tendencies.'[10] In either case the same problem arises which gave Bulgakov pause when he attempted to analyze agricultural development in Marxist terms. Either the investigator's predictions concerning the future depend (at least in part) on a picture drawn from non-empirical sources, such as value judgments, faith or intimations, in which case the 'positive' status of the predictions may be challenged; or the predictions are inferences based on evidence drawn from the past or the present, in which case they should not be accepted as valid until they are verified by the actual course of events:

> The boldest theories of progress do not get further in their predictions than the visible historical future, and the historical eye does not see very far. Even supposing that the destiny of humanity in the twentieth century is known to us, we still know absolutely nothing about what awaits it in the twenty-first, twenty-second, twenty-third centuries and so on. The scientific

[10] 'Osnovnye problemy teorii progressa,' p. 123, n. 2.

theory of progress is like a dim candle which someone has lit at the head of an interminable, dark corridor. The candle provides meager illumination for a distance of a few feet, but the rest of the space is enveloped in deep darkness. Positive science does not have the power to reveal the destiny of humanity in the future, it leaves us in a state of *total uncertainty* about it.[11]

The effort to avoid this conclusion by arguing the future is knowable because it is the product of antecedent forces merely enslaves the future to the past. It can also cause an investigator to overlook the significance of data which do not conform with his or her picture of what the future is going to look like. Bulgakov exposed this error in *Capitalism and Agriculture*. Marx 'believed that it was possible to measure and determine the future according to the past and the present, while in fact every epoch brings forward new facts and new forces of historical development – the creativity of history is not diminishing.'[12]

Thus Bulgakov rejected the scientific pretensions of progressivism. At the same time he was fascinated by this peculiarly modern, atheistic faith. Marx, Comte and other progressivists were all convinced that humanity is the end of cosmic evolution, that history has an intelligible goal. Nowhere in the materialist worldview can grounds for such a belief be found, nor is it explained why a belief of this sort is needed. Nevertheless, the progressivists hold firmly to their conviction and in so doing come to resemble the theological and metaphysical thinkers whom they think they have overthrown.

The analogies between progressivism and religious faith are innumerable. The doctrine of progress may be seen as an atheist 'theodicy,' that is to say, 'a disclosure of highest reason, of supreme purposiveness in the world' which justifies the ways of cosmic and historical evolution to human beings. Moreover, just as 'every religion has its *Jenseits* – the belief in the eventual fulfillment of its hopes,' so progressivism entails 'ideas of the destiny of a free, proud and happy humanity in the future,' that is to say, its own sort of 'eschatology.'[13] Divinity is not lacking, either, as promethean humanity assumes the role. Humanity

---

[11] 'Osnovnye problemy teorii progressa,' p. 127.
[12] *Kapitalizm i zemledelenie*, 2:457–8.
[13] 'Osnovnye problemy teorii progressa,' pp. 120–3, 154.

also achieves immortality: 'the individual human being is mortal, but humanity is immortal; the individual human being is limited, but humanity possesses the capacity for endless development.'[14] The ethical principles of progressivism also betray an element of faith. Materialism ought to produce a fairly straightforward eudemonism in ethics; but Bulgakov finds no progressivist ideology in which eudemonism 'is advanced consistently as the exhaustive principle.' On the contrary, a belief in the perfectibility of human beings always enters in to qualify the present-oriented ethics of eudemonism.[15]

In short, progressivism manifests the dynamics of faith, for which reason Comte was quite right to call it 'the religion of humanity.' His error lay in thinking he had left the limitations of traditional religion and metaphysics behind. On the contrary, he and other progressivist doctrinaires demonstrated in an ironic way the human need for faith and metaphysical illumination.[16] Comte, and Marx after him, would have us construe religion, metaphysics and science in serial succession, the last of the series dislodging the other two. But in the light of the role played by religious and metaphysical 'contraband' in positivist ideologies, Bulgakov insists the series be construed cumulatively rather than disjunctively. 'Religion, metaphysical thinking and positive science all answer to fundamental demands of the human spirit, and their development leads to mutual clarification, not destruction.'[17]

---

[14] 'Osnovnye problemy teorii progressa,' pp. 128–32. Bulgakov calls progressivist-humanist immortality 'a dead immortality' and, borrowing a phrase from Hegel, 'a bad infinity.'

[15] 'Osnovnye problemy teorii progressa,' pp. 136–41.

[16] 'Osnovnye problemy teorii progressa,' p. 116; cf. pp. 150–2.

[17] 'Osnovnye problemy teorii progressa,' p. 113. Bulgakov's appreciation of the dynamics of faith forms the core of his article on the leading nineteenth-century Russian radical thinker Aleksandr Herzen: 'Dushevnaia drama Gertsena,' *Ot marksizma do idealizma*, pp. 161–94. 'S.N. Bulgakov had been the first to state clearly the proposition that Herzen – before he became immersed in émigré politics and embittered towards the end of his life – had been seeking for a spiritual solution to the problem of human freedom. The search for a solution to this question and of man's spiritual dignity had been the two polestars of his entire life and thought.' Marc Raeff, 'Enticements and Rifts: Georges Florovsky as Russian Intellectual Historian,' *Georges Florovsky: Russian Intellectual and Orthodox Churchman*, ed. Andrew Blane (Crestwood, NY: St Vladimir's Seminary Press, 1993), p. 252.

'Fundamental Problems of the Theory of Progress' thus turns out to be an essay on faith – not Christian faith, but a modern secular faith. The secularism is ironic if not paradoxical because faith by definition cannot define itself completely in terms of the *saeculum*, the here and now. A self-transcending, absolutizing impulse is integral to any sort of faith, as one sees from the faith-elements (one could say dogmas) of modern progressivism. The appearance of the dynamics of faith in ideologies which supposedly reject religion serves to demonstrate the universality of faith. Bulgakov puts the point nicely in a later work: 'A human being is a *believing* animal called to faith and to life on the basis of faith, although not all people recognize this with equal clarity.'[18]

Bulgakov's view is virtually identical to Paul Tillich's theory of faith as 'ultimate concern.'[19] Tillich's theory, in turn, can help us appreciate Bulgakov's findings. Tillich's important distinction between pseudo-religions and quasi-religions is particularly relevant at this point. A pseudo-religion is a fake; it relies on 'an intended but deceptive similarity.' A quasi-religion shows 'a genuine similarity, not intended, but based on points of identity.'[20] The practical implications of the distinction are considerable. On Tillich's view modern secular ideologies cannot simply be unmasked and dismissed, as traditionalist critics might be tempted to suppose; they must be taken seriously *as faiths*, encountered in a critical dialogue about faith. 'Fundamental Problems of the Theory of Progress,' the fruit of a dialogue going on in Bulgakov's own life, may be viewed as just such an encounter.

---

[18] *Avtobiograficheskie zametki*, pp. 31–2.
[19] The best concise exposition of Tillich's definition of faith as 'ultimate concern' is his book *Dynamics of Faith* (New York: Harper & Row, Publishers, 1957). The affinity between Bulgakov and Tillich was not accidental but derived from their connection with Schelling's philosophy of revelation. Bulgakov came to Schelling via Soloviev; Tillich wrote two dissertations on Schelling. See Jerome Arthur Stone, 'Tillich and Schelling's Later Philosophy,' *Kairos and Logos: Studies in the Roots and Implications of Tillich's Theology*, ed. John J. Carey (Macon, Georgia: Mercer University Press, 1984), pp. 3–35.
[20] Paul Tillich, *Christianity and the Encounter of the World Religions* (New York and London: Columbia University Press, 1963), p. 5.

A PROGRESSIVE FAITH

Bulgakov's conversion from Marxism to idealism represented a dramatic break in his intellectual and spiritual life, but there was also some continuity in it. After rejecting positivism and materialism, Bulgakov still had to decide what to do with the religion of humanity. Should he cast it aside and embrace a completely different faith, or should he explore the possibility of justifying humanistic faith on other grounds besides Marxism – on the basis of Christianity, for example? Choosing the latter course, Bulgakov stripped the theory of progress of materialist ideology and refounded it on the postulates of 'Christian theism,' namely, human freedom, the absolute value of the personality, a moral world-order, and a divine mind at work in nature and history.[21] Bulgakov believed such a procedure repatriated the theory of progress to its rightful home, for 'the doctrine of progress is in reality a specifically Christian doctrine' which modern ideologists have secularized. This argument facilitated the transposition of the values of humanity and progress from Marxism to Christianity. Bulgakov rejected faith in progress only to embrace a progressive Christian faith.

The first Russian thinker to make such a move was of course Vladimir Soloviev. In a remarkable essay Soloviev had already hailed Comte's idea of humanity as one of the most seminal ethical and religious concepts of modern times and called upon Orthodox Christians to provide it with the theological foundation it deserved.[22] Soloviev admired Comte for seeing more clearly than other philosophical radicals that the reference point of humanity as an ethical ideal is obscure. Those who take humanity to mean individual beings do so at the price of abstracting human beings from their actual life-situation, which is everywhere profoundly corporate. On the other hand, those who identify humanity with a corporate entity, such as the family, the state or a social class, diminish it by substituting the part for the whole. This leads to statism, nationalism, revolutionary terror and other perversions of humanity. Comte's greatness lay in recognizing the profoundly relational nature of

---

[21] 'Osnovnye problemy teorii progressa,' pp. 147–8.
[22] 'Ideia chelovechestva u Avgusta Konta.' See Ch. 6, n. 51 above.

human experience while rejecting premature or foreshortened constructions of this relatedness. The logic of his position led him to posit a cosmic or hypostatic humanity, 'a collective whole which in its inner essence, not just externally, surpasses every individual human being and completes him both ideally and in a totally real sense.' This 'Great Being,' as Comte called it, is 'not a personified principle but a Person in the form of a Principle [*Printsipial'noe Litso*], or Person-Principle, not a personified idea but a Person-Idea,' a worthy object of positive faith. Soloviev regarded Comte's concept as an intimation of the humanity of God.[23]

In the light of Bulgakov's fascination with the religious pathos of progressivism, it is not surprising he found the theologically bountiful idealism of Soloviev a more inspiring model than Neo-Kantianism when he sought a place for himself in the world of idealism. Neo-Kantianism was near its zenith in European thought around 1900, and many of the Russian liberals with whom Bulgakov collaborated between 1900 and 1917 stood closer to it than to the Solovievian tradition. Bulgakov knew the Kantian tradition well and carried on a continuous dialogue with it for more than two decades. But Neo-Kantianism did not meet the needs which counted most for him after his break with Marxism. Critical idealism, as the name implies, is at its best when making distinctions. Bulgakov was looking for wholeness. In an important essay of 1903 he asked what Soloviev's philosophy offered the modern mind. He answered that it offered

a balanced and harmonious synthesis of modern thought and knowledge, an integral worldview in which the demands of

---

[23] Solov'ev, 'Ideia chelovechestva u Augusta Konta,' *SS VSS*, 9:178, 186. Cf. p. 192: 'When in the future authoritative representatives of Christianity focus their attention on the fact that our religion is above all and par excellence a divine-human religion and that humanity is not some sort of appendage but an essential, formative aspect of the Humanity of God, they will resolve to expel from their historical pantheon some of the inhumanity that has casually slipped in during the course of so many centuries and to replace it with a little more humanity. At that time it will behoove them to remember [Comte], who, in spite of his great errors and the limitedness of his theoretical horizon, surpassed everyone else in our now waning nineteenth century in his feeling for and efforts to promote the human side of religion and historical Christianity.'

critical philosophy, metaphysical creativity and natural science are all taken into account and harmonized ... [Moreover] the philosophy of Vladimir Soloviev organically merges with Christian metaphysics, standing, as it were, as a critical introduction to theology and actually realizing the ideal of 'free theosophy.'[24]

Soloviev joins together what most modern philosophers and theologians put asunder.

Wholeness was not the only Solovievian characteristic that appealed to Bulgakov. He was also drawn to the philosopher's activism, the passion for reform in state and church. Bulgakov admired Soloviev's Christian politics, his grasp of Christianity as an active force wrestling with the problems of modern society:

The greatest sin of Byzantium, as Soloviev pointed out more than once, was to recognize only a domestic and cultic Christianity while leaving the whole sphere of social and political life to the dark, baser forces in human nature. Contemporary life presents somewhat the same picture, and it is the duty of every true Christian to work for the elimination of such an abnormal state of affairs.

The struggle must proceed 'along two fronts: unmasking the anti-Christianity of those [Christians] who have Christ's name on their lips but crucify Him by the way they live, and of those [secularists] who serve Him in deed but disclaim all thought of Him.'[25] Here as in the critique of the theory of progress, Bulgakov seeks 'a middle way' between the extremes of anti-Christian secularism and Christian hatred of the secular world.[26] Bulgakov commends Soloviev's political legacy on four

---

[24] 'Chto daet sovremennomu soznaniiu filosofiia Vladimira Solov'eva?,' *Ot marksizma k idealizmu*, p. 238.
[25] 'Chto daet sovremennomu soznaniiu filosofiia Vladimira Solov'eva?,' pp. 241–2.
[26] In 'Fundamental Problems of the Theory of Progress' Bulgakov assesses the prospects for 'a metaphysics of history' (general theory of the meaning of history) and suggests that it can only be found in 'a middle way' (*srednii put'*) between absolute rationalism (as in Hegel) and despairing skepticism. 'Osnovnye problemy teorii progressa,' pp. 144–5. As we shall see, Bulgakov often tried to resolve issues by seeking a middle way.

critical issues of modern Russian life: religious freedom, social justice, law, and the national question in the Russian empire. On the religious issue Soloviev continued the work of the early Slavophiles, who were the first to point out the harm done to Orthodoxy by its subordination to the state. But Soloviev was also zealous, as the Slavophiles usually were not, for the liberty of non-Orthodox faiths in the empire and for the welfare of the minorities generally. Bulgakov also praises Soloviev for his vigorous criticism of anti-Semitism, a vice to which the Slavophiles were prone.[27] Social justice, too, was an integral part of Soloviev's free theocracy, an ideal so generous that it accommodated even 'the truth of socialism.'[28] Soloviev also did ground-breaking work on the theory of law by promoting the concept of natural law and breaking ranks with his Slavophile friends by insisting on the need for formal juridical guarantees in Russia.[29]

On the national question in Russia, namely the twofold question of how the Russian nation should be defined and how relations between the various nationalities of the Russian Empire should be construed, Bulgakov identifies with Soloviev's search for a middle ground between the extremes of 'cosmopolitanism' and 'zoological patriotism,' an approach which would be 'national' in spirit while subject to the claims of 'Christian universalism.' In Bulgakov's opinion, however, Soloviev did not carry his 'left Slavophilism' far enough. An element of political romanticism kept him from wholeheartedly embracing 'the political credo of Russian Westernism,' although the latter was 'the only consistent conclusion' to be drawn from his call for a state system based on the rule of law.[30]

---

[27] 'Chto daet sovremennomu soznaniiu filosofiia Vladimira Solov'eva?,' pp. 244–5; cf. p. 258, n. 1.
[28] 'Chto daet sovremennomu soznaniiu filosofiia Vladimira Solov'eva?,' p. 248. Bulgakov was less impressed by the specifics of Soloviev's economic ideas, observing that 'political economy is in general the Achilles' heel of [this] philosopher, and in the field of strictly economic questions the reader who has been properly schooled in economics will find much that is incorrect and misleading, much that fails to measure up to the overall teaching of the philosopher' (p. 249).
[29] 'Chto daet sovremennomu soznaniiu filosofiia Vladimira Solov'eva?,' pp. 250, 258–9.
[30] 'Chto daet sovremennomu soznaniiu filosofiia Vladimira Solov'eva?,' pp. 250–9. 'Left Slavophilism' occurs on p. 257.

Bulgakov combined theoretical advocacy of progressive Christianity with political activism. He entered the inner circle of Russian liberalism at an early date thanks to his association with Petr Struve (1870–1944). He collaborated in Struve's militant journal *Liberation*, published in Stuttgart from 1902 to 1905. Again with Struve he was one of the founders of the Union of Liberation, an illegal political organization that began operations in 1903. When open political activity became possible in Russia during the Revolution of 1905, the Liberationists took the lead in forming the Constitutional Democratic (Kadet) Party, the largest party in the First and Second Dumas (1906–7), and the standard-bearer of Russian liberalism for the rest of the imperial period. Bulgakov's political principles on the eve of 1905 were close to what became Kadet liberalism.[31]

During the revolutionary years, however, Bulgakov's political position grew more complicated. He did not join the Kadet Party as he might have been expected to do. Allying himself instead with a few liberal Slavophiles, he formed the Union of Christian Politics, which advocated Christian socialism.[32] The

---

[31] See Akulin's discussion of Bulgakov's article 'Idealism and Social Programs' (1904). Bulgakov claimed the political principles of idealism are 'the natural and inalienable rights of man and citizen, the rights of the human person, the freedom or more precisely the freedoms of this person, the whole aggregate of freedoms,' including speech, religion, assembly and national self-determination. Akulin, 'S.N. Bulgakov,' *Khristianskii sotsializm*, p. 13.

[32] For an analysis of Bulgakov's politics at the time see Bastiaan Wielenga, *Lenins Weg zur Revolution: Eine Konfrontation mit Sergej Bulgakov und Petr Struve im Interesse einer theologischen Besinnung* (Munich: Chr. Kaiser Verlag, 1971), pp. 241–65; Akulin, 'S.N. Bulgakov,' *Khristianskii sotsializm*, pp. 14–17; and Evtuhov, *The Cross and the Sickle*, pp. 101–14. Evtuhov regards Bulgakov's Christian socialism as inspired by Soloviev's ideas of *bogochelovechestvo* and Christian politics. The welfare-liberalism of Soloviev's *The Justification of the Good* with its defense of the 'right to a dignified existence' may also be cited. A comparison with Paul Tillich is instructive. Tillich entered the theological arena in Germany shortly after World War I with a philosophy of culture advocating 'religious socialism.' Religious socialism challenged both the individualism of secular liberalism and the mechanistic collectivism of Marxism; it sought to transcend autonomy and heteronomy in theonomy. Bulgakov's Christian socialism was similar in that it was not a rejection of liberalism, as Marxism was, but a quest for a more inclusive ideal. On Tillich's socialism, see John R. Stumme, *Socialism in Theological Perspective: A Study of Paul Tillich 1918–1933*, American Academy of Religion Dissertation Series, no. 21 (Missoula, Montana: Scholars Press, 1978); and Ronald H. Stone, *Paul Tillich's Radical Social Thought* (Atlanta: John Knox Press, 1980).

initiative revealed Bulgakov's discomfort with certain aspects of Kadet liberalism. The secularism of the Kadets, which Bulgakov interpreted as religious indifferentism, left him cold. He was also put off by what he took to be their lack of sympathy for the organic and collective values to which Sololviev's religious philosophy had attuned him. Bulgakov's gifts as a political organizer proved meager, however. The Union of Christian Politics failed to attract much support and soon ceased to exist, although Bulgakov remained politically active. In 1907 he was elected to the Second Duma from the Orel region. Officially an independent, he stood closest to the Kadets on most issues. The dissolution of the assembly in June 1907 put an end to his parliamentary career.

At this point in his life Bulgakov was not yet the inside player in church affairs he would be by the time of the Revolution of 1917–18. As a prominent publicist he gave strong support to the Orthodox conciliar movement of 1905–6, the most important church-political development during the Revolution of 1905.[33] Moreover, his intellectual evolution pointed clearly to reconciliation with historic Orthodoxy. Yet his role in 1905–6, even in the religious sphere, remained that of an intellectual, not a churchman. Only late in 1907 did Bulgakov return to the sacramental life of Orthodoxy.[34] This is worth remembering when assessing the Russian religious renaissance, as the return of intellectuals and artists to Orthodoxy is sometimes

---

[33] The conciliar movement sought to free the Russian Orthodox Church from the dependence on the state to which the church 'reform' of Peter the Great had subjected it in the eighteenth century. The restoration of conciliar government in the church was the chief demand. See James W. Cunningham, *A Vanquished Hope: The Movement for Church Renewal in Russia, 1905–1906* (Crestwood, New York: St Vladimir's Seminary Press, 1981); Nicolas Zernov, *The Russian Religious Renaissance of the Twentieth Century* (New York and Evanston: Harper & Row, Publishers, 1963), pp. 63–85; John Meyendorff, 'The Russian Bishops and Church Reform,' *Russian Orthodoxy Under the Old Regime*, eds Robert L. Nichols and Theofanis G. Stavrou (Minneapolis: University of Minnesota Press, 1978), pp. 170–82; and Paul Valliere, 'The Idea of a Council in Russian Orthodoxy in 1905,' ibid., pp. 183–201.

[34] Bulgakov wrote of his emotional struggle to embrace the sacramental life of the church in an autobiographical digression in *The Unfading Light* (1917): *Svet nevechernii: sozertsaniia i umozreniia*, ed. V.V. Sapov, afterword by K.M. Dolgov (Moscow: Izdatel'stvo 'Respublika', 1994), pp. 14–15.

called.[35] The drama of the conversion of unbelievers to religious faith makes it is easy to overlook the fact more was going on than a return to tradition. The intelligentsia did not arrive at the household of faith with empty bags, but with a load of liberal and reformist values which they had no intention of surrendering. The encounter between modernity and Orthodox tradition was dynamic: it operated in both directions.

Bulgakov was always clear about this. At the dawn of his return to faith he embraced idealism because it offered a transcendental grounding of the moral law; but not for a moment did he suppose faith in the transcendent meant disengagement from the world. On the contrary, he regarded as

> pitiful the person in our day who cannot see the radiance of the absolute moral ideal in the hearts of those who give themselves to the service of the proletariat in its struggle for human dignity, who live and die for the cause of freedom, the person who does not perceive [the moral ideal] in the dull and prosaic paragraphs of the factory law or in the constitution of a labor union and so on.[36]

We can hear the same Bulgakov speaking more than three and a half decades later when, in his Paris exile, he rose to the defense of progressive Christianity before a much more conservative Orthodox audience than the one he faced in Russia between 1900 and 1917:

> While confessing all the falsehood of [my youthful] nihilism, I must also bear witness to the truth of my intransigence toward the servility and enslavement of Russian life, and church life in particular, so characteristic of [that] period. I could not accept this, nor should I have, and I do not repent of this refusal. In a sense I can say that I have continued in it 'even unto this day,' and to the end of my days I wish to remain faithful to the principles of freedom and the protection of human dignity, intransigent toward every sort of 'totalitarianism.' In this respect I wish to remain in the ranks of

---

[35] Zernov, *The Russian Religious Renaissance of the Twentieth Century*. Bulgakov uses the phrase 'our Russian renaissance' (without special reference to religion) in his 1903 article 'Ob ekonomicheskom ideale,' *Ot marksizma k idealizmu*, p. 287.
[36] 'Osnovnye problemy teorii progressa,' p. 149.

Russian 'progressive' society (I do not even want to disclaim this word).[37]

Returning to 'his Father's house' Bulgakov renounced the sins of his youth; he did not renounce the virtues.

HEROISM AND HUMILITY

Bulgakov was not alone in calling for a rapprochement between the religion of humanity and the church of the humanity of God in Russia in the first years of the twentieth century. The new religious consciousness in Russian art and literature, the new liberalism in social and political thought and the conciliar movement in the Russian Orthodox Church all responded in one way or another to the same prospect. So did the celebrated Religious-Philosophical Meetings that brought intelligentsia and churchmen together to discuss problems of contemporary religion and society.[38] Yet while rapprochement was in the air, few of its advocates were prepared for the test to which the ideal was put by the Revolution of 1905. The revolution caught most Russian intellectuals and even the professional revolutionaries by surprise. The radical parties unexpectedly found themselves in command of the streets, the Orthodox Church found itself planning its first national council in over two hundred years, intellectuals found themselves sitting in Russia's first democratically elected parliament. Ideas which had merely been talked

---

[37] *Avtobiograficheskie zametki*, p. 27. The passion for social and political issues is one of the characteristics that distinguish the Russian school from Neopatristic thinkers beginning with Florovsky. The contrast is well drawn by Marc Raeff: 'Even the members of the intelligentsia who returned to the Christian faith after abandoning their positivistic and Marxist enthusiasm did not cease to give social issues a central position in their thinking (e.g. N.A. Berdiaev, S.N. Bulgakov, S.L. Frank, and later G.P. Fedotov). But in the case of Florovsky there never seems to have been any interest in social questions as such; his concern was always exclusively for philosophy, culture, theology, and scholarship.' 'Enticements and Rifts: Georges Florovsky as Russian Intellectual Historian,' *Georges Florovsky*, ed. Blane, p. 244.

[38] See Peter Scheibert, *Die Petersburger religiös-philosophischen Zusammenkünfte von 1902 und 1903* (Berlin, 1964) and Jutta Scherrer, *Die Petersburger religiös-philosophischen Vereinigungen: Die Entwicklung der religiösen Selbstverständnis ihrer Intelligencija-Mitglieder (1901–1907)* (Berlin, 1973).

about suddenly had to be put into practice. Religious ideas enjoyed no immunity from the demands of the 'moment of truth,' as the Revolution of 1905 has been described.[39]

Bulgakov reassessed the idea of a rapprochement between the religion of humanity and the church in 'Heroism and Humility,' which appeared in *Landmarks: A Collection of Essays on the Russian Intelligentsia* (1909).[40] *Landmarks* was the work of seven leading Russian thinkers, most of them political liberals. Bulgakov spoke for the whole group when he wrote in the opening lines of his essay: 'Russia has lived through a revolution. This revolution has not brought what was expected from it.' The revolution did not bring about national reconciliation, it did not renew the state or reinvigorate the national economy. To make matters worse, post-revolutionary Russia suffered from 'an unprecedented rise in crime and a general deterioration of morals,' while a wave of pornography and sensationalism saturated Russian literature.[41]

Who was to blame for this disappointing outcome? Reactionary forces, to be sure. Yet this explanation, as far as the *Landmarks* group was concerned, was insufficient because it absolved the makers of the Revolution of any responsibility for what had happened. If 1905 was in some sense the intelligentsia's revolution, its failure was also the intelligentsia's. In any case Bulgakov believed 'Russia [could] not be renewed without first renewing her intelligentsia (and much else besides),' a task which first of all demanded 'self-criticism.'[42]

Bulgakov's critical reflections led him to the clear, if distasteful, conclusion that practical co-operation between Christianity and modern humanism is as difficult as the

---

[39] Teodor Shanin, *Russia, 1905–07: Revolution as a Moment of Truth*, vol. 2 of *The Roots of Otherness: Russia's Turn of Century* (New Haven and London: Yale University Press, 1986).

[40] Sergei Bulgakov, 'Geroizm i podvizhnichestvo (Iz razmyshlenii o religioznoi prirode russkoi intelligentsii),' *Vekhi: sbornik statei o russkoi intelligentsii*, 2nd ed. (Moscow: Tipografiia V.M. Sablina, 1909; reprint, Frankfurt am Main: Izdatel'stvo 'Posev', 1967), pp. 23–69. A fine English translation and background article are included in *Sergii Bulgakov: Towards a Political Theology*, ed. Rowan Williams, pp. 55–112. Williams translates the title 'Heroism and the Spiritual Struggle.'

[41] 'Geroizm i podvizhnichestvo,' pp. 23–4.

[42] 'Geroizm i podvizhnichestvo,' pp. 24–7.

theoretical gap between them is wide. This view represented a clear shift from the position he held before 1905. In his earlier essays, as we have seen, Bulgakov rejected the theoretical worldview of the religion of humanity but called for practical co-operation between humanists and Christians on the basis of a shared progressivist agenda. But the hard school of politics in a time of revolution taught him theoretical differences generate differences of practice. The atheist-humanist and Christian worldviews, when consistently applied, result in conflicting approaches to social action: in the one case, an ethic of revolutionary 'heroism,' in the other, an ethic of saintly 'humility.'[43] The 'chasm' between the two is not easily bridged. A person passes from one side to the other by *metanoia*, by repentance and conversion.[44]

Those who embrace the heroic or atheist-humanist worldview 'deny Providence and any sort of primordial plan being worked out in history, they put themselves in the place of Providence and see themselves as their own savior.' In this they carry the religion of humanity to its extreme: 'the divinity of humanity' (*chelovekobozhie*).[45] This absolutizing of human beings casts the spell of revolutionary 'maximalism' upon the ends and means of social action. The maximalism of ends leads radicals to treat remote possibilities, such as a socialist republic, as 'immediate tasks of the moment' and to despise liberals who advocate more moderate goals.[46] The maximalism of means leads to the attitude that 'everything is permitted,' to the

---

[43] *Podvizhnichestvo*, which I translate 'humility' in this context, is a word from the Orthodox monastic tradition for which there is no adequate equivalent in English. *Podvizhnichestvo* is the quality of a *podvizhnik*, i.e. a saint, ascetic, witness, or martyr. But the saintly self-denial which is always integral to the meaning of *podvizhnichestvo* is understood in active, not passive terms. A *podvizhnik* is a person who accomplishes *podvigi* (feats, labors, achievements), an athlete of faith. The root indicates movement, advancement. The humility Bulgakov is speaking about, then, is an energetic value, a constructive force, not a pious euphemism for passivity or indolence. That 'humility' is a valid translation for *podvizhnichestvo* in 'Heroism and Humility' is supported by the fact Bulgakov uses and even italicizes the ordinary Russian word for humility (*smirenie*) to define the specific quality which distinguishes *podvizhnichestvo* from heroism. The relevant passage is quoted below at n. 48.

[44] 'Geroizm i podvizhnichestvo,' p. 58.

[45] 'Geroizm i podvizhnichestvo,' p. 36.

[46] 'Geroizm i podvizhnichestvo,' p. 39.

rejection of ordinary morality, hence to the acceptance of violence and amoralism. Individual conscience is set aside in favor of ideologically prescribed morality.[47]

The Christian ethic is quite different. Its most elementary virtue is one which the radical intelligentsia least wishes to entertain:

> In intelligentsia circles there is no word less popular than *humility* (*smirenie*). Few concepts suffer from greater misunderstanding and distortion or give intelligentsia demagogues a handier object to sharpen their teeth on. And this, better than anything else perhaps, reveals the spiritual nature of the intelligentsia, exposes its haughty, self-deifying heroism. Yet humility is, by the unanimous witness of the Church, the first and fundamental Christian virtue, and even beyond the boundaries of Christianity it is an extremely precious quality and, in any case, evidence of a high level of spiritual development.[48]

Humility is the active expression of faith in divine Providence. The Christian *podvizhnik* 'sees history and every individual human life as the realization of a divine plan. While the plan is incomprehensible to him in its details, he humbles himself before it through an act of faith.' In consequence he is freed from the spell of heroic pretensions and ready for the day at hand. 'His attention is focused on his immediate business, his actual duties and the strict and prompt execution of the same.'[49] The contrast with the heroic revolutionary could not be sharper. The revolutionary rejects and if need be represses today for the sake of tomorrow. The Christian leaves tomorrow to God and ministers to the needs of today.

Bulgakov takes pains to emphasize the active character of Christian humility. He rejects the commonplace view of humility 'as outward passivity, as making peace with the forces of evil, as inertia and even servility.' The stereotype results from taking the monastic expression of Christian humility as the normative one, when it should be seen as only one of the

---

[47] 'Geroizm i podvizhnichestvo,' pp. 44–8.
[48] 'Geroizm i podvizhnichestvo,' p. 49.
[49] 'Geroizm i podvizhnichestvo,' p. 48.

options. '*Podvizhnichestvo* as an inner disposition of the personality is compatible with every sort of outward activity as long as the latter does not contradict its principles.'[50] Bulgakov develops this thought with reference to modern secular vocations, a concern which was central to Orthodox renewalism already in Bukharev's day, but which Bulgakov deepens with the help of Max Weber's famous theory:

> The doctor and the engineer, the professor and the political activist, the manufacturer and his worker may all be guided in the performance of their obligations not by personal interest, be it spiritual or material, but by conscience, by the commands of duty. This discipline of obedience, 'worldly asceticism' (in German: 'innerweltliche Askese'), had a profound impact on the formation of personality in Western Europe in various fields of endeavor, a development which makes itself felt to this very day.[51]

The point of Bulgakov's digression is to emphasize the contrast between revolutionary and Christian forms of activism. The revolutionary way is marked by 'maximal pretensions ... with minimal personal preparation in the scientific field as well as in practical experience and self-discipline.' The Christian way, by contrast, is characterized by 'maximalism in personal life, in the demands one makes upon oneself,' but 'moderation' in ends and means.[52]

The many contrasts between the heroic-revolutionary and Christian paths lead Bulgakov to the inescapable conclusion that a choice must be made; or to put it another way, that the issue of 'the ultimate criterion' cannot be dodged:

> Is this criterion of self-evaluation to be supplied by the image of the perfect Divine personality incarnate in Christ or by the

---

[50] 'Geroizm i podvizhnichestvo,' p. 53.

[51] 'Geroizm i podvizhnichestvo,' pp. 54–5. Bernice Glatzer Rosenthal discusses Bulgakov's effort to deal with the problem of Orthodoxy and modern vocations in 'The Search for an Orthodox Work Ethic,' *Between Tsar and People*, eds Edith W. Clowes, Samuel E. Kassow and James L. West (Princeton: Princeton University Press, 1991), pp. 57–74. See also Iu. N. Davydov, 'Veber i Bulgakov (khristian-skaia askeza i trudovaia etika),' *Voprosy filosofii*, 1994/2: 54–73.

[52] 'Geroizm i podvizhnichestvo,' pp. 51–4.

self-deifying human being in one or another of his limited earthly guises (humanity, the people, the proletariat, the superman), i.e. in the last analysis by his own ego standing before him in a heroic pose.[53]

Bulgakov rejects conceptions of the relation between Christianity and modern humanism which obscure this issue. He opposes those who would ' "correct" the image of Christ by freeing it from "ecclesiastical distortions" and portraying [Jesus] as a social democrat or socialist revolutionary.' Yet no less blasphemous to Bulgakov's ears is the self-proclaimed 'new religious consciousness' of Merezhkovsky and others who would christianize revolution by simply 'replacing the name of Marx or Mikhailovsky with the name of Christ, and *Capital* with the Gospel, or even better with the Revelation of John (which they conveniently cite).' In its more extreme forms this approach leads to 'an ecclesiastical revolutionism' which counterposes 'its own new holiness' to the historic church. The problem with all these conceptions is that they leave the heroic spirituality of the intelligentsia unchallenged.[54]

Bulgakov was convinced revolutionary maximalism was the last thing Russia needed in 1909. What was needed was a rapprochement between the intelligentsia and the nation so the division of the country 'into two irreconcilable halves, into right and left blocs, into black-hundredism and red-hundredism,' could be overcome. Christian humility was the key to a rapprochement because it would lead the intelligentsia to address the immediate problems of the country while at the same time striking a sympathetic chord in the hearts of the Russian people, a people whose 'ideal is Christ and His teaching,' whose 'norm is Christian holiness.'[55]

'Heroism and Humility' deepened the theology of the humanity of God in modern Orthodoxy. While a synthesis of Christianity and modern culture remained his goal, Bulgakov achieved a new sophistication about it. He became more skeptical toward modern culture and more sympathetic toward ecclesiastical Christianity. When Bulgakov ended 'Heroism and

---

[53] 'Geroizm i podvizhnichestvo,' p. 50.
[54] 'Geroizm i podvizhnichestvo,' pp. 56–8.
[55] 'Geroizm i podvizhnichestvo,' pp. 61–7.

Humility' by calling for the formation of a 'church intelligentsia' in Russia he meant something more than a vaguely religious intelligentsia. He was calling his colleagues to the Orthodox Church.[56]

While the primary target of Bulgakov's skepticism was revolutionism, one should not suppose Bulgakov had lost interest in progressive faith or the engagement between Orthodoxy and the modern world. Bulgakov and other Orthodox renewalists of the post-1905 period were simply coming to see that the dynamics of this engagement were more complicated than their predecessors realized. Archimandrite Feodor questioned the split between a culturally disengaged church and an engaged, but unbelieving secularism. Bulgakov, drawing on a longer history and on his own firsthand experience of secular radicalism, recognized that secularism in some of its forms is just as disengaged from culture as religious traditionalism. Revolutionism, proposing to save Russia while rejecting the beliefs and institutions of the historic Russian nation, was a case in point. In its way it resembled Orthodox traditionalism, which preached the incarnate Word but shunned contact with the world of flesh and blood. From opposite ends of the ideological spectrum traditionalism and revolutionism share a common antipathy for the present. Traditionalism spurns the present for an idealized yesterday, revolutionism for an improbable tomorrow. The *podvizhnik*, attending to the business of today, seeks the indwelling humanity of God.

When he celebrated Christian humility in *Landmarks*, Bulgakov did not know how soon his ideal would be put to the test in his own life. Bulgakov was a family man. At the age of twenty-six he married Elena Ivanovna Tokmakova. Their daughter Maria was born in 1898; their son Fyodor in 1901. A second son, Ivan, was born in 1906. Ivashechka, as he was called, was a sweet but sickly child who died in 1909 after an agonizing struggle with nephritis. The blow fell on the Bulgakov family with tremendous force. Sergei's brief memoir of the ordeal, written a few years later, speaks of desperate grief as

---

[56] 'Geroizm i podvizhnichestvo,' p. 67.

well as of mystical illumination.[57] The loss – or was it gain? – was a defining moment in Bulgakov's spiritual life. Ivashechka became for him, like little Ilyusha (Ilyushechka) for Alyosha and the schoolboys in *The Brothers Karamazov* (Epilogue, ch. 3), the measuring rod of Christian *podvizhnichestvo*, an example which would challenge Bulgakov, inspire him and bring him to tears for the rest of his life.

[57] For Bulgakov's description of his family's trauma over Ivashechka's death see *Svet nevechernii*, pp. 17–18; and Evtuhov, *The Cross and the Sickle*, pp. 133–7.

II

The Philosophy of Economy

In 1912, after a dozen years of lecturing, writing and political activism, Bulgakov brought out *The Philosophy of Economy*.[1] In the preface he tells his readers the work 'has unique significance for the author, for it sums up the whole phase of his life colored by economic materialism and [so] represents the author's philosophical obligation with regard to his own past.'[2] The book does, in fact, occupy a special place among Bulgakov's works in that here more than anywhere else Bulgakov the economist and Bulgakov the religious thinker collaborate on a single task. *The Philosophy of Economy* may also be seen as a response to some of the issues raised in 'Heroism and Humility.' That essay, by probing the complexities of the project of Christian engagement with modern civilization, showed the need for a deeper understanding of the cultural process. In *The Philosophy of Economy* Bulgakov addresses this need by offering a general theory of cultural activity.

The Philosophy of Economy follows Soloviev's lead. One will recall that in *The Critique of Abstract Principles*, Soloviev pledged himself to three philosophical-theological projects: free theosophy, free theocracy and free theurgy. By the first he meant pure theoretical philosophy, the study of being, to which he applied himself in parts of his early works and in *Theoretical Philosophy* (1899) late in his career. He treated free theocracy in the theocratic and ecumenical works of his mid-career and in *The Justification of the Good*. He never wrote a theurgy, although one may see some of his essays on literature and esthetics as preliminary sketches. Bulgakov's *Philosophy of Economy* fills this gap in Soloviev's program. Taking economy

---

[1] Sergei Bulgakov, *Filosofiia khoziaistva* (Moscow: Izdatel'stvo 'Put'', 1912; reprint, New York: Chalidze Publications, 1982).
[2] *Filosofiia khoziaistva*, p. i.

as the basic paradigm of cultural activity, he constructs a Solovievian theurgy, that is to say, a philosophy of culture as a divine-human process.

Bulgakov planned *The Philosophy of Economy* as a two-part work. In the volume of 1912 he investigates 'the general foundations of the economic process, its ontology'; in the second volume he intended to deal with '*the justification of economy* – its axiology and eschatology,' including 'the problem of the relation of flesh and spirit (the ethics of economy) and the meaning of history and culture.' The second volume never appeared.[3] After 1912 Bulgakov dealt with his concerns under religious and theological rubrics rather than continuing with the philosophy of economy.

Some of these rubrics appear already in *The Philosophy of Economy*, notably sophiology. The Sophia chapter in *The Philosophy of Economy* is Bulgakov's first sustained essay of sophiology.[4] Since sophiology is the most notorious and least understood aspect of Bulgakov's theological legacy, his first sketch merits attention.

THE HUMANIZATION OF NATURE

For Bulgakov the philosophy of economy, like all philosophy, begins with wonder about reality, in this case wonder over 'the problem of human beings in nature and nature in human beings.'[5] How is it that human beings, who think of themselves as free agents, are so profoundly dependent on a nature which is external to them and not of their own making? At the same

---

[3] *Filosofiia khoziaistva*, p. iv. A fragment of the projected second half of *The Philosophy of Economy* appeared as a monograph comparing Platonist and Christian approaches to economics: *Osnovnye motivy filosofii khoziaistva v platonizme i rannem khristianstve*, vol. 1, pt 3 of *Istoriia ekonomicheskoi mysli*, eds V.Ia. Zheleznov and A.A. Manuilov (Moscow: Moskovskii nauchnyi institut, 1916).

[4] 'O transtsendental'nom sub"ekte khoziaistva,' *Filosofiia khoziaistva*, ch. 4. Some of the themes of Bulgakov's sophiology are adumbrated in his essay 'Nature in the Philosophy of Vladimir Soloviev' (1910): 'Priroda v filosofii Vl. Solov'eva,' in S.N. Bulgakov, *Sochineniia v dvukh tomakh*, eds S.S. Khoruzhii and I.B. Rodnianskaia, 2 vols (Moscow: Izdatel'stvo 'Nauka', 1993), 1:15–46.

[5] *Filosofiia khoziaistva*, p. i.

time, how is it that an ostensibly sovereign and all-encom-passing nature is subject to human influence and direction?

Wonder is not the only motive for the philosophy of economy. Another is the need to understand the economic materialism of modern civilization. The view that life is above all an economic process 'hypnotizes modern minds,' leading them to accept the science of economics as 'the authoritative law-giver' not only on economic matters but on other issues as well. Yet the grounds for this authority are not self-evident, for 'the science of economics is one of the most dependent and philosophically least independent of disciplines.' The gap between practical might and theoretical weakness demands philosophical treatment.[6]

Moreover, some of the commonest concepts in the science of economics stand in need of clarification, even though many economists do not realize it. The concept of wealth is a case in point. Economists agree their science analyzes and measures wealth. Yet the concept is hazy; it has the 'amorphousness and diffuseness which normally characterize our most vital concepts.' As a result the science of economics divides into conflicting schools of thought depending on how narrowly (Adam Smith) or broadly (List, Ruskin) wealth is defined.[7] The definition of labor is equally tricky, as Marx and others found out when they tried (and failed) to devise a labor theory of value.[8] A philosophy of economy is needed to define concepts, mediate between the schools and formulate the unity of the discipline.

The philosophy of economy also responds to the growing recognition by social scientists of the role of personal creativity in the shaping of an economy. Weber, Sombart and others have shown '*economy is a phenomenon of spiritual life* in the same measure as all other aspects of human activity and labor,' hence that one may speak of 'the *spirit of economy* (e.g. "the spirit of capitalism").'[9] Clearly the study of spirit involves something more than quantitative analysis of economic processes.

[6] *Filosofiia khoziaistva*, pp. 2–7.
[7] *Filosofiia khoziaistva*, pp. 275–9.
[8] *Filosofiia khoziaistva*, pp. 104–6.
[9] *Filosofiia khoziaistva*, p. 238.

Finally, in addition to the intellectual grounds for undertaking a philosophy of economy there is an existential reason. The philosophy of economy addresses the human predicament of living under the shadow 'of death, of dead mechanism, of oppressive necessity,' as a result of which life may appear to be 'some sort of accident, some sort of indulgence or condescension on the part of death.' People often take the apparent 'compatibility of life and death' for granted, speaking, for example, of their 'mortal life,' even though this phrase makes no more sense than 'hot ice' or 'black whiteness.'[10] Life is a continual struggle against death, as economic activity shows more clearly than anything else. Economy (*khoziaistvo*) in the broadest sense of the word is 'the struggle to protect, affirm and extend life against the hostile forces of nature, the effort to rule and tame them, to make oneself their *master* (*khoziain*).' Since true mastery entails not just external dominion but the assimilation of that which is mastered, the aim of the economic process in ideal terms may be said to be 'the transformation of the entire cosmic mechanism into a potential or actual organism by the overcoming of necessity by freedom, mechanism by organism, causality by teleology, as the *humanization of nature*.' How this end can be accomplished is not clear, however, because economic victories over necessity are partial and temporary. Moreover, despite its ideal aspect, economic activity remains '*a function of death*, called into being by the necessity of life to protect itself,' hence 'an unfree activity.'[11]

What is the fundamental question which the philosophy of economy attempts to answer? Bulgakov puts it in the idiom of Kantian idealism: '*How is economy possible?*' That is to say, what are the conditions which must be assumed in order to account for the phenomenon?[12] Now the basis of all economic activity is labor, 'the production or accumulation of vital goods, material or spiritual, as a result of *work*.' Labor, as distinct from instinct and free gifts, implies a complex interaction between human beings and the world; it envisages, implements and usually achieves a reshaping of the world. Another way of

---

[10] *Filosofiia khoziaistva*, pp. 38–40.
[11] *Filosofiia khoziaistva*, pp. 43–5.
[12] *Filosofiia khoziaistva*, p. 52.

asking how economy is possible, then, is to ask: 'How is objective influence possible? How is it that [human] will becomes a force that transforms objects?'[13]

It is obvious from the way in which Bulgakov addresses the philosophy of economy that he regards economic activity as something more than the manipulation and exploitation of material resources. He views it as creative activity, 'a continual modeling or projecting of reality,' like art or science.[14]

The philosophy of economy must do justice to all aspects of the phenomenon it studies: the embeddedness of human beings in nature, the creative freedom of human beings, and the responsiveness of nature to human initiative. Most approaches to the subject are too one-sided to meet this demand. Dogmatic materialism does justice to the dependence of human beings on nature but not to human freedom. Critical idealism does justice to the freedom of the human subject, but cannot make sense of the involvement of the subject in nature. Neither doctrine appreciates the responsiveness of nature to human creativity. What is needed is a philosophical position beyond dogmatism and criticism, which Bulgakov finds in the concrete idealism of Schelling and Soloviev. Schelling's two revolutionary ideas, 'the identity of subject and object, and the understanding of nature as a living, developing organism,' make it possible to see 'nature as unconscious spirit and spirit as nature that has become aware of itself.' This view corresponds with what we see happening at every moment in the economic process, namely, the interpenetration of subject and object, 'the constant passage from I to not-I' in an ongoing process of synthesis.[15] The identity of subject and object (spirit and nature) is not itself the product of economic activity, however, because every act of economy presupposes it; it is that which makes economy possible. Identity is a cosmic reality, an aspect of the way things are.

The philosophy of economy thus forms part of what Schelling

---

[13] *Filosofiia khoziaistva*, pp. 45–8, 69; cf. pp. 49–50, where Bulgakov equates his concept of 'objective influence' (*ob"ektivnoe deistvie*) with Marx's 'Praxis'; and p. 105, where he calls labor 'the supreme principle of economic life.'
[14] *Filosofiia khoziaistva*, p. 95.
[15] *Filosofiia khoziaistva*, pp. 59–60, 95.

called *Naturphilosophie*, the philosophy of nature or cosmic process:

The problem of 'economic materialism' – the effect of economy and, in it, of nature on human beings, and of human beings in their turn on economy and, in it, on nature – is above all a problem of *Naturphilosophie*, and only as a result of a philosophical misunderstanding does the Marxist school take the idealist intellectualist Hegel for its godfather, not recognizing that the *Naturphilosoph* Schelling is incomparably more suitable for its purposes.[16]

Bulgakov will not make the same mistake. As a Christian philosopher he is ready to recognize the promise of the Schellingian approach in any case because 'Schelling, in the philosophical language of his time, expressed one of the most fundamental truths of Christianity,' namely, 'its doctrine of the human being as *incarnate spirit*, as a living unity of [spirit and flesh].' This is the view on which 'the possibility of the deification of the flesh accomplished by the incarnation of God is based.' As the religion of the incarnation Christianity stands 'equally far from both materialism and subjective idealism' but naturally gravitates toward the concrete idealism of Schelling and Soloviev.[17]

The affinity between concrete idealism and the theology of incarnation provides the conceptual basis for some of Bulgakov's boldest suggestions about Christianity and economy in *The Philosophy of Economy*. As he sees it, Christianity is the quintessential economic religion; economic activity, the primordial incarnational enterprise.

These connections stand out in Bulgakov's analysis of the two most basic economic activities: consumption and production. Consumption in all its forms manifests 'the physical communism of being' and 'metaphysical unity' of the consumer with the world.[18] In every act of consumption the consumer assimilates a portion of the world to himself, thereby manifesting also his incorporation in the world. In a sense the consumer and the consumed actually become each other. In an elementary act of

---

[16] *Filosofiia khoziaistva*, p. 74.
[17] *Filosofiia khoziaistva*, p. 65.
[18] *Filosofiia khoziaistva*, pp. 76, 85.

consumption such as eating, for example, human beings participate in '*a natural communion, a partaking of the flesh of the world.*'[19] By patterning its supreme sacrament on eating and drinking Christianity confirms its prefiguration in the natural history of the human race, affirms its solidarity with the everyday world and prefigures the transformation of all flesh into the eschatological spiritual body of the future.

Production also is incarnational. Every productive act involves envisioning some sort of impact on nature and attempting to realize that vision in an object of some kind – a tool, for example. Technology is the sum of these objects. In classical economic thought technology is much discussed but poorly understood because of a one-sided concern with technical details and the applied aspects of technology, i.e. with the tools themselves as distinct from technological production as a whole. When one focuses on the art as a whole one sees that it relies on the responsiveness of nature to human initiative and human ends.

While absolute attunement between human beings and nature is an 'immeasurably distant' prospect, it remains the goal, 'the eschatology of economy.' In other words, economic production implies faith in a common destiny for nature and human beings: '*Nature is being humanized*, it has the capacity to become the peripheral body of human beings, submitting to their consciousness and in them becoming conscious of itself.' The idea is comparable to Paul's vision of the liberation of the cosmos from its bondage to futility and death through the revelation of the children of God (Rom. 8:19–21). Every productive act is a foreshadowing and partial consummation of that liberation. 'In economy, in the conscious re-production of nature, one can see a prototype, a prefiguration of that liberation of *natura naturans* from the fetters of *natura naturata* in its current state.'[20]

In a famous poem Wordsworth suggested that contemplation of nature prompts intimations of immortality. For Bulgakov, one could say, contemplation of economy – of human beings at work in nature – prompts intimations of the humanity of God.

[19] *Filosofiia khoziaistva*, p. 84.
[20] *Filosofiia khoziaistva*, pp. 106–8.

NATURE, CULTURE AND SOPHIA

Bulgakov's meditations on the humanization of nature lead directly to sophiology, the investigation of divine Wisdom. The concept of Sophia is moored to the central argument of *The Philosophy of Economy*. The argument, as we have seen, is that the cultural process is concerned with the humanization of nature, the transformation of the cosmos into the humanity of God (theosis). We have noted also that, while theosis is an eschatological reality, intimations of it are given in the cosmicizing, transformative works of culture. Sophiology is the enterprise of gathering, sorting and synthesizing these intimations in an ever-expanding appreciation of the humanity of God.

Sophia is 'the transcendental subject of economy.'[21] That is to say, Sophia is Bulgakov's name for that which accounts for the unity and coherence of the cultural process in all fields, including economics, politics, science and the arts. Although the process is unfinished, human agents must believe it is basically coherent, for without this assumption they would be incapable of sustaining creative work. Sophiology is the systematic expression of this faith.

In elaborating a sophiology Bulgakov continues in the tradition of Soloviev and Schelling. Unwilling to accept the Neo-Kantian reduction of the transcendental subject of human culture to 'the epistemological subject,' much less to the isolated individual, and of course refusing to eliminate the need for a transcendental subject by acquiescing before the blind force preached by materialists, Bulgakov posits a super-individual ground of humanity, a human hypostasis in God:

> *There is one who knows, the many come to know.* This one, this transcendental subject of knowledge, is of course not the human individual but humanity as a whole, the World Soul, Divine Sophia, the Pleroma, Natura Naturans – by various names and in various guises it presents itself in the history of thought.

'World steward' (*khoziain, oikonomos*) and 'demiurge' are additional names. The fluidity of the terminology, a feature also

---

[21] *Filosofiia khoziaistva*, pp. 109–59.

of Soloviev's sophiology, allows Bulgakov to annex a variety of thinkers to the presumed sophiological tradition, including Plato, Plotinus, Dionysius the Pseudo-Areopagite, Maximus the Confessor, Gregory of Nyssa, John Scotus Erigena, Jacob Boehme, Franz Baader, Schelling, Vladimir Soloviev and S.N. Trubetskoi.[22] But Sophia is the pre-eminent name not just because it is biblical – the predictable references to Proverbs 8, Wisdom 9 and other sapiential texts follow shortly – but because the name best fits the specific task of sophiology. Sophiology evaluates cultural creativity, the production of wisdom. It is not a purely speculative enterprise tacked on to cultural pursuits. On the contrary, '*human creativity* – in knowledge, in economy, in culture, in art – is *sophianic*,' i.e. sophianic already.[23] Sophiology is not a gnostic quest for truths beyond the world but reflection on creative processes taking place within the world. It does not warrant an ethic of detachment or stillness (*hesychia*) but 'an ethic of joyful and creative labor,' as Evtuhov puts it.[24]

While Russian sophiology is concerned with culture in general, I have argued that it is bound up with the challenges of modern civilization in particular. The fact that Bulgakov's sophiology emerges from the study of economics, one of the new sciences of modern times, offers corroborating evidence for my thesis. Bulgakov's own assessment of his cultural situation is another piece of evidence. In *The Philosophy of Economy* he observes that while economic activity 'creates culture' at all times and in all places,

> our generation has been seized by this creative impulse especially forcefully, [and] all limits defining the possible are being lost. 'The world is plastic,' it may be recreated, and even in a variety of ways. Our children will live under different conditions than we do, and as for our grandchildren we cannot even begin to guess ... We are impressed by the growing might of an economy which opens up boundless perspectives for 'the creation of culture.' And so that we

---

[22] *Filosofiia khoziaistva*, pp. 119–20.
[23] *Filosofiia khoziaistva*, p. 139.
[24] *The Cross and the Sickle*, p. 155.

might relate with philosophical awareness to this doubtless grand and majestic fact which stands before the modern Oedipus as the riddle of the Sphinx – at times a sinister sign, at other times a prophetic augury – we must first of all answer for ourselves the question: what exactly is this human 'creation' of culture and economy, how and by what power do human beings create here?[25]

Bulgakov weighs three different answers to the riddle of modern civilization. The first is that modernity represents 'the coming of age of humanity,' the end of humanity's tutelage to nature and tradition. The second is that modern civilization and its works are 'wonders of the Anti-Christ,' an attempt to usurp the power and prerogatives of the creator. The third is that modernity is an evolutionary accident which may be superseded by some other accident in the future, such as the emergence of a Superman.[26] Eliminating the last (Nietzschean) answer as extremely dubious, Bulgakov divides his attention between the other two. That is to say, he embraces the classic problem of Orthodox renewalists beginning with Archimandrite Feodor: how to reconcile an ecclesiastical culture which regards modern civilization in hostile terms ('wonders of the Anti-Christ') with a secularist culture which asserts human rights without reverence for nature or God. Sophiology deals with this problem by offering a theonomous interpretation of cultural creativity, that is, by relating cultural activity in all fields to its ground in the humanity of God.

Sophiology also serves to justify Bulgakov's progressive Christianity. In 'Heroism and Humility' Bulgakov rejects utopianism but leaves room for a progressivism based on faith in Providence.

---

[25] *Filosofiia khoziaistva*, p. 135. Gachev, too, sees the need to read Bulgakov's sophiology in terms of the existential concerns that motivated it. 'The word-enigma "Sophia" will only lead us into a labyrinth of scholasticism (if we begin with it); but if we come to it with some sense for what Sergei Bulgakov the man and thinker lived for, if we understand what pained him, what he loved, what he wanted – then even this will readily be cleared up.' Contrasting Bulgakov with the aristocratic Berdiaev, Gachev sees Bulgakov as concerned above all with sanctifying the earth and walking humbly with his God in everyday life. 'Bulgakov's philosophy is the worldview of a Russian peasant-farmer lifted to the very heights of intellect.' *Russkaia duma*, pp. 223, 227.

[26] *Filosofiia khoziaistva*, pp. 135–6.

As an Orthodox Christian, however, Bulgakov could scarcely be expected to settle for abstract providentialism – the inscrutable Providence of Calvinism, for example. Sophiology cosmicizes Providence:

> Sophia directs history as Providence, as its objective conformity with law, as the law of progress (which the positivist sociologists try so unsuccessfully to ground empirically). Only the sophianic character of history guarantees that something will come of it, that [history] will bear some sort of general result, that the integral of these endlessly differentiating series is a possibility.

Sophia is what Hegel called 'the cunning of reason' which lures all things to fulfillment.[27] By providing a theonomous (Soloviev's 'theurgic') analysis of human creativity, sophiology empowers progressive Christianity to break the stale-mate between secularist autonomy and traditionalist heteronomy.

The pertinence of sophiology to the engagement of Orthodoxy with the modern world explains Bulgakov's abiding enthusiasm for it. But like all solutions sophiology generates new problems. The most glaring is the problem of reconciling the cosmism of sophiological faith with the anti-cosmic phenomena in the world, such as disorder, evil, sin and finitude. Sophia performs the 'synthesizing function thanks to which unity is introduced in diversity and connectedness in multiplicity' in the world.[28] Yet the world is not a harmonious whole, not yet a perfect cosmos. Why not? Where does the resistance to Sophia come from?

A second problem concerns the impact of anti-cosmic resistance on the integrity of Sophia. In order to shape the world process, Sophia must enter into it, she 'must be "subjected to the futility of decay" that hangs over all creation.' But since Sophia-in-bondage is not perfect Sophia, a distinction must be made between 'extra-temporal, heavenly Sophia and empirical Sophia, [between] metaphysical and historical humanity.'[29] The motive for this distinction is clear, but not the distinction itself,

---

[27] *Filosofiia khoziaistva*, p. 157.
[28] *Filosofiia khoziaistva*, pp. 121–2.
[29] *Filosofiia khoziaistva*, pp. 122, 150.

which appears to undermine the unity and coherence of Sophia, in effect to de-cosmicize her.

Predictably, Bulgakov looks to the theology of incarnation for answers to these questions. Unlike Plato, whose doctrine of eros expressed but could not fulfill the desire for union between the two Sophias, Christians know 'the living link' to be 'Christ the incarnate Logos, whose body is the Church, heavenly Sophia.'[30] Yet while this declaration indicates the way in which Christians might approach the questions raised, it does not really answer them. It simply translates the problem from sophiological into ecclesiological terms. One must still ask how the church, the body of Christ, relates to the ongoing world process, the continuing history of empirical humanity. In other words, the problematics of engagement appear again, albeit in more nuanced terms than those employed by anti-secular traditionalists and doctrinaire secularists.

Another challenge to sophiology concerns the conformity between creative activity and Christian piety. Like Soloviev before him, Bulgakov would have sophiology be a branch of christology in that Christ is the link between heavenly and earthly Sophia. Yet Bulgakov sometimes models the protagonist of the sophiological drama on other prototypes. He compares earthly Sophia to 'the bright hero and demigod' Heracles cleaning the Augean stables, to Prometheus struggling 'with a capricious, despotic governor of the world,' to Siegfried contesting 'the dark forces of universal fate,' to Orpheus liberating Euridice from Hades.[31] To the extent that all of these heroes suffer for a divine or at least a cosmic cause, they resemble the suffering Messiah. Yet the likeness is not strong enough to establish these heroes as types of Christ or models of Christian piety – least of all, one should think, for the author of 'Heroism and Humility.' *The Philosophy of Economy* thus stands in an ironic relation to Bulgakov's famous essay of 1909: the heroes expelled there rush in again here. Heracles, Orpheus and the others might be more attractive role-models than utopian revolutionaries, but they are heroes all the same. They

---

[30] *Filosofiia khoziaistva*, pp. 150–1.
[31] *Filosofiia khoziaistva*, pp. 122–4.

are not the Lamb of God. Clearly Bulgakov has not thought through his sophiology to the end.

Then there is the problem of the Anti-Christ. Revisiting the theme of 'Heroism and Humility,' Bulgakov distinguishes between 'two religions: the divinity of humanity [*chelovekobozhie*], for which the human being is not a creature but a creator, and Christianity, for which the human being is a creature but, as a child of God, receives the mission of re-creation, of stewardship in the creation of his Father.' Bulgakov recognizes the creative power of human beings 'can be darkened by the spirit of satanism, can lose the awareness of its true character and lead to human satanism, to Anti-Christ.' He promises to explore the problem in his projected study of the eschatology of economy.[32] In *The Philosophy of Economy*, however, the ambiguity persists. It is inherent in the very proposition of modernism as Bulgakov states it: 'the world is plastic.' How far should this idea be pushed? In Bulgakov's day, after all, there were intellectuals who believed that even God was plastic – Nietzscheans, for example, and the utopian 'god-builders' (*bogostroiteli*) on the romantic fringe of the Bolshevik party. One could even argue the Solovievian concept of theurgy, reflecting willy-nilly its roots in magic, implies the plasticity of the divine, thereby reinforcing the ambiguity of creativity in the sophiological tradition. In a world where Anti-Christ is at large, this ambiguity is a dangerous thing, for the Adversary is, among other things, the supreme manipulator of divine things.

Bulgakov tries to address some of these difficulties with the help of Schelling's celebrated essay, *Philosophical Inquiries Into the Nature of Human Freedom* (1809). There Schelling offered a theory of the pretemporal fall or self-alienation of Sophia-Humanity from the divine ground of being and interpreted the cosmo-historical process as the drama of alienated Sophia's struggle to be reunited with her heavenly ground. Schelling's essay helps Bulgakov to be more precise about the nature of the problems which confront his sophiology, but it does not solve them. The crucial question – how to bridge the gulf between heavenly and earthly Sophia – remains unanswered, as Bulgakov has the candor to admit: 'The question of the relation

---

[32] *Filosofiia khoziaistva*, pp. 141, 145.

between the metaphysical fall of the world-soul and the fall of the first human being is one of the most difficult for religio-metaphysical speculation (it remained obscure in both Schelling and Vl. Soloviev).' Less admirable is his next sentence: 'For our discussion this question does not have independent and decisive significance, and consequently we prefer to leave it aside.'[33] Like it or not, the question does have decisive significance for what Bulgakov is trying to do. If a convincing answer cannot be found, sophiology as a speculative project must fail.

PHILOSOPHY AND FAITH

While Bulgakov averted his eyes from the most glaring flaws of his sophiology, he seems to have recognized that if he wanted to continue with the project he would have to come up with a fresh approach. At the end of the sophiology chapter of *The Philosophy of Economy*, for example, he suggests moving from a philosophy of 'discursive, theoretical knowledge based on the dichotomy of subject and object' to a Schellingian 'philosophy of revelation' based on the mythology and symbols of religious traditions. The philosophy of revelation deals with the glimpses of Sophia which have been afforded to saints and seers:

> The accounts of saints' lives are full of these visions of Truth. But the latter are not unknown to the non-Christian world, either, in the persons of thinkers and holy people of exceptionally intense religious contemplation (Plotinus' light, Socrates' 'daimon,' Buddhist monks' and Brahmins' experience, etc.).[34]

Presumably the collation and systematization of these insights will produce a more satisfactory sophiology than the one in *The Philosophy of Economy*. In any case Bulgakov recognized that the sophiological project had to be pursued in closer relation to positive religion.

Bulgakov's respect for positive religion grew rapidly after his return to the practice of Orthodoxy, as can be seen in his essay

---

[33] *Filosofiia khoziaistva*, p. 150, n. 1.
[34] *Filosofiia khoziaistva*, pp. 157–9.

of 1908, 'On Early Christianity.'[35] In this article he sought to refute the notion that the earliest form of the gospel was a rational ethical teaching which the church subsequently mystified. This view was popular among liberal and radical intellectuals of the day because it opened the way to presenting Jesus as a proto-socialist, or a prophet of Tolstoyanism, or a preacher of some other modern ideology. Through studying the New Testament, the latest western biblical criticism and especially the work of S.N. Trubetskoi, Bulgakov came to see that Christianity was from the beginning a positive religious phenomenon with dogmatic content.[36] 'The first Christians had a genuine, immediate experience of Divinity, they felt themselves to be in real and immediate communion with Christ, they burned with the joy of adoring the Risen One.' Moreover, in making this observation about the early church Bulgakov came to see that it applies to Christians of all eras, including his own:

I stop, for I sense that here I am approaching the limit of what can be expressed in words or should be treated in print. To lift the veil and approach that which is ordinarily so distant from us, look more attentively into the faces of those who were in living communion with heaven, in whom you sensed this incomprehensible power. In their brief, modest, restrained descriptions of what they experienced, in their religious experience, you will see the power of early Christianity. And even if we abandon these heights bathed in heavenly light to which only the chosen ascend and turn instead to everyday religion, we have only to look around us a little more

[35] Sergei Bulgakov, 'O pervokhristianstve: o tom, chto bylo v nem i chego ne bylo. Opyt kharakteristiki,' *Dva grada: issledovaniia o prirode obshchestvennykh idealov*, 2 vols (Moscow: Tovarishchestvo tipografii A.I. Mamontova, 1911), 1: 234–303.
[36] In his important essay 'Ethics and Dogmatics' Sergei Trubetskoi (1862–1905) criticized the anti-dogmatic approach of Ritschl, Harnack and Russian moralists such as Tolstoy who postulated a fundamental disjunction between the religion of Jesus and the religion of the church. Like Soloviev in *Three Dialogues*, Trubetskoi argued that the essence of Christianity is Christ himself and the relationship between God and humankind established in and through him. See 'Etika i dogmatika,' in *Sobranie sochinenii Kn. Sergeia Nikolaevicha Trubetskogo* (Moscow: Tipografiia G. Lissnera i D. Sobko, 1908), 2:134–60. See Bulgakov's tribute to Trubetskoi: 'Filosofiia kn. S.N. Trubetskogo i dukhovnaia bor'ba sovremennosti,' *Dva grada*, 2:243–54.

attentively to see points of light here, too, however weak and broken. Who has not seen, in some dark corner of a church or even in the midst of everyday life, living faith and dedication to God in simplicity, humility and tears?[37]

As we have seen, the problem that undoes speculative sophiology is the difficulty of conceptualizing the link between heavenly and creaturely Sophia, which is to say the link between the eternal humanity of God and actual human beings. The problem is as challenging for positive religion as it is for religious philosophy, but it is approached there in a different way, a way so homely and common that uncommon minds tend to overlook it. Ordinary religious people deal with the difficulty of imagining the link between God and the world by means of 'living faith,' to use Bulgakov's words in the passage just cited. That is to say, ordinary believers are justified by faith. They believe where they cannot prove, trust where they do not understand, accept the fact they see divine things through a glass darkly. Historically speaking, faith is the sturdiest mediator between heaven and earth in the middle-world inhabited by human beings, steadier by far than philosophical speculation. Admittedly, living by faith amounts to less than bathing in divine light, but it is more than groping in the dark. Moreover, the limits of faith's theoretical horizon do not vitiate its moral and spiritual worth. Drawing on Bulgakov's distinction in 'Heroism and Humility,' one might say that if speculation assumes the role of 'hero' in the quest for religious insight, faith takes the part of the *podvizhnik*.

In *The Unfading Light*, published in 1917, Bulgakov presents his philosophy of revelation. True to his new appreciation for the life of faith, he tells us in the author's preface his book is comprised of 'contemplations connected with [my] life in Orthodoxy.' The incorporation of brief but significant autobiographical pages deepens the work's existential coloring.[38]

---

[37] 'O pervokhristianstve,' p. 293.
[38] See Ch. 10, notes 34 and 57 above. Bulgakov took the title of *Svet nevechernii* (lit. the non-evening light) from a beautiful poem by the lay theologian Aleksei Khomiakov. The poet describes a radiant nightfall in language redolent of the Song of Simeon and other elements of Orthodox Vespers. 'The Gracious Light' would have comparable resonance in an Anglican setting.

In general, however, *The Unfading Light* is not a confessional or autobiographical work. Moreover, Bulgakov's claim in the preface that the volume is no more than 'a motley collection of chapters' (a phrase from Pushkin) is authorial posing. *The Unfading Light* has a clear systematic design. At least in outline it is the sort of 'critique of religious reason' the author identifies as the logical aspiration of post-Kantian religious philosophy.[39] The book opens with a well-organized prolegomenon in which basic terms in the phenomenology of religion (religion, faith, dogma, myth, etc.) are defined and major problems in the modern philosophy of religion are described. The body of the work is founded on the distinction between two types of theology: negative or apophatic theology, which reflects upon the divine transcendence, upon the unknowable God who forever remains 'a NO-thing (and a NO-how, and NO-where, and NO-when, and NO-why)' to the human mind; and positive or kataphatic theology, which examines the revelation of God in the creation and salvation of the world.

For obvious reasons Bulgakov spends less time talking about apophatic theology than about its counterpart, for how can one describe or systematize that which is in principle unknowable? However, the history of apophatic theology may be described. Beginning with Plato and ending with Jacob Boehme, Bulgakov catalogs the themes and tensions of apophasis, taking pains to distance himself from the 'impersonalism' to which some apophatic theologians incline. He also makes the important observation that the practitioners of apophatic theology were for the most part God-intoxicated thinkers who enriched the 'No' of apophasis with 'a mystical YES' that kept them within the household of faith. Were it otherwise, apophatic theology would be indistinguishable from atheism or agnosticism, leaving nothing but 'a gaping void' in its wake.[40]

The discussion of kataphatic theology in *The Unfading Light* (Parts 2 and 3) is cut from a fairly conventional pattern, although certain parts of it show a more original design. Bulgakov begins by discussing the creation of the world *ex nihilo*, proceeds to the creation of human beings (the First

[39] *Svet nevechernii*, p. 27.
[40] *Svet nevechernii*, p. 94.

Adam), next to the salvation of humanity (the Second Adam) and finally to the theology of history, including some remarks on the pathos of modern civilization. Needless to say, this is a lot of ground to cover in about two hundred pages, but it conforms with Bulgakov's ambition to outline a comprehensive philosophy of revelation. The outline is not without its defects. Particularly surprising is the paucity of space devoted to the discussion of salvation (the Second Adam) and the virtual absence of the Solovievian concept of the humanity of God.

This last fact should not be taken to mean Bulgakov was tiring of the Solovievian tradition. Rather, he seems to have used *The Unfading Light* as an occasion to give himself an education in the primary sources that inspired Soloviev. Soloviev's preferences are evident in the heavy representation of mystical and gnostic theologians in Bulgakov's theological reading list and in the focus on German Idealist philosophy of religion. As one might expect, Bulgakov devotes the most sustained attention to Schelling's *Philosophy of Revelation* (1841–2), but he is also concerned to fix his position in relation to Kant, Hegel, Schleiermacher and Hartmann.[41] What emerges from this exercise is a Bulgakov still standing in the Solovievian tradition but able to express that tradition in a more general idiom.

Sophiology finds a prominent place in *The Unfading Light*, where it serves to complement and also to complicate Bulgakov's discussion of the createdness of the cosmos. The doctrine of Sophia qualifies the traditional theology of creation *ex nihilo* by positing a heavenly dynamic as immanent in the creaturely world. A more complex theology of creation thereby emerges, since the cosmos is viewed as being governed not just by the condescension of the divine in creation and salvation but by the heavenwards aspiration of all creatures. This two-way energeticism, as it might be called, is one of the most distinctive features of *The Unfading Light* and the one which most directly connects the book to *The Philosophy of Economy*.

Yet if one looks to *The Unfading Light* for a resolution of the

---

[41] Bulgakov calls *Philosophy of Revelation* Schelling's 'most accomplished and thoroughly articulated system,' *Svet nevechernii*, p. 129. He appropriates Schelling critically, however. For instance he rejects Schelling's (and Soloviev's) ambition to 'deduce' trinitarian dogma (pp. 173–5).

theoretical impasse which stalled Bulgakov's sophiology in the earlier work, one will not find it. The old problem reappears in a new form. In *The Philosophy of Economy* Bulgakov tries to bridge the gap between God and the world by distinguishing between 'heavenly' and 'creaturely' Sophia, in effect splitting Sophia in two. In *The Unfading Light* he preserves Sophia's integrity, presenting her as an undivided 'fourth hypostasis' of the divine life, a manifestation of divinity *ad extra*, standing outside the Trinity and facing creation. As soon as he starts to apply this concept, however, he reaps a harvest of contradictions. He refuses to admit Sophia to the inner life of the Trinity (which would explode Orthodox doctrine) yet insists Sophia is 'uncreated.' He denies Sophia is 'the Absolute or God' yet claims 'she has what she has immediately from God or *in an absolute manner.*' He claims Sophia transcends temporality yet exists in 'sophianic time ... *eternal time*, as one can say without fear of contradictio in adjecto.' He avers that Sophia occupies 'a *middle* position between time and eternity.'[42] In all these cases one can see that Bulgakov has safeguarded the integrity of Sophia at the cost of stranding her in a metaphysical limbo between the divine and creaturely worlds. Seeking to make Sophia the crucial link in the philosophy of revelation, Bulgakov has in fact disconnected her on all sides.

To appreciate Bulgakov's Sophia-problem and the direction his sophiology took after *The Unfading Light*, we must return to my thesis about the nature of modern Russian sophiology. I have suggested sophiology be read as a representation, virtually a dramatization, of Orthodoxy's struggle to engage with the modern world. *The Unfading Light* offers strong corroborating evidence for this view, beginning with the terms in which Bulgakov presents the book to his readers:

> Difficult is the path through modernity [*sovremennost'*] to Orthodoxy and back again. Yet can we free ourselves of all difficulty, and should we be trying to free ourselves from it? As passionately as I thirst for a grand simplicity, for its pure light, I just as heartily reject false and self-deceptive simplification, flight from one's spiritual destiny, from one's

---

[42] *Svet nevechernii*, pp. 185–9.

historical cross. As a seeker of religious unity of life, [a unity] sought but not yet possessed, do I step forward in this book. The spirit of modernity is ulcerated by problems and exhausted by doubts; nevertheless, faith is not waning in her heart, hope still shines. And we see that in this painful complexity a religious opportunity awaits us, a particular task is given, [a task] appropriate to our historical stage of growth; and this whole problematic of ours with its presentiments and portents is a shadow cast by Him that cometh [*Griadushchim*]. To become aware of oneself and one's historical legacy in Orthodoxy and through Orthodoxy, with all one's historical flesh, to attempt to grasp [Orthodoxy's] age-old truth through the prism of the modern world and to see the latter in its light – such is the burning, ineradicable need which we have clearly felt since the 19th century; and the longer it continues, the more acute it becomes.[43]

While this passage alone suffices to orient *The Unfading Light* to the concern for Orthodox engagement with the world, Bulgakov presses the point even further. He observes that modern spiritual life is pervaded by 'immanentism.' Unchecked, immanentism ends in one or another kind of pantheism which contradicts the substance of Orthodox dogma. Nevertheless, immanentism must not be summarily dismissed. Immanentism, by affirming the inherent value of the world, provides a necessary corrective to the spirit of world-denial which 'so easily works its way into Orthodox consciousness,' infecting the latter with a one-sided 'transcendentism.' The vocation of modern religious thought is 'to unite the truth of both [immanentism and transcendentism], to discover not "a synthesis" but the living unity [between them], to know God in the world and the world in God.' Bulgakov concedes this task is difficult and can lead to neurotic 'Hamletism,' or division of mind. But modern believers must rise to the occasion, knowing that 'what is impossible for human beings is possible for God.'[44]

The apparent contradiction between immanentism and transcendentism, besides bedeviling the relations between

---

[43] *Svet nevechernii*, p. 3.
[44] *Svet nevechernii*, pp. 5–6.

Orthodoxy and modern secularism, is also precisely the problem which plagues Bulgakov's sophiology. His persistence in sophiology against the logical odds, so to speak, can thus be seen as a gauge of his determination not to abandon the engagement of Orthodoxy with modernity.

That we are dealing with an integral, not accidental connection between sophiology and engagement with the modern world can be inferred from an imaginative neologism employed by Bulgakov in the sophiological chapters of *The Unfading Light*: 'cosmodicy'. Bulgakov introduces the term while discussing Plato's theory of forms, which he regards as the first sophiology. The discovery of the sophianic nature of the world is 'the essence of the cosmodicy of Platonism.'[45] Bulgakov's terminology clearly shows what sophiology is about: not theodicy, the justification of the ways of God to human beings; but cosmodicy, the justification of the world to the guardians of divine truth. Adumbrated by Plato and the biblical Wisdom tradition, cosmodicy comes into its own in modern times when the creaturely world, with modern secularism as its tribune, steps forward to claim its rights.[46]

Seeing the connection between sophiology and the engagement of Orthodoxy with the modern world opens the way to a fresh diagnosis of the conceptual problems of sophiology. Perhaps Bulgakov's difficulties resulted from trying to solve a practical or existential problem by purely theoretical means, that is to say, by applying speculative sophiology to a set of problems which cannot be settled by speculation in any case. Ironically, by the time Bulgakov wrote *The Unfading Light* he had already grasped this point to some extent, but he had not yet applied it to his sophiology. He had come to appreciate the pivotal role of faith in religious life but did not yet see that he needed to exchange his would-be theoretical sophiology for a sophiology justified by faith. To put it another way, Bulgakov did not heed his own advice when he invited modern religious

[45] *Svet nevechernii*, p. 189.
[46] S.S. Khoruzhii is right to observe 'the fundamental motive of Bulgakov's philosophical thought is *the justification of the world* – the convinced, often passionate affirmation of the value and coherence of earthly life and the material cosmos.' *Posle pereryva*, p. 76. The same insight led L.A. Zander to entitle his magisterial study of Bulgakov *Bog i mir* (God and the World).

philosophers 'to discover not "a synthesis" but a living unity' between immanentism and transcendentism. If theoretical sophiology as Bulgakov had been practicing it were to succeed, that is to say, if the link between God and the world could be fully intellectualized, then 'a synthesis' would in fact be achieved. Bulgakov cannot have it both ways. Religious philosophy cannot be justified by faith and by *theoria* at the same time.

Far from being destructive of Bulgakov's sophiology, these observations suggest a better way of going about it. The key lies in recognizing a definitive synthesis of Orthodoxy and modernity would not be desirable in any case because such a thing would surely produce a new stasis, a new formula for stagnation. What is needed instead is a dialogue, which differs from a synthesis in being justified by faith, not works; by a fruitful, expanding yet forever unfinished conversation about divine and human things, not by gnosis.

To be sure, Bulgakov is not the only modern religious philosopher who fails to heed his own best insights into the dynamics of faith. To a significant degree he inherited his difficulties from the philosophy of revelation which he borrowed from Schelling and Soloviev. Philosophy of revelation suffers from ambiguity with respect to its theoretical ambitions. To the extent that it gathers, compares and systematizes the data of positive religion, philosophy of revelation generates a phenomenology of religion; but a phenomenology of religion is not a system of theological truths. If, on the other hand, philosophy of revelation claims to generate a body of theological truths, one may ask about the basis of the truth claim. Are the truths of revelation justified on the basis of theoretical argument? If so, then philosophy of revelation turns out to be a handmaiden of theoretical philosophy, theoretical philosophy sits as the arbiter of theological truth, and one may wonder why anyone should speak of a philosophy of *revelation*. If, on the other hand, the truths of revelation are established by extra-theoretical means – taken seriously as divine revelation, for example, or existentially justified – then philosophy of revelation should not present itself as a purely speculative or theoretical enterprise. In this case one may ask why anyone should speak of a *philosophy* of revelation – rather than dogmatic theology, for example.

The prospect of dogmatic theology is of course the clue to the path which Bulgakov eventually took. Already in *The Unfading Light* there are passages where the author finds himself heading in this direction. The assessment of Sophia as a 'fourth hypostasis' of the divine life is an instance which has already been cited. But Bulgakov was not yet prepared to handle himself on the terrain of dogmatic theology because he did not conceive of *The Unfading Light* in a way that gave dogma its due.

The formal definitions of dogma and related terms in *The Unfading Light* are not the problem; in fact, these serve to document Bulgakov's budding interest in dogmatics. He already knows, for example, that '*all religion is dogmatic,* [that] it establishes a relation not to Divinity in general, but to a definite God who has his own "name." ' He knows that 'faith is not abstract, but concrete, which means that *faith necessarily generates dogma* of one sort or another; or conversely, [that] dogma is the formula of that which is identified by faith as transcendent being.' In short Bulgakov sees that dogma is the idiom of faith.[47] What *The Unfading Light* lacks is not respect for dogma but the actual practice of dogmatics. The occasional references to the discipline are woefully inadequate, as when Bulgakov describes dogmatics as 'the external systematization of dogmas' or 'the compiling of an inventory' of dogmas, descriptions which construe dogmatics as a mechanical operation devoid of creativity. More promising is Bulgakov's hope that his philosophy of revelation will end in what he calls 'critical dogmatism,' which seems to promise a more creative approach.[48] But it is hard to see how critical dogmatism can get very far before dogmatics as such enters the picture; or to put it another way, how a philosophy of revelation can complete its work before revelation is more adequately represented than it is in *The Unfading Light.*

This assessment does not necessarily imply that dogmatics, when it makes its appearance, will eliminate the need for philosophy of revelation. The outcome depends on how the philosophy of revelation is conceived. If it is conceived as an autonomous, self-authenticating discipline, then conflict with

---

[47] *Svet nevechernii*, pp. 50–7.
[48] *Svet nevechernii*, p. 82.

dogmatics is inevitable. The weakness of *The Unfading Light* in systematic terms lies here, for Bulgakov does appear to practice philosophy of revelation as an autonomous discipline. This results in a dilemma paralleling the familiar problem of his theoretical sophiology: as Sophia hangs in metaphysical limbo between God and the world, so philosophy of revelation hangs in methodological limbo between philosophy and theology. If on the other hand, philosophy of revelation is conceived as the construction of a dialogical matrix, a set of rules, procedures and agenda for the conversation between dogmatics and philosophy (and the other human sciences), then a polarizing conflict is avoided. For the dialogue to begin, however, dogmatic theology has to enter the field.

When dogmatic theology joins the conversation, it enters the force-field of modern 'creativity.' That is to say, when dogmatic theologians enter into dialogue with partners from secular vocations and the human sciences, they must practice their discipline in a way that differs in some respects from traditional approaches to the subject. For example, they have to embrace the project of dialogue with modern civilization in the first place and must be willing to carry that project into dogmatics itself, the inner sanctum of theology. The humanist side, too, is challenged by the dialogical situation. So, for example, approaches to the humanities relying on a methodological *cordon sanitaire* excluding religious faith must be rejected. As a result of these adjustments, the dialogue catalyzed by the philosophy of revelation ceases to be an exchange of mutually unintelligible views about divine and human things and becomes a divine-human conversation. Mirroring the humanity of God, the conversation challenges each side in a distinctive way. Theology is challenged to orient itself not just to divine things, not just to God as it were, but to the humanity of God. The other side is challenged to deal not just with human things, but with God-filled humanity. The goal is an irenic collaboration of the two sides, without division or confusion.

Bulgakov devoted the last phase of his remarkable career to dogmatic theology, producing a large body of work culminating in the trilogy *On the Humanity of God* (1933–45). By undertaking a dogmatics of the humanity of God, Bulgakov embarked on a project which had not been attempted before in the history of Orthodoxy. He fostered a new level of integration in Orthodox theology by weaving Solovievian and other modern ideas with traditional patristic themes in a bold new theological corpus.

Exactly when Bulgakov decided to devote himself to dogmatic theology is debatable. Because of the catastrophes of revolution, war and exile that separate the lay religious philosopher of 1917 from the priestly dogmatic theologian of the 1920s and 1930s, one is naturally tempted to construe Bulgakov's late career as a break with all that came before it. Such a view is valid to the extent that the Bulgakov of 1917 could not possibly have imagined the circumstances in which he would be working in 1927 when he published his first dogmatic works. With respect to the inner logic and systematic needs of his thought, however, Bulgakov's turn to dogmatics was a natural step after *The Unfading Light*, a step which he might have taken even earlier if his life had not been turned upside down by the tragedy of Russia. Be that as it may, the case for the discontinuity of Bulgakov's late career collapses when one examines the substance of his dogmatic theology. There, as we shall see, he deals with the same themes, concerns and problems which occupied him before, albeit in a new professional context and in a radically changed historical environment. This is not surprising. Established intellectuals with thirty years of experience behind them rarely change their mind about fundamentals, even if the most creative individuals go on learning, growing and revising particular positions, as Bulgakov certainly did.

On the personal level, of course, the changes in Bulgakov's life after 1917 were profound. He greeted the February Revolution with skepticism although he made common cause with liberal public opinion at the time. But he did not enter the political arena as he had done in 1905.[49] His chief preoccupation during

---

[49] Constitutional monarchy remained Bulgakov's ideal, at least as far as the future of Russia was concerned. In his memoirs he recalls attending a meeting of liberal intelligentsia in December 1916 where a friend recently back from the front argued the time had come 'to replace the chauffeur' (of the Russian state). When the tsar abdicated a couple months later Bulgakov claims that he 'saw absolutely clearly, knew with a sixth sense, that the Tsar was not a chauffeur who could be replaced but the rock upon which the hooves of the Russian horse suspended in mid-air find their footing.' *Avtobiograficheskie zametki*, pp. 89–90.

the first year of the Revolution was the Local Council of the Russian Orthodox Church, which opened in August 1917. Bulgakov was one of the most prominent lay delegates, occupying a centrist position and supporting the restoration of the patriarchate.[50] He was personally and politically close to Archbishop Tikhon (Bellavin), who was elected to the patriarchal throne in October. Among the hierarchs Tikhon occupied a centrist position much like Bulgakov's. He was considerably more moderate than the other leading contender for the office, Archbishop Antony (Khrapovitsky), yet more traditionalist than the left wing of the council, which opposed restoration of the patriarchate. Archbishop Tikhon was well aware of the challenges facing the Orthodox Church in the modern world, not just in Russia but abroad, for he had served for almost a decade as bishop of the Orthodox community in North America.[51]

At Pentecost, 1918, Bulgakov himself entered the ranks of the Orthodox clergy. With some of his oldest friends from the intelligentsia looking on, he was ordained to the diaconate and the priesthood on successive days in the Danilov Monastery in Moscow.[52] By this time, however, Russia was descending into civil war. Bulgakov's family had already moved to Crimea. Two weeks later, with the patriarch's permission, he joined them there. He would never see Moscow again. For a while he taught at the University of Simferopol, but when Bolshevik authority was established in Crimea he lost his job. He was eventually arrested and expelled from Russia by order of the Soviet government. He and his family left their native land in December 1922.

[50] The council and Bulgakov's role in it are well described by Catherine Evtuhov, *The Cross and the Sickle*, pp. 189–206. See also her article, 'The Church in the Russian Revolution: Arguments for and against Restoring the Patriarchate at the Church Council of 1917–1918,' *Slavic Review* 50 (1991): 497–511.

[51] For a survey of Patriarch Tikhon's life and work, see M. Vostryshev, *Patriarkh Tikhon* (Moscow: Molodaia gvardiia, 1997). Tikhon directed the North American mission of the Russian Orthodox Church from 1898 to 1907 and was responsible for moving the seat of the diocese from San Francisco to New York. In 1989 he was canonized as a saint by an episcopal synod of the Moscow Patriarchate.

[52] Bulgakov left a memoir of his ordination: 'Moe rukopolozhenie,' *Avtobiograficheskie zametki*, pp. 34–48. Among those attending were Pavel Florensky, Nikolai Berdiaev, Evgeny Trubetskoi, Mikhail Gershenzon and Lev Shestov.

12

A Theologian in Exile

In exile Bulgakov settled first in Prague, where he taught church law at a university institute for Russian émigré scholars organized by his old friend, Pavel Novgorodtsev. In the spring of 1925 the Bulgakov family moved to Paris, where Father Sergii became founding dean and professor of dogmatic theology at the Orthodox Theological Institute. St Sergius, as the institute was called in honor of its patron, the fourteenth-century Russian monk Sergii of Radonezh, owed its existence to the collaboration of three networks: the western European diocese of the Russian Orthodox Church; Russian scholars in exile; and philanthropic Protestant ecumenists, especially the American Methodist clergyman and YMCA leader, John Mott. All three associations figured prominently in Bulgakov's life and work for the next twenty years.[1]

Bulgakov's bishop was Metropolitan Evlogy (Georgievsky, 1868–1946).[2] Evlogy hailed from the Orthodox heartland province of Tula and was educated at Moscow Theological Academy. He spent most of his ecclesiastical career before the

[1] For a description of the conditions in which Russian intellectuals lived and worked in the emigration, see Marc Raeff, *Russia Abroad: A Cultural History of the Russian Emigration, 1919–1939* (New York: Oxford University Press, 1990); and Zernov, *The Russian Religious Renaissance*, chs 8–12. For Bulgakov's home base, see Donald A. Lowrie, *Saint Sergius in Paris: The Orthodox Theological Institute* (London: SPCK, 1954); and Alexis Kniazeff, *L'Institut Saint-Serge: De l'Académie d'autrefois au rayonnement d'aujourd'hui* (Paris: Éditions Beauchesne, 1974). Mott's extensive contacts with the Orthodox world and the Russian emigration are described by C. Howard Hopkins, *John R. Mott, 1865–1955: A Biography* (Grand Rapids: William B. Eerdmans Publishing Company, 1979).
[2] Evlogy's autobiography is an important primary source for the whole period: *Put' moei zhizni: vospominaniia Mitropolita Evlogiia (Georgievskogo), izlozhennye po ego rasskazam T. Manukhinoi* (Moscow: Moskovskii rabochii, Izdatel'skii otdel vsetserkovnogo pravoslavnogo molodezhnogo dvizheniia, 1994). The original edition was published by YMCA-Press in 1947.

Revolution in the religiously mixed Polish and western Russian provinces of the empire. He was well acquainted with Russian politics, having served as a deputy in the Second and Third Dumas (1907–12). In 1917 he was a member of the planning body that prepared the Local Council. He was a strong supporter of the restoration of the patriarchate.

Emigrating in 1920, Evlogy was asked by an episcopal synod which had constituted itself in exile to direct the western European parishes of the Russian Orthodox Church. He accepted the responsibility but took steps to have his appointment confirmed by Moscow. In 1921 Patriarch Tikhon officially designated him exarch of a new western European diocese. Meanwhile, however, the episcopal synod in exile was evolving into a rival jurisdiction which rejected Tikhon's authority on the grounds his proximity to Soviet power compromised his independence. The synod was also strongly committed to restoring the Russian monarchy. The schism placed Evlogy and his flock in a difficult position, which grew worse in 1927 when the *locum tenens* of the Moscow Patriarchate, Metropolitan Sergii (Stragorodsky), issued a declaration of loyalty to the Soviet state. Advised by Bulgakov and others to maintain his ties to Moscow, Evlogy held out for a few more years.[3] In 1931, however, following a gratuitous scolding by Metropolitan Sergii for alleged anti-Soviet activities, Evlogy led his diocese into the canonical jurisdiction of the Ecumenical Patriarch in Istanbul.

From 1925 until his death in 1944 the Orthodox Theological Institute was Bulgakov's home base. During the first two decades of its existence, the institute was one of the finest theological schools in the world. After World War II, St Sergius emerged as one of the centers of the Neopatristic theology which would dominate Orthodox thought for the rest of the century. For the first two decades of its existence, however, the institute was the center of the Russian school. The faculty roster of the 1920s and 1930s shows this very clearly. Bulgakov held the chair of dogmatics until his death. Church history was taught by A.V. Kartashev, who had been removed from a

---

[3] Evlogy notes Bulgakov's pro-Moscow stance at the time in *Put' moei zhizni*, pp. 566–7.

comparable position at the pre-revolutionary St Petersburg Theological Academy on account of his liberal views. (Kartashev went on to become the Minister of Confessions in the Provisional Government of 1917.) Moral theology fell to B.P. Vysheslavtsev, whose most important book, *The Ethics of Transformed Eros*, betrays in its title the author's platonizing approach to Christian ethics.[4] V.V. Zenkovsky and V.N. Ilyin, both deeply grounded in continental idealism, taught philosophy. G.P. Fedotov, who promoted liberal democratic values on theological as well as humanistic grounds, taught hagiography and western church history. Florovsky, who held the chair of patristics, was the exception and often found himself in the minority on issues that divided the faculty.

Bulgakov began composing dogmatic theology soon after leaving Russia. His first contribution, *St Peter and St John*, dealing with apostolic authority, grew out of his lectures on church law in Prague, although it did not come out until 1926.[5] In 1927 Bulgakov published two more dogmatic works, *The Burning Bush* on the Virgin Mary and *The Friend of the Bridegroom* on John the Baptist. These volumes combined with *Jacob's Ladder*, an essay on angels published in 1929, form Bulgakov's first dogmatic trilogy.[6] A second and larger trilogy, bearing the general title *On the Humanity of God* deals with the incarnation, the Holy Spirit and the church: *The Lamb of God* (1933), *The Comforter* (1936) and *The Bride of the Lamb* (1945).[7] Dogmatic works not incorporated in the trilogies include *Icons and Their Veneration* (1931), *The Gospel*

---

[4] See Ch. 14, n. 44 below.

[5] *Sviatye Petr i Ioann: dva pervoapostola* (Paris: YMCA-Press, 1926).

[6] *Kupina neopalimaia: opyt dogmaticheskogo istolkovaniia nekotorykh chert v pravoslavnom pochitanii Bogomateri* (1927); *Drug zhenikha (Io. 3:28–30): o pravoslavnom pochitanii Predtechi* (1927); *Lestvitsa iakovlia: ob angelakh* (1929). All were published in Paris by YMCA-Press.

[7] *O bogochelovechestve*, pt 1: *Agnets bozhii* (1933); pt 2: *Uteshitel'* (1936); pt. 3: *Nevesta agntsa* (1945). All were published in Paris by YMCA-Press. In the present study I cite the original editions of pts 1 and 2, and the reprint edition of *Nevesta agntsa* (Gregg International Publishers Limited, 1971). French translations of the first two volumes are available: *Du Verbe incarné. (Agnus Dei)*, vol. 1 of *La Sagesse divine et la théanthropie*, trans. Constantin Andronikof (Paris: Aubier, Éditions Montaigne, 1943); and *Le Paraclet*, vol. 2 of *La Sagesse divine et la théanthropie*, trans. Constantin Andronikof (Paris: Aubier, Éditions Montaigne, 1946).

Miracles (1932) and *The Revelation of John* (1948).[8] Bulgakov also wrote many articles on dogmatic and ecclesiastical topics, some of which were published in French, English or German translation.

All of Bulgakov's major works of dogmatic theology were published by YMCA-Press. Created in 1921 by John Mott, 'Imka' found a permanent home in Paris in 1925, where it became the most important Russian-language publisher in the emigration. Most of the works of the faculty of St Sergius in the 1920s and 1930s bore its imprint, which is to say that many of the classics of twentieth-century Orthodox theology came out under the auspices of a Protestant ecumenical organization.

This unusual arrangement was one of the reasons for the strong commitment to ecumenism among the first generation of Russian Orthodox intellectuals in exile. Another factor was Soloviev's legacy. Soloviev was the philosophical mentor of the whole generation of religious thinkers who came to maturity in Russia in the two decades before the Revolution. Bulgakov, Berdiaev and other Russian thinkers who became involved in ecumenical activism after World War I regarded ecumenism as part of their intellectual tradition. Still another inducement was the maturation of the Ecumenical Movement in the 1920s and 1930s. The period was the golden age of ecumenism in that the movement had advanced far enough to show some impressive results while the conflicts which would plague it later in the century were present only in embryo.[9]

Bulgakov's interest in the ecumenical idea was also sharpened by his shock at the collapse of Russia in 1917–21. Prior to this time he had not concerned himself in a direct way with ecumenism; his work focused on Russian Orthodox issues. The collapse of Russia altered Bulgakov's horizon, opening his eyes to what he called the 'wide road of ecumenical Orthodoxy freed

---

[8] *Ikona i ikonopochitanie: dogmaticheskii ocherk* (1931); *O chudesakh evangel'skikh* (1932); *Apokalipsis Ioanna: opyt dogmaticheskogo istolkovaniia* (1948). All were published in Paris by YMCA-Press.
[9] For a detailed account of the Orthodox role in modern ecumenism see Nicolas Zernov, 'The Eastern Churches and the Ecumenical Movement in the Twentieth Century,' *A History of the Ecumenical Movement 1517–1948*, eds Ruth Rouse and Stephen Charles Neill, 2nd ed. with rev. bibliography (Philadelphia: The Westminster Press, 1967), pp. 645–74.

from provincialism.'[10] While he was living in Crimea during the Civil War, he experienced an intense attraction to Roman Catholicism thanks to a friendship with an uprooted Polish priest. In Istanbul – his first stop on the way to exile in Europe – he paused in St Sophia's Cathedral to ponder the ironies of world history.[11] The great church of the Christian Roman Empire and *pium desideratum* of the Russian Slavophiles was still a Turkish mosque. In his reverie Bulgakov found himself admiring the discipline and sincerity of the Muslim worshipers. He rejoiced that the sanctuary had not been recovered for Orthodoxy by 'the bloody boots' of a Russian army. Ceasing to regard St Sophia's as a monument to Orthodox tradition alone, he came to see it as a prophetic symbol of 'the Universal Church and universal humanity' to be realized at the end of history.

Once established as a professor of dogmatic theology Bulgakov could speak for Orthodoxy with authority at ecumenical meetings. He and Metropolitan Evlogy were delegates to the Lausanne Conference on Faith and Order in 1927, a worldwide gathering that significantly advanced the institutionalization of the Ecumenical Movement. At Lausanne Bulgakov was elected to the Continuation Committee charged with shepherding the Faith and Order movement until the next international meeting set for Edinburgh in 1937. Father Sergii also achieved prominence at Lausanne by delivering an impassioned plea to the Protestant majority to embrace the veneration of the Virgin Mary, whom he hailed as the mystical 'Unifier' of the worldwide church. Bulgakov's proposal was so controversial that the section chairman, a Congregationalist, blocked the speech for a week on the grounds that mariology was not among the conference agenda.[12]

The year after Lausanne Bulgakov became a founding member of another ecumenical venture, the Fellowship of St Alban and St Sergius. Based in England, which Bulgakov now visited fairly often, the fellowship was dedicated to promoting Anglican–Orthodox friendship. The commonalities of the two communions were clear enough: a polity of the catholic but not

---

[10] *Avtobiograficheskie zametki*, p. 50.
[11] 'V. Aia-Sofii,' *Avtobiograficheskie zametki*, pp. 94–102.
[12] Evlogii, *Put' moei zhizni*, pp. 537–8.

Roman type, a high regard for the patristic heritage, a liturgically based identity and a history of state establishment. There was also a record of relatively frequent contacts between Anglican churches and the Russian Orthodox Church dating back to the first half of the nineteenth century, a history free of missionary turf-wars and other types of inter-church rivalry. Although he was based in Paris, where contacts with Roman Catholics were a natural outlet for ecumenism, Bulgakov focused on Anglicanism. The same was true of Metropolitan Evlogy, whose ecumenical activism antedated World War I.[13] The studied remoteness of the Roman Catholic Church from the Ecumenical Movement before Vatican II was one of reasons for Bulgakov's choice, although not all Paris-based Orthodox shared his preference. Berdiaev, for example, directed his ecumenical activism mainly toward Roman Catholics.[14]

One of the results of Bulgakov's high visibility in Anglican circles was an invitation to visit North America through the offices of the Episcopal Church of the United States.[15] Sailing from Hamburg on a German ocean liner decorated with the swastika and loaded with Jewish refugees, Bulgakov arrived in New York on 4 October 1934. He stayed until early December, carrying out an ambitious program of visits, lectures and fund-raising events.

[13] Metropolitan Evlogy discusses his ecumenical activities in *Put' moei zhizni*, pp. 523–51. About Anglicanism he writes: 'Our frequent efforts at rapprochement with the Anglicans, it seems to me, had a huge significance both for them and for us. Together we exchanged and shared the treasures of church life. We [Orthodox] opened to the Anglicans the profound, mystical depth and boundless breadth of our Orthodox faith, and the inexpressible beauty and grandeur of our worship. They [opened] to us their firm sense of church discipline, their reverential and sensitive approach to what goes on in the church, to what is said and sung there, as well as their special talent for putting Christian ideals to work in practical life. We gave them depth of insight into the mysteries of Christianity; they showed us wisdom in the building of Christian life' (pp. 549–50).

[14] Bulgakov was by no means unknown to budding Roman Catholic ecumenists. The young Yves Congar reports paying 'several visits to Father Sergius Bulgakov' in 1936 and cites his work frequently. See Yves M.-J. Congar, *Dialogue Between Christians: Catholic Contributions to Ecumenism*, trans. Philip Loretz, (London and Dublin: Geoffrey Chapman, 1966), p. 17.

[15] Bulgakov's travel diary of his trip to North America is in *Avtobiograficheskie zametki*, pp. 114–35. One of his North American lectures was published: 'Social Teaching in Modern Russian Orthodox Theology,' *The Twentieth Annual Hale Memorial Sermon* (Evanston, Illinois: Seabury-Western Theological Seminary, 1934).

He spent the first couple of weeks at the General Convention of the Episcopal Church, which was meeting in Atlantic City. He was impressed by the splendid hotel, the friendliness of his reception, the high level of organization and the African-American gospel choir singing music that was new to him but reminded him of Russian folk songs. On the other hand, he was surprised at how little American Episcopalians knew about Orthodoxy and astonished by their lack of interest in fundamental theology. Their theological apathy vexed him more than anything else on his journey. His diary entry after a day of lecturing at the university and seminary in Princeton is typical: 'These grand halls, libraries, all this splendor, this power of organization – somehow these do not lead to genuine theologizing, and you have to descend to a child's level.'[16] At General Theological Seminary, Wellesley College, Seabury-Western Theological Seminary, Nashotah House in Wisconsin and other venues on his itinerary he was faced with the same situation. People were interested in Bolshevik Russia, Russian literature, the social mission of Christianity and other contemporary issues, but not in theology as such.

Bulgakov's ecumenism was bold and open to experiment. The nature of his approach can be sensed in a proposal he made in 1933 to the Fellowship of St Alban and St Sergius to practice a limited form of intercommunion (sharing of eucharist) at society gatherings. His idea was to have the Anglicans members submit to a special blessing by an Orthodox bishop authorizing their participation in Orthodox eucharist at services conducted during Fellowship meetings. Although it was rejected by the majority of the Fellowship, Bulgakov's proposal demonstrated his conviction that the mystical unity of the church could be made manifest even in the absence of doctrinal agreement and canonical union; in other words, that the eucharist itself could serve as a symbol and means of church unity.[17]

In 1937 Bulgakov attended both the Oxford Conference on

---

[16] *Avtobiograficheskie zametki*, p. 123.
[17] On Bulgakov's proposal and the controversy surrounding it, see Zernov, *The Russian Religious Renaissance*, pp. 265–8; *Georges Florovsky*, ed. Blane, p. 65; and Evlogii, *Put' moei zhizni*, pp. 546–7. Bulgakov's proposal for intercommunion is probably best understood as a reflection of his intense eucharistic piety. Bulgakov's sense of the charisma of the eucharist was evident in his manner of celebrating the rite 'with a trembling reverence,' as Metropolitan Evlogy put it (*Put'*

Church, Community and State and the Edinburgh Conference on Faith and Order. These were the gatherings which finalized plans to create the World Council of Churches. At the time Bulgakov was still generally regarded in the Ecumenical Movement as the most distinguished Orthodox theologian.[18] At Edinburgh he was re-elected to the Continuation Committee of Faith and Order. But his career as an activist was drawing to a close. A cancer operation in 1939 forced him to withdraw from international meetings. His place on the Continuation Committee was taken by Georges Florovsky.

In the Solovievian tradition the ecumenical mission of mending the unity of Christendom is closely associated with the imperative of improving Jewish–Christian relations. This connection was not as prominent in Bulgakov's career, however. Before the Revolution he wrote relatively little about Judaism or Jewish–Christian relations. The same was true of his career in exile until just before the end, in 1941–2, when he wrote two important essays on the persecution of the Jews in Nazi-dominated Europe.[19] The articles are valuable in

moei zhizni, p. 410). Alexander Schmemann recorded the same characteristic: 'Father Sergii really put himself into the liturgy [deistvitel'no liturgisal]. There was something primal and elemental in his manner of serving, in his awkwardness and impetuosity ... He thoroughly, totally blended into [the service], leaving the impression that the liturgy was being served for the first time, that it was falling from heaven and being lifted up from the earth for the first time.' Quoted in Monakhinia Elena, 'Professor Protoierei Sergii Bulgakov,' p. 148. It is not surprising, then, that Bulgakov found it painful to stand on the sidelines at a eucharistic service. At St Luke's Episcopal Church in Evanston, Illinois in 1934, the priest in charge invited Father Sergii to assist. 'I declined, of course,' Bulgakov noted in his diary, 'but my refusal caused me grave suffering. In general I experienced this mass as unquestionably the sacrament of eucharist.' Avtobiograficheskie zametki, p. 126.

[18] The esteem in which Bulgakov was held, if eminent company is any indication, can be inferred from his collaboration in a volume of essays prepared on the eve of the Edinburgh Conference: Gustav Aulén, Karl Barth, Sergius Bulgakoff, M.C. D'Arcy, T.S. Eliot, Walter M. Horton and William Temple, Revelation, eds John Baillie and Hugh Martin (New York: The Macmillan Company, 1937). Bulgakov's contribution (pp. 125–180) is one of the best summaries of his dogmatic-theological position in English.

[19] Bulgakov's writings on the Jews and Jewish–Christian relations are collected in Sergii Bulgakov, Khristianstvo i evreiskii vopros (Paris: YMCA-Press, 1991). See also Nikita Struve, 'S. Bulgakov et la question juive,' Cahiers du monde russe et soviétique 29 (1988): 533–42; and 'Bulgakov and Anti-Semitism,' Sergii Bulgakov, ed. Williams, pp. 293–303.

dogmatic-theological terms. Bulgakov condemns racism as anti-Christian, stresses the purely Jewish character of the early church, affirms the Pauline theology of the validity of Israel's election even under the New Covenant and rejects the application of Matthew 27:25 ('His blood be on us and on our children') to the Jewish people collectively. In an interesting interpretation of the New Testament genealogies of Jesus (Mt 1:1–17; Lk 3:23–38), he shifts the focus of anti-racist apologetics from affirming the humanity of the Jews – as if that were open to question! – to affirming the Jewishness of humanity, a counter-intuitive dogmatic truth that overturns racism on the ontological level. It must be admitted, however, that Bulgakov's essays are less interesting in practical terms. In one respect they represent a step backwards: Soloviev's Christian Question has become 'the Jewish Question' again.[20]

The most notorious episode in Bulgakov's career in exile was the Sophia Affair of 1935. In that year, in a rare if not unique instance of concord, the Moscow Patriarchate and the rival émigré synod of the Russian Orthodox Church condemned Bulgakov's sophiology as heretical, an accusation which called into question Bulgakov's right to teach Orthodox theology. Again Metropolitan Evlogy found himself in difficult straits. Bulgakov was the star of his faculty, his deputy in the Ecumenical Movement and a personal friend. But heresy charges could not be ignored, even though Evlogy and his flock were not subject to the prosecuting jurisdictions. Furthermore, there was opposition to Bulgakov's sophiology at the Orthodox Theological Institute. Florovsky in particular was known to be opposed. So was Florovsky's younger contemporary Vladimir Lossky (1903–58), who played a key role in supplying evidence to the Moscow Patriarchate in the Sophia Affair. Lossky was not a member of the St Sergius faculty, but he was well-placed in the Russian community as the son of the distinguished philosopher Nikolai O. Lossky and as a promising scholar of Orthodox theology in his own right. Evlogy responded to the dispute by appointing a faculty commission to investigate the heresy charges but otherwise took no action prejudicial to Bulgakov. The commission never concluded its work, although a

---

[20] See *Khristianstvo i evreiskii vopros*, pp. 93 and 148. For Bulgakov's discussion of the New Testament genealogies, see pp. 143–7.

minority report resulted in Father Sergii having to appear before a panel of bishops to explain his views.[21] Bulgakov continued to express his sophiological views to the end of his life.

One might be tempted to think Metropolitan Evlogy protected Bulgakov mainly for political reasons. Bulgakov was 'his' man; the accusers, his ecclesiastical adversaries. But this is only part of the story. Evlogy's autobiography makes it clear he felt an intellectual and spiritual kinship with Bulgakov. He may not have agreed with everything Father Sergii wrote and taught, but he supported Bulgakov's project. Evlogy saw the need to bring Orthodoxy closer to the world, to play the melody of theology in a new key. In his spare time he read modern novels, kept an eye on contemporary journals, took an interest in art and the natural world.[22] He excoriated the 'self-sufficient' mindset and 'inertia and isolation' that often govern Orthodox attitudes toward other churches and traditions.[23] He cherished Christian liberty so deeply he devoted the closing pages of his

---

[21] No thorough, dispassionate study of the Sophia Affair has yet been made. For the accusations and Bulgakov's response see O Sofii premudrosti bozhiei: ukaz moskovskoi patriarkhii i dokladnye zapiski prof. prot. Sergiia Bulgakova Mitropolitu Evlogiiu (Paris, 1935), which includes Bulgakov's answer to an earlier (1927) attack on his sophiology by the émigré synod; Dokladnaia zapiska Mitropolitu Evlogiiu prof. prot. Sergiia Bulgakova po povodu opredeleniia Arkhiereiskogo sobora v Karlovtsakh otnositel'no ucheniia o Sofii Premudrosti Bozhiei, Prilozhenie k zhurnalu 'Put'' (Paris: YMCA-Press, 1936); and V. Losskii, Spor o Sofii: 'Dokladnaia Zapiska' prot. S. Bulgakova i smysl Ukaza Moskovskoi Patriarkhii (Paris, 1936). The outcome of the Affair has not been clarified. Andrew Blane writes that the bishops who examined Bulgakov demanded and got a retraction of the latter's views, but there is no evidence for this besides a conversation which Blane had with Florovsky several decades later. See Georges Florovsky, ed. Blane, pp. 65–8; cf. Sergii Bulgakov, ed. Williams, p. 175, n. 44.

[22] 'I do not understand or take pleasure in narrow fanaticism, and the polemical attitude "he who is not for us is against us" in my view contradicts the spirit of the Holy Gospel ... All that is good and truly human contains a spark of God and should not be alien to us. Perhaps this orientation of my spirit to the world, my wish to understand the soul of every human being, to find God, explains my love for nature, art, literature and basically for everything beautiful in life. People often ask me, "What, you're still reading novels?" With some embarrassment I answer: "Yes, I am." And it's true: I love to follow literature, I try not to miss a single volume of Sovremennye zapiski [Contemporary Notes]. Perhaps I err in this, for it befits me to devote my leisure hours to the spiritual literature of the church. [Yet] I believe that secular literature is one of the great means for the education of the human soul, almost as effective as nature; and the religious–educational significance of nature is immense.' Put' moei zhizni, pp. 599–600.

[23] Put' moei zhizni, p. 523.

autobiography to it. His words on the subject are poignant, heart-felt, free of pedantry. To appreciate the true value of these pages, however, one must read them in the light of Evlogy's handling of the Sophia Affair. Nothing is easier in hierarchical churches than celebrating Christian liberty in principle while denying it in practice. Evlogy did not fall into this syndrome. He defended not just the concept of Christian liberty but the liberty of individual Christians. Unlike many Orthodox churchmen of his day, Evlogy knew the modern world was a freer place than any which the church had known before, and that an unprecedented degree of freedom would have to be allowed in the church if Orthodoxy was to address the civilization around it. In the last analysis the Sophia Affair was not about the fate of an individual or even about sophiology. It was about Orthodox engagement with the modern world. The issue was the extent to which interpretations of Orthodox faith not clearly attested in antecedent tradition could or would be accommodated in the church.[24] The resolution of this issue did not rest with Bulgakov. He was the creative genius set upon by critics, but he was not the hero of the Sophia Affair. The hero was Metropolitan Evlogy. Three-quarters of a century earlier Archimandrite Feodor complained about the tendency among the guardians of Orthodoxy to express zeal for their faith in such a way as 'to desiccate all that is alive and fruitful in Christianity.' Evlogy had a different attitude toward the new, the fresh, the untried in the life of the church. 'I consider patience to be a great creative force,' he writes in the last paragraph of his autobiography. 'One must know how to wait for the shoots to appear from the sown earth, and then, blessing the new plants, one must take all possible measures to help them grow, heating them with the warmth of love and prayer; but even here patience is needed: the process of growth is mysterious, and there is no point in forcing it artificially in the hope of a rapid flowering, you just end up interfering; one can only try to create conditions conducive to development. Everything alive in the Church is born in this way, grows, flowers and bears fruit in this way. This is a great mystery of the Church.'[25]

[24] This issue is discussed in Ch. 15 below.
[25] *Put' moei zhizni*, p. 602. Archimandrite Feodor's words are cited in Ch. 2, n. 17 above.

13

Dogmatics of the Humanity
of God

CHURCH-AND-WORLD DOGMATICS

Bulgakov's dogmatic works bear the stamp of the Orthodox ecclesiastical tradition more than any of his previous writings. The first trilogy is patterned on the deisis, or prayer row, the canonical arrangement of icons depicting Christ, the Mother of God, John the Baptist and the holy angels that governs the iconostasis of any Orthodox church. The second trilogy, *On the Humanity of God*, parallels the economy of salvation in the New Covenant: the sacrifice of the Lamb of God, the sending of the Holy Spirit and the ministry of the church. *The Revelation of John* (1948) deals with the eschatological fulfillment of salvation. In all of these works Bulgakov demonstrates a level of expertise in patristic and liturgical sources that shows the seriousness with which he applied himself to his new profession. Bulgakov liked to say that 'one should imbibe theology from the bottom of the Eucharistic Chalice.'[1]

Yet the chalice was not the only cup from which Bulgakov the theologian drank. His debt to Soloviev's religious philosophy is as plain in his dogmatics as in his earlier works. The second trilogy features the most familiar of all Solovievian terms in its title: *bogochelovechestvo*, the humanity of God. *The Lamb of God* begins with two chapters of sophiology. In the preface to *The Comforter* Bulgakov invites his readers to join him in hoping for 'a DIVINE-HUMAN [*bogochelovecheskogo*] revelation about the HUMAN, the world, the human being ... [for] the new gift of an all-inclusive [*vseedinoi*] Pentecost.' *The*

---

[1] Monakhinia Elena, 'Professor Protoierei Sergii Bulgakov,' p. 151.

Bride of the Lamb presents 'the doctrine of the Church, or ecclesiology broadly and profoundly understood as sophiology,' an equation that makes sense only if one knows that in the Solovievian tradition Sophia embodies (among other things) the whole of humanity destined for incorporation in the Universal Church.[2] Accordingly Christ can be viewed as the pan-human person: 'a Human Being in the sense of the Pan-Human Being [*Vsechelovek*], His Person contained all human images, it was the Universal Person [*Vselichnost'iu*].'[3] Throughout his dogmatics Bulgakov employs the unmistakable theo-philosophical vocabulary fashioned by Soloviev.

The linguistic and terminological affinity is matched by a deep programmatic bond between Bulgakov's dogmatics and the Solovievian tradition. Soloviev did not write or contemplate writing a dogmatics. He made use of dogmatic material and wrote a number of essays on dogmatic topics, but he did not take up dogmatic theology systematically. This suggests the possibility that in his later works Father Sergii saw himself as extending and presumably enriching the Solovievian tradition by writing the kind of dogmatics Soloviev might have written had the latter applied himself to it.[4] As we have seen, Bulgakov did something like this once before in *The Philosophy of Economy*, which can be read as the theurgy or philosophy or culture which Soloviev projected but did not write.

The title of Bulgakov's second trilogy, indicating that the work is a thematization of the humanity of God, lends weight to this hypothesis. A dogmatics of the humanity of God would be a dogmatics taking the incarnation as its starting point and main theme, which is exactly what we find in the second trilogy. The series begins with a christological study (*The Lamb of God*), proceeds to pneumatology (*The Comforter*) and ends with an ecclesiological study, that is to say, an essay on the community

---

[2] *Nevesta agntsa*, p. 5.

[3] *Agnets bozhii*, p. 229.

[4] Bulgakov implies as much in *The Lamb of God*. Discussing Sophia as 'eternal humanity' in God he observes: 'This thought was put forward by V. Soloviev in his youthfully brilliant *Lectures on the Humanity of God*, but unfortunately [Soloviev] did not develop these sagacious ideas into a theological doctrine; rather, he muddied and distorted them with gnostic images.' *Agnets bozhii*, p. 137, n. 2. Clearly Bulgakov's aim is to develop the theological doctrine.

founded upon the incarnate Word (*The Bride of the Lamb*). Unlike dogmatic theologians in scholastic and rational-theological traditions, Bulgakov does not begin his work with a general doctrine of God, nor even with a dogmatics of the Father. He begins with the Son, proceeds to the Spirit, deals with the Father in an epilogue and eschews the abstract doctrine of God in favor of a sophiology.[5]

The incarnation is the theme of Bulgakov's first dogmatic trilogy, too, although titular reference is lacking. The trilogy is patterned on the deisis. In dogmatic terms the deisis is the full icon of the Word made flesh. A picture of Christ alone is also an icon of the incarnation, of course, but a minimalist one. In a complete picture of the incarnation an Orthodox Christian also expects to see the Mother of God who bore the Word into the world, John the Forerunner who heralded and consecrated him, and the holy angels who, though not incarnate themselves, implemented the divine will-for-incarnation in obedience and awe. This is the deisis. The first trilogy also resembles the second in that the narrative focus falls not on the beginning of the biblical story, but on the christological and mariological middle.

The connection between incarnational theology and Solo-vievian philosophy must not be construed to imply that every theology of incarnation must be Solovievian, as if Soloviev invented the idea of incarnation. On the contrary, the doctrine of the incarnation was the source of the Solovievian idea of the humanity of God. Bulgakov's project is thus rather complex. Construing Orthodox dogmatics in terms of the humanity of God, he is at the same time re-evaluating Soloviev's concept in the light of its roots in the Orthodox dogmatic tradition.

Bulgakov's focus on the incarnation invites comparison with similar initiatives elsewhere in modern theology. Indeed, an incarnational or christological focus governs many creative projects in Christian dogmatics in modern times. The nineteenth-century theologies of kenosis, which had an interde-nominational appeal, are an early example. In the twentieth century the incarnation became the dominant theme of Anglican dogmatics, while Barth's christocentrism swept the field in the Reformed tradition. All of these experiments were prompted in

---

[5] The epilogue on the Father is in *Uteshitel'*, pp. 406–47.

one way or another by the principal intellectual challenge facing dogmatic theology in modern times, namely, how to reconcile dogma, i.e. non-optional faith propositions handed down by tradition, with the intellectual freedom and creativity claimed by modern civilization. In Russian Orthodoxy, as we have seen, Archimandrite Feodor was the first to address this issue in his pioneering theology of the kenosis of the Lamb. Bulgakov honored this precedent when he entitled the inaugural volume of his second trilogy *The Lamb of God*.

In the annals of religious thought since the Enlightenment a variety of strategies for dealing with the tension between dogma and freedom have been tested. One, sometimes called liberalism but better described as rationalism, is to interpret dogmas in such a way as to take the mystery out of them in the hope of showing them to be reasonable propositions after all. A related strategy is to deny integral status to dogma in Christianity in favor of a simpler, more original, more immanent gospel. The Social Gospelers and Tolstoyans of Bulgakov's day took this approach. Another strategy, which may be called dualism, summons not rationalism but irrationalism to the defense of dogma, bifurcating human experience into a secular-historical sphere and, over against it, a privileged spiritual or ecclesiastical sphere where dogmas abide in all their purity and authority. Finally there is the strategy usually called fundamentalism, better termed literalism, in which dogma is formulated in such a way as to override the claims of rationality as such.

Bulgakov had no difficulty rejecting theories which isolate dogma from the world or block the modern critical assessment of dogmatic claims. He regarded such approaches as a pretext for 'lazy obscurantism.'[6] He also steered clear of moralistic rationalism, which he criticized masterfully in his essay 'On Early Christianity.'[7] Philosophic rationalism, on the other hand, presented him with a more serious challenge. Like Soloviev and Bukharev, Bulgakov regarded 'the light that enlightens every human being who comes into the world' (Jn 1:9) to mean the Word of God dwells in all human beings and can be discovered

---

[6] *Agnets bozhii*, p. 207.
[7] See Ch. 11, 'Philosophy and Faith' above.

by them in their innermost selves.[8] This view may be taken to suggest some type of religious philosophy may eventually replace dogmatic religion. In Hegel's philosophy of religion, for example, dogmas are handled as objects that can be fully rationalized, i.e. expressed in logical concepts. Because Hegelian reason is not reductionistic, these concepts prove to be rich and profound. Still, at day's end when the owl of Minerva takes wing, it is rational concepts, not theological dogmas, which she surveys.[9]

This was not an outcome Bulgakov could condone. For one thing, his career reversed the Hegelian progression, since he began as a religious philosopher but ended his days as a dogmatic theologian. Moreover, by his ordination to the Orthodox priesthood Bulgakov accepted responsibility in a very personal way for upholding the distinctive witness of the church in matters of faith. There is little room for the church in the household of intellect as Hegel and other rationalists construe it.[10]

Yet Bulgakov could not simply turn his back on idealism. Besides forcing a break with Soloviev, to whom he owed so much, such a move would undermine the project of dialogue with modernity, for Bulgakov regarded idealism as the supreme embodiment of modern intellectuality. As we have seen, Bulgakov sought a way out of his dilemma by taking up the Schellingian strand of idealism. Schelling accused Hegel of reducing reality to rational concepts and, by focusing on concepts alone, of severing philosophy's connection with the living, pulsating whole of things. The key word in Schelling's critique was 'positive.' A positive philosophy focuses not on concepts alone but on the continuing interaction between

---

[8] Bulgakov notes that the much-cited Johannine verse has a liturgical as well as a biblical setting. In the first hour of the daily office one prays to 'Christ, the light of truth, enlightening and sanctifying *every human being* that comes into the world' (Bulgakov's italics). *Kupina neopalimaia*, p. 67.

[9] That Hegel's philosophy is rationalistic does not disqualify it from being religious. I.A. Il'in, a Russian philosopher of Bulgakov's generation, explicated this dimension of Hegel's thought in *Filosofiia Gegelia kak uchenie o konkretnosti Boga i cheloveka* (1918).

[10] The subordination of church to state in Hegelianism is an important consequence of the rationalistic elimination of dogma. See Walicki's observation on Hegel and Soloviev quoted in Ch. 6, n. 43 above.

concepts and the life-process which generates them, a process with which rational concepts always stand in tension because they are necessarily abstractions. In the case of religion a positive philosophy does not construe religious ideas as objects that can be exhausted by logical analysis but seeks to appreciate their historical, experiential and existential significance, dimensions of meaning which have enduring validity in life as it is actually lived. Purely conceptual interpretations of religious ideas, by contrast, supplant the ideas which they interpret, just as in social and political philosophy a thoroughgoing rationalism subordinates the church to the state or even eliminates the church altogether.

In the Schellingian tradition, to be sure, there is a danger dogmatic religion will be dissolved into philosophic mysticism, an outcome that tempted Soloviev from time to time. The antidote lies in recognizing 'positive' realities are by definition concrete, particular, historical things. A mysticism which dissolves the multiplicity of positivities into a singular Positive defeats the program of positive philosophy as surely as Hegelian rationalism; it merely delivers the fatal blow at the end of the game rather than at the beginning. Respect for the positive in religion, on the other hand, means honoring the concrete idiom in which faith expresses itself, thereby limiting the degree to which dogma can be rationalized. To earn such respect, however, dogmatic theologians must be able to show how dogmas are connected with human experience, how they function as positive religious ideals. Merely reiterating traditional formulas will not do.[11]

Bulgakov's handling of the Chalcedonian dogma is a good example of the positive approach to dogma. Proclaiming two natures united in the one person of Christ, the fathers at Chalcedon expressed the essence of the incarnation. As an Orthodox theologian Bulgakov reveres the Chalcedonian formula as 'a dogmatic crystal'.[12] He has no interest in revising it; rather, he makes it the dogmatic cornerstone of *The Lamb of*

---

[11] The positive method also implies that the meaning of a dogma is not exhausted by the doctrine which expresses it. As Bulgakov puts it, 'dogmatic facts are prior to theological doctrines.' *Kupina neopalimaia*, 'Ot sostavitelia.'

[12] *Agnets bozhii*, p. 80.

God. But as surely as the cornerstone is not the finished house, the Chalcedonian formula is not a finished christology. In fact, Bulgakov does not believe an adequate, much less a complete dogmatics of the Chalcedonian definition can be found anywhere in the patristic tradition:

> Having the force of a divinely inspired, *dogmatic* definition, the Chalcedonian formula is not, with respect to its content, a *theological* achievement. On the contrary, being theologically ahead of its time (and to some extent also ahead of our own), it has remained unclarified and unrealized in theological thought – more an outline than a doctrine.[13]

Bulgakov goes on to observe that in patristic theology the Chalcedonian definition functioned mainly as a negative criterion. It fixed the boundaries of christological reflection by clarifying that which could not be said about Christ, e.g. that he was not human, that he was not divine, that the two natures were not distinguished, and so on. 'But about the *positive* relationship of the two natures [in Christ], the dogma is silent.'[14]

The positive truth Bulgakov finds lacking in patristic expositions of the incarnation is an appreciation of the humanistic implications of the doctrine. Seeking to conceptualize the union of natures in Christ, patristic theology 'could not explain it otherwise than by a general appeal to the omnipotence of God.'[15] But in stressing divine omnipotence to the exclusion of the human element the fathers risked reducing the incarnation to a *deus ex machina*. They affirmed the human truth of the incarnation theoretically but ignored it in practice.

While believing a more humanistic account of the incarnation was needed, Bulgakov did not consider it an easy task to come up with one. The rare pioneers of a more positive view, lacking precedent to guide them, fell into confusion or heresy. Apollinaris, who taught the divine Logos replaced the human hypostasis of Jesus, was one of these. But his effort should not be dismissed because of its unsatisfactory outcome. Apollinaris

---

[13] *Agnets bozhii*, p. 74.
[14] *Agnets bozhii*, p. 221; cf. p. 79.
[15] *Agnets bozhii*, p. 28.

was right to see 'the union of divine and human nature in the God-human is not an external and ontologically arbitrary act of uniting the un-unitable, the totally alien and different, but an ontologically grounded and predetermined union of Prototype and image, of heavenly Man and earthly'; he was right to focus his teaching 'on the *correlation* of heavenly and earthly man, i.e. on the Humanity of God.'[16] While patristic theology did not pursue this theme, modern theology must do just that, for

> the Chalcedonian dogma is not just a doctrinal norm by which the mind of the Church is to measure itself; it is given to human thought as the supreme and final problem for theological and philosophical comprehension ... We like to think that our time in particular is called – in its search for a theological synthesis – to be a Chalcedonian epoch in history, called to a new religious and theological discovery and appropriation of this gift of the church.[17]

Bulgakov's call for a more positive Chalcedonianism reveals the connection between the classical doctrine of the incarnation and the Solovievian idea of the humanity of God on which his dogmatics turns. The humanity of God is the doctrine of the incarnation construed as a positive religious ideal. The construct may be termed modern in that it is not found in the fathers; yet it may be considered traditional, too, to the extent that it respects, affirms and extends the classical doctrine.

While placing the incarnation at the center of his dogmatics, Bulgakov does not treat it as an exceptional case. He applies his view that Orthodox dogma is an unfinished business, a field for creative projects beyond the scope of the fathers, to the whole gamut of dogmatics. To mariology, for example: 'Orthodox dogmatic theology – partly because of hostility to Sophia [*sofieborstvo*] and partly because of polemical tendentiousness in the struggle against one-sided Roman Catholic positions – to this day has not realized the treasure of revelation concerning the Mother of God which is contained in the church's veneration of Her.'[18] To biblical theology:

---

[16] *Agnets bozhii*, p. 26–8.
[17] *Agnets bozhii*, p. 80.
[18] *Agnets bozhii*, p. 232.

While it is customary to think, or at least to pretend, that all is well in this area, that all the christological questions have essentially been resolved, this is in fact far from the case, and at the key point no less – namely, how to view the image of Jesus Christ in the Gospels in the light of the fundamental dogmatic definitions accepted by the Church.[19]

To *communicatio idiomatum*: 'When applied to emphasize theosis, [this principle] can be kept within bounds and rightly interpreted only if it is also made to show the influence of human nature on the divine. But here we see a total lack of clarity [in patristic theology].'[20] To kenosis: 'It is stated – that's the important thing – but not elaborated in patristic theology.'[21]

Bulgakov's call for a positive Chalcedonianism has a dissonant ring to it in the context of later twentieth-century Orthodox theology. Since Bulgakov's time, indeed beginning already in the 1930s, Neopatristic scholars effected a reorientation of Orthodox theological reflection to the apophatic path. Apophatic theology honors the transcendence of God by avoiding positive propositions, stating the truths of revelation by means of negation instead: God is not a creature, not remote from his creation, the Persons of the Trinity are not reducible to each other, the two natures in Christ are neither divided nor confused, and so on. Finding a handy tool in the alpha-privative, a common adjectival prefix in Greek, apophasis established itself as a popular mode of theologizing in the patristic period. Whether and to what extent the Greek fathers actually privileged apophatic theology is an issue worth debating, but it is not the issue here. The relevant point is that modern Neopatristic theologians privileged apophatic theology both in their reading of the fathers and in their own theological constructions. Since

---

[19] *Agnets bozhii*, p. 232. Bulgakov's *The Gospel Miracles* is an example of his determination to vindicate the humanity of the gospel even in a matter (miracles) where discussion typically focuses on divinity. 'In the patristic age the acts of Christ were regarded above all in relation to His Divinity. For us the question of their relation to His Humanity has status in its own right inasmuch as all the fullness of divine nature was united without diminishment with all the fullness of human nature in Christ the Humanity of God.' *O chudesakh evangel'skikh* (Moscow: Russkii put', 1994), p. 3.
[20] *Agnets bozhii*, pp. 237–8.
[21] *Agnets bozhii*, p. 239.

most contemporary western students of Orthodox theology were introduced to the subject by Neopatristic scholarship, the apophatic bias established itself among them as well.[22] Thus a certain amount of historical imagination is required to appreciate an Orthodox theological environment where the preeminence of apophatic theology was not taken for granted. For Bulgakov the

> negative formula of the Council of Chalcedon cannot ... be understood as a *ban* on positive definitions, but only as a *preliminary* definition, not complete, not exhaustive, but awaiting continuation. The removal of the question concerning the positive relationship of the two natures into the preserve of apophatic (negative) theology therefore lacks foundation.[23]

The humanity of God, or the incarnation as a positive religious ideal, is a prime example of what Bulgakov means by a 'continuation' of Chalcedon.

---

[22] Vladimir Lossky's brilliant and haunting brief for apophatic theology, *Essai sur la théologie mystique de l'Église d'Orient* (Paris, 1944), was particularly influential. English trans.: *The Mystical Theology of the Eastern Church* (London & Cambridge: James Clarke & Co. Ltd, 1957). Examining this book in the light of Bulgakov's concern for positive theology is an interesting exercise. Lossky's initial claim for apophatic theology sounds modest: 'In the present work ... the term "mystical theology" denotes no more than a spirituality which expresses a doctrinal attitude' (English trans., p. 7). The issue is whether the spirituality which Lossky speaks of is one among a number available to Orthodoxy, or a higher, privileged, exclusive spirituality. One soon discovers the latter is the case, as when Lossky says of Origen ('this great Christian thinker') that 'an attitude which was not fundamentally apophatic made the Alexandrine teacher a religious philosopher rather than a mystical theologian, in the sense proper to the eastern tradition' (p. 32). Here apophasis is a distinguishing characteristic of the theological as opposed to philosophical enterprise. From then on Lossky assumes 'the apophatic basis of all true theology' (p. 33).

[23] *Agnets bozhii*, p. 221; cf. p. 135. Bulgakov applies the positive approach to other doctrines besides the incarnation, e.g. to *creatio ex nihilo*, a favorite locus of apophatic theology because of the sharp distinction between God and the world which it implies. For Bulgakov there are two dimensions to the doctrine of creation: 'If the negative definition that "God created the world from nothing" excludes the idea of any sort of non-divine or extra-divine principle of creation, then the *positive* content of the idea can only be that God created the world through Himself, from His own nature ... The *positive* content of the being of the world is every bit as divine as its foundation in God, for no other source exists for it.' *Agnets bozhii*, pp. 148–9. This thought points clearly in the direction of sophiology.

As a guiding concept the humanity of God supports the engagement of Orthodoxy with the modern world because it posits a dynamic link between dogma and experience, underscoring the mutual interaction between God and the world signaled by the incarnation. To explicate the interaction Bulgakov delves into the rich store of relational categories and divine-human meetings preserved in Christian dogma. In each of his dogmatic works Bulgakov explores one or more of these encounters in detail: Mary as Mother of God in *The Burning Bush*; the friendship between John the Forerunner and Jesus in *The Friend of the Bridegroom*; the engagement of the holy angels with human beings in *Jacob's Ladder*; the world-creating and world-redeeming Dyad of Son and Spirit in *The Lamb of God* and *The Comforter*; the yoked destiny of church and world in *The Bride of the Lamb*. Each of these relationships is irreducibly particular, and in that sense unique; but each also manifests God's positive relatedness to the flesh-and-blood world, to creation. The deity of Bulgakov's dogmatics is not Godhead-in-Itself but the God-for-others, divinity manifesting itself *ad extra* as divine love. The relationships generated by divine love are so intimate that the divine and human terms, while distinguishable in the abstract, cannot be separated in actual life; rather, each relationship in its own way embodies the humanity of God, the integral divine-human connection which pervades all being. Explicating these relationships is the business of dogmatics as Bulgakov understands it. Besides representing the humanity of God effectively (concretely, not abstractly) this approach also serves the ecclesiastical tradition, since the latter is a prime record – sometimes the unique record – of the relationships which the theologian explicates.

A good example of Bulgakov's affinity for relational categories which factor the world into dogmatic formulas is his discussion of ecclesiastical primacy in *St Peter and St John*. Discussions of primacy typically focus on the ministry of Peter, with Orthodox and Roman Catholics parting company over the issue of whether Peter's seat is occupied by one bishop seated above the others or by the worldwide company (*sobor*) of bishops. As an Orthodox theologian Bulgakov holds the latter view, but this is not his main concern in *St Peter and St John*. His aim is to complexify the concept of primacy by positing a 'second' primacy alongside Peter's, paradoxical as this may sound: the primacy of John the Theologian, the beloved disciple. Peter, designated rock of the church by Jesus, holds a primacy of authority. Following Peter's martyrdom his primacy passed to his episcopal successors, including the bishop of Rome as *primus inter pares*. John's is a primacy of love based on his special relationship to Jesus and also to Mary, whom John lodged and cared for after Jesus' ascension.

Another dimension of John's primacy is attested by the legend of his miraculous death, which as we have seen figures also in Soloviev's 'Brief Tale of the Anti-Christ.' When it came time for him to fall asleep in the Lord, John lay down in his grave with the words, 'Receive me, damp earth.' Thereafter his body was nowhere to be found. The *stikhira* for his feast describes John as 'settling apart from the earth yet not leaving the earth, but dwelling [here] and waiting for the dread Second Coming' (Slav. *ot zemli preseliaiushchagosia i ot zemli ne otstupaiushchago, no zhivushcha i zhdushcha strashnoe vtoroe prishestvie; Gk. ek gês methistamenon kai gês ouk aphistamenon*). Bulgakov glosses this text by saying John 'invisibly shepherds his flock [by] prophetically inspiring it.' Johannine primacy is thus a primacy of prophecy as well as of love, which again distinguishes it from Peter's primacy of office and authority. The distinction between Petrine and Johannine primacies shows that primacy in the church is not unitary but 'di-une, complex' (*dvuedinyi, slozhnyi*).[24]

Legends such as the story of John's death, widely accepted in Orthodoxy yet not dogmatically codified, serve as an important means of experientializing dogmatic theology. Bulgakov's thesis of a Johannine primacy is an effort to validate the prophetic principle in the church alongside the priestly-episcopal principle embodied in Peter and his successors. It also gives Bulgakov a way to suggest the prophetic principle is somehow bound up with the historical destiny of the eastern church, with which John the Theologian was closely identified already in antiquity. The faith of Orthodox renewalists that Orthodoxy has a

---

[24] *Sviatye Petr i Ioann*, pp. 79–90. The translation of John the Theologian is commemorated on September 26.

prophetic word to speak to the modern world finds theological grounding here.

Dogmatic theology is necessarily affected by the Johannine primacy. To be sure, dogmatics must speak with the voice of Peter, the voice of authoritative tradition. But no less should it speak with the living, prophetic voice of John. In the church of Peter dogmatics is a retrospective discipline; it expresses what has been duly taught by the line of successors going back to the rock of the church. In the Johannine church dogmatics is a prospective discipline; it expresses what is yet to come or just beginning to dawn. This, too, is an apostolic calling, though necessarily more provisional, more experimental, more conversational than the Petrine vocation. The prophetic principle reminds the dogmatic theologian that 'no pre-established forms are prescribed for church tradition – the Spirit living in the Church blows where it wills.'[25]

Having gone this far to justify the prophetic principle, however, Bulgakov bars the door to the type of prophetism that would explode the whole edifice of Orthodox dogma. Among the advocates of the new religious consciousness in Bulgakov's generation there were voices prophesying the so-called Third Testament or Testament of the Holy Spirit, a dispensation transcending historic Orthodoxy and abolishing the distinction between church and world. Bulgakov, too, believed the Third Person of the Trinity needed as concrete a realization in the world of flesh and blood as the Son; but unlike the prophets of a Third Testament, he was convinced such a revelation was given already in the New Covenant, in Mary the Mother of God, who from the beginning to the end of the gospel is intimately linked with the Holy Spirit:

> A more complete dwelling of the Holy Spirit in creation, in human being or angel, than that which occurred in the Mother of God cannot be imagined ... She is the Spiritual Human Being in heaven seated at the right hand of the God-human ... Thus it is foolish and impious to expect a new, Third Covenant involving a personal revelation of the Third Hypostasis, since the revelation of the Third Hypostasis, to

[25] *Drug zhenikha*, p. 193.

the extent possible and appropriate, has already happened in the Mother of God.[26]

Bulgakov's rejection of the Third Covenant idea was not only an act of dogmatic conservatism natural for any Orthodox priest, but a means of defending the specific character of his dogmatic project. Third Testament prophecy is in effect a form of utopianism. By abolishing the distinction between church and world, it destroys relational categories by erasing the tension on which they depend. Bulgakov, by contrast, drew upon the incarnation and other relational categories given in biblical and ecclesiastical tradition to clarify the relationship between Orthodoxy and the modern world. As he practiced it, dogmatic theology was neither a strictly ecclesiastical affair, a church dogmatics pure and simple, nor a Nietzschean or Merezhkovskian super-dogmatics. Bulgakov sought a church-and-world dogmatics founded on the humanity of God.

The centrality of relational categories in Bulgakov's dogmatics explains the ample role he assigned in it to sophiology. Sophia is by definition a relational category, especially when we recognize her as representing the dialogue between Orthodoxy and the modern world. In a church-and-world dogmatics sophiological discourse is a means of speaking about God–world linkages.

In Bulgakov's dogmatics sophiology occupies the place reserved for abstract doctrine of God or natural theology in scholastic and rationalistic dogmatics. Nowhere does Bulgakov attempt to prove the existence of God, to isolate the God-category conceptually or submit it to analysis while wondering how one might enter into a relationship with this God. Bulgakov proceeds as a biblical and church theologian, proclaiming the God in whose presence human beings and the cosmos already stand. Sophiology is a means of inscribing this point in categorical terms. In its bearing on the concept of God, sophiology is reducible to a single axiom: God cannot be thought of apart from the world. This not to say God cannot be thought of apart from our picture of the world at a given point in time; that would be too parochial a view. The 'world' as a dogmatic

[26] *Kupina neopalimaia*, p. 175.

category is first and foremost the world which God envisions and loves within himself from all eternity. Bulgakov's name for this world is divine Sophia.[27] Human beings cannot gaze at this world directly but experience it on the basis of analogies drawn from the created world, for the latter, being grounded in the divine world, bears the image of its source. Creaturely Sophia is Bulgakov's name for this matrix of analogies. The formulation and evaluation of these analogies is the work of constructive sophiology. The business may get complicated, but its axiom remains simple: the living God can be thought of only as Being-in-relation, as Lover of the world. 'There is no God without the world and no world outside of God: the world is in God.'[28]

The alliance between sophiology and dogmatics enhances both enterprises. By accommodating a sophiological perspective dogmatics equips itself to deal more self-consciously with the divine-human dialogue, especially as this occurs in culture-building activities such as science, the arts or economics. Dogmatics thereby better serves the humanity of God. No longer the science of 'divinity,' as it is sometimes called in English, dogmatics becomes more self-consciously a divine-human enterprise: humano-theology, church-and-world dogmatics. For its part, sophiology gains in clarity by attending to the positive religious ideals embedded in dogmatics rather than spinning a cocoon of theosophical speculation, the fatal flaw of sophiology when it proclaims itself an independent discipline. Moreover, engagement with dogmatics is necessary if sophiology is to accomplish its mission of cosmodicy, the justification of the world to the guardians of divine revelation.

Obviously sophiology must observe certain limits if the alliance with dogmatics is to work. It must forgo the ambition of realizing itself in a theoretical system. This is not a reasonable aspiration for an enterprise which is designed to generate positive ideals. Because new content is being produced by the world process at all times, sophiology must remain unfinished,

---

[27] '[Sophia] is the divine world, its foundation or idea in God, the world in God prior to its creation (prior, of course, not in the chronological but the ontological sense).' *Kupina neopalimaia*, p. 247.
[28] *Agnets bozhii*, p. 428.

open, in process, if it is to do its work. A definitive sophiological system would turn Sophia into an abstract principle.

Another constraint is that sophiology must not aspire to invent dogma. Sophia is the Lilac Fairy, not the Sleeping Beauty of dogmatic theology. She energizes dogma in all sorts of enchanting ways – galvanizing, crystallizing, illuminating, extending, elaborating; but she does not discard received dogmas or fashion new ones. Only the church can do that. The mission of sophiology is to foster conversation, not dominate it; to catalyze relationships between dogma and culture, not abolish the distinction. Sophia guides theologians over the terrain, mostly uncharted, where dogma meets experience, church meets world, Christianity meets culture, Orthodoxy meets modernity.

Bulgakov's admission of Sophia to the realm of dogmatic theology precipitated bitter disputes in his day and thereafter. A recent characterization of the sophiological tradition in modern Russian Orthodox thought as 'seductive and poisonous' represents the standard view of the matter on the part of traditionalist and Neopatristic Orthodox theologians.[29] This sort of challenge makes it important to ask whether anything essential would be lost if sophiology were discarded from Bulgakov's dogmatics. Frederick Copleston, for example, doubts 'whether [Sophia] is an essential element in the doctrine of Godmanhood.' He fails to see why 'in treating of the spiritualization of humanity the theologian cannot get on well enough with the doctrines of the Incarnation and the indwelling of the Holy Spirit.'[30] Copleston is not necessarily quarreling with the idea of a relational dogmatics; he simply believes the traditional dogmatic concepts are sufficient to sustain this project. Is he right?

One could defend Bulgakov by arguing that incorporating sophiology into dogmatic theology underscores the open-ended character of dogmatics, since Sophia is a process category. But this is a rather formalistic defense; one can imagine other means of keeping dogmatic theology open-ended besides sophiology. A

[29] Lewis Shaw, 'John Meyendorff and the Heritage of the Russian Theological Tradition,' in *New Perspectives on Historical Theology: Essays in Memory of John Meyendorff*, ed. Bradley Nassif (Grand Rapids, Michigan and Cambridge, UK: William B. Eerdmans Publishing Company, 1996), p. 20.

[30] Frederick C. Copleston, *Russian Religious Philosophy: Selected Aspects* (Notre Dame, Indiana: Search Press, University of Notre Dame, 1988), pp. 98–9.

more substantive defense runs as follows. Copleston holds that in treating 'the spiritualization of humanity,' the theologian can get on well enough with the doctrines of the incarnation and the indwelling of the Holy Spirit. He may be right about that. But he is wrong to suppose the spiritualization of humanity is all that Bulgakov's theology is about. As the thematizer of the humanity of God Bulgakov deals not just with the spiritualization of humanity but with *the humanization of the spiritual*, the humanization of the divine. Seriousness about this dimension of the humanity of God is what distinguishes his dogmatics from patristic dogmatics. The dogmatics of the humanity of God expresses the Word of God, but it speaks human words as well – fully human words. A fully human word is a free act, a task imagined and projected by an autonomous self, an expression of creativity (*tvorchestvo*, a key sophiological term for which no real equivalent exists in the vocabulary of patristic theology). One may call the fairy of creativity by another name if Sophia is disliked for some reason; but then the quarrel is about names, not substance. Bulgakov's point stands.

Some might suppose Bulgakov's point has the effect of subordinating the Word of God to human initiative; but this is a misinterpretion. Subordination of this sort would violate the humanity of God as surely as the opposite extreme. It is the Word of God, not some other word, to which human beings respond; only they do so with words that are truly their own. Genuine response is a creative act, a going-out-to-meet the Lord, a *podvig*.[31] This last term, brimming with movement, energy, aspiration, shows that Orthodox tradition always recognized

---

[31] Bulgakov rejected the concepts of 'imitation of Christ' and 'walking in His steps.' 'In Him each person must seek and find himself, his own, eternal, ideal [*umoposti-gaemyi*] face ("until Christ be formed in you"), yet this is never accomplished by way of outward, uncreative imitation ... This is always the *creative* path of finding precisely *one's own* cross and bearing it after Him in one's own way.' *Drug zhenikha*, pp. 227–8. The divinely inspired prophet is no exception: 'The words "who has spoken through the prophets" must be understood in the sense of an enabling influence of the Third hypostasis, who inspires the prophets, but not in relation to the *content* of the word itself, which comes from the Word [the Second hypostasis]. Thus it is wrong to understand the inspiration of the holy scriptures as a mechanical dictation of words of truth which the prophet passively writes down. We are dealing with the inspiration of the prophet himself by the word of truth which he has found deep within his own humanity through the activity of the Third hypostasis.' *Uteshitel'*, p. 217.

the dynamism of human response to the gospel. But it would be difficult to show that dogmatic theology as traditionally practiced brought that dynamism to the fore or gave an adequate account of it in systematic terms. Traditional theologizing was too wedded to church dogmatics to imagine the kind of church-and-world dogmatics in which Bulgakov is engaged. Church dogmatics is concerned with 'the vindication of tradition' (Pelikan). A church-and-world dogmatics must be concerned also with the vindication of reception, the justification of a God-seeking, God-interrogating, God-intoxicated humanity.

The vindication of reception affects the way dogmatic theology handles its subject matter. The business of dogmatics everywhere is to present the contents of the gospel – personages, stories, sayings, images, ideas – in such a way as to make plain the message of salvation. The business of dogmatics in so far as it is concerned with the vindication of reception is to interpret the same materials in the light of human freedom, human rights, human creativity; and to do so not just as an act of courtesy but in the faith that these values, too, inhere in the gospel, coinhere in divinity. In this sense one may say (at the risk of being misunderstood) that a dogmatics vindicating reception seeks to 'humanize' the gospel in the service of a fuller, better, more responsible appreciation of the humanity of God.

All of Bulgakov's dogmatic writings serve this end. In each work he treats one or more of the core relationships which constitute the gospel story, such as Mary as Mother of God and the friendship of John the Forerunner. He handles each relationship with as much concern for the dynamics of reception as for the divine initiative, recognizing such a balance is essential to an adequate representation of the meaning of the incarnation:

> [The incarnation] is possible only given the reception of God and the meeting with God [*bogopriiatie i bogovstrecha*] by the human race ... The justification of Wisdom in the Incarnation is accomplished through the union of Divine Wisdom in the descending and incarnate Son of God with Divine Wisdom in humanity in the persons of the Mother of God and the Forerunner.[32]

---

[32] *Drug zhenikha*, p. 214.

Bulgakov's biblical-dogmatic portraits of these two primal receivers and of others who welcome the Messiah into the world are as it were pictures at an exhibition illustrating 'the all-embracing humanity of the gospel' (*ego vysochaishaia vsechelovechnost'*).[33]

It is crucial, of course, that a sophiological dogmatics reject the prometheanism and utopianism which the rhetoric of humanization so often inspires in modern times. Bulgakov himself flirted with prometheanism in *Philosophy of Economy*. In the dogmatic enterprise, however, godless humanism and superhumanism are checked by the holy dogmas of Orthodoxy, which judge and cleanse humanity at the beginning of the gospel story, and sanctify and trans-figure it at the end. The dogmas save sophiology from destruction by protecting the conditions that make the divine-human conversation possible. Radical humanism does the opposite: it destroys its interlocutors and with them its potential as a humanizing enterprise. In sophiological dogmatics, then, one has a method for drawing new meaning out of traditional dogmas while at the same time respecting the integrity of the conversation. To be sure, the project depends on faith: faith in dogma as an inexhaustible source of meaning, and faith in dialogue itself, trust in the productivity of the conversation. Unlike utopianism, prometheanism and even certain types of church dogmatics, Bulgakov's faith does not demand a leap out of the world into the wholly other future of utopia, but an open-ended series of small leaps into the world in the confidence that one meets God Incarnate there.

THE HUMANITY OF THE GOSPEL (1): THE DEISIS

'The all-embracing humanity of the gospel' is the theme which connects the voluminous and variegated chapters of Bulgakov's dogmatic theology together. In the first trilogy Bulgakov's concern is to capture the deisis – John the Forerunner, Mary the Mother of God and the holy angels – in his humanizing lens. In the second trilogy he extends the theme

---

[33] *Agnets bozhii*, p. 229.

to the Holy Trinity, to the Son in *The Lamb of God*, to the Spirit in *The Comforter*. The humanity of the church is the theme of *The Bride of the Lamb*.

The deisis proclaims the humanity of the gospel by depicting 'intercession and prayer for the human race in its *earthly* life.'[34] It portrays beings of otherworldly holiness praying for the welfare of the world. All of them are connected with the created order in some way. Christ, the glorified man Jesus, is God Incarnate; Mary and John are human beings; the archangels are also created beings, although not human. In other words, createdness is integral to the holiness depicted in the deisis. The composition is an illustration of Bulgakov's claim that the incarnation 'is possible only when the human race is ready to receive and encounter God.'[35]

It might be objected that one over-humanizes the deisis by focusing on the human beings in it, since the composition includes the archangels as well. As we shall see, however, Bulgakov's angelology vindicates the humanity of the Gospel every bit as much as his mariology and treatment of John the Forerunner do. Bulgakov will argue that the angels, while not incarnate by nature, participate in the world of flesh by grace of the incarnation and thereby experience a plenitude of being that would not have been available to them otherwise. In other words, the angels are not merely attendants or executors of the gospel but beneficiaries. The humanity of God transfigures them along with the rest of creation.

The humanity depicted in the deisis is not generic but particularized in the persons of Mary, John and Jesus in glory. The personal character of the deisis conveys a message about prayer and the praying community. One does not see isolated individuals at prayer but a prayer-group, 'not just [John and Mary] standing next to each other at prayer, *but a union* in Christ and through Christ.' Their praying is not an ascent of the alone to the Alone, but 'two – or three if we count the Son of Man seated on the throne – gathered in His Name, and He

---

[34] *Drug zhenikha*, p. 202.
[35] *Drug zhenikha*, p. 214.

himself is in the midst of them.' The prayer of the deisis is 'all the more powerful by virtue of being ecclesiastical.' Yet the saints do not surrender their individuality in prayer. On the contrary, the deisis demonstrates 'the Church is not only unity in multiplicity [*mnogoedinstvo*] but multiplicity in unity [*edinomnozhestvo*] . . . in the image of the Holy Trinity, the one in three and three in one.'[36] The view of the church as a web of dynamic personal relationships illustrates the relational categories which structure Bulgakov's dogmatics.

Since the deisis stands for the whole church at prayer, one might ask why Mary and John are featured in it rather than other saints as well. The most obvious explanation is that Mary and John are attested by scripture as the two individuals most directly responsible for ushering the incarnate Word into the world. But why were John and Mary chosen for this honor in the first place? What qualified them for their role in the drama of the incarnation and thereafter for 'primacy in prayer, a headship of the Church at prayer?'[37] This is the question which Bulgakov's first trilogy is designed to answer.

Mary comes first in the biblical narrative as well as in Bulgakov's trilogy. Nevertheless it is better to begin our investigation with John. His case is less complex than Mary's in dogmatic terms. Moreover, Bulgakov grew clearer about the theme of his dogmatics in the process of composing it. In *The Burning Bush* he set for himself the limited task of refuting the modern Roman Catholic dogma of the immaculate conception of Mary, although the book deals with other issues as well. In *The Friend of the Bridegroom*, unencumbered by a polemical purpose, Bulgakov addresses his primary dogmatic theme more fluently and elegantly.

The key term in the dogmatics of John the Forerunner – 'johannology,' as Bulgakov calls it[38] – is found in the words John utters upon learning that Jesus, whom he had baptized, was pursuing a ministry of his own:

> You yourselves are my witnesses that I said, 'I am not the Messiah, but I have been sent ahead of him.' He who has the

---

[36] *Drug zhenikha*, p. 202.
[37] *Drug zhenikha*, p. 201.
[38] *Drug zhenikha*, p. 201.

bride is the bridegroom. The friend of the bridegroom, who
stands and hears him, rejoices greatly at the bridegroom's
voice. For this reason my joy has been fulfilled. He must
increase, but I must decrease. (Jn 3:28–30)

John is the friend of the Messiah, the friend par excellence, the
first to be called Jesus' friend in the gospel narrative. Jesus' other
friends, such as the disciples, his friend Lazarus and other interlocutors, do not alter John's primacy in this respect.

Bulgakov approaches his inquiry philosophically as well as
exegetically. Before delving into the biblical record of John's
friendship with Jesus, and into John's unusual mode of life, he
asks why Jesus needed a friend in the first place. Jesus was the
Messiah, the Lord of lords, the only Son of the Father. Why did
he need a friend? How, indeed, could such a one even have a
friend, for must not friends be peers in some sense?

These questions might lead one to expel the category of
friendship from the gospel. On the other hand, when one
considers that the gospel is not about God the Absolute but God
Incarnate, the case becomes clearer. Assessing the category of
friendship in the perspective of the incarnation, one comes to see
it is not just admissible but indispensable. An unapproachable
Messiah could be Lord of lords but could not embody the
humanity of God. When John the Forerunner hailed Jesus he
saw more than the divine king; he discerned a human being and
dared to befriend him. '*The Lord was met in the world.* He was
not alone, for *a friend, ready and worthy to receive Him*, came
out to meet him. The *friend* in this meeting represented *all
humanity.*'[39]

Naturally enough, the focus of exegetical attention in johannology usually falls on the Epiphany, the descent of the Holy
Spirit upon Jesus in the form of a dove and the voice from
heaven proclaiming his divine sonship. But for Bulgakov the
divinity of the Epiphany is only half of the event. Equally
important is the Messiah's 'appearance to the people, [His]
meeting with the human race.' The Messiah 'must not dwell in
solitude and isolation from the human race, though of course
this meeting must be a worthy one, i.e. it must be a genuine

---

[39] *Drug zhenikha*, p. 21.

meeting.'[40] Bulgakov's interpretation is an example of the vindication of reception in his dogmatics. He will not have an
Epiphany in which humanity participates as the passive
recipient of divine gifts. Humanity plays an active role in the
coming of the kingdom. The Messiah does not enter the world
like a stone thrown through a window. Someone goes out to
meet him, to greet him, to befriend him – and not just anybody,
but a person worthy of the task, the friend of the bridegroom.
Thanks to John's initiative Jesus averts the danger of isolation
from the humanity he comes to save. He becomes a sociable
Messiah, a Messiah with friends and companions. Bulgakov's
interpretation of John's reception of Jesus is the dogmatic equivalent of A.A. Ivanov's 'The Appearance of Christ to the People,'
the painting so admired by Archimandrite Feodor.[41] Like
Bukharev and Soloviev, Bulgakov promotes the meeting
between humanity and holiness, between Orthodoxy and the
world.

John's friendship with Jesus raises two questions: Why did the
Word's meeting with humanity in Mary's womb need to be
supplemented by a relationship with John? Second, what was it
about John that made him worthy to meet the Messiah?

To answer the first question Bulgakov appeals to the
psychology of human relationships. The danger threatening an
un-met Messiah is isolation. Jesus' 'Most Pure Mother could not
liberate him from this loneliness, for as the one who bore Him
She composed as it were a single whole with Him and for that
reason could not be "other" to Him, a friend (or, as we say, not
a second but a "third person").'[42] A mother cannot take the
place of a friend. Friendship requires a dimension of otherness
which a mother cannot supply. Otherness involves the risk of
competition and conflict, which can be sensed in the tensions
swirling just below the surface of the gospel narrative about
Jesus and John. Following his baptism by John, Jesus founded
a movement of his own which, humanly speaking, was in

---

[40] *Drug zhenikha*, p. 89.
[41] See Ch. 2, 'The Humanity of Jesus' above.
[42] *Drug zhenikha*, p. 17. The statement works well in Russian because of the play
on words between 'friend' (*drug*) and 'other' (*drugoi*). Cf. p. 112: '[John's] joy is
not over himself and not in himself but over another, over the *Friend* [*o drugom, o
Druge*].'

competition with the Baptist's. The gospel narrative glosses over the tension but cannot hide it. Jesus did not join John's movement, nor did John become a follower of Jesus.[43] The potential for rivalry between John and Jesus was a necessary condition for friendship.

Friendship is not homologous with either kinship or sexual attraction. Sex and family involve relations of commonality which make two individuals in some sense one; friendship is a turning toward another in conversation and regard in which a certain distance must be preserved. The fruits of friendship are also different. Mary ushers the Word into the world by bearing and nurturing Jesus. John, through baptism, confers spiritual birth. Epiphany was 'Christ's Pentecost,' a unique personal Pentecost which brought Jesus to maturity as the human being fit to be the Christ. In John the Forerunner Jesus found a second birth-giver, 'the spiritual parenting' he needed to clarify his vocation. For this reason Bulgakov can speak of 'the participation of the Forerunner in the work of the Incarnation.'[44]

The idea of John as a spiritual parent for Jesus brings rigor to Bulgakov's concept of friendship. He treats friendship not primarily as sentiment but as shared profession. Through his encounter with John, Jesus clarifies that which he is called to profess – the kingdom of God; and John recognizes in Jesus a colleague destined to carry their mission to a new level. The equality between them is not the static, distributive equality of identity, but the dynamic equality born of mutual commitment to a grand project.

What was it about John that made him worthy to be the Messiah's friend, the one chosen to meet Jesus on behalf of all humanity? Bulgakov gives the traditional Orthodox answer to this question: John was the greatest ascetic who ever lived. 'All types of human asceticism come together in the Forerunner: [he is] "preacher of Christ and Baptizer, angel, apostle, martyr, prophet, forerunner, priest, close friend, seal of the prophets, most honorable of those born of women." '[45] The list of John's

---

[43] Bulgakov discusses the complicated relations between John's and Jesus' movements in *Drug zhenikha*, ch. 3, pp. 68–74.

[44] *Drug zhenikha*, pp. 21–3; cf. pp. 26–7.

[45] *Drug zhenikha*, p. 20. Bulgakov is quoting a *stikhira* for John the Forerunner.

offices illustrates the richness of the concept of *podvig*. Asceticism means not just mortification of the flesh but the inner concentration and outward discipline required for spiritual achievements of any kind. It requires human aspiration and will-power, which is one of the reasons why classical Protestantism with its doctrine of justification by faith alone rejects most of the traditional forms of asceticism. Orthodoxy, unencumbered by the *sola fide* doctrine, sees prophecy, martyrdom and other spiritual attainments as requiring human effort and conforming with the ideal standard of human virtue, although it regards these achievements as fruits of divine grace at the same time.

Bulgakov is comfortable with this understanding of asceticism because it conforms so well with the conceptuality of the humanity of God. He portrays John the Forerunner as the *podvizhnik* who epitomizes the grandest of human aspirations and readies them for effectuation in the kingdom of God through the baptism of repentance. Baptism can thus be seen as a gracious gift and the crown of human ambition at the same time:

> The *thirst* for baptism had to awaken in Old Testament Judaism, the Baptist was its awakener, awakening it not just with words but with an actual deed, a baptizer summoning to baptism ... [His baptism] was not the sacrament [*tainstvom*] conferring the supernatural gift of the Holy Spirit, but it was, if we may put it this way, a natural-sacramental action [*prirodnym tainodeistviem*]: all the finest powers given to the human soul at the time of its creation were harnessed, awakened, concentrated in prayer, repentance, faith. The *natural* side of baptism, namely, that which is demanded *from the human being* for the reception of the *grace* of baptism is fully evident here.[46]

In other words John the Forerunner was both divinely appointed herald and paragon of human virtue. In John the *podvizhniki* of all ages went out to receive the Lord.

How is asceticism a qualification and preparation for friendship? The common term is self-sacrifice, or more precisely, self-realization through self-sacrifice. Asceticism is a

---

[46] *Drug zhenikha*, p. 71.

creative response to 'the antinomy of the sinful nature of human beings, who in order to affirm their authentic human nature, to save their souls, must give themselves away completely, destroy their souls.'[47] John's friendship for Jesus was like this: he lay down his life for him, lost himself for his friend and so doing completed his vocation as the Forerunner. When John's disciples came to him with the news that Jesus' disciples had begun a ministry of their own, John responded not with self-assertion but with self-diminution: 'He must increase, but I must decrease.' He spoke not out of frustration, nor for that matter just to please God or fulfill prophecy, but from his own joy at the coming of the kingdom which he and Jesus jointly professed. 'The friend of the bridegroom, who stands and hears him, rejoices greatly at the bridegroom's voice. For this reason my joy has been fulfilled' (Jn 3:29).

Bulgakov calls John's discourse in this passage 'a hymn' and likens it to the Song of Songs, an association prompted by John's use of the word 'bridegroom.' Yet there is a difference. The Song of Songs is a love song celebrating the union of Christ with his church, but the great Song 'does not know of a friend of the bridegroom.' John's hymn, while referring to the same wedding feast, is not a love song because, as we have seen, friendship differs from sexual love. The Song of Songs

> speaks of the joy and blessedness of the union of the divine with the human, of the deification of [human] nature; it does not speak of the *podvig* and joy of self-diminution, of the self-mortification of human nature as the precondition for this union, of the triumphant joy of humility which is the marital joy of the Forerunner, the friend of the Bridegroom. The friend has found the bride and delivers her to the Bridegroom.

The same dynamics operate in every person aspiring to lead a holy life:

> Every soul that comes to Christ must become not only a bride but also a friend of the Bridegroom, i.e. has to pass through the sacrificial immolation of human self-will, human

---

[47] *Drug zhenikha*, p. 20.

self-assertion, and indeed not just human but luciferian self-assertion, to reject self-deification and the divinity of humanity [*chelovekobozhie*], to taste the voluntary death of self-sacrifice.[48]

The point of greatest tension in John's ministry comes when he is imprisoned by Herod Antipas. What interests Bulgakov about the Passion of the Forerunner, as we may call these events, is the embassy which John sends to Jesus from prison asking, 'Are you the one who is to come, or are we to wait for another?' (Mt 11:3). The question is most unexpected from the one who hailed the Christ, baptized him, saw the heavens open and the Spirit descend upon him. How could John have failed to know the answer to his question? Bulgakov resolves the issue by calling this part of the story John's Gethsemane, his moment of hesitation and self-doubt, '*the temptation of the Forerunner as Forerunner.*' Like Jesus, John endures 'God-forsakenness' near the end of his earthly path, causing him to ask his 'tragic' question. His anguish underscores the humanity of the gospel. In the last days of his earthly ministry John 'was left to his human capacities, he had to find his path as Forerunner relying on these alone, he had to seek *in a human way* the Messiah he already knew by grace.' Jesus did not relieve the tension when he responded to John's question by saying, 'And blessed is anyone who takes no offense at me' (Mt 11:6). This was 'not an answer, but rather a greeting from the One who is to come to the one who is passing away.' Again John was thrown back upon himself to work out his salvation in faith, fear and trembling, lest anyone suppose John's knowledge of the Messiah was given to him '*free of charge.*' John's grandeur was not achieved without 'labor, *podvig*, effort.'[49]

One can see in Bulgakov's portrait of John a strong interest in humanizing the Baptist by relating him to the general pattern of human aspiration and moral struggle. The Forerunner is 'the key to a Christian anthropology' and 'the norm of human life in so

---

[48] *Drug zhenikha*, pp. 110–14.
[49] *Drug zhenikha*, pp. 139, 143–4.

far as it proceeds down the correct path.'[50] Yet this treatment, valuable as it is, does not do justice to the whole picture of John in the New Testament or later Orthodox tradition. John was not an urbane, Socratic sort of prophet. His desert abode, hair shirt, diet of locusts and wild honey, vehement rhetoric and message of a fiery apocalypse made him an exotic figure in his day. Post-scriptural traditions concerning John color the picture even more brightly. John is said to have conducted a ministry in the under-world as the herald of Christ's harrowing of hell. He is said to occupy the place in heaven where Lucifer once stood. In icons he is sometimes shown bearing his severed head in a eucharistic chalice. He is often depicted with wings, that is to say as a kind of angel. And of course he occupies a place of honor in the deisis.[51]

Most of the exotic features of John are concentrated in the picture of the winged angel of the desert. The point of this iconographic convention is to indicate John's realization of an 'angel-like' (*angelopodobnyi*) way of life on earth. Patristic interpretation of this tradition focused on the mystery of a mortal human being possessing the ascetical fortitude and grace to live as an angel while still in the flesh. Bulgakov, as thematizer of the humanity of God, is interested not just in how a human being could become an angel but how an angel could become a human being. How could angelic being – immortal, intellectual, collective[52] – be realized in a mortal, embodied, individual human life?

The bridging of the gulf between the human and angelic

---

[50] *Drug zhenikha*, pp. 149, 152.

[51] For these and other examples, see *Drug zhenikha*, chs 9–10. On the connection between John and Lucifer, see also pp. 239–40, where Bulgakov observes that the temptation of Jesus in the wilderness by Satan follows immediately after his baptism. As the friend of the bridegroom the Forerunner remedies the loss of the archangelic friend whose company the Son enjoyed in heaven prior to Satan's rebellion.

[52] 'Angels form an *assembly* or *host* [*sobor, voinstvo*], whereas human beings form a *human race* [*rod*] ... The fundamental distinction between a human being and an angel lies in the fact that only the human being possesses the *fullness* of the Image of God. He is the bearer of [the Image] not only in hierarchical union with all others; rather, *each* person [bears it] in himself.' *Drug zhenikha*, pp. 236–7. For the same distinction in somewhat more abstract language, see *Kupina neopalimaia*, p. 40.

worlds can be appreciated, if never fully comprehended, as one of the consequences of the incarnation. At first glance it might appear the angelic world is left out of the mystery of the incarnation because the kenosis of the Son takes the form of being-made-human, not being-made-angel. Angels are messengers of the divine will, including the divine will for incarnation, as when Gabriel makes the great announcement to Mary. But if we define angels strictly in terms of the role of messenger we put them forever at a certain remove from the goods which they announce or deliver. The incarnation in particular is problematic for the angelic world, since angels are bodiless. Conversely, the angelic world is problematic for the incarnation, since if the latter is to be pan-cosmic, it must embrace the whole created order, which includes the angels. These problems are solved by the establishment of a new relationship between the angelic and human worlds in the person of John. The Forerunner is as it were 'an angel-made-human [*vochelovechivshiisia angel*] or angelic human being, the living and personal link between the two worlds.' By virtue of John's becoming an angel-human (*angelochelovek*), the angelic world gains 'indirect co-reception and co-inclusion in the incarnation.'[53]

Angelochelovek suggests an analogy with *Bogochelovek*, the God-human: as divine being was made human in Jesus, so angelic being was made human in John. Bulgakov does not go on to coin the term *angelochelovechestvo*, although he certainly could have done so because the word expresses the theme of his angelology: the humanization of the angels and the angelization of humanity.

The bond between human beings and angels makes possible their mutual incorporation in a single church. 'The union of angels and human beings in the one Church, a consequence of the incarnation, is for the angelic world, too, a kind of new creation, an expansion and enrichment of angelic nature through a new intimacy with human [nature].'[54] The parallelism

---

[53] *Drug zhenikha*, pp. 183–6.
[54] *Drug zhenikha*, p. 241. Cf. *Kupina neopalimaia*, p. 228, where Bulgakov asserts the humanization of the angelic world was anticipated by the prophets of Israel. In Ezekiel 1:5, for example, the prophet sees heavenly creatures which appear to be 'of human form.' Bulgakov explains: 'the Glory of the heavenly world corresponds to

with human salvation is reinforced when we consider that the new creation is not something the angels could have secured for themselves. An angel, as a purely intellectual being, cannot become a human being. However, since human nature 'stands ontologically higher than the angels,' i.e. incorporates all dimensions of created being, a human being can become an angel.[55] This is what happened in John. His *podvig* perfected him to be the Forerunner, the angel in the flesh preparing the way for the Word made flesh. In John the angelic messengers who figure in the history of salvation are humanized.

John's ministry as angel in the flesh suggests an analogy with the work of Mary, in whose womb the Word was made flesh. As seen by Orthodox tradition, John and Mary have much in common. Their life-stories are linked at the beginning of the New Covenant in Luke 1, the 'earthly prologue' to the gospel as Bulgakov calls it.[56] They are also the paradigms, female and male, of moral purity under the law of Israel. For this reason they stand first among 'the children of Wisdom' (cf. Lk 7:35) and sometimes appear on icons of Sophia.[57] Both John and Mary are virgins. They are also linked to each other through the person of John the Theologian, traditionally regarded as the only virgin among the apostles. In Orthodox tradition John the Theologian is viewed as having been one of John the Forerunner's followers and thus a witness to the baptism of Jesus. Mary is believed to have lived in the Theologian's house after Jesus' ascension, an appropriate domicile in the light of the beloved disciple's intimacy with her son, itself a continuation of the friendship extended to the Messiah by the Forerunner.

For Bulgakov these connections are important because they vindicate the factor of human receptivity in the gospel. They show

---

the Glory of the human world and – in this sense – is human, hence the animal and human characteristics of the ranks of angels on whom the Lord rests, "seated on the cherubim." ' The likeness of a human being on the divine throne – noted also in the visions of Daniel 7 and Revelation 4–5 – 'testifies directly to the heavenly eternity of the human image.' Bukharev read Ezekiel 1, Revelation 4–5 and comparable texts in much the same way; see pp. 88–9 above.

[55] *Drug zhenikha*, p. 183.
[56] *Drug zhenikha*, p. 39. John 1 is the 'heavenly prologue.'
[57] *Drug zhenikha*, pp. 213–16; *Kupina neopalimaia*, p. 189.

the Mother of God and the Forerunner to be creative receivers, not passive recipients, of the Word made flesh. Bulgakov's quarrel with the Roman Catholic dogma of the immaculate conception of Mary – the proposition promulgated by Pope Pius IX in 1854 that Mary was conceived free of original sin in her mother's womb – turns precisely on this point. Bulgakov sees Mary as an agent, not an instrument. While the annunciation was surely a divine miracle, a human grandeur also was involved.

Mariology presents a textbook case of the development of dogma in Christian tradition. Unlike classical Protestantism, which insists on a scriptural basis for dogmas and therefore rejects most mariology, Orthodoxy and Roman Catholicism accept church tradition as well as scripture as a source of dogmatic truth. Thus Bulgakov does not object to the dogma of the immaculate conception on the grounds it is not attested in the New Testament. Most johannology also lacks scriptural sanction for that matter.[58] Nor does Bulgakov fault the dogma because it is a modern innovation, although here he shows himself to be more open-minded than many Orthodox theologians. While not opposed to the development of dogma in principle (recognition of tradition as a source of dogma implies some sort of development), the Orthodox Church has utilized this concept much more sparingly than Rome, with Orthodox conservatives taking the view that most important dogmatic issues were settled by the fathers of the seven ecumenical councils (325–787). Bulgakov is much more heavily invested in the idea of tradition as an ongoing, organic process. He is especially critical of traditionalism, that is to say, the reduction of tradition to the particular historical forms which it takes at a given point in time. As Bulgakov saw it, 'no preordained forms are prescribed for church tradition – the Holy Spirit, living in the Church, blows where it wills.'[59] New dogmas concerning Mary therefore lie within the realm of possibility. They may even be necessary if Bulgakov is right to observe that the Orthodox

---

[58] Icons depicting John holding a cross or a chalice link him to the paschal and eucharistic mysteries. Bulgakov recognizes 'there is not even a hint' of these ideas in the gospel. *Drug zhenikha*, pp. 191–2. Naturally the same is true of the traditions concerning the glorification of John.

[59] *Drug zhenikha*, p. 193.

Church 'has not yet realized the treasure of revelation concerning the Mother of God which is contained in the church's veneration of Her.'[60]

Nevertheless, Bulgakov rejects the Roman Catholic dogma of the immaculate conception because it seems to him to diminish the moral grandeur of Mary by releasing her from original sin. To be sure, Bulgakov affirms the 'personal sinlessness' of Mary.[61] The issue is how this purity came about. Was it the result of a divine miracle, or was it in some measure also Mary's personal accomplishment? The dogma of the immaculate conception affirms the former in a radical way, dispelling the tension in the idea of personal sinlessness through a dogmatic *deus ex machina*. As a result Mary is alienated from the human condition: 'removed from original sin, Mary [is] removed from humanity.'[62] This in turn makes it impossible to regard Mary's life as a *podvig*, a winning-through to purity by means of asceticism, virtue and piety. The immaculate conception dehumanizes Mary either by reducing her to a subhuman tool or by transforming her into a superhuman goddess. If Bulgakov is right to believe that one of the faults of traditional dogmatics is insufficient appreciation for the human side of the incarnation, then the dogma of the immaculate conception clearly represents a step backwards.

A further problem with the dogma is that it alienates Mary from history by eliminating 'the whole human side of the preparation for the Incarnation.' The immaculate conception makes it impossible to construe history as 'the *common task* of humanity, a single and connected action having the incarnation as its center.' In particular the dogma undermines the status of Israel as the people called to moral and cultic purity for the cause of human salvation. A dogmatics of Mary which abolishes her moral achievement denigrates the grandeur of Israel because Mary's moral horizon, the standard of purity she accepted and fulfilled, was defined exclusively by the law of Israel. Hence Mary's personal sinlessness was 'not just Her personal accomplishment [*podvig*] but the accomplishment of the whole Old

---

[60] *Agnets bozhii*, p. 232.
[61] *Kupina neopalimaia*, p. 70.
[62] *Kupina neopalimaia*, p. 108.

Testament church of all [her] forefathers and fathers in faith as well.'[63] Israel's legal and prophetic traditions are short-circuited by the immaculate conception because a miracle of this kind could not have been 'anticipated' by the prophets and teachers of Israel. Salvation becomes an arbitrary 'amnesty.'[64]

Bulgakov's respect for historic Israel is not limited to Mary. In his johannology he also stresses the Jewishness of his subject. John's righteousness was that of a man who fulfilled the law of Moses 'to the extent that it can be fulfilled by a human being.' To objections based on Paul's teaching that human beings are not justified by the works of the law, Bulgakov replies 'the impossibility of being justified [by the law] by no means signifies the impossibility of fulfilling it, [for the law] was given not only for awareness of sin but for fulfillment unto salvation, to be the norm of Old Testament piety, as Psalm 118 [119] eloquently testifies.'[65] The law of Israel is a positive divine good.

Bulgakov handles the teaching and preaching ministry of Jesus similarly. Rather than construing Jesus' works in absolute terms as 'the word of the Word about the Word, of truth about Truth,' he prefers to see Jesus as 'a prophet like the other prophets' of Israel who stood in need of the inspiration of the Holy Spirit. This view, affirming the continuity of Jesus' ministry with those who came before him, agrees with the 'kenotic self-diminution of the Lord.'[66] Just as the Word made flesh was not a Superman but the Son of Man, so Jesus was not a Superprophet, but a prophet of Israel like the rest. No more than Mary were the prophets tools in the hands of God. 'In prophetic ministry and in the very act of prophesying the *humanity* of the prophet is in no way eliminated.' Likewise in Jesus, 'the word of divine truth proclaimed by Truth itself was at the same time a *human* word, inexhaustible in its depth but directed at human beings and accessible to them.'[67] The

---

[63] *Kupina neopalimaia*, p. 70.
[64] *Kupina neopalimaia*, pp. 92–3. In an interesting extension of his point Bulgakov observes that the doctrine of the immaculate conception opens 'a path leading straight to Calvinism with its doctrine of arbitrary predestination.'
[65] *Drug zhenikha*, pp. 154–5.
[66] *Agnets bozhii*, pp. 354–5.
[67] *Agnets bozhii*, p. 354; cf. pp. 279–81.

pan-dogmatic scope of Bulgakov's theme is clear: the humanity of God entails not just the humanity of the gospel but the humanity of all scripture, the humanity of all Israel, the humanity of all revelation.

Of course an assessment of divine-human mutuality in Mary must be based on more than contemplation of her grandeur as a human being. Her special connection with the divine must be considered as well. Bulgakov leaves plenty of room for this dimension in his mariology. Yet even here the humanization of the divine figures as prominently as the spiritualization of humanity.

In dogmatic terms Mary's link to the divine may be expressed as a special connection with the Holy Spirit. The archangel's words at the annunciation are explicit about this: 'The Holy Spirit will come upon you, and the power of the Most High will overshadow you' (Lk 1:35). Through the Spirit's visitation Mary became Mother of God (*Bogomater'*). Her moral purity and receptivity made her 'transparent for the Holy Spirit.' The permeation of Mary's being by the Spirit was so complete that she should be regarded not just as a supremely 'spiritual' person but as 'the Spirit-bearing Person' (*Dukhonosnym Chelovekom*). Mary received the Holy Spirit with her whole being and bore its unique gift – the Son – into the world. She was the 'Spirit-bearer' (*Dukhonositsa*), the Spirit's 'living abode' in the world. The last of these terms is very expressive in Russian: *priiatelishche* (abode, lit. 'receiving-place') connotes active hospitality and friendship (*priiatel'*, 'friend').[68] The term suggests yet another analogy between Mary and John the Forerunner: as the friend of the bridegroom received the Second Person of the Trinity into the world, so Mary, the friend of the Holy Spirit, received the Third.

Bulgakov draws an even bolder analogy when he likens Mary's relationship with the Third Person to Jesus' relationship

---

[68] *Kupina neopalimaia*, p. 141. The word *priiatelishche* is liturgical, used of Mary in a *stikhira* and doxology of the service for the Nativity of the Virgin (8 September). Bulgakov got the idea of using the word to enrich the theology of friendship from Pavel Florensky. See Florensky, *The Pillar and Ground of the Truth*, trans. and annotated by Boris Jakim, with an intro. by Richard F. Gustafson (Princeton, New Jersey: Princeton University Press, 1997), pp. 310–11 and p. 568, n. 774.

with the Second. In Mary the Holy Spirit found its perfect human image, just as the Son found his perfect image in Jesus. As Spirit-bearer Mary co-ordinates humanity with Trinity by linking it to the Third Person as Jesus the God-human links it to the Second. A restored humanity in the image of the Holy Trinity will therefore manifest both *bogochelovechestvo* and *bogomaterinstvo*, the humanity of God and the motherhood of God, as in the icon of the Mother of God with her child. 'The God-human and the Spirit-bearer, the Son and the Mother, revealing the Father through the Second and Third hypostases, respectively, manifest also the fullness of the divine image in humanity, or conversely, of the human image in God.'[69]

This formulation makes for a powerful mariology. At the same time, Bulgakov recognizes a distinction must be made between Christ and Mary to avoid what would otherwise be two divine incarnations – Christ/Christa, Divine Male/Divine Female, God Incarnate/Goddess Incarnate and the like. The problem with such an outcome, aside from the offense to the Orthodox dogmatic tradition, is it collapses personal identities on both the human and the divine level, merging Mary with Jesus, and Spirit with Son. This produces a generic humanity and quasi-unitarian divinity, hence an abstract rather than a personal humanity of God. The antidote is to be found in basic trinitarian dogmatics, that is to say, in respecting the distinctions between the three Persons and their respective vocations. The Son is 'begotten' by the Father and executes the divine will for the world through incarnation. The Spirit 'proceeds' from the Father and executes the divine will for the world through vivification ('the Giver of Life') and sanctification. Bulgakov sees these distinctions reflected in the creaturely images of the divine hypostases. Hence Mary is not God incarnate because incarnation is not the Spirit's work. As the humanity of the Holy Spirit she is the perfectly sanctified, revivified, deified human being, to such a high degree that her mortal flesh is glorified and assumed into heaven at the dormition. But Mary does not anticipate Jesus' work any more than Jesus recapitulates hers. Their missions are distinct, though co-ordinated and equally integral to the humanity of God.

[69] *Kupina neopalimaia*, pp. 139–42.

More needs to be said about Mary's work. Bulgakov's name for it is *bogomaterinstvo*, a term which obviously parallels *bogochelovechestvo*. Like the latter, it is derived from a traditional title (*Bogomater'*, the Mother of God), although Bulgakov's thematization of the concept in abstract-nominal form is modern. In effect Bulgakov does with mariology what Soloviev did with christology: taking traditional dogmatic material, he broadens its application to generate a positive religious ideal.

That which *bogomaterinstvo* adds to *bogochelovechestvo* may be clarified by considering the translation of the term into English. If *bogochelovechestvo* may be translated as the humanity of God, then *bogomaterinstvo* may be translated as the motherhood of God. The translation involves predicating motherhood of God as well as of Mary, which may offend traditionalist ears; but it expresses what Bulgakov had in mind when he fashioned the word. If we suppose *bogomaterinstvo* refers simply to Mary's motherhood, not God's, we are left without a basis for stating what was special or different about Mary except her offspring was special, i.e. he was not just any child, but the God-human. But a statement about the child does not communicate the full mystery of Mary because, standing alone, it could be taken to imply the Virgin's womb was a passive receptacle, and any womb would have served just as well. The error is comparable to the one which Bulgakov criticized in the dogma of the immaculate conception. Such a view also skips too gingerly over the inherent paradox of *bogomaterinstvo*, namely, Mary could not have given birth to God by virtue of her humanity alone, since human beings cannot generate the divine. *Bogomaterinstvo* is a divine mystery, albeit one in which the human being Mary plays a creative role.

A better appreciation of *bogomaterinstvo* can be had by reviewing once again the analogy between Mary as Spirit-bearer and Jesus as God-human. As Jesus is the perfect image of the Word, the perfect image of divine sonship, so Mary is the perfect image of the Holy Spirit, the perfect image of divine – what? The answer must have to do with the Spirit's particular role in the creation and salvation of the world. Now the Spirit gives life, as on the first day of creation when it brooded over the face of the watery abyss; and the Spirit sanctifies, that is to say, inspires, nurtures and strengthens the children of God. In both respects the Spirit's work may be described as a kind of mothering. Even in the inner life of the Trinity the Spirit has a maternal function. Bulgakov states this unambiguously:

> The Holy Spirit, proceeding from the Father to the Son, finds the Son already begotten but actualizes Him for the Father through Itself. In this sense the Spirit is as it were a hypostatic motherhood proceeding from the Father to the Son, 'the giving of life' being the special property of the Holy Spirit.[70]

For Bulgakov, then, *bogomaterinstvo* is a life-giving and life-nurturing force far vaster than the motherhood of Mary, although the latter is the perfect creaturely image of it. The work of the Spirit is nothing less than 'a kind of universal, cosmic motherhood of God' (*nekotoroe vseobshchee, kosmicheskoe bogomaterinstvo*). Annunciation looks ahead to Pentecost and beyond when 'creation will appear as Christ in the process of being born, human existence as the God-bearing womb, the whole world as the Mother of God.'[71]

Bulgakov's mariology is a highly original dogmatic composition combining both traditional and modern motifs. The pan-cosmic scope of Mary's motherhood is attested throughout the Orthodox world by popular veneration of Mary as 'guardian of all creation ... sovereign of the seas, helper of crops, fragrant flower, protectoress of cities and kingdoms, guardian of the plant world.'[72] This kind of veneration resonates also with Bulgakov's philosophy of economy, his longstanding fascination with the stewardship of productive forces. Bulgakov's understanding of Mary's capacity for virginal conception runs along similar lines. Mary's body, like the human body in paradise before the Fall, was 'the obedient tool of the spirit ... Her body was endowed with that spiritual plasticity by virtue of which it became capable of realizing a

---

[70] *Kupina neopalimaia*, pp. 148–9. The Russian is: *Dukh Sv., iskhodiashchii ot Ottsa k Synu, nakhodit uzhe rozhdennogo Syna, no Ego dlia Ottsa Soboiu osushchestvliaet. V etom smysle On est' kak by ipostasnoe materinstvo, iskhodiashchee ot Ottsa k Synu, 'zhivotvorenie,' kak narochitoe svoistvo Dukha Sviatogo.*

[71] *Kupina neopalimaia*, pp. 160–1.

[72] *Kupina neopalimaia*, p. 206.

movement of the spirit.'[73] Bulgakov's speculation here is as much informed by the *naturphilosophisch* intimation of a sympathy between nature and spirit as by the traditional reverence for the body of Mary. In other words Bulgakov both honors and transforms traditional material. He honors dogmas by believing in them. He transforms them by reconceptualizing, thematizing and systematizing them, coining terms when necessary, and turning an episodic piety into a comprehensive intellectual program.

The extensive development of the idea of the motherhood of God in Bulgakov's dogmatics raises the issue of whether Bulgakov should be regarded as a forerunner of what is now called feminist theology. Brenda Meehan is probably right to caution interpreters against reading Bulgakov in this way.[74] The concern with gender and power and the programmatics of inclusiveness are lacking in his thought. At the same time, one cannot deny the motherhood of God, Sophia and related themes effect a rather striking feminization of dogmatic categories in Bulgakov's theology. The best way to explain this phenomenon is probably to relate it to the humanity of God. If, as I am arguing, the humanity of God means not just the spiritualization of the human but the humanization of the divine, and if concrete humanity is always gendered ('male and female he created them'), then one of the things an exposition of the humanity of God will require is the feminization of categories used to speak about the divine, including those pertaining to the inner life God, as in Bulgakov's feminized trinitarianism. Whether feminized theology necessarily leads to feminist theology is an issue to be explored in contexts where it arises. Bulgakov's historical context was not one of these.[75]

---

[73] *Kupina neopalimaia*, pp. 171–2.

[74] Brenda Meehan, 'Wisdom/Sophia, Russian Identity, and Western Feminist Theology,' *Cross Currents* 46 (1996): 149–68.

[75] For a discerning analysis of gender-categories and related issues in Bulgakov's thought see the essay by Bernice Glatzer Rosenthal, 'The Nature and Function of Sophia in Sergei Bulgakov's Prerevolutionary Thought,' *Russian Religious Thought*, eds Kornblatt and Gustafson, pp. 154–75.

THE HUMANITY OF THE GOSPEL (2):
TRINITY AND CHRIST

The interest in the human and cosmic connections of the Trinity evident in Bulgakov's mariology is a feature of his trinitarianism generally. It could scarcely be otherwise. A theologian explicating the humanity of the gospel must seek to contemplate the humanity of the Trinity, for the Trinity is the ground of the gospel.

Bulgakov's favorite term for the human and cosmic connections of the Trinity is of course Sophia, a usage which his traditionalist critics condemned as implying a fourth person of the Godhead or, alternatively, a unitarian Godhead of which the Persons are merely modes. In fact neither heresy is to be found in Bulgakov's dogmatics. His trinitarianism cannot even be called revisionist, if by this term one means a scheme which undoes the trinitarian relations as traditionally defined. What we are dealing with here, as elsewhere in Bulgakov's dogmatics, is Orthodox theology in a new key, a creative reconstruction of dogma in a modern idiom, unprecedented but not ungrounded in antecedent tradition.

Bulgakov's trinitarianism is first of all a good example of the Greek patristic approach to the Trinity in its rigorous regard for the distinctions between the Persons and its rejection of modalism and other tendencies to unitarianism. Also absent is the Augustinian interest in putative 'vestiges' of the Trinity in the created world. While Bulgakov is profoundly interested in the Trinity's activity in the world, he views this activity as the hypostatic self-manifestation of unique Persons, not the placid reflection of a generic triad.

Bulgakov exploits trinitarian distinctions in order to celebrate the mystery of mutuality in difference. So, for example, when distinguishing between Christmas and Pentecost, the birthday of Christ and the birthday of the church, he draws on the distinctive vocations of Son and Spirit. The Son becomes incarnate in an individual human being; the Spirit does not become incarnate but 'descends and rests upon human beings.' The vocations are not interchangeable, although they effect 'one salvation' and 'one humanity of God.' The unity of purpose is evident in the preparatory role of each divine Person in the other's saving work: the Spirit makes Christmas possible by 'overshadowing' Mary (Lk 1:35), the Son makes Pentecost possible by 'sending' the Spirit (Jn 15:26).[76]

Mutuality in difference can also be seen in the work of the Holy Trinity in the creation of the world. The Father is the creator, the initiating hypostasis, but he works through the Son, who provides the 'foundation and content' of the world ('All things came into being through him,' Jn 1:3). The Son accomplishes his work silently in deference to the Father. In the creation of the world we hear not the Word per se but 'the words of the Word'; only in the incarnation does the Son reveal himself in person. The Spirit, too, plays a role in the creation of the world, brooding over the pre-cosmic waters and engendering life. But like the Son, the Spirit manifests itself as a silent servant of the Father, not hypostatically. At the same time the Spirit's work in the creation of the world differs from the Son's. The Son gives the world its 'words' or founding principles; the Spirit actualizes the Son's 'words' by giving them life, actuality, concreteness. The Son is the 'demiurge' or craftsman of all things; the Spirit is the 'cosmo-urge,' the enlivener or life-force of all things.[77]

The most important refinement in Bulgakov's trinitarianism is the distinction between the monarchy of the Father and 'the Dyad' of Son and Spirit. Following patristic tradition, Bulgakov sees a hierarchy in the Trinity to the extent the Father always reveals himself, not another, whereas Son and Spirit reveal the will of the Father as well as themselves. The Father, on the other hand, reveals himself not to the world directly but to Son and Spirit, whereas Son and Spirit are the revelatory or 'sophianic' hypostases, emptying themselves into the world to manifest the will of the Father.[78] But if Bulgakov follows tradition in accepting the monarchy of the Father and rejecting 'abstract equality' as foreign to the spirit of trinitarianism,[79] his interest

---

[76] *Uteshitel'*, p. 404.
[77] *Uteshitel'*, pp. 223–6. For 'demiurge' and 'cosmo-urge' see *Agnets bozhii*, pp. 134–5.
[78] The distinction is consistently observed. The Father is *otkryvaiushchiisia*, Son and Spirit are *otkryvaiushchie*, e.g. *Agnets bozhii*, p. 334. For Son and Spirit as the 'sophianic' hypostases see *Uteshitel'*, p. 216.
[79] *Agnets bozhii*, p. 335.

does not lie in the divine monarchy. It is the sophianic hypostases linking Trinity to the world and unleashing the dialogue of the divine with the extra-divine which capture his imagination. One can see Bulgakov's interest in the dialogue of Orthodoxy with the world inspiring his trinitarianism at this point.

Bulgakov's focus on the Dyad shapes the trilogy *On the Humanity of God*. *The Lamb of God* presents a dogmatics of the Son; *The Comforter*, a dogmatics of the Spirit; *The Bride of the Lamb*, a dogmatics of the church, the community of Son and Spirit in the world. The dogmatics of the Father, as already noted, appears only as an addendum to the second volume. *On the Humanity of God* is thus a dogmatics of the Dyad rather than of the Triad, a dogmatics of Trinity-in-the-world.

To elaborate his trinitarianism Bulgakov draws on the resources of kenotic theory. As he sees it, the whole Trinity, not just the Son, stands in a kenotic relationship to the world, although each Person has its own distinctive mode of kenosis. The kenosis of the Father is the creation of the world out of nothing. In traditional dogmatics *creatio ex nihilo* figures as the touchstone of divine transcendence and omnipotence. For Bulgakov the case is more complicated. 'The creative "Let there be ...," the command of divine omnipotence, also expresses the sacrifice of divine love, the love of God for the world, of the Absolute for the relative, by virtue of which the Absolute itself becomes Absolute-Relative.' The act of creation is not just a manifestation of divine might, but 'a voluntary self-diminishment, a metaphysical kenosis,' whereby the divine Absolute admits the existence of beings outside itself. Moreover, the creatures of the world are not passive material in the hands of the creator but are endowed with a life of their own, a freedom of their own, a creaturely divinity so to speak, precisely because they bear the image of their divine creator. 'In its awareness of itself as the relative-absolute, the creature reflects that Absolute-Relative from Which ("Let there be ...") and in relation to Which ("For in him we live and move and have our being") its being is defined.'[80] In his critique of a one-sided emphasis on

---

[80] *Agnets bozhii*, p. 150. Cf. *Uteshitel'*, p. 398: 'The condescension of absolute Divinity to relative being is accomplished by God in the creation of the world, at which moment [the world] is posited as an other [*kak inobytie*] alongside God.'

divine omnipotence in the doctrine of creation, Bulgakov arrives at a position close to that of Anglo-American process theology.

The kenosis of Son and Spirit takes the form of being sent into the world by the Father, although in two different ways. The Son is sent to become incarnate in the man Jesus, the Christ, and to suffer death upon the cross as the sacrificial Lamb of God. The Spirit is sent into the world to guide the community founded on the sacrifice of the Son by imparting glorious divine gifts to it. In other words, the Son reveals himself but conceals his divinity; the Spirit manifests its divinity but conceals itself. The kenosis of the Son consists in 'taking the form of a slave, being born in human likeness' (Phil. 2:7); the kenosis of the Spirit consists in being the servant of the Son and therefore concealing its own identity or 'Face' (*Lik*) until the end of the age.[81]

The kenosis can also be formulated as the divine regard for the integrity of created being, 'the subjection of the Measureless to a measure.' The Son respects the human measure in Jesus; the Spirit respects it in those whom it sanctifies, incorporating them into the divine life '*not measurelessly* but from measure to measure.' The Spirit 'does not force human freedom but persuades it,' winning it over with patience and humility in an 'ongoing Pentecost' or 'final kenosis' which will continue until the end of the age.[82]

The difference in modes should not be taken to imply the kenosis of each divine Person takes place in isolation. On the contrary, the Trinity is the quintessential image of communion. So, for example, while the Son and only the Son is sent into the world to die on the cross, both Father and Spirit participate in the Son's Passion. The Father suffers by sending his beloved Son into the world in the first place, and he too is 'orphaned' by the crucifixion. Moreover, 'in the human crucifixion of the Son and divine co-crucifixion of the Father, that very love, the hypostatic Love of Father and Son, the Holy Spirit, the joy of love, the One who unites [the Son] with the Father, is crucified as well.'[83]

The mutuality manifested in the pan-trinitarian kenosis sets

---

[81] *Uteshitel'*, pp. 315–23.
[82] *Uteshitel'*, pp. 398, 318–23.
[83] *Agnets bozhii*, p. 383.

the pattern for the relationship of the Son to humanity in the incarnation. Schooled in the Trinity to do his work while respecting that of the other Persons, the Son as incarnate Word respects 'the *independence* [*samobytnost'*] of human nature in its freedom. Christ's humanity does not take the place of our natural humanity but co-lives, co-suffers, co-abides [*so-zhivet, so-strazhdet, so-prisutstvuet*] with it.'[84] Bulgakov's verb forms bear witness to the incarnate Word as Immanuel: God with us.

Bulgakov's trinitarianism, anticipating Neopatristic personalism, places him in the mainstream of twentieth-century Orthodox dogmatics. Yet Bulgakov did not believe the dogmatics of the Trinity could be formulated in personalistic categories alone. While the triune God subsists as three divine Persons, the hypostases share a common nature, or *ousia*. The divine *ousia* does not exist apart from the Persons, but it cannot be reduced to them, either, for 'if we view ousia only under the aspect of *personal* being, for all practical purposes we eliminate it.' This is bad theology because it makes God 'poorer than created spirit,' construing his personhood as 'an empty, abstract *ego* rather than as a vital spirit with a nature of its own.' The concept of *ousia* enhances trinitarianism by challenging us to envision the divine nature 'not just as power and depth, but as self-manifesting content.'[85] Since the rather formalistic patristic term *ousia* is not very expressive in this regard, Bulgakov introduces some non-traditional terms to give more body to the concept: the whole of things (*vseedinstvo*), integrity (*tselomudrie*), and of course Sophia. 'Sophia, as the divine world [*bozhestvennyi mir*], *is* in God and in some sense *stands before* God and *possesses* Him in all his divine reality and authenticity.'[86]

Considering the concreteness Bulgakov ascribes to Sophia as well as the degree of personification involved in the use of the proper noun, one can appreciate why some critics accused him of postulating a fourth divine hypostasis. In fairness to Bulgakov, however, one should point out this reading of his sophiology glosses over the distinction between the *ousia* and

[84] *Agnets bozhii*, p. 378.
[85] *Agnets bozhii*, pp. 124–6.
[86] *Agnets bozhii*, p. 129.

the hypostases of the Trinity, a distinction Bulgakov consistently observes. Sophia 'is not a hypostasis at all,' even though her manifestations bear the character of personality because they involve the activity of the divine Persons.[87]

Even so, the idea of a 'world' in God remains problematic as a speculative postulate. If one takes the divine world to be the prototype of the visible universe, the postulate seems to imply a kind of pantheism. If, on the other hand, one imagines the divine world to be radically unlike the visible universe, the postulate leads to some sort of gnosticism, an outcome as antagonistic to classical trinitarianism as pantheism, although for the opposite reason. By disconnecting God from the world gnosticism undermines the God-givenness of creation and the possibility of a real incarnation.

It is easy to understand why the gnostic option never held any appeal for Bulgakov. The anti-cosmic dualism of gnosticism solves no problems for the Orthodox seeker of dialogue with the world. On the contrary it aggravates his situation, especially when it conceals itself under the mantle of Orthodox asceticism. Bulgakov rejected world-denying or 'sophioclastic theism' (*sofieborcheskii teizm*), so named to suggest a parallel with the abstract, anti-incarnational monotheism of the medieval

---

[87] Bulgakov admits there is 'a fundamental difficulty, insuperable for many people, in the doctrine of divine Sophia: namely, how one can affirm of Sophia that she is at one and the same time the revelation of both the Son and the Holy Spirit or, more exactly, of Son *and* Holy Spirit. People want a simple, rationalistic *identification* of Sophia with *one* of the hypostases of the Holy Trinity, although Sophia is in fact not a hypostasis at all; and they are amazed when one says that the Wisdom of God, as the self-revelation of the Father, is the dyadic unity of the revelation of the *Two* revelatory hypostases.' *Uteshitel'*, p. 217. Bulgakov tried to clarify his position by distinguishing between 'hypostasis' (*ipostas'*) and 'hypostatic character' (*ipostasnost'*). By the latter he meant receptivity or transparency to the activity of hypostases/Persons. See 'Ipostas' i ipostasnost' (Scholia k *Svetu Nevechernemu*),' in *Sbornik statei posviashchennykh Petru Berngardovichu Struve ko dniu tridtsatipiatiletiia ego nauchno-publitsisticheskoi deiatel'nosti* (Prague, 1925), pp. 353–71. See the brief but helpful discussions of Bulgakov's later sophiology in *Sergii Bulgakov*, ed. Williams, pp. 165–7; and Aidan Nichols, 'Bulgakov and Sophiology,' *Sobornost* 13/2 (1992):17–31. Barbara Newman offers a more detailed, patristically oriented analysis in 'Sergius Bulgakov and the Theology of Divine Wisdom,' *Saint Vladimir's Theological Quarterly* 22 (1978):39–73. See also Sergius Bulgakov, *The Wisdom of God: A Brief Summary of Sophiology*, preface by the Rev. Frank Gavin (New York: The Paisley Press, Inc.; London: Williams and Norgate Ltd, 1937).

Iconoclasts. Pantheism, by contrast, was a view for which Bulgakov confessed a deep affinity. He knew that absolute pantheism leads to 'the impious deification of the world,' but he was honest enough to confess his sophiological vision 'is *also* pantheism, only of a thoroughly pious kind.' He softened the point by using the term 'panentheism' (all-in-God-ism) to describe his position. But the issue is not one of terminology. Bulgakov firmly believed pantheism is 'a dialectically indispensable moment in sophiological cosmogony,' i.e. something the Christian theologian should not try to avoid. The sophianic foundation of the world, the ground of all its truth and beauty, may indeed be called the world's 'pantheism.'[88]

So what distinguishes Bulgakov's 'pious' pantheism from the other kind? For a substantive answer one has to consider the problem of pantheism in the light of the humanity of God. When Bulgakov postulates a world in God, he does not mean a world with the human or personal element filtered out. On the contrary, the point of the postulate in the first place is to make it possible to speak about *bogochelovechestvo*, the eternal humanity of God. The profound link between divinity and humanity manifested in the creation of human beings and in the incarnation 'signifies not just the divinity of human beings but also a kind of humanness [*chelovechnost'*] in God.' God's

---

[88] *Uteshitel'*, pp. 232–3. The speculative parameters of the problem of pantheism in sophiology are outlined by Robert Slesinksi, *Pavel Florensky: A Metaphysics of Love* (Crestwood, New York: St Vladimir's Seminary Press, 1984), pp. 193–213. Although Slesinski's analysis deals with Florensky's sophiology, not Bulgakov's, it applies to the latter at least as far as the problem of pantheism is concerned. Faulting both Neopatristic and Whiteheadian approaches to the problem, Slesinski sees the Thomist concept of analogy as offering the most promising basis for a solution. Of course if sophiology is something other than a purely speculative project, a theoretical concept cannot 'solve' its problems. It is interesting in this regard that Slesinski concludes his discussion not with a theory but with an existential appeal: 'There is one last constant to bear in mind in any consideration of Florensky's sophiology, namely, that both its point of departure and point of arrival concern an experience of love. In the sophianic vision, God's infinite love is grasped to be the true, creative cause of the ordered beauty of the cosmos' (p. 212). The idea that Sophia is the expression of a supra-logical yet productive experience of the world brings us back to the 'positive' philosophy of Schelling and Soloviev where sophiology began and suggests the need to start the whole discussion over again with an eye to the practical, as opposed to merely theoretical, challenges at stake. This is what I have tried to do in the present study.

world, or Sophia, is a humanized world: 'Sophia is the Wisdom of God, the Glory of God, Humanity in God [*Chelovechestvo v Boge*], the Humanity of God [*Bogochelovechestvo*], the Body of God (or what is the same thing, the "rainment" [*riza*] of God), the Divine World existing in God "before" the creation.'[89] If this is so, then no doctrine which suppresses the human element or assigns it a secondary role in the cosmos can be acceptable to a Christian theologian. Yet this is precisely what absolute pantheism does: it dehumanizes the world in order to deify it, for it cannot imagine the humanity of God. So doing, pantheism falls short of its goal, for the world it deifies is no longer the actual world, which always contains a human or personal dimension, but a 'world' of its own devising, an intellectual abstraction. This is its impiety: not the deification of the world, which the gospel itself promises at the end of the age, but the replacement of the divinely grounded, living world by a depersonalized abstraction. By means of sophiology Bulgakov seeks a middle way between the extremes of abstract pantheism (a deified world lacking humanity) and abstract trinitarianism (a super-essential Trinity disconnected from the world).[90]

The middle way, because it is oriented to the actual world and hence always under construction, will never possess the completeness or polish the extreme positions appear to have. This is a weakness in a purely speculative context and in theological contexts where doctrinal purity is valued above relevance to everyday human experience. The point of Bulgakov's theology is to generate positive religious ideals, and

---

[89] *Agnets bozhii*, pp. 136, 140.
[90] Another way of accounting for Bulgakov's rejection of pantheism and other impersonalist doctrines is to focus on his concept of personhood (*lichnost'*) in its own terms. The concept is superbly presented by Michael A. Meerson, 'Sergei Bulgakov's Philosophy of Personality,' *Russian Religious Thought*, eds Kornblatt and Gustafson, pp. 139–53. If not complemented (and complicated) by sophiology, however, Meerson's reading results in an over-personalistic Bulgakov – a Bulgakov who looks too much like Berdiaev, for example. A thoroughgoing personalist is never tempted by pantheism. Bulgakov, as we have seen, not only confessed to this temptation but embraced a position (panentheism) not all that far removed from pantheism in certain respects.

positive ideals are by definition incomplete, even ragged and torn, because they pertain to a world in process.[91]

Grammatical aspect, a distinctive feature of the Russian language, offers Bulgakov an effective means of expressing the tension inherent in positive religious ideals. Aspect is a device for distinguishing between completed and uncompleted action. In Russian the distinction is encoded in every verb in the language, which keeps Russian-speakers mindful of the phased nature of the processes denoted by verbs. In Russian it is not just possible but natural to construe a process and its outcome as an integral whole. This is a significant asset for someone who would speak about positive ideals. So, for Bulgakov, the creation of human beings in the image of God and the redemption of human beings in Christ are 'givens' (*dannosti*), yet at the same time 'mandates' (*zadannosti*) which human beings have yet to fulfill. 'Salvation' (*spasenie*) was accomplished once for all by Christ; yet 'the process of being saved' (*spasanie*), i.e. the incorporation of all things into Christ, continues.[92] Christ spoke once for all in the Gospels; yet he also continues speaking in the sense that his words are still being assimilated. 'Every characterization [of Christ's words] is inadequate, for human beings are not capable of grasping the full measure of the words [*izmerit' slova*] of the God-human; but people do have the capacity always to learn more about what the measure of those words might be [*ikh neprestanno izmerivat'*].'[93] Humanity itself is a positive, hence unfinished ideal, 'an essence just beginning to be disclosed [*raskryvaiushchaiasia*] which will be fully disclosed [*raskroetsia*] only when "God will be all in all." '[94]

Bulgakov's realistic yet hopeful grasp of the tensions in positive religious ideals steadies his hand as he sketches his portrait of Jesus in *The Lamb of God*. As the humanity of God

---

[91] Aidan Nichols' characterization of Bulgakov's position as 'an incomplete pantheism,' a repartee to Bulgakov's characterization of Palamas' theology as 'an incomplete sophiology,' is perceptive; but in the last analysis it is unfair to Bulgakov because it privileges the theoretical extremes (pantheism, hesychasm) and excludes the middle way (dogmatics of the humanity of God). See Nichols, 'Bulgakov and Sophiology,' p. 28.

[92] *Agnets bozhii*, p. 169; *Kupina neopalimaia*, p. 201.

[93] *Agnets bozhii*, p. 356.

[94] *Agnets bozhii*, p. 136.

in person, Jesus is the measure of humanity everywhere. Bulgakov takes Pilate's salutation, 'Here is the man!' (Jn 19:5), as containing a criteriological affirmation: behold the 'perfect' human being, 'the one true human being.'[95] However, as no one has yet taken the full measure of Christ, the definition of humanity must be regarded as still in process. Bulgakov approaches the business of christology in this spirit. He is open at all times to new discoveries – not of a new Christ, to be sure, but of a grander Christ than the one known to traditional exegesis, grander not just in divinity, but in humanity as well.

Bulgakov's chief aim in the dogmatics of the Son in *The Lamb of God* is to dispute the docetic and monophysite tendencies of patristic exegesis by offering readings of the Gospels that emphasize the Son's humanity. The general proposition is that 'uninterrupted humanity in the God-human is the basic fact and basic premise of the gospel narrative.'[96] Take, for example, the reports in all the Gospels that Jesus prayed. Bulgakov wants to know why the sinless God-human prayed? Was it something he had to do, or, as some patristic expositors thought, did Jesus pray merely to set a good example for sinful human beings? Bulgakov rejects the latter theory as tantamount to saying that Jesus 'prayed without [really] praying.' The humanity of the Son is affirmed only if one recognizes Jesus prayed for the same reason other human beings pray: to draw closer to God. His divine nature, far from making prayer superfluous, intensified it, inspiring his human nature to perpetual prayer.[97]

Or take the temptation of Jesus by Satan. John of Damascus wrote 'the Evil One assailed Christ from the outside, not in his inner thoughts.' Bulgakov rejects this interpretation as a species

---

[95] *Agnets bozhii*, pp. 229, 301, 349.

[96] *Agnets bozhii*, p. 306. In patristic exegesis, Bulgakov complains, 'human flesh, though [regarded as] assumed in hypostatic union for purposes of redemption, is treated as if it were outside the life of the God-human, it remains a tool (St John of Damascus), or a veil, or some sort of annex or accident in the manifestation of God, but not nature, not *ousia* existing also for the Godhead itself. And it is remarkable that on this de facto elimination of all participation of the flesh in the God-human's own life, all the warring christological schools concurred (except perhaps that of Apollinaris)' (p. 285). Bulgakov traces the source of the problem to 'the absence of an appropriately framed and consistently pursued idea of kenosis' (p. 277, n. 1, referring specifically to John of Damascus).

[97] *Agnets bozhii*, pp. 283–4; cf. pp. 309–10.

of docetism. When the Word assumed human nature it assumed human freedom, which involves the capacity to err. The startling discovery which the human race made in Jesus was that 'an unexercised capacity to err is a creaturely possibility.' Jesus achieved this *podvig* not through divinity operating in him mechanically as it were but through a synergy of the divine and the human in which the contribution of human effort – spiritual toil, asceticism, prayer – must not be minimized. Human freedom in Jesus 'was not paralyzed or eliminated by His Divinity, but only inspired by it.'[98] Jesus' victory in the desert, and at Gethsemane and on the cross, was a 'human victory' as well as the fulfillment of a divine plan.[99]

Bulgakov applies the same principle to the threefold ministry of Christ as prophet, priest and king. All three vocations should be valued not just as divine dispensations but as human accomplishments as well.

Bulgakov's insistence on the humanity of prophecy has already been noted. 'In the mouths of the prophets the *Divine Word* [is] a *human word* . . . The prophet [is] a living mediator between God and human beings, not an oracle, which would be nothing but a mechanical tool for delivering messages unintelligible even to the prophet himself.'[100] Jesus was no exception to this rule. Take, for example, his summary of prophetic morality in the Sermon on the Mount. As Bulgakov sees it, the Sermon is fatally misconstrued if it is boiled down to 'an anonymous doctrine' imposing 'abstract morality of little vitality and loaded with impossible demands, oriented to utopian maximalism and lacking a religious connection.' The Sermon should not be handled as an oracle or manifesto of the Absolute Word, but as a prophecy of the incarnate Word inviting a human response. To appropriate the Sermon in human terms, however, one has to figure 'earthly, relative, transitory values' into the equation. The difficulty of the task cannot be eased. 'The proper diagonal of the earthly and heavenly, the temporal and eternal, is found by each person only in his own creative work.'[101] Like Soloviev in *Three Dialogues*,

---

[98] *Agnets bozhii*, pp. 325–6.
[99] *Agnets bozhii*, p. 316.
[100] *Agnets bozhii*, pp. 352–3. See n. 31 above.
[101] *Agnets bozhii*, pp. 356–7.

Bulgakov appreciates the non-formulaic, existential character of evangelical ethics. Over against the unitary moralism of Tolstoyanism and other forms of utopianism, he looks to an ongoing, ever-dynamic relationship between Son, Sermon and humanity. Over against the authoritarian divine Teacher of patristic exegesis, he sees a kenotic Son granting human beings the space and time they need to respond creatively to the Word.

Bulgakov humanizes Jesus' apocalyptic prophecies in much the same way. Apocalyptic was a visionary form of prophecy known already in Old Testament times to Jeremiah, Ezekiel and Daniel. Yet the visions granted to these prophets were 'far from clear' even to the visionaries themselves and should be appreciated for the 'ontology, not the concrete history' which they contain, i.e. for the hopeful, future-oriented view of life and lively expectation of the kingdom of God. 'We must not forget the *humanity*, hence also the relativity of the prophetic visions if we are to have a correct view of them, free from exaggerations.'[102] No less an authority than the divine Son applies the same criterion to his prophecies of the end of the age: 'But about that day or hour no one knows, neither the angels in heaven, nor the Son, but only the Father' (Mk 13:32). This saying, along with other instances in the Gospels where Jesus' knowledge is portrayed as deficient, was a stumbling block to patristic expositors. Bulgakov, by contrast, takes it as stunning evidence of the kenosis of the Son and as a vindication of the centrality of human reception in the gospel.

> One of the meanings of Jesus' testimony about not knowing the time of the end of the world may be that this time is determined not just by the will of God but by human response [*vstrechnym dvizheniem chelovechnym*]. The latter has yet to be completed and represents a variable, undetermined quantity, the sphere of free, human creativity. The Son of Man takes the side of humanity here and, on its behalf, faced with an unconsummated and as yet unknown future with respect to which prophecy is *conditional*, speaks about His (the Son of Man's) ignorance [of the end of the age].[103]

[102] *Agnets bozhii*, p. 360.
[103] *Agnets bozhii*, p. 334; cf. pp. 454–5.

Bulgakov's humanizing purpose with respect to the priestly ministry of Christ appears in the breadth of his concept of priestly sacrifice. The self-offering of the Lamb of God on the cross for the sins of the world is the defining moment of Christ's high priesthood, to be sure, but not the one and only moment. Kenotic theory enables Bulgakov to see the priesthood of the Son at work long before and long after the sacrifice on the cross. The creation of the world, an act of self-sacrificial divine love, may be regarded as a priestly work. The demiurge or Logos through whom all things were made may thus be seen as a priest and identified with the Lamb that was slain 'before the foundation of the world.'[104] At the other end of the drama of salvation, Christ's descent into hell may be regarded as a continuation of his kenotic priestly work.[105] Even the resurrection can be appreciated in these terms, for the Son does not glorify himself but is glorified by the Father who accepts his pure sacrifice. The Son's victory over the grave should not to be viewed through the prism of conventional triumphalism but as 'a kenotic glorification, a glorification in humiliation.'[106]

The kenotic Christ is not a passive Christ. A priest is always an agent, an active mediator between the divine and the human, someone with work to do. Resurrection is not just divine but also human work, the work of making human nature spiritually worthy of receiving immortality. In this sense immortality may be regarded as 'an act of co-operation, of the synergism of God and the human being.'[107]

The concept of synergy applies also to the ascension. Like resurrection, ascension should not be regarded as 'a unilateral creative act of divine omnipotence, [but as] an act of co-operation (synergism) of God the Father and the God-human' through which human nature 'attains such a fullness of deification in Christ that it becomes capable of wanting what divine nature wants,' namely, ascension into heaven. A problem arises

---

[104] *Agnets bozhii*, p. 374.
[105] *Agnets bozhii*, pp 405–6.
[106] *Agnets bozhii*, pp. 410–11. Analogously, Christ's death on the cross should not be viewed through the prism of heroism, but as sacerdotal work, *podvizhnichestvo* (pp. 398–9).
[107] *Agnets bozhii*, p. 412.

here, however. Unlike resurrection (immortality in a body), which Bulgakov deems a natural human desire, ascension into heaven involves 'a metaphysical removal from the world.' Why, then, does the ascension of Christ not signify his 'disincarnation and disengagement from humanity' (*razvoploshcheniem i raschelovecheniem*)?[108]

As the ascended high priest Christ remains linked to the world of flesh and blood in two ways. First, the ascension involves the bodily incorporation of Christ into the Trinity – not in flesh as we know it, but 'as the whole energy of the incarnation, a spiritual image, a truly spiritual body ... *the body of the Body*, the ideal image of divine Sophia in union with creaturely Sophia, their connection and identity.' The 'absolute energeticism' of Christ's heavenly body makes his real presence in the eucharist possible, thereby securing for him an ongoing priestly (sacramental) ministry on earth.[109] Second, the ascended Christ exercises a priestly ministry by supplicating the Father to send the Spirit into the world to complete the work of salvation through the lifting up of all humanity:

> The meaning of the ascension is not exhausted by the glorification of the Lord, for, besides the ascension that has been completed, there is one that *is still being completed*, the glorification of creaturely, as yet unglorified earthly humanity, which however is by nature identical with the humanity of Christ.[110]

The ascension does not disconnect Christ from the world because, in effect, the world is destined to follow him, destined to inherit a spiritual body of its own. Through Christ 'the dualism of God and creation is being overcome and the monodualism of the Humanity of God is being established.'[111] The investigation of this process in its own right, however, belongs to the dogmatics of the Spirit, not the Son.

In Bulgakov's account of the priestly ministry of Christ the long-standing Orthodox preference for an ontological as

[108] *Agnets bozhii*, pp. 420–1.
[109] *Agnets bozhii*, p. 425.
[110] *Agnets bozhii*, p. 429.
[111] *Agnets bozhii*, p. 427.

opposed to juridical theory of redemption finds fresh expression in the humanizing idiom of church-and-world dogmatics. The continuity of the process of salvation throughout the cosmos is the central theme. What is modern is the degree of world-affirmation allowed and indeed demanded by church-and-world dogmatics. For Bulgakov the dogmatic theologian, the unbreakable mutual relatedness of God and world is neither a problem to be solved nor a threat to be parried but an axiom from which to proceed:

> There is no God without a world, no world outside God: the world is in God ... Creation, Providence, Incarnation, ascension, the sending of the Holy Spirit and so on – all of these are acts of the mutual coming-to-be of God for the world and of the world for God [*vzaimostanovleniia Boga dlia mira i mira dlia Boga*]. This fundamental theological antinomy cannot be further elucidated but must be accepted as axiomatic.

God *and* the world: the emphasized conjunction expresses the heart of Bulgakov's positive Chalcedonianism.[112]

Bulgakov's account of the royal ministry of Christ follows in the same vein. He criticizes the tendency to present the kingship of Christ in terms of divine omnipotence, as when all manifestations of divine power in Jesus' life, such as miracles, resurrection, descent into hell or ascension, are interpreted as royal functions. Bulgakov faults this approach first for its imprecision, since it assigns to the royal ministry works which are better regarded as belonging to the prophetic ministry or high priesthood of Christ. But the chief problem lies in the one-sided definition of royal ministry in terms of power, for this falsifies the very concept of ministry, which is that of service. The Son entered the world through incarnation, 'taking the form of a slave, being born in human likeness' (Phil. 2:7). His royalty should not be construed in such a way as to negate his mode of being in and with the world. Rather, after the incarnation 'God

---

[112] *Agnets bozhii*, p. 428. 'The transcendent God has united himself with the world, has become God and the world, and this *And* is the union of the two natures in one divine hypostasis, divine and human, without division and without confusion, in a single life. The Chalcedonian dogma retains its significance even in heaven' (ibid.).

reigns over the world *in a new way*, in human beings and through human beings in the God-human.' The royal ministry, like the others, depends on a synergy of the divine and the human. Human beings are granted 'co-rule with Christ, co-participation in His royal ministry.'[113]

To elucidate what co-rule with Christ means in concrete terms Bulgakov focuses on a peculiarity of the royal ministry, namely, that this ministry was not completed or even openly exercised by Christ during his earthly life. The prophetic work of Christ, richly described in the Gospels, was essentially completed during his lifetime. His priestly work, while extending far beyond the limits of earthly life, could be seen in his suffering and death on the cross. The royal ministry, by contrast, is manifested only after Christ's glorification at the right hand of the Father; it is accomplished in heaven, not on earth. This peculiarity lends an 'especially mysterious character' to the royal ministry. 'Christ is King in the world, but He does not rule in the fullness of the Kingdom of God, he is still only beginning to accede to it.'[114] To the extent that images of Christ's reign on earth are given at all in the New Testament, they appear in laconic apocalyptic passages and in the enigmatic scenarios of the Revelation of John, all of which are notoriously difficult to interpret. Why such reticence about the royal ministry?

Bulgakov's answer once again vindicates the humanity of the gospel. 'The fundamental premise regarding the royal ministry of Christ is that His accession is being accomplished in history as a whole, with the latter culminating in eschatology.' That is to say, the indeterminate character of the earthly reign of Christ is the condition which makes a substantive human history possible. New Testament apocalyptic provides an inspiring vision of the end of history, of its 'sophianic determinism' or ontology; but actual history is a divine-human process involving human creativity as well as divine will.[115] The kenosis of the Son, far from being terminated by his accession to a royal ministry, is actually extended by it.

---

[113] *Agnets bozhii*, pp. 445, 458.
[114] *Agnets bozhii*, p. 447.
[115] *Agnets bozhii*, pp. 447–8, 462.

Bulgakov's interpretation of the royal ministry of Christ in *The Lamb of God* can be compared with Bukharev's *Studies on the Apocalypse* and Soloviev's free theocracy. All three are expressions of a world-affirming, historically engaged Orthodox faith seeking to sanctify the ever-expanding range of human vocations. Bukharev and Soloviev would agree wholeheartedly with Bulgakov that

> history is not an empty corridor which must be got through somehow in order to be liberated from this world into the other one, it belongs to the work of Christ in His Incarnation, it is an apocalypse striving for eschatological fulfillment, a divine-human work on earth.[116]

Bulgakov's handling of apocalyptic literature was much more sophisticated than Bukharev's, thanks to the progress of Russian theological scholarship in the intervening decades; but their interest in the subject was fundamentally the same:

> The action of Christ is not exhausted by *personal* Christianity and the *personal* life in Christ of individuals ... The whole of human history after Christ, with all its warped and strange dialectics, is essentially a *Christian history*, linked with Christ's Church as its inner teleology. This is exactly what the Apocalypse bears witness to when it depicts the destinies of the nations as a single connected whole (just as the Old Testament prophets Isaiah, Jeremiah, Daniel and others did in their philosophy of history).[117]

The words are Bulgakov's, but they express Bukharev's position exactly.

Bulgakov's link to Soloviev's theocratism is evident on all levels, including methodology and vocabulary as well as positive ideals. The main difference is that Bulgakov never wrote a historiosophical treatise of the type of *The History and Future of Theocracy* or *La Russie et l'Église universelle*. Instead he pleaded the case for a world-affirming theocratism before the bar of Orthodox dogmatic theology. His treatment of the royal ministry of Christ in *The Lamb of God* was the first installment.

---

[116] *Agnets bozhii*, p. 464.
[117] *Agnets bozhii*, pp. 459–60.

For a fuller treatment of the 'dynamic pan-christism'[118] of the world-historical process one must look to *The Comforter* and *The Bride of the Lamb*, for in the last analysis the theocratic theme is not christological but pneumatological. Christ is king, but it is the Holy Spirit who brings in the kingdom.

---

[118] *Agnets bozhii*, p. 463.

14

The Church of the Humanity of God

Much traditional ecclesiology, Orthodox as well as Roman Catholic and Protestant, is explicitly or implicitly dualistic. Church and world, Christianity and humanity, city of God and city of man, are viewed as basically separate bodies, although their coexistence as a *corpus permixtum* in historical time is recognized. The most conventional form of dualism is confessionalism, which equates the church with a particular ecclesiastical establishment and regards the rest of humanity as being more or less outside the church. In certain circumstances dualism may inspire a confessing as opposed to a merely confessional church, a community bearing heroic witness to Christ against earthly powers. Piety of this type has prophetic appeal in times of persecution, unspiritual prosperity, religious indifferentism or other circumstances which offer little incentive for questioning the distinction between church and world.

The dogmatics of the humanity of God cannot found its ecclesiology on any sort of dualism. Once humanity is recognized along with divinity as an active and creative principle of the incarnation, a new appreciation of the historical process outside the visible church becomes possible. The church may still be regarded as the focal point of the kingdom of God, and for that reason the mission of christianizing the world may still be affirmed. But because humanity encounters Christ not just in the church but in the depths of humanness, a second quest becomes imaginable: not the christianization but the 'christification' of the world, that is to say, the clarification and effectuation of the divine-human principle at work in every human being and every human community. To a significant extent extra-ecclesial humanity discovers this principle for itself, albeit indirectly:

> This free self-determination of the human being is accomplished as it were in the semi-darkness of twilight, not in relation to Christ himself but nevertheless in relation to the principle of Christ – to goodness, to conscience, to Divinity. The whole of human history after Christ travels along a new highway by virtue of this dynamic pan-christism.[1]

If the ongoing priestly ministry of Christ in history unfolds first of all through the christianizing mission of the church, the theocracy or royal ministry – Christ's accession to kingship over all humanity – advances first of all through the work of christification:

> The history of humanity after Christ is the history not just of Christian humanity but of Christ's humanity [*Khristovo chelovechestvo*] ... The affairs [*dela*] of this humanity, scattered and contradictory though they be, are all being synthesized into the cause [*delo*] of Christ.[2]

The distinction between christianization and christification raises the ecclesiological issue of where the Universal Church is to be found. Identifying the church with historic Christianity – e.g. with the Orthodox confession – will not do. But the Universal Church must not be simply equated with humanity without qualification, for this would dissolve the church altogether and produce a utopian humanism. As we have seen, there were tendencies in this direction in Soloviev, who used the terms Universal Church and pan-humanity interchangeably. A milder form of the equation occurs in Bulgakov when he calls the church 'Christ's humanity.'[3] On the other hand, phraseology

---

[1] *Agnets bozhii*, p. 463. Bulgakov cites Peter's words to the Roman centurion Cornelius: 'God has shown me that I should not call anyone profane or unclean ... God shows no partiality, but in every nation anyone who fears him and does what is right is acceptable to him' (Acts 10:28, 34–5).

[2] *Agnets bozhii*, p. 459.

[3] Soloviev, *Chteniia o bogochelovechestve*, p. 180; Bulgakov, *Agnets bozhii*, p. 456. Bulgakov's equation of ecclesiology with sophiology in the preface to *The Bride of the Lamb* ('ecclesiology understood in all its breadth and depth as sophiology') is another instance of the Solovievian equation of the Universal Church with pan-humanity (*vsechelovechestvo*).

such as Bulgakov's and Soloviev's may also be interpreted as a means of talking about the universality of the body of Christ as the humanity of God. The concept of the humanity of God, when taken seriously, bars the way to any sort of ultimate division between church and world. 'The force field of the Humanity of God coincides with the boundary of the Church; or to say it better, there is really no boundary at all, for the entire world [*mirozdanie*] belongs to the Church; [the world] is her periphery, her cosmic face [*lik*].' Having said this, however, Bulgakov hastens to add that an ecclesiology consisting of ultimate statements alone will not suffice, for 'in such a definition of the catholicity of the Church everything dissolves in infinity.' Critical distinctions must be made, beginning with 'the Church as an institution of grace separate from the rest of the world that lies outside of it "in darkness and the shadow of death." '[4]

The ecclesiological issue may be clarified by comparing it to the problem of pantheism already discussed. Bulgakov's postulation of a world in God is pantheistic, but his position is held back from absolute pantheism by 'the mono-dualism of the Humanity of God,' the ongoing dialogue between God and the world.[5] The result is a moderate panentheism. The ecclesiological issue plays itself out in much the same way. The resemblance of Solovievian and Bulgakovian theocratism to utopian humanism is real but ultimately limited by the mono-dualism of the humanity of God. Pan-humanity and the Universal Church may be one and the same eschatologically; but a reduction of the categories from two to one, however appealing as a theoretical position, violates the actual dynamics of life and the search for positive religious ideals. Humanity stripped of the church resembles the absolute-pantheist cosmos stripped of humanity: both are abstractions. The world-historical process as we know it is a dialogue between divinity and humanity, between church and world. Positive religious ideals may therefore be humanely ecclesiastical, or reverently humane, or both, but not unitary.

---

[4] *Nevesta agntsa*, pp. 291–2.
[5] *Agnets bozhii*, p. 427.

Thus when Bulgakov writes of 'the pan-christism' of world history, 'the pan-christianity' of the history of religions and 'the limitless pan-christism and pan-pneumatism' of human nature, he should be read not as a utopian humanist but as a prophetic enthusiast for the mutual engagement of church and world.[6] Like the utopian, Bulgakov seeks the 'humanization of the world' [ochelovechenie mira];[7] unlike the utopian, Bulgakov recognizes God and the church are already at work in the world to be humanized. He also sees the humanization of the world in the name of humanity alone absolutizes humanity as it understands itself at a given point in time, which is to mistake the part for the whole. Positive religious ideals address humanity-in-the-making.

The dynamic connection between church and world as Bulgakov construes it finds dogmatic validation in the doctrine of the Holy Spirit. All theologians agree the church is the fruit of the descent of the Holy Spirit on Pentecost Day. They also agree the church conducts its mission to the world through the guidance of the Holy Spirit. The gifts of the Spirit separate the church as the realm of grace from the unsaved world. Ecclesiological dualism arises when this separation is taken to be the defining principle of the church. However, restricting the gifts of the Spirit to the fruits of Pentecost leads to a narrower view of the Spirit than that which is found in the Bible and classical dogmatics. In both of these sources the Spirit is seen not just as the church-giver on Pentecost, but as the life-giver on the first day, and as the enlivener and beautifier of creation every day. Seen in this perspective, the gift of Pentecost is best described not as new life, which may suggest discontinuity with that which precedes it, but as renewal or 'newness of life,' in the felicitous expression of the Book of Common Prayer. Because the Holy Spirit is the life-giver of both church and world, these two realities must be regarded as ontologically linked, no matter how separate they appear to be in the fallen state of humanity.

Bulgakov adduces some common conventions of the Orthodox commemoration of Pentecost to support this

---

[6] *Agnets bozhii*, p. 463; *Uteshitel'*, pp. 278–9; *Nevesta agntsa*, p. 285.
[7] *Agnets bozhii*, p. 465.

dogmatic point. Cosmos, represented as an old man, is often depicted on Pentecost icons to indicate the scope of the Spirit's vivifying work. Orthodox churches are festooned with green boughs and flowers at Pentecost 'as if to expose [the natural world] together with [the worshipers] themselves to the nourishing rain of heavenly fire.'[8]

Bulgakov's dogmatic position involves a particular theory of divine grace which must be considered here. In western Christianity since Augustine, and especially since the Reformation, 'nature' and 'grace' have tended to be viewed disjunctively. If some power or dignity can be shown to belong to a creature by nature, that good thing is not regarded as grace. The latter term is reserved for supernatural gifts falling outside the common pattern of creaturely existence, such as the sacraments of the church or faith in predestination to salvation. In the Orthodox East the theory of grace has been less discussed and is less fixed than in the West.[9] One of the reasons for this is the conservatism of Orthodox theology since the end of the patristic age – a conservatism, let it be noted, which has not protected Orthodoxy from western influence. But Orthodox theologians have also kept their distance from the debate about nature and grace because of their instinctive dislike for the compartmentalizing tendency of western theology. With its ideals of *sobornost'* and symphony, and an appreciation for cosmic beauty which is the common legacy of Greek-speaking theology since Plato, Orthodoxy has never found a sharp disjunction between nature and grace to be an attractive theoretical position.

Bulgakov's view of grace may be cited as a case in point of the emerging consensus among modern Orthodox theologians that they have a healing word to speak to the schizophrenic West on

[8] *Uteshitel'*, pp. 388–9. 'The descent of the Holy Spirit on Pentecost happened *in the world*, and, although He rested upon the apostles' heads in visible ("as of") tongues of fire, He descended by virtue of His unseen fire upon the whole natural world, for, of course, His activity was not confined by the walls of the chamber on Zion' (ibid.).

[9] 'The concept of grace, although it stands at the center of the doctrine of the Church, does not possess the clarity and stability one would expect, either terminologically or theologically ... Theology, generally speaking, prefers to occupy itself with particular questions about the various forms and applications of grace rather than with the essence of the subject; moreover, the doctrine has attracted much more attention in western theology than in eastern.' *Nevesta agntsa*, p. 318.

this subject. The key to the Orthodox position is the concept of 'natural grace.' The idea is that all creation, by virtue of its being and beauty, reflects the divine ground from which it springs:

> The beauty of the world is the effect of the Holy Spirit, of the Spirit of Beauty, and Beauty is Joy, the joy of being: 'Joy eternal nourishes / The soul of God's creation.' This effect of the natural grace of creation, this breath of the Holy Spirit in creation, the continuing, ongoing *'brooding'* of the Holy Spirit over the 'waters' of creation, is the *positive* power of being.[10]

All cosmic activity, from angelic contemplation to the mating of insects, conforms with divinity 'in as much as creation bears within itself the living image of the creator and stands in a relationship with him.'[11] This ontological relationship is a divine gift, the original endowment bestowed on creatures by their creator as 'the precondition for [their] sanctification through reception of the Holy Spirit.'[12] Western theology recognizes original sin but not original grace. Bulgakov's theory, like Dostoevsky's lyrical portrait of Dmitry Karamazov, makes room for both.

Original grace is the foundation for all subsequent works of sanctification, including the outpouring of the Holy Spirit upon the church. Were there no link or likeness between that which is sanctified (nature) and that for which and into which it is sanctified (the divine life), sanctification would lack an intelligible basis, and the elaborate sacramental ministries of the Orthodox Church would be called into question. The blessing of material things so exuberantly practiced in Orthodoxy – blessing of water, oil, bread, wine, crops, buildings, viands, and so on – would have to be dismissed as superstition or justified by some sort of magical theory. Indeed, rationalism and occultism, while usually viewed as opposites, are essentially equivalent

---

[10] *Uteshitel'*, pp. 233–4. The two lines of verse are from Schiller's ode 'To Joy' which Dostoevsky places on the lips of Dmitry Karamazov in *The Brothers Karamazov*, 1.3.3.

[11] *Nevesta agntsa*, p. 242.

[12] *Uteshitel'*, p. 255.

with respect to the dynamics of sanctification, for both envision the world as a closed mechanical system. Sanctification is imaginable only if one sees the world standing in a coherent relationship ('likeness') to a divine reality beyond it. Sanctification is the lifting-up of the creature to the One whose image it bears by the grace of its creation. Stating the concept in the idiom of his dogmatics, Bulgakov writes that sanctification depends on the kenosis of the Spirit in the form of natural grace. Grace itself he calls 'the power of sophianization,' the capacity of all creatures to conform to the goodness and beauty of God.[13]

Adherents of a disjunctive view of nature and grace might ask at this point: Do creatures have the power to conform themselves to God, or are they brought into conformity by a power from on high? Bulgakov, with his synergistic view of the divine-human relationship, rejects this dichotomy in principle. The Holy Spirit, whose work is to promote the reception of the incarnate Word throughout the world, respects the limits of creaturely being in the world just as the Son did in Jesus:

> If the fullness of the divine life in Christ is determined by the measure of human nature, then here, too, human freedom plays a determining role in the measure to which the Holy Spirit is received. Grace does not force freedom but wins it over by persuasion. A kind of *duel* between freedom and grace, between creaturely humanity and the gifts of the Holy Spirit, is going on.[14]

If it were otherwise, an unbridgeable gulf would open between Son and Spirit, incarnation and Pentecost. But the Spirit of Pentecost respects the kenotic terms of the salvation effected in and through Christ.

The doctrine of original grace provides a conceptual bridge for mediating the relationship between church and world. By holding the grace-filled being of the world before the eyes of the church Bulgakov validates a certain boldness, even optimism about the prospects for the christification of humanity. He also

---

[13] *Uteshitel'*, pp. 254–5. For grace as 'the power of sophianization' (*sila osofieniia*), see *Nevesta agntsa*, p. 247.
[14] *Uteshitel'*, pp. 318–19.

reinforces his rejection of an isolationist or merely custodial approach to the church's mission. As far as Bulgakov is concerned, ecclesiastical isolationism is a kind of heresy, albeit not recognized as such by the historic church. It is 'the heresy concerning the world,' the idea that 'the world is not Christ's but belongs to itself,' in effect 'unbelief in the royal ministry of Christ.'[15] The doctrine of original grace, by contrast, implies the locus of spiritual life is to be sought in the midst of the world, not outside of it or on its margins. The challenge is to forge creative linkages between the original grace which sanctifies all creation and the pentecostal or ecclesial gifts revealed to the historic church.

Bulgakov's theory of grace raises some interesting questions about the degree to which the Holy Spirit can be said to be revealed in the scripture and tradition of the church. For example, Bulgakov points out the New Testament contains no gospel of the Holy Spirit. Even the Acts of the Apostles, while it describes many episodes of sanctification, does not paint a clear picture of the hypostatic or personal revelation of the Spirit. Indeed, one might not infer that Acts was speaking about such a revelation at all were it not for Jesus' words, reported in John's Gospel (14:16, 26), about the sending of a Comforter. The picture of the Holy Spirit in Acts is really no different than the Old Testament accounts of outpourings of the Spirit on the prophets, kings and sages of Israel.[16] The testimony to the Son, whose portrait is painted in four glorious and detailed Gospels, is incomparably richer. Does one have to conclude from this that the New Testament's pneumatology is somehow deficient?

As Bulgakov sees it, the defect lies not with the New Testament but with a theological conceptuality which fails to appreciate the distinctiveness of the Spirit's work in the economy of salvation. The Spirit does not recapitulate the work of the Son. The Son, concealing his divinity, reveals himself by appearing in the world as a human being; the Spirit, concealing itself, reveals its divinity by descending upon the world in a shower of divine gifts. Moreover, unlike the Son the Spirit knows no ascension but stays in the world to effect 'the

---

[15] 'K chitateliu,' *Agnets bozhii*, p. 6.
[16] *Uteshitel'*, pp. 304–6.

continuing Pentecost.'[17] To see the Spirit at work one must look to where that work is going on, namely, to the unfolding world-historical process. The case of the Son is fundamentally different. For a clear picture of him one looks to the Gospels, for the man Jesus is no longer in the world. *Non est hic*! Resurrected and ascended, he sits at the right hand of the Father whence the church awaits his coming again. But the Spirit has not ascended. Its works of grace are seen most clearly not in scripture or tradition but in the world, the actual world of the present including the present-day life of the church. A church dogmatics based on scripture and tradition might elaborate a passable doctrine of the Son, but not a passable doctrine of the Spirit. To think seriously about the Spirit one needs a church-and-world dogmatics. Bulgakov never tires of reminding the church that 'the descent of the Holy Spirit on Pentecost took place *in the world*.'[18]

The Spirit is known to the world through its divine gifts, divine in the sense of endowing all things with being and beauty and making apparent the connectedness of the world to its divine ground. Human beings, by virtue of their creation in the image and likeness of God, are capable of receiving the full range of the Spirit's gifts. They are by nature 'spirit-bearers.'[19]

All gifts of the Spirit are mutually related, but in the fallen human condition this relationship is only gradually being clarified and sometimes is not recognized at all. The separation of church and world can and should be contested: this is what the royal or theocratic mission of the church is about. But the gulf between the two shores will not be closed before the end of the age. This means the gifts of the Spirit will appear to pertain to separate spheres, such as nature, church, secular humanity and so on. For purposes of discussion the gifts of the Spirit may be sorted into two classes: those known outside the church and those particularly associated with the church.

The spiritual gifts known outside the church are those discoveries, vocations and institutions which effect the humanization of the world. Human beings are the natural priests of creation,

---

[17] *Uteshitel'*, pp. 321–3, 387–8.
[18] *Uteshitel'*, p. 388 (Bulgakov's italics).
[19] *Uteshitel'*, p. 258.

mediators of the unity of nature and spirit. Their humanity contains the sophianic substance of all things. But as Sophia is not isolated or abstract humanity but Christ the humanity of God, the humanization of the world entails the christification of the world. Every act of humanization advances the process of christification.

The christification of the world proceeds through the agency of human vocations, including vocations known from time immemorial as well as new vocations discovered by exploring the sophianic substance of the world. We have seen that the sanctification of secular vocations was a prominent concern of philosophic Orthodoxy already in Bukharev's day. In Bulgakov's pneumatology this concern finds a firm dogmatic basis.

A vocation, as distinct from a job or career, is a function of human beings as spirit-bearers, hence a priestly function. As the crystallization of a creative inspiration, every vocation may be described as an outpouring of the Spirit upon the flesh, a natural, partial or little pentecost. In content, that is to say, with respect to the good or goal served, every vocation may be described as 'a sophiophany,' a concretization of an aspect of divine Wisdom in a particular historical context.[20]

Bulgakov sees the whole gamut of creative human activities in pneumatological terms. So, for example, the Muse known to pagan antiquity, the power animating all genuine poetic vocations, is a natural revelation of the Spirit.[21] So are the piety and prophecy of extra-biblical religions. The ever-loyal student

---

[20] 'The objective basis and content of this inspiration is determined by its connection to creaturely Sophia. Consequently one should not say that every human inspiration is *directly* from the Holy Spirit and in this sense divinely inspired. This is not the case. It is the case, however, that creaturely Sophia, creaturely being itself, has been invested by the Holy Spirit with the power of life and inspiration as its sophianic foundation ... The heights and depths of the world become accessible to human beings through creative discovery ... Inspiration is limitless, as is the human world that exists by virtue of the image of God; inspiration is natural grace in human beings, just as the life-force is the natural grace of the pre-human world.' *Uteshitel'*, pp. 245–6. For 'sophiophany' and 'partial and little pentecosts,' referring to the religion of the Old Testament, see pp. 228–9; for 'natural Pentecost,' referring to pagan religions, p. 276.

[21] *Uteshitel'*, pp. 246–8. Bulgakov expresses indebtedness to G.P. Fedotov for this insight.

of Schelling and Soloviev, Bulgakov takes a generous view of world religions. He sees the rejection of pagan spirituality by the prophets of Israel and the early Christian fathers as 'only a *relative* truth,' justifiable 'pedagogically,' but not categorically. The Israelite prophets and church fathers, in their zeal for pure doctrine, were 'blind to the authentic and profound content' of pagan religion. Scripture, on the other hand, is not blind. Bulgakov gazes in wonder at the portrait of the priest-king Melchizedek emerging 'from the darkness of paganism' to bless Abraham and offer him gifts of bread and wine prefiguring the holy eucharist (Gen. 14:17–24). In the meeting of Abraham with Melchizedek we see 'an encounter of two representatives of the Old Testament – [one] from the chosen people and [one] from paganism.' The pagan prophet Balaam who foresaw Israel's glorious destiny when 'the Spirit of God came upon him' (Num. 24:2) is another example of this encounter, as is the Roman poet Virgil whose *Fourth Eclogue* anticipated the messianic age. These and other examples verify Bulgakov's proposition that 'the pagan world is *not* devoid of the promptings of the spirit of God, neither in its religion nor in its culture.'[22]

Bulgakov also values the 'humanistic neopaganism' and 'religious atheism' of modern times wherever these are found 'doing the works of love and sacrificing themselves therein.' Writing in the 1930s at the apogee of Stalinism, Bulgakov recognized that the larger part of his Russian Orthodox audience would not warm to this point. Yet the case was clear to him: to deny the Spirit works even among atheists and apostates amounts to 'measuring the kenosis of the Spirit and its gifts by the dimensions of human understanding.'[23] True philanthropy, even when practiced apart from religious belief, is always a gift of the Spirit.

So is philosophy. Philosophizing is inspired by an erotic *daimon* or 'spiritual love' which will eventually lift the mind to God, as the examples of Socrates, Plato and Plotinus show.[24]

---

[22] *Uteshitel'*, pp. 273–5. Cf. p. 269, where Bulgakov calls pre-Christian paganism 'a natural Old Testament.'
[23] *Uteshitel'*, p. 280.
[24] *Uteshitel'*, pp. 358–9.

How indeed could Bulgakov think otherwise about the vocation which bears the very name of Sophia?

Science, too, is a Spirit-filled vocation. Bulgakov always took a lively interest in the sciences. He was especially drawn to vitalist and energeticist concepts of matter, for these appeared to support two of his long-standing convictions about the order of things: his *naturphilosophisch* conviction that nature and spirit spring from a common ground and hence are transparent and coherent to each other, and his love for 'the religious materialism' of Orthodoxy, the church's countless rituals sanctifying the material world. These influences, along with the Solovievian critique of abstraction, led Bulgakov to the belief there is no such thing as 'dead nature' or 'abstract matter.' Matter belongs to a living cosmos, a world pervaded by 'the primal energy of life,' which is the original gift of the Spirit:

> Matter, understood simply as reality or as the power of being, is the direct effect of the Holy Spirit in the act of creation, in the *primordial* Pentecost before the first day of creation. Spirit is not only not opposed to matter but, as energy, is to be identified with it, it is the *power* of matter.[25]

Bulgakov also believed evolution and the origin of species could be appreciated theologically. The hexameron, or six days of creation, shows that the creative activity of God manifests itself not once for all on the threshold of time but kenotically in time, according to the measure of creaturely life. 'The multi-staged and gradual character of being is characteristic of the life of the world, for the creative "Let there be!" always rings out in the world in a *variety* of forms; creation always involves *a future which is about to be*, [it is] not just *nata* but *natura*.' The ongoing 'Let there be!' of creation is a concretization of natural grace.[26]

The implication of Bulgakov's view is not only that the church has nothing to fear from the natural sciences but that theology and science are destined to converge. In the investigation of the material-energetic evolution of the world, 'theology (sophiology

[25] *Uteshitel'*, pp. 389–91.
[26] *Uteshitel'*, pp. 254–5.

in particular) meets natural science, and science is destined to become the theology of nature.'[27]

Statecraft, military leadership and all the arts and crafts are also gifts of the Spirit. Like Bukharev, Bulgakov relished the Old Testamental picture of a nationwide collaboration of vocations in the building up of Israel. Kings, judges, warriors, artisans and others, each with a God-given talent, worked together for the prosperity of the chosen people; and the Spirit of God strengthened them. In all of these activities Bulgakov sees a synergy of human talent and divine inspiration resulting in 'a divine-human union of two natures, two wills, two energies, without division and without confusion, in a single human hypostasis.' That is to say, he sees the Chalcedonian formula inscribed in a limited yet powerful way in particular vocations, each of which is thereby dynamically linked to the work of the incarnate God-human.

The synergy is especially evident in the vocation of prophecy. With the Old Testament prophets and their extraordinary intimacy with the Spirit one begins to approach the inner sanctum of Pentecost. But even here humanity is not negated. 'The great prophets are also great people, thinkers, patriots, saints, people not just favored [udostoennymi] with revelation, but worthy [dostoinymi] of this favor, for which reason the Church venerates them as saints.'[28] The prophets of Israel, like the apostles and saints of the church whom they anticipate, do not surrender their humanity at the gate of holiness. Holiness energizes and elevates their humanity, prepares it for incorporation into the kingdom of God.

From the prophets of Israel it is only a short step to the pentecostal gifts proper, the work of the Spirit in the visible church. The special function of the ecclesial gifts is to signify the deification of the world. Even a short list of these gifts suffices to establish their exalted status. The first gift, evident in the earliest days of the church as described in the Acts of the Apostles, is a powerful sense of communion (*koinonia, sobornost'*) in the love of Christ. Its focal points are the eucharistic fellowship and 'the

---

[27] *Uteshitel'*, p. 244.
[28] *Uteshitel'*, pp. 266–7.

catholic sense of church unity' symbolized by the apostles' miraculous multilingualism on Pentecost. A sense of direct guidance by the Holy Spirit is another gift to the earliest church: 'For it has seemed good to the Holy Spirit and to us . . .' (Acts 15:28). Interestingly, Bulgakov regards inspiration of this type as proper to the apostolic age rather than as a universal norm of church life such as *koinonia*.[29]

As the life of the church unfolds in New Testament and patristic times more gifts are showered upon the community: prophecy, hierarchy, new forms of asceticism, new forms of sacramentalism, gifts of love and many others. Taken together these endowments give content to the distinctive identity of the church as an institution in, but not of, the world. Symbolizing the life which comes from above and empowering the saints to begin living that life in the flesh, the ecclesial gifts foreshadow the deification of the world. Penultimately, they promote the christianization of the world.

Because they signify the deification of the world, ecclesial gifts are often regarded in traditional theology as divine gifts pure and simple. The view is understandable but not accurate because all gifts of the Spirit have a divine-human character. The distinction has practical implications, of which the first is the church's gifts should not be presented as if they were inherently foreign to the world or unprecedented in it. Bulgakov is not the sort of theologian for whom a Christian belief or practice is

---

[29] *Uteshitel'*, pp. 323–7. The danger in claims to direct guidance by the Spirit is that 'magical suggestion or a mechanistic *deus ex machina* [may] take the place of the fullness of divine-human life in the Church.' The evaluation of claims to special inspiration by the Spirit became even more problematic (and urgent) with the rise of Pentecostalism in twentieth-century Christianity. While Pentecostalism as such was not a phenomenon Bulgakov had to deal with, one should not suppose his sense of sobriety alone would have determined his approach. Bulgakov feared pious excess, but he also feared quenching the Spirit in the name of piety. His staunch support of a group of early twentieth-century hesychast revivalists against a rationalizing hierarchy is a case in point. 'The name-worshipers' (*imiaslavtsy*) cultivated a charismatic approach to prayer based on their belief that the revealed name of God (Jesus Christ) was itself divine. They represented a charismatic renewal movement in twentieth-century Orthodoxy. For an account of the controversy and Bulgakov's role in it, see *Sergii Bulgakov*, ed. Williams, pp. 8–13; and Evtuhov, *The Cross and the Sickle*, pp. 210–18.

diminished if it cannot be shown to be unique. On the contrary, anticipations, approximations and replications of the church's gifts in other contexts confirm for him the universality of the gospel. This point bears on the way Bulgakov construes the relationship between the Old and New Covenants. In his view most of the ecclesial gifts of the New Covenant were known already in one form or another under the Old Covenant. Even the outpouring of the Spirit upon all flesh on Pentecost was anticipated by the prophet Joel (Joel 2; Acts 2).[30] The difference lies in the degree to which the pentecostal mystery is realized and generalized. Before the messianic age inaugurated by the Lamb of God, the gifts of the Holy Spirit were experienced as partial, episodic, discontinuous; in the New Covenant, they are an ever-flowing stream.

A second implication of the divine-human character of the ecclesial gifts is the demand for a humanizing as well as a deifying ministry. The humanization of the world is going on even apart from the church, of course, thanks to the Spirit's life-giving work in the cosmo-historical process. Yet there is another humanizing ministry to be considered as well: the humanization of the church itself. The divine-human gifts of the Spirit humanize the church even as they empower the church to advance the deification of the world. That the doctrine of the incarnation or humanity of God implies a deified cosmos has always been recognized in Orthodox theology. That the same doctrine implies a humanized church has not been as clearly recognized. As a result countless forms of inhumanity have been tolerated, sometimes even cultivated, by traditional Orthodoxy. The modern Russian school addresses this situation with its own version of *ecclesia semper reformanda est*: the humanity of God is ill served by an inhumane church. The christianization of the world must go hand in hand with the humanization of the church.

One way Bulgakov presses the case for a more humane church is by asking his co-religionists to appreciate the human element involved in ecclesiastical arrangements in the first place. This is a humanizing discovery because it exposes the relativity of many ecclesiastical forms and so challenges the absolutizing of

[30] *Uteshitel'*, pp. 265–6; cf. p. 331.

tradition to the detriment of humanity and the gospel. Bulgakov's discussion of the hierarchical structure of the church is a case in point. He observes hierarchy in its historic form is not among the gifts of the Spirit enumerated in the New Testament. 'The organic and creative life of the Church ontologically *precedes* the hierarchical principle, which in its organized form arose in the Church later on.' The difference between primitive Christianity and the later church 'has enormous significance for our [ecclesiological] principles' because it shows 'the hierarchical-sacramental organization is not an adequate or absolute manifestation of the church.' A measure of 'relativity' is thereby introduced into the hierarchical structure of the church.[31]

Yet Bulgakov does not absolutize relativity, either. He rejects as 'a reactionary utopia' radical Protestant ecclesiology based on a return to supposedly original forms of church organization. Even if such reversion were possible, which it is not, the theory is defective because it presents church history as 'a historical Fall and withering away of the Spirit.' Such a view amounts to denying the continuity of the Spirit's work.[32] Church history is a continuing Pentecost. The fact hierarchical arrangements can be seen as involving human invention does not mean they are not gifts of the Spirit bearing 'the stamp of the divine will.' A dichotomy here is alien to a rightly guided ecclesiology. Church history is neither a purely divine nor a purely human process but a divine-human process. Hierarchical and other institutions emerging organically and functioning coherently in this process can be appreciated as *ius humanum* and *ius divinum* at the same time, precisely as one would expect in the community of the humanity of God.[33]

The virtue of Bulgakov's position is it affirms the catholic forms of church life while at the same time providing a theological basis for critically evaluating them. The distinction between the ontology and the organization of the church calls into question not just Protestant radicalism but also many

---

[31] *Nevesta agntsa*, pp. 286, 298.
[32] *Nevesta agntsa*, p. 293. Bulgakov cites the famous study by Rudolph Sohm, *Kirchenrecht* (1892), as an example of the defective view.
[33] *Nevesta agntsa*, pp. 298–9.

received forms of catholicism, both Roman and eastern. So, for example, Bulgakov rejects

> the dogmatic fiction set up for the Catholic Church by the Council of Trent, but taken over later by eastern theology as well, that all the sacraments were personally and directly established by Christ and have been handed down from Him through the holy apostles in the apostolic succession [of bishops].

The concept of apostolic succession in this literalistic and totalizing sense produces as fanciful a view of church history as Protestant primitivism. A second misguided notion is that of a supreme 'vicar of Christ,' which violates the principle of the living headship of Christ in the church. Another violation to which hierarchicalism is prone is the diminishment of the role of the laity in the church. 'But you are a chosen race, a royal priesthood, a holy nation, God's own people' (1 Pet. 2:9). Bulgakov notes Peter's words apply to the whole church, not just to bishops and other clergy:

> Only from the principle of the royal priesthood of all, the hierarchism of the *whole* Church, can we grasp and receive the *distinction* of hierarchical functions and avoid the exaggeration that lets clerical absolutism creep in and undermine the very principle of ecclesiastical hierarchism, splitting the church into two parts: the rulers and the ruled.[34]

Bulgakov's critique of church history is refreshing for its candor about the extent to which Orthodoxy has committed the very errors which it tirelessly criticizes in Roman Catholicism. The rejection of the Roman papal monarchy, for example, has been a commonplace of Orthodox ecclesiology for centuries. Bulgakov, too, opposes papalism; only he points out papalism comes in two forms, the 'individual' papalism of Rome and the 'collective' or eastern papalism which absolutizes the episcopate as such. Eastern papalism mistakes the *sobor* of bishops for the *sobornost'* of the church, encouraging 'the general belief that the hierarchical organization *is* the

[34] *Nevesta agntsa*, p. 303.

Church.'[35] But no part of the church can stand for the whole, not even a council. The same is true of the sacraments. Not one of them, nor even the entire sacramental system, is equivalent to the sacramental reality of the church, for 'the sacrament of all sacraments, the pan-sacrament [*vsetainstvo*], [is] the Church itself as the Humanity of God, the abiding Incarnation of God and Pentecost of the Spirit in their ongoing power.'[36] The ontological reality of the church transcends all historical forms.

But if the church as a whole must not be compromised or diminished by the claims of the parts, neither should the parts be oppressed in the name of the whole. The affirmation of multiplicity, diversity and individual freedom in the church is the second humanizing principle of Bulgakov's ecclesiology. The being of the church, as he sees it, is not an abstract unity (*edinstvo*) but a multiunity (*mnogoedinstvo*).[37] The unity of the church is nourished by the sacramental and hierarchical gifts of the Spirit. These take the form of a transmittable pattern, reproducible in time and space. They compose a tradition. But there are limits to tradition in the church. Many of the Spirit's gifts to the church are not traditionalizable at all, such as the gifts cataloged by Paul in 1 Corinthians 12:8–10: the utterance of wisdom, the utterance of knowledge, faith, gifts of healing, the working of miracles, prophecy, the discernment of spirits, various kinds of tongues, the interpretation of tongues. And of course this is only a partial list. 'Irregularity is the law for such manifestations of the Spirit ... The power of these gifts is entrusted to no one sacramentally, it remains in God's hands as an immediate, continuing Pentecost.'[38] These gifts manifest divine power, but they also have a humanizing effect by virtue of the receptivity which must exist in the church which hosts them. A church which is not open to exploration, individual expression, the non-traditional, the unprecedented, in a word a church lacking liberty, cannot receive, much less benefit from the prophetic gifts of the Spirit.[39] Human creativity is integral to sanctification.

---

[35] *Nevesta agntsa*, pp. 299–300; cf. p. 287.
[36] *Nevesta agntsa*, pp. 296–7.
[37] *Uteshitel'*, p. 345; *Nevesta agntsa*, p. 282.
[38] *Nevesta agntsa*, pp. 315–16.
[39] See Bulgakov's appeal to Paul's recommendation of Christian liberty to the Galatian church, *Uteshitel'*, p. 351.

Organized Christian asceticism presents an interesting case for Bulgakov's theory of sanctification. Monasticism is one of gifts of the Spirit to the church. In theory it is essentially a prophetic gift because it is based on the renunciation of normal modes of social life for the sake of the kingdom of God. Like all prophetic witness, monasticism bears 'the character of creative *daring*, often accompanied by struggle, by the breaking of fleshly and spiritual ties.' It is 'in the full sense a free, even self-appointed act' and in any case a highly individual one, for no Christian is required to become a monk or a nun. In practice, however, monasticism long ago formed an ecclesiastical tradition with its own rules and patterns, its own institutions, even its own canon of texts, such as the corpus of mystical and ascetical texts known as the *Philokalia* (Russ. *Dobrotoliubie*). Bulgakov reveres the monastic tradition as a record of some of the church's most intimate experiences of the Spirit, but he also recognizes monasticism is vulnerable to a spirit of 'legalism' subversive of Christian liberty. At its worst this legalism means 'slavery to grand and little inquisitors, with their pretensions to infallibility and assertion of spiritual despotism under the pretext of spiritual guidance [*monasheskogo 'starchestva'*].'[40] When cultivated with love and regard for all people, however, monasticism enriches the whole church.

The generous yet critical spirit of Bulgakov's assessment of monasticism is typical of his approach to ecclesiastical tradition generally. He is as fierce as any Protestant in his rejection of legalism, yet he also rejects an ecclesiology which would expel organized asceticism from the church. A mountain of evidence exists to show monasticism is as rich in spiritual gifts as the more worldly traditions of piety prized by Protestants. To reject monasticism is to turn one's back on a significant aspect of the continuing Pentecost which is the life of the church. Yet monasticism must conform with the humanity of God; its other-worldly orientation provides no exemption here. A genuinely Christian (divine-human) asceticism will be a humane asceticism.

No matter how much it treasures the traditional forms of spirituality, however, a healthy church will not seek to

[40] *Uteshitel'*, pp. 345–56.

channel all its inspiration into pre-established patterns. The *Creator Spiritus* must always be acknowledged. 'There cannot be a *Philokalia* of creativity, for creativity is extra-legal and irregular.'[41] This important insight is connected with Bulgakov's observation about the absence of a gospel of the Holy Spirit in the New Testament. There is an inherent tension in the concept of 'a canon' of spirituality, for the Spirit blows where it wills. So, while there can be a pneumatological canon in a loose and metaphorical sense of the word – the *Philokalia* is a case in point – such a corpus differs in a fundamental way from the christological canon. The latter can be full-bodied and definitive, for it portrays the incarnate Word, the historic Christ. But the Spirit manifests itself differently than the Son, concealing its personal hypostasis until the end of the age while continuing to shower divine gifts on church and world. A pneumatological canon is therefore unfixed and open to novelty in principle, hence not a canon at all in the strict sense of the word.

Nowhere is the humanizing tendency of Bulgakov's ecclesiology more evident than in his discussion of love in the church. To say that love is one of the gifts of the Spirit is of course to say the obvious. Yet differences of opinion arise as soon as one tries to specify the type of love affirmed by this statement. In dualistic ecclesiologies a categorical distinction is made between *eros* and *agape*, *amor* and *caritas*, human love and spiritual or divine love.[42] The distinction more or less expels erotics from pneumatology. Bulgakov, with his doctrine of natural grace and his sophianic ecclesiology, could not accept this dichotomy. Moreover, erotics finds an ally in the theme of creativity, which figures so prominently in his dogmatics. With Plato, Bulgakov believes all creative activity is an expression of erotic longing, hence the stamp of eros is not lost even in the most highly spiritualized forms of creative expression. Thus he can speak of prophecy as '*the eros of the spirit*' and 'creative eros in the

---

[41] *Uteshitel'*, p. 356.
[42] Bulgakov was familiar with Anders Nygren's *Agape and Eros*, which more than any other book shaped the discussion of love in twentieth-century Protestant theology. See *Uteshitel'*, p. 364, n. 1.

Church, in Spirit-bearing humanity.'[43] In some sense, then, Bulgakov envisions the church not just as a caritative community but as an erotic community. The sense in which erotic values apply to the church must be spelled out, however, because it is obvious a good deal of eroticism deals in sin and death. Like Dostoevsky, Bulgakov believed the love of divine beauty dwells in Sodom as well as Eden, but he was not prepared to abandon the distinction between the two, to equate 'Venus and Madonna, heavenly lilies and poisonous "flowers of evil." '[44]

One way to investigate the matter is to examine the body of material in the Bible which may be categorized as erotic and ecclesiological at the same time, such as the Psalm 45, the Song of Songs, Ephesians 5:21–33, Revelation 19–22 and other texts which present the love between Christ and the church in erotic terms. The importance of these texts for Bulgakov can be gauged by the fact that he took the title of the ecclesiological volume of his dogmatics from one of them: 'Come, I will show you the bride, the wife of the Lamb' (Rev. 21:9).

Bulgakov believes most interpretations of eroticism in the Bible result in an impoverished and one-sided view of the subject. '[Biblical] definitions of Sophia [= Church] as Bride, Woman and Body have long led to misunderstanding, whether in the direction of an excessive spiritualism that eliminates the power of the image by dissolving it into allegory, or an excessive romanticism in which poetry, emotions and even carnal passion predominate.'[45] Of the two errors, spiritualism is the more frequently encountered in Orthodoxy. By neutralizing the sense of wonder about the imagery of love in the Bible, traditional allegorization effectively removes erotics from the theological

---

[43] *Uteshitel'*, pp. 333, 336.
[44] *Uteshitel'*, pp. 236–8. For a contemporary example of an Orthodox love-ethic which is Bulgakovian in spirit without being influenced directly by Bulgakov, see Vigen Guroian, *Incarnate Love: Essays in Orthodox Ethics* (Notre Dame, Indiana: University of Notre Dame Press, 1987). Among Bulgakov's contemporaries B.P. Vysheslavtsev, professor of moral theology at Saint Sergius, presented Orthodox ethics in much the same spirit in *The Ethics of Transformed Eros: Etika preobrazhennogo erosa*, intro. and notes by V.V. Sapov (Moscow: Izdatel'stvo 'Respublika', 1994). The work was originally published by YMCA-Press in 1931 and bore the subtitle 'Problems of Law and Grace.'
[45] *Nevesta agntsa*, p. 289.

agenda. For his part Bulgakov marvels at biblical eroticism. About the Song of Songs he writes: 'the presence of this book in the canon, so questionable and incomprehensible for people of anti-erotic spirit past and present, is a true miracle revealed by the Holy Spirit; [the Song is] "the Holy of Holies" of the Bible, as Christian and Jewish interpreters call it in comparison with the other canonical books.'[46] This sense of wonder prompts inquiry into the ontological link between eros and *ecclesia*. That such a link exists is implied by Bulgakov's sophianic ecclesiology. Indeed, as the place where philosophic eros joins hands with ecclesial conscience, sophiology is a specific instance of the connection.

For all his interest in the sanctification of eros, however, Bulgakov cautions against 'excessive romanticism.' While the specific reference is not clear, Bulgakov might be referring to the exploitation of religious imagery in some of the poetry and philosophy of the Russian Silver Age, which elaborated a fleshly Solovievianism or carnal piety difficult to reconcile with classical Orthodoxy. Be that as it may, Bulgakov's aspiration to transcend the dichotomy between spiritual allegory and fleshly poetry conforms with the overall purpose of his ecclesiology, which is to vindicate the humanity of God in the life of the church. As an anthropological given and a gift of the Spirit at the same time, eros is a divine-human good. Neither the mortification of eros nor its apotheosis penetrates to the heart of the mystery.

Bulgakov does not seek a single mode of erotic-caritative expression to which all loves in the church should conform. On the contrary, he envisions a church in which many ways of loving are practiced, each responding to a particular divine-human gift while leaving room for other ways. The human experience of love is so 'antinomic', it is unrealistic to expect a total synthesis of its elements, even if such a thing were reconcilable with free inspiration in love.[47] The challenge is to

---

[46] *Uteshitel'*, p. 371. Cf. *Nevesta agntsa*, p. 288, where Bulgakov calls the Song of Songs 'the Old Testamental Apocalypse' and 'a verbal *miracle*.'

[47] 'In the dual character of ecclesial love as agapic love and eros the abovementioned antinomic duality of the Christian life as asceticism and creativity, repentant humility and creative inspiration, appears.' *Uteshitel'*, p. 366.

keep potentially creative antinomies from degenerating into deadening dichotomies.

So, for example, Bulgakov does not reject monasticism because of its asceticism, or marriage because of its worldliness. There is an antinomy here which can be resolved only on the level of personal vocation. At the same time personal vocations should not be pursued in isolation but should stay connected with each other in the living matrix of the church. Interaction between vocations checks the tendency to one-sidedness in all of them. Thus monks and other ascetics should not aspire to de-eroticize human beings, not even themselves. 'The fiery element' of eros, far from dying out in asceticism, fuels the passion that belongs to every true vocation. As for the more worldly expressions of eros, these will not be coherent or even all that gratifying without a spiritual discipline. There is 'an *ascetics* of love, its method and work, so to speak,' which need to be culti-vated along with love itself.[48]

One of the gravest tensions in the human experience of love as Bulgakov understands it is the antinomy between eros and sex. As an original endowment of human nature eros precedes the Fall, whereas sex is a consequence of the Fall. The inherent antagonism between the two remains unresolved. Bulgakov takes a fairly negative view of most attempts to 'desexualize' human beings, as in certain ascetical traditions, and does not rule out the possibility of a certain 'harmonization' of sex and eros.[49] Yet he remains suspicious of sex because it does not belong to original human nature. Adam and Eve in paradise knew eros but not sex. They could have reproduced humankind in Eden, but this would have happened by 'an extra-sexual and super-sexual means of reproduction,' through 'virginal conception' comparable to that which occurred in Mary's womb.[50] By the same logic Bulgakov denies that Jesus experi-enced sexual passion. 'In this respect Christ *differed* from the rest of the human race, for in Him the original chastity and virginity of [humanity] were re-established.' The temptations

---

[48] *Uteshitel'*, p. 359. For 'the fiery element' see p. 370.
[49] *Uteshitel'*, p. 370.
[50] *Kupina neopalimaia*, pp. 164–5.

Jesus endured were those inherent in original, not post-lapsarian, human nature.[51]

The forms of love which Bulgakov envisions as flourishing in the church are for the most part traditional. There is no evidence in his work of openness to active homosexuality or extra-marital sex. The feminist problematization of traditional gender roles is also absent from his thought. It would be wrong, therefore, to say Bulgakov sought a radical revision of the understanding of love in the church. His aim was to humanize, not to revolutionize, the church.

Bulgakov's approach to friendship in the church illustrates the distinction. In his love for Pavel Florensky, Bulgakov knew the experience of passionate, even romantic friendship between men. In *The Comforter* he identifies such 'spiritual pairing or *syzygy*' as a gift of the Spirit which has a rightful place in the life of the church. He credits Florensky with 'a true theological discovery' for offering a theology of friendship in *The Pillar and Ground of the Truth* (1914). Bulgakov's praise of the defunct ritual of 'brothering' (*adelphopoiêsis*, Russ. *bratotvorenie*) in the Orthodox Church is for all practical purposes a call for reinstitution of the practice. He also appears ready to extend the sanctification of erotic friendship to heterosexual pairs outside the context of marriage.[52] For Bulgakov, then, the church was not just an association of the saved but a community of friends. He was not prepared to accept the sexualization of friendship, however.[53]

---

[51] *Agnets bozhii*, pp. 329–30.

[52] *Uteshitel'*, pp. 363–6. For Florensky's 'discovery,' see Letter Eleven: Friendship (ch. 12) of *The Pillar and Ground of the Truth*, trans. Jakim. Robert Slesinski offers a balanced and theologically informed analysis of Florensky's theory of 'the metaphysical roots of friendship' in *A Metaphysics of Love*, pp. 215–32. Florensky was a married priest and family man, although his marriage came as a surprise to some of his close friends, who expected him to take monastic orders. See Bulgakov's memoir, 'Sviashchennik o. Pavel Florenskii,' in Bulgakov, *Sochineniia v dvukh tomakh*, ed. Khoruzhii and Rodnianskaia, 1:538–47. For a recent discussion of brothering and related practices, see John Boswell, *Same-Sex Unions in Premodern Europe* (New York: Villard Books, 1994). Boswell's rendering of *adelphopoiêsis* as 'same-sex union' is problematic, but his presentation remains very valuable.

[53] 'Of course the erotic character of this inspiring love is devoid of the tension that characterizes love between the sexes. In this sense it is necessary to liberate the concept of "erotic" love from the admixture of sexuality. The latter attaches itself to the concept in the vulgar use of the word "erotic," but even in Plato it is not

His theory, like his love for Father Pavel, was edenic, not carnal.

Whether Bulgakov's theology of eros could be used to sanction untraditional forms of love in the church is an issue to be pursued in the appropriate contexts. Bulgakov certainly believed no traditional inventory of gifts could ever sum up the Spirit's work in the church 'inasmuch as the continuing life of the church brings to light ever new forms of holiness.'[54] This is as true in the erotic sphere as in any other. But novel expressions of love have to be subjected to the same scrutiny as the old ones. While unprecedented forms of holiness are continually being generated in the church, so are new forms of one-sidedness, new abstract principles, new ways of simplifying, reducing and negating the humanity of God.

---

inherent in the concept (on the contrary, Alcibiades' encomium of Socrates in *The Symposium* testifies to the overcoming of sexuality).' *Uteshitel'*, pp. 364–5.
[54] *Uteshitel'*, pp. 349–50.

I5

Conclusion: The Limits of Tradition

Despite his prominence in the Orthodox world at the end of his life, Bulgakov had no heirs in the field of dogmatic theology. Lev Zander and Nicholas Zernov were executors of his legacy in their ecumenical work and in the contributions which each made to the study of Bulgakov and the Russian religious renaissance. Zernov, who lived for many years in Oxford, played an especially important role in keeping interest in Bulgakov alive in the English-speaking world. The cultural historian and publicist G.P. Fedotov (1886–1951), whose *Russian Religious Mind* served a generation of English-speakers as a primer in Russian Orthodoxy, also stood in the tradition of Bulgakov.[1] So did the Rev. Alexander Schmemann to a greater extent than is commonly recognized. Schmemann was old enough to have studied under Bulgakov at Saint Sergius, and some of his English-language publications evinced an interest in promoting the Bulgakovian (and Solovievian) legacy.[2] In the lecture course on Russian religious thought which he taught for a number of years at Columbia University as well as in radio broadcasts to the Soviet Union, Schmemann's debt to the Russian school, which he always acknowledged, was even clearer. However, the degree to which Schmemann promoted the concerns of the Russian school was limited by his recognition of the virtues of the Neopatristic method for liturgical theology, the field in

---

[1] George P. Fedotov, *The Russian Religious Mind: Kievan Christianity* (Cambridge, Massachusetts: Harvard University Press, 1946); vol. 2: *The Middle Ages, The Thirteenth to the Fifteenth Centuries*, ed. with a foreword by John Meyendorff (1966).

[2] See especially *Ultimate Questions: An Anthology of Modern Russian Religious Thought*, ed. with an intro. by Alexander Schmemann (New York, Chicago, San Francisco: Holt, Rinehart and Winston, 1965).

which he made his greatest scholarly contribution, and by the relatively marginal status of philosophic Orthodoxy in the ecclesiastical environment in which he worked.[3]

The most impressive work of the Russian school after Bulgakov's death was V.V. Zenkovsky's *A History of Russian Philosophy*, published in Paris in 1948. Translated into English by George L. Kline in 1953, Zenkovsky's book served as the standard history of Russian philosophy for more than a generation. Zenkovsky was an Orthodox priest and long-time faculty member of the Orthodox Theological Institute. While his purpose in writing *A History of Russian Philosophy* was to present a balanced account of the whole of modern Russian thought, he devoted plenty of attention to the theological dimension. His portrait of Russian theology is anything but Neopatristic, however. Zenkovsky believed the theological creativity of modern Russian Orthodoxy did not derive from the inner logic of Orthodoxy alone but from the momentous meeting of Orthodoxy with the modern western world. Zenkovsky's *History of Russian Philosophy* was thus a response to Florovsky's *Paths of Russian Theology*. It celebrated the engagement of Orthodoxy with the modern world.

It would be wrong, of course, to portray the shift from the Russian to the Neopatristic school solely in terms of individuals or important books. The changing historical context of Orthodox theology in the 1930s was the most important factor. A new generation was emerging for whom the Russian religious renaissance of the late imperial period, so fundamental for Bulgakov and his generation, was a thing of the past. Even if some members of the younger generation had completed their higher education in Russia before the revolution, they did not enjoy the kind of memories Bulgakov and his contemporaries

---

[3] Father Thomas Hopko's contribution to the study of Bulgakov should also be mentioned. Hopko's edition of *The Orthodox Church* made this concise summary of some of Bulgakov's ideas readily available in English again. See Sergius Bulgakov, *The Orthodox Church*, with a foreword by Thomas Hopko, trans. Lydia Kesich (Crestwood, New York: St Vladimir's Seminary Press, 1988). Hopko's foreword is a good example of the mixture of admiration and ambivalence toward Bulgakov in the Neopatristic ranks. See also Myroslaw Tataryn, 'Sergius Bulgakov (1871–1944): Time for a New Look,' *St Vladimir's Theological Quarterly* 42 (1998):315–38.

did: memories of inspired student activism, cultural prominence, weighty responsibilities in the universities, the Duma, the Council of 1917, and so on. The new generation came of age professionally in a small emigré community in the West where Orthodoxy was the faith of a tiny minority. For them the brave new world could scarcely be found in memories of Russia and its 'renaissance.' Moreover, Europe in the 1930s, the Europe of Hitler and Stalin, was scarcely a place to nurture dreams of cultural renaissance. The pessimism about human civilization and humanism itself which pervades Neopatristic theology must be seen against this background. In this respect the Neopatristic movement in Orthodox theology invites comparison with the vigorous counter-cultural trends in western theology at the time, such as Karl Barth's Neo-Orthodoxy.

If the early Neopatristic theologians were invariably countercultural, they were not necessarily anti-western. Western theology actually became something of an ally in the field closest to the heart of the Neopatristic school, namely, patristic studies, which were flourishing in the West at the time. The tendency of western patristic scholarship had swung away from the antidogmatic, liberal Protestant approach of Harnack and his school toward a deeper appreciation for the dogmatic content of early Christianity. In other words western theology was moving in a direction Orthodox scholars could approve of. As a result Orthodox scholars found themselves speaking a common language with some of their most sophisticated western Christian neighbors. They even found themselves in demand because of their mastery of patristic sources. For the new generation, in effect, patristics was the brave new world. Unlike the Russian religious renaissance, which had become a formula for cultural isolation, the Neopatristic path led somewhere. It offered opportunities for dialogue while at the same time licensing claims to a specific Orthodox identity. The combination of cosmopolitanism and particularism was irresistible for young Orthodox theologians who saw that their future lay in the West.

There were so many good reasons for the Neopatristic option that one can easily appreciate why it swept the field. Unfortunately the sweep was so complete that Orthodox theologians soon forgot that, despite the undeniable gains of the

Neopatristic option, something important was lost. As time passed and the memory of the divisions which once existed in the Paris community faded, a harmonizing portrait of Orthodox theology emerged which emphasized consensus and relegated divisive issues to the periphery, a picture promoted by Neopatristic theologians because it corresponded to their ideal of 'the mind of the fathers.' Of course, the keenest observers of modern Russian theology knew such a harmonious picture was simplistic. But since there was almost no one vigorously representing the Russian school on the Orthodox scene after the middle of the twentieth century, recognition of the diversity that once existed in Paris (and before) had no practical consequences. The view that Orthodoxy theology should go 'beyond the fathers' came to seem alien. Few could have said what the phrase was supposed to mean.

'Beyond the fathers' or 'back to the fathers?' The rhetoric is stirring. But unless one assumes this distinction involves nothing more than differences of style or taste, one must identify the theological issue at stake in it. This issue, in turn, will offer a vantage point from which to take a final, retrospective look at the intellectual tradition represented by Bukharev, Soloviev and Bulgakov.

One should begin by noting the issue is not whether the fathers are indispensable for Orthodox theology. For the Russian as well as the Neopatristic school the 'patristic foundation' was taken as a given.[4] The issue concerns that which is added to the foundation. Does it involve substantive additions and new discoveries, or does it simply entail new ways of expressing, articulating or defining that which the church has always known and preached?

The latter is the Neopatristic position. The underlying concept is, to quote Schmemann again, 'the holy Tradition of the Church.' That is to say, the Neopatristic position is not merely that theology should follow the lead of the fathers, but that in the works of the fathers one finds a singular and comprehensive tradition which provides the pattern for Orthodox theologizing. Such an assumption is necessary if Neopatristic

---

[4] See Schmemann, 'Russian Theology: 1920–1972,' quoted in the Introduction, n. 1 above.

theology is to acquire shape, since patristic literature as a historical phenomenon is an extremely variegated corpus of texts comprising a wide range of opinions. In Neopatristic theology tradition does not depend on the fathers; the fathers depend on tradition. Moreover, the same tradition must be assumed to underlie the whole of the church's patrimony, that is to say, not just patristic literature but scripture, liturgy, canons and other institutions as well. Otherwise a gap would open between the singular tradition of the fathers and the being of the church, for the church as a historical entity is even more variegated than patristic literature. In short, only as tradition does the church find its shape. John Meyendorff states the Neopatristic view perfectly when he writes 'tradition is the sacramental continuity in history of the communion of saints; in a way, it is the Church itself.'[5] This strong statement makes it clear that the concept of tradition is not just one of a number of formative or organizing concepts in Neopatristic theology, but the hegemonic concept, the central idea, the practical absolute.

The hegemonic concept of tradition entails as its corollary the rejection of the historical development of dogma except in the formal sense. Thomas Hopko states the Neopatristic position:

> The Orthodox Church does not have a teaching of 'dogmatic development.' Orthodox believe that expressions of Christian faith and life can change and indeed must change as the Church moves through history. But the Orthodox interpret these changes as being merely formal and not in any sense substantial. They would never agree that there can be anything in the Church of Christ today that was not essentially present at any moment of the Church's life and history.[6]

This view clearly excludes the possibility that dogmatic theology could be substantively affected by its historical environment, as the Russian school tended to assume. In Neopatristic theology tradition governs dogma; dogma does not shape tradition, except of course at the originating moment of dogma and tradition alike.

[5] John Meyendorff, *Living Tradition: Orthodox Witness in the Contemporary World* (Crestwood, NY: St Vladimir's Seminary Press, 1978), p. 16.
[6] *Women and the Priesthood*, ed. Thomas Hopko (Crestwood, New York: St Vladimir's Seminary Press, 1983), p. 177.

What are the dangers of such a strong concept of tradition in theology? Are there dimensions of the gospel or of the life of the church that are likely to be obscured, distorted or left out of account when so much of the church's life is subsumed under the category of tradition? In short, does it make sense, logically and theologically, to say that tradition is 'in a way, the Church itself?'

One way of responding to these questions, which are obviously crucial for the Neopatristic project, is to say they are the kind of questions western theologians typically raise with regard to Orthodoxy. One might then argue, like it or not, Orthodox theology takes the hegemony of tradition as a given and anyone who wishes to have a dialogue with Orthodox theology must recognize this is how it works. But is it the case that Orthodox theology always works this way? In the century of theologizing represented by Bukharev, Soloviev and Bulgakov one finds a large and rich corpus of Orthodox theology in which tradition is not the hegemonic concept and certainly not the practical absolute. Even the word tradition (*predanie*) does not become prominent in the Russian school until Bulgakov's later works. By then Bulgakov had become aware of the nascent Neopatristic movement and had made some concessions to it, though not to the extent of surrendering his whole conceptuality. Of course the absence of a particular word from someone's vocabulary does not necessarily betoken the absence of the phenomenon described by that word. A Neopatristic historian could argue, for example, the principle of tradition is inconspicuous in Bukharev's theology not because Archimandrite Feodor doubted its axiomatic status but because the principle was so unchallenged in his time he felt no need to emphasize it. Yet this line of reasoning is tricky for the Neopatristic case because it implies the concept of tradition fashioned by Neopatristic theologians is a response to the challenges of *their* time and hence historically relative to some extent.

To be clear about the issue at stake here, however, one must return to the point about the patristic foundation of Orthodox theology. Bukharev, Bulgakov and even Soloviev would agree the Orthodox Church and its theology rest on a patristic foundation. They would also agree the concept of tradition is wider, richer and deeper in Orthodoxy than in western theology, where a tendency to compartmentalization generates distinctions which Orthodox see as artificial, e.g. the categorical distinction between scripture and tradition. But accepting tradition as foundational for theology is not the same thing as taking tradition to be the criterion by which all else is measured. Such traditio-centrism is foreign to the Orthodox theology described in this study.

To state the point more systematically, the theologians of the Russian school recognized the limits of tradition. They accepted tradition as a guide but did not think it sufficed for all the paths of mission and ministry which the Orthodox Church was called to explore.

One must not oversimplify the Neopatristic position in the process of criticizing it. The Neopatristic school was not so naive as to imagine that Orthodoxy in the modern world did not have to heed anything but the voice of tradition. Neopatristic thinkers were and are sophisticated modern theologians. They know they live in a complex world which, while full of dangers for Orthodoxy, also offers unprecedented means for promoting it, such as critical-historical scholarship, the freedoms of a democratic society and the world-shrinking devices of modern communications. Moreover, Neopatristic theology has always qualified its concept of tradition by making a couple of distinctions designed to avoid the formalism to which traditio-centrism would otherwise incline.

First, a distinction is drawn between Tradition and traditions, that is to say, between the essential, unchanging, divine deposit of faith and the many customary, culturally relative arrangements which also attach themselves to the historic church but which the church is free to alter because they are human products. A distinction is also drawn in one way or another between 'living' and 'dead' tradition. Jaroslav Pelikan's famous formulation, 'tradition is the living faith of the dead, traditionalism is the dead faith of the living,' is a rightly celebrated case in point.[7] The virtue of this distinction, besides calling attention

---

[7] Jaroslav Pelikan, *The Vindication of Tradition* (New Haven and London: Yale University Press, 1984), p. 65. While Pelikan's conversion to Orthodoxy is recent, Neopatristic elements have been evident in his work for many years.

to the spiritual reality of tradition, is that it accommodates the idea of change or growth. 'True tradition is always a *living* tradition,' writes John Meyendorff. 'It changes while remaining always the same. It changes because it faces different situations, not because its essential content is modified. This content is not an abstract proposition; it is the Living Christ Himself, who said, "I am the Truth." '[8] Aided by these two distinctions Neopatristic theologians fashioned a concept of tradition flexible enough to find application in all sorts of contexts, and nuanced enough to avoid the pitfalls of formalistic piety and stand-pat conservatism. To say it another way, the Neopatristic concept of tradition is broad enough to make it difficult for those who embrace it to see why anyone should view it as deficient, unless of course that person were inspired by values fundamentally irreconcilable with Orthodoxy.

Yet both of the distinctions employed by Neopatristic theologians are problematic for the following reason. Tradition, as the Latin (also Greek) term makes clear, is by definition something handed down, i.e. received from others. If something cannot be received from others, it cannot be termed tradition. The mistake of Neopatristic theology is to extend the category of tradition to realities that are not traditional and then to discourse about those realities as if they were. When, for example, in the passage already cited John Meyendorff writes that the 'content' of tradition is 'not an abstract proposition [but] the Living Christ Himself,' he is extending the concept of tradition and *tradita* (things handed down) to something which cannot possibly be so construed, namely, the living Christ. The same sort of problem is evident when he writes that 'tradition is the sacramental continuity in history of the communion of saints; in a way, it is the Church itself.' To justify this statement one must either extend the concept of tradition beyond its boundaries to accommodate a mystical reality, or else impoverish the concept of church by defining the church in terms of its *tradita* alone. The qualifier 'sacramental' does not remedy the logical flaw here. A sacrament is by definition both an outward and visible sign and an inward and spiritual grace, but only in the first respect is it a *traditum*, something handed down. The

---

[8] Meyendorff, *Living Tradition*, p. 8.

spiritual reality of a sacrament is just that: spiritual, inward, unseen, present, existential, personal, hence not traditional. Let it be noted this argument does not introduce a dualism of spirit and matter into sacramental theology. What is at issue here is not the divine-human plenitude which is the sacramental being of the church, but the extent to which the conceptuality of tradition adequately describes that reality.

The same critical point can be made with respect to the distinction between Tradition and the traditions. As a way of discriminating between the central and the peripheral in the history of the church, this distinction is reasonable and indeed indispensable. But Neopatristic theologians almost always take the distinction further by supposing that it parallels the distinction between the eternal and the historically relative, the divinely revealed and the merely human. This is to disregard a logical sticking point, namely, that while tradition may be said to signify, prompt, structure or otherwise mediate a perception of the eternal, it does not accomplish this end *by virtue of its traditionality or historicity alone*. Tradition, like everything else in the church, is justified by faith and eternalized by the life-giving Spirit. Faith and the Holy Spirit abound in the church, irradiating the church and transfiguring tradition into Tradition. But they abound *as* faith and the Spirit operating upon tradition. Tradition has no eternity without them, only historicity. Similarly, historical science cannot demonstrate the eternity of a tradition, only its continuity. Historical continuity is important; it can serve as a powerful goad to faith and as a device for opening the mind to the Spirit. But faith and the Spirit must complete the equation.

The confidence which Neopatristic theologians vest in the self-authenticating character of historic traditions can be sensed in Florovsky's approval of Marc Bloch's statement that 'Christianity is a religion of historians.' The statement is correct, Florovsky argues, because 'Christianity is basically a vigorous appeal to history, a witness of faith to certain particular events in the past ... as "mighty deeds" of God, *Magnalia Dei*.'[9] The

[9] Georges Florovsky, 'The Predicament of the Christian Historian,' *Christianity and Culture*, vol. 2 of *The Collected Works of Georges Florovsky* (Belmont, Massachusetts: Nordland Publishing Company, 1974), p. 31.

problem with Florovsky's argument is not that it affirms the importance of history in Christian faith but that it underemphasizes, indeed overlooks, the very real tension between an appeal to history and an act of faith. An act of faith can only happen 'now' as opposed to 'then'; it can never be a *traditum*. An act of faith takes place in that mysterious gap between the not-yet-historical and the already-historical where human life is actually lived. Only by disregarding this tension can Florovsky pronounce Christianity to be a 'religion of historians.' On the other hand, Florovsky's pronouncement certainly suggests that Christianity is viewed by Neopatristic theologians as a religion of historians, a position which is not all that surprising considering most Neopatristic theologians have been historians. Here one sees another contrast between them and the thinkers of the Russian school presented in this book. None of the latter were historians. Bukharev was a biblical theologian, Soloviev a philosopher, Bulgakov an economist and dogmatic theologian. The theological distortions resulting from disciplinary factors should not be disregarded in their case, either. But for an Orthodox theological scene dominated for decades by historians, Bukharev, Soloviev and Bulgakov offer a healthy change of perspective.

One might object that my argument depends on a rigoristic definition of tradition alien to the fullness of the Orthodox concept. But this objection is misplaced if its aim is to defend Neopatristic methodology. One of the greatest virtues of the latter is the rigor with which it construes the concept of tradition when applying it to the history of the church. Neopatristic theology is part of what Pelikan has called 'the scholarly rediscovery of tradition,'[10] a process which has vastly expanded our appreciation for the integrity and continuity of the Christian tradition. This virtue would be impaired if a looser concept of tradition were put in place of the one that Neopatristic theologians actually use in their historical scholarship. What is needed is not a looser definition of tradition, but a recognition that tradition, in theology and in ecclesiastical practice, has limits.

What concept or concepts might be placed alongside that of tradition in theology? The phrase 'living tradition' provides the

[10] *The Vindication of Tradition*, p. 12.

clue. As Neopatristic theologians usually apply it, the phrase is another case of the conflation of the traditional with the a-traditional. A living thing, *qua* living thing, cannot be a tradition, for its life is immanent, its own, not received from others. Even a tradition becomes something more than traditional when it is put into practice in a living moment. The same is true of the act of tradition. That which is handed down is by definition a *traditum*, and even the action of handing down can be viewed as a tradition to the extent that it follows an antecedent pattern (which it almost always does). But the act itself, because it issues from someone's free decision, is new every time it is performed. An a-traditional and untraditional-izable element – the 'living' element – has entered in. Embedded in the concept of living tradition, in other words, is the assumption of a continuing, hence open dialogue between tradition and life in the various senses of the latter term (individual experience, contemporary world, world-process, potentiality, etc.). Living tradition thus construed is not so much a concept as a project.

The dialogic implications of the concept of living tradition can be appreciated even more clearly when one examines the origins of the term in Orthodox theology. In point of fact the concept of living tradition was not introduced into Orthodox theology by Neopatristic theologians at all, but by Bulgakov and those who rallied to his defense in the Sophia Affair. In 1937 this group published a volume of essays titled *Living Tradition: Orthodoxy in the Modern World*.[11] The aim of the book was to oppose a theological proposition which, as the authors be-lieved, sanctioned the attack on Bulgakov and threatened to diminish the freedom and scope of Orthodox theologizing: the proposition that patristic tradition should be the primary guide of Orthodox theology and Orthodox life. In other words, the concept of living tradition made its debut in Orthodox theology as a means of protesting the fundamental assumption of the nascent Neopatristic movement.

The fact that Bulgakov and his allies titled their book *Living*

---

[11] *Zhivoe predanie: pravoslavie v sovremennosti* (Paris: YMCA-Press, 1937). I cite the new Russian edition (Moscow: Sviato-Filaretovskaia moskovskaia vysshaia pravoslavno-khristianskaia shkola, 1997).

Tradition was itself a sign of the changes taking place in Orthodox theology at the time. The concept of tradition was capturing the theological agenda to such an extent that even critics of the new wave, by now very much on the defensive, had to present their case in their opponents' idiom. Still, no one who reads the eleven articles of *Living Tradition* can fail to see that the purpose of the collection was to expose the limits of tradition as a theological concept; or to put it more positively, to show that other concepts besides tradition should play a central role in the structuring of Orthodox theology.

Acknowledging his debt to *Living Tradition* in the introduction to a book of his own bearing the same title, John Meyendorff observed that 'the impact of the [earlier] collection was not as strong as it could have been because the Western world was not at that time sufficiently attuned to the authors' witness, and [because] their native country was totally closed to them.'[12] While Meyendorff's two points are well taken, one must add that *Living Tradition* had a limited impact also for reasons internal to Orthodox theology. The book represented the losing side of a bitter in-house debate. The Neopatristic group, rightly sensing that Orthodox theological opinion was shifting in its favor, saw the Russian school was in a tight spot. To the extent that *Living Tradition* affirmed the task of recovering patristic tradition, Neopatristic scholars knew they could do this job better than the generation whose thinking dominated *Living Tradition*. To the extent that the purpose of *Living Tradition* was to question the basic assumption of Neopatristic theologizing, the new group had no interest in promoting the book.

Living Tradition is exceptionally valuable as a summary of the theology of the Russian school, for in defending their position the authors deploy virtually all of the school's leading concepts and concerns, beginning with the humanity of God. To the Neopatristic demand for a return to tradition, Bulgakov and his allies reply: yes, but! Tradition, yes, but only if it is construed in divine-human terms rather than being asserted as a divine formula pure and simple, a holy thing untouched by human

---

[12] Meyendorff, *Living Tradition*, p. 11. Meyendorff mistakenly dated the publication of *Zhivoe predanie* to 1930.

384

experience, human history, the world outside the church or the cosmos itself. As the writers put it in the preface to the volume, 'the Church is a divine-human organism in which the fullness and immutability of divine truth are disclosed within human history, with all the limitations and relativity of each of its epochs.'[13]

Creativity is another concept that knits the *Living Tradition* group together. The church, as they see it, is obligated to preserve tradition but must do this 'creatively, for tradition is not just a fact but an act, not just statics but dynamics ... Tradition does not just preserve itself; it also creates itself, for it is a living thing [*ne tol'ko khranitsia, no i tvoritsia, ibo zhivet*].'[14] The *Living Tradition* group viewed the Neopatristic call for a return to the fathers as a threat to creativity in the church. They lashed out at what they viewed as a new 'scribalism' in theology, 'a rabbinical approach to the writings of the fathers,' an Orthodox Christian 'talmudism.' The panicked tone of these accusations, which is to be explained by the bitterness of the Sophia Affair, does not bring the authors much credit. No one today would deny the Neopatristic turn sparked a remarkable outburst of creativity in Orthodox theology. But if we lay aside polemics and grant that both the Russian and Neopatristic schools were creative in their time, we may still ask which of the two understood the *concept* of creativity better.

On this point the Russian school has the stronger claim. Bulgakov formulated the critical insight in a comment already cited: 'there cannot be a *Philokalia* of creativity, for creativity is extra-legal and irregular.'[15] In other words there cannot be a canon of creativity because creativity is not a *traditum*. Here is the basis for criticizing the Neopatristic conceptuality. If creativity means only a new application of an idea or institution which is already completely defined and understood, then the creative process is not in dialogue with tradition but has been subordinated to it. In actuality creativity reshapes the material on which it works. That is precisely what is creative about it. The Russian school accepted this point; the Neopatristic school

---

[13] *Zhivoe predanie*, pp. 6–7.
[14] *Zhivoe predanie*, p. 7.
[15] *Uteshitel'*, p. 356, cited in Ch. 14, n. 41 above.

did not. While frequently employing the language of creativity, Neopatristic scholars did not allow the idea to complicate the hegemony of tradition in their theology.

Cosmodicy, or the right of the world to theological status, is another idea in *Living Tradition* with a long history in the Russian school. Archimandrite Feodor's dialogue between Orthodoxy and the modern world, Soloviev's vision of the humanity of God and Bulgakov's church-and-world dogmatics all clearly involve the idea. In Neopatristic theology, by contrast, cosmodicy is not a concern at all. Neopatristic theologians might be willing at times to concede the world did not receive sufficient attention in patristic theology, hence one of the tasks of modern Neopatristic theology is to apply patristic concepts more clearly to contemporary problems. But as always, this concession pertains only to the application, not the substance, of tradition. N.N. Afanasiev speaks for the *Living Tradition* group as a whole when he discerns in the Neopatristic movement 'a certain exit of the Church from the world: there is only one path – from the world into the Church, but there is no path from the Church into the world.'[16] Afanasiev sees church and world linked together in a more dynamic and mutual relationship. 'The face of the Church is turned not to the desert but to the world, in relation to which she has creative and constructive work to do ... Through the historical forms of her existence the Church does not just exist in history, but history exists in the Church itself.'[17] G.P. Fedotov puts the point even more boldly in an essay reaffirming the Russian school's longstanding commitment to the dialogue between Orthodoxy and modern humanism. He challenges Orthodox theologians to recognize that in some arenas of modern life 'the Church is nurtured by the world, just as in earlier times the world was nurtured by the Church.'[18] Fedotov's idea is comparable to the distinction between christianization and christification in Bulgakov's dogmatics.

---

[16] N.N. Afanas'ev, 'Neizmennoe i vremennoe v tserkovnykh kanonakh,' *Zhivoe predanie*, p. 93.
[17] 'Neizmennoe i vremennoe v tserkovnykh kanonakh,' *Zhivoe predanie*, pp. 108–9.
[18] G. Fedotov, 'Drevo na kamne,' *Zhivoe predanie*, p. 130.

Now if 'history exists in the Church itself,' and if Afanasiev was not talking about merely superficial aspects of church life when he made this statement, then one must assume that history also exists in dogma, not just dogma in history. In other words, one must assume there is such a thing as dogmatic development. As one might have expected, Bulgakov contributed the essay on this issue in *Living Tradition*. The lead essay of the volume, 'Dogma and Dogmatics,' strongly reiterates the case for substantive dogmatic development in Orthodoxy:

> The fullness of Revelation and the fullness of life are built into the Divine foundation of the Church – *divinely*. But in the *divine-human* mind of the Church, to the extent that this involves temporality and relativity, this fullness enters in only gradually and partially, for which reason the *history* of dogmas can and does exist, as we can in fact observe. New dogmas arise, and in this sense dogmatic development, too, exists.[19]

To illustrate his point Bulgakov lists some of the specific issues which, as he believes, are open to investigation because they were not settled or even seriously discussed at the seven ecumenical councils. These include such fundamental dogmatic issues as pneumatology (which receives surprisingly little attention in patristic theology), the world and the human being, Providence and predestination, ecclesiology, grace and sacraments, theology of history, eschatology and mariology. To this list Bulgakov adds a set of church-and-world issues standing in need of 'dogmatic interpretation': Christianity and culture, Christian social ministry, church–state relations and ecumenism.[20] For Bulgakov dogmatics is more than the discipline of discerning, reappropriating and proclaiming the church's historic teachings. It entails 'dogmatic *searching*' (i.e. searching *for* dogma) based on 'creative intuition, factual investigation and dogmatic construction (i.e. religious philosophy or, more accurately, metaphysics).'[21]

While Bulgakov does not catalog the contributions of the

---

[19] Sergii Bulgakov, 'Dogmat i dogmatika,' *Zhivoe predanie*, p. 20.
[20] 'Dogmat i dogmatika,' *Zhivoe predanie*, pp. 8–10, 22.
[21] 'Dogmat i dogmatika,' *Zhivoe predanie*, p. 9.

modern Russian school to dogmatic theology, these may be cited as further illustrations of the reality of dogmatic development in Orthodoxy. The list is impressive: the thematization of the humanity of God (*bogochelovechestvo*), the concept of the whole of things (*vseedinstvo*), the idea of cosmodicy, the greatly expanded doctrine of kenosis, sophiology, the theory of the trinitarian Dyad, the relational logic of church-and-world dogmatics, dogmatic applications of the idea of pan-humanity (*vsechelovechestvo*), the dogmatic case for a humane church (the divine-human imperative) and other ideas. Neither Bulgakov nor anyone else in the Russian school claimed finished dogmatic status for these constructions. Bulgakov called them 'doctrine' (*doktrina*), by which he meant provisional teachings, dogma-in-the-making as it were, which theologians submit to the church for discussion, reflection, prayer, testing, revision, adoption when appropriate and further development. Unfortunately Orthodox traditionalists had little tolerance for such experiments with truth and found in Neopatristic theology an effective means of diverting attention from them.

To be fair, one must say the traditionalists usually saw themselves as doing no more than enforcing a patristic standard in Orthodox theology. One need not impugn their motives. So, for example, one is not compelled by the evidence (as I read it) to doubt that Metropolitan Sergii of Moscow and Vladimir Lossky honestly believed they were combatting 'pantheism' and 'gnosticism' in the Orthodox Church when they attacked Bulgakov's sophiology. But one needs to be clear about the broad scope of their attack. The Sophia Affair was not a quarrel about the concept of Sophia alone. It was a dispute about two different approaches to dogmatic theology, a debate between Neopatristic classicism and modern Russian reconstructionism. The evidence for this is readily found in the documents composed by Bulgakov's opponents. Neither the Moscow Patriarchate's *ukaz* nor Vladimir Lossky's rebuttal of Bulgakov's reply confines itself to sophiology. The *ukaz*, for example, cites Bulgakov's doctrine of kenosis as an example of his betrayal of patristic tradition. Lossky attacks Bulgakov's trinitarianism, his use of gender analogies in theology, his pan-human ecclesiology and the concept of the humanity of God. All of these ideas,

Lossky alleges, 'confuse personhood and nature'; they subject the history of salvation to 'a sophianic-natural process that annihilates freedom.'[22]

Lossky's accusation and the philosophical assumptions underlying it are worth debating, although the debate cannot be pursued here as it would require a detailed exposition of Lossky's theology. A preliminary observation may be offered, however. Many of Lossky's criticisms revolve around the Russian school's commitment to cosmodicy, the theological justification of the world. Lossky could expel categories of nature and history from dogmatic theology with an easy conscience because, as a rigorous apophaticist, he assigned little positive theological status to the world to begin with.[23] Bulgakov, on the other hand, could not set aside these categories without abandoning the enterprise to which the Russian school was committed from the beginning, namely, the engagement of Orthodoxy and the modern world.

While the substantive objections of Bulgakov's opponents in the Sophia Affair were important, a formal issue also figured in the debate. Bulgakov's critics believed many of his ideas lacked patristic precedent and rejected them for that reason. This was not a false charge. Many of Bulgakov's concepts did lack patristic precedent to one degree or another. But this is to say no more than that Bulgakov embraced the project of the Russian school. The Russian school from the beginning was dedicated to innovation and reconstruction in Orthodox theology.

Despite their commitment to change, however, the theologians of the Russian school were not radicals. They recognized that innovation has limits just as tradition does. Their aim was not a revolutionary theology but a theological middle way combining tradition and freedom. If they did not discourse at

---

[22] Losskii, *Spor o sofii*, p. 82.

[23] Lossky's anti-cosmic position can be sensed in his definition of Christian freedom: 'Is not [Christian freedom] first of all freedom from "one's own," even from "one's own" nature, "one's own" will?' *Spor o sofii*, p. 87. One wonders whether this view of Christian freedom sprang fully armed from 'the mind of the fathers' or owed something to the existentialist and personalist philosophies which were popular in Europe in Lossky's day. The role of modern philosophical influences on Neopatristic theology deserves much more attention than it has received.

length about the limits of innovation, this was because of their assessment of the needs of contemporary Orthodoxy. When Bulgakov and his supporters surveyed the modern world they saw a host of opportunities for Orthodox mission and renewal, but almost all of these opportunities required Orthodox people to overstep traditional boundaries, to rise to unprecedented challenges, to do something new.

The challenge of modern ecumenism, discussed by Lev Zander in a brilliant essay in *Living Tradition*, is a case in point. A theologian's attitude toward ecumenism reveals quite clearly how he thinks about the limits of tradition, for ecumenism by definition is a conversation with those who stand outside one's own tradition. The only way for an ecumenist to avoid conceding that his own tradition is limited in some respects is to adopt the view of ecumenism voiced by Florovsky in a candid moment:

> As a member and priest of the Orthodox Church I believe that the Church in which I was baptized and brought up *is* in very truth *the Church*, i.e. *the true* Church and the *only* true Church ... I am compelled therefore to regard all other Christian Churches as deficient, and in many cases I can identify these deficiencies accurately enough. Therefore, for me, *Christian reunion is just universal conversion to Orthodoxy.*[24]

Many Orthodox participants in ecumenical conversations have shared Florovsky's view, but the Russian school did not. Zander explicitly rejects it because it reduces ecumenism to 'proselytism.'[25] For Zander the Ecumenical Movement is 'a genuine encounter of churches' predicated on the assumption 'all Christians are Christ-bearers' and all churches have something to contribute to an understanding of the living Christ. For Florovsky, the Ecumenical Movement simply provides an opportunity for Orthodox Christians to bear

---

[24] Quoted by Alexander Schmemann, 'Roll of Honour,' *St Vladimir's Seminary Quarterly* 2 (1954): 9.
[25] L. Zander, ' "I soglasno slavim vsesviatago Dukha": o sushchnosti ekumenich-eskogo dvizheniia,' *Zhivoe predanie*, p. 147.

witness to Christ. For Zander, the Ecumenical Movement per se witnesses to Christ; it is itself 'a christophany.'[26]

One of the most interesting features of Zander's discussion is the prominence of process terms in it. The search for Christian unity is 'an ecumenical process' in which traditional concepts such as church, sacrament and even heresy 'lose their stony precision and widen their boundaries.' The 'boundaries of the Church' are reassessed in the light of the emerging ecumenical fellowship.[27] Zander uses a rare Russian word to denote this fellowship: *soborovanie*, a noun derived from an imperfective form of the root verb 'gather,' hence 'gathering-process.' The significance of the term becomes clear if one compares it with the related term *sobornost'*. Both words pertain to the conciliar fellowship of the church, but they refer to it in different aspects. *Sobornost'* refers to the fellowship of the church as a perfected mystical plenitude, *soborovanie* to fellowship-in-the-making, the ecclesial process. Ecumenism as Zander understands it affirms both. Ecumenists of the Florovskian school affirm *sobornost'* but not *soborovanie*, ecumenicity but not ecumenification. The error results from the absolutizing of historic tradition.

Archimandrite Kiprian Kern's essay 'Levitism and Prophecy as Types of Pastoral Ministry' deals with challenges and opportunities for Orthodox pastoral ministry. Kiprian's theme is the responsibility of Orthodox pastors to own both the priestly and the prophetic dimensions of their office. When only the former is embraced, a legalistic or 'levitical' distortion of the pastoral vocation occurs. This can be prevented only if pastors recognize they are also prophets, by which Kiprian means free agents who involve themselves in the moral, social and political struggles taking place in the world around them. Archimandrite Kiprian's distinction reveals yet another instance of the limits of tradition. The priestly office is a canonical office; prophecy is not, for it speaks a new word and testifies to a new thing happening in the world. As there can be no *Philokalia* for creativity, so there can be none for prophecy. Archimandrite Kiprian gives the name

---

[26] ' "I soglasno slavim vsesviatago Dukha," ' *Zhivoe predanie*, pp. 143–5.
[27] ' "I soglasno slavim vsesviatago Dukha," ' *Zhivoe predanie*, pp. 152–5.

'pastorology' to the theological discipline charged with helping Orthodox pastors grasp the two dimensions of their vocation.[28] The name is quite suggestive if we take it as a process term paralleling Zander's *soborovanie*. As Zander envisions a continuing ecumenical process, so Kiprian envisions a continuing pastoral ministry, a ministry which cannot be fixed by tradition because it is prophetic and changing. Pastorology requires theology to go beyond patrology. A pastoral church is more than a patristic church.

One might object to the analogy between ecumenism and pastoral ministry by arguing the latter, unlike ecumenism, is an internal process, the care of the church community. But this is not the case. Pastoring in the prophetic mode happens not just in the church but *between* church and world. A prophetic pastor must always venture beyond the limits of tradition.[29] Zander's startling extension of the Creed at the end of his essay on ecumenism applies equally well to Archimandrite Kiprian's discussion of pastoral ministry: 'I believe in the Holy Spirit, the Lord, the Giver of life, Who proceeds from the Father; He has spoken – *and speaks* – through the prophets.'[30]

Theology of nature is another enterprise that reveals the limits of tradition. Nature, whatever it is, is not a tradition; and a theologian who would deal with it in its own terms (kataphatic terms) must utilize sources of evidence and inspiration which are not to be found within the limits of tradition alone. The intellectual challenge involved here does not arise in historical contexts where theology of nature is not a pressing concern or serves only as a prolegomenon to apophatic theology. But in the modern world, shaped so fundamentally by the natural sciences and technology, nature demands theological attention in its own right. The Russian school recognized this from the beginning, in part because of the role played by *Naturphilosophie* in the

---

[28] Arkhimandrit Kiprian, 'Levitstvo i prorochestvo, kak tipy pastyrstvovaniia,' *Zhivoe predanie*, p. 160.
[29] The experimentalism of Russian Orthodox thinking about pastoral ministry in the nineteenth and early twentieth centuries is beautifully described by Jennifer Hedda, 'Good Shepherds: The St Petersburg Pastorate and the Emergence of Social Activism in the Russian Orthodox Church, 1855–1917' (PhD diss., Harvard University, 1998).
[30] ' "I soglasno slavim vsesviatago Dukha," ' *Zhivoe predanie*, p. 158.

formation of the modern Russian philosophical tradition. Bukharev's fascination with science and technology, while intellectually primitive because of his lack of scientific education, was an indication of the importance which these concerns would assume in the Russian school. Soloviev's concept of the whole of things (*vseedinstvo*), his essays on beauty in nature and the meaning of love, Bulgakov's philosophy of economy and modern Russian sophiology all involved experiments with theology of nature to one degree or other.

V. V. Zenkovsky's contribution to *Living Tradition*, 'The Problem of the Cosmos in Christianity,' is an especially lucid presentation of the challenges and opportunities for Orthodox theology on this subject. Zenkovsky argues that while Christianity was from the beginning a cosmic faith, a revelation of the salvation of all creation through 'the freedom of the glory of the children of God' (Rom. 8:21), tendencies to 'acosmism' complicated the picture at an early point.[31] The church fathers, with ancient Greek cosmism and the biblical view of the world as the creation of a benevolent God to guide them, never abandoned cosmism. While insisting (against pagan thought) that the cosmos was a created, not a divine reality, they still saw the world as a kind of theophany, an effulgence of the creative energies of God. The problem was they developed this vision in a one-sided way, contrasting the glory of God with the nothingness of the creature while overlooking the extraordinary affirmation of creaturely being which can also be inferred from Christian cosmism. Acosmism thereby found a theoretical base in Orthodoxy, and issues concerning the nature, scope and dignity of creatures in their own right went uninvestigated. Zenkovsky believes modern Orthodox theology must face up to the problem of the cosmos in Christianity, citing Russian sophiology as an admirable, if far from perfect, effort to do so.[32] Effectively summarizing the Russian school's case for

---

[31] V.V. Zen'kovskii, 'Problema kosmosa v khristianstve,' *Zhivoe predanie*, p. 71.
[32] Zenkovsky eventually distanced himself from Bulgakov's sophiology and is usually numbered among the critics of the enterprise. This makes the forceful last sentence of his *Living Tradition* essay all the more interesting to consider: 'The construction of an Orthodox sophiology has only just begun in our time – there are

393

cosmodicy, Zenkovsky's essay can also be read as a criticism of the radical apophaticism that was making itself felt in Orthodox theology in his day.

Kartashev's essay on 'The Freedom of Scientific-Theological Research and Church Authority' discusses the demands of modern intellectual freedom in the theological arena. This is an appropriate issue with which to conclude the discussion of *Living Tradition* because it concerns the practice of theology in all branches. Kartashev defends intellectual freedom as a value worth cherishing not just *for* the church (the freedom enjoyed by the church in a liberal society) but *in* the church, that is to say, as a value which can be justified theologically and should be expected to have an impact on the way theology is practiced.

Kartashev rejects two extreme ways of handling intellectual freedom in modern theology. The first is the radical liberty claimed by so called ' "free" theological science which is independent of church authority and sometimes even of Christianity itself,' as seen in some liberal Protestant circles. The second is the suppression of intellectual freedom in the name of tradition, a common error in the Orthodox world. The trouble with the first extreme is that 'the problems of the relationship between freedom and dogma' never arise because the dogmas of the church are not confessed at all. Theology is free but lacks dogmatic content, which is to say it is scarcely theology at all. The other extreme oppresses theological creativity and, by harnessing tradition to the cause, distorts tradition.

Kartashev devotes most of his essay to criticizing the traditionalist extreme because it was the weightier factor in his Orthodox environment. The issue, as Kartashev sees it, is not

many difficult and complicated problems here which await elaboration (especially the problem of evil in human beings and of disharmony in nature); but another way to solve the problem of [theology of] the cosmos in the spirit of the Christian Gospel besides the one projected here does not and cannot exist.' *Zhivoe predanie*, p. 91. There is no contradiction here once we recognize Zenkovsky's reservations about Bulgakov's sophiology had to do with the particulars, not with the kind of project it was, namely, a species of cosmodicy. Zenkovsky did not identify with Neopatristic critics who rejected the sophiological project as such. For Zenkovsky's later assessment of the Sophia Affair see Vasilii Zen'kovskii, 'Delo ob obvinenii o. Sergiia Bulgakova v eresi (glava iz neizdannykh vospominanii),' *Vestnik russkogo khristianskogo dvizheniia* 149 (1987):61–5.

loyalty to tradition as such but how tradition is defined and hence delimited. 'It is an indisputable, elementary truth that in the church we stand upon the solid rock of apostolic tradition … Without the authority of apostolic tradition we fall into religious vacuity and illusionism. The issue is: what is the content of [tradition] and where are its limits?' Rather than addressing these questions in a probing way, traditionalists subject tradition to 'a process of absolutization' that freezes it at a certain point in time.[33]

The force of Kartashev's criticism should not be blunted by observing Neopatristic scholars often affirmed the value of intellectual freedom. So they did; and even if they had not, it would be easy to show they could not have done their work without the freedom available to them in their Paris home. But the systematic issue does not lie here. As with creativity, the question is which of the two schools had the clearer understanding of the concept of intellectual freedom and its implications for the life of the church. Unfortunately for the Neopatristic side, the Sophia Affair must figure in the evidence. Whatever one thinks of Bulgakov's sophiology, no one who values intellectual freedom will find it easy to admire the procedures employed by his opponents to attack it. The case against Bulgakov was brought without his knowledge; he had no opportunity to defend himself before judgment was rendered; the assessment of his views was based on decontextualized excerpts from his writings cobbled together by his opponents; and judgment was passed without consultation, publicity or debate. If Bulgakov went too far when he complained of the Moscow Patriarchate's 'romanizing absolutism,'[34] his error lay in the gratuitous swipe at Rome, not in the charge of absolutism leveled at Moscow.

It must be admitted Bulgakov and his allies made their share of mistakes in the Sophia Affair. In his defense of the Moscow Patriarchate's condemnation of Bulgakov, Lossky makes a couple of points which Bulgakov's theological sympathizers would still do well to heed. The first concerns the use of

---

[33] A. Kartashev, 'Svoboda nauchno-bogoslovskikh issledovanii i tserkovnyi avtoritet,' *Zhivoe predanie*, p. 31.
[34] *O Sofii premudrosti bozhiei*, p. 50.

historical analogies. Complaining about the lack of discussion and debate in the Sophia case, Bulgakov tried to argue that the utility of 'factions' as a means of discovering truth in the church was already recognized by Paul (1 Cor. 11:17–19) and could be seen even more clearly in the christological debates of the fourth and fifth centuries. Lossky has little trouble convincing us Paul was not thinking of the modern dialectical concept of the search for truth when he scolded the Corinthians for infractions against churchly propriety, or that the fourth- and fifth-century fathers (who anathematized their opponents) would scarcely have regarded the christological disputes as 'a normal and desirable phenomenon of church life,' as Bulgakov appeared to view them.[35] Lossky has the better of this argument for the simple reason intellectual freedom in the modern sense did not exist in the patristic period, nor would the fathers of the church have been quick to embrace it if it had. Greater candor about the differences between ancient and modern approaches to intellectual culture would surely have served Bulgakov better than forced historical analogies.[36]

There is also something to be said for the distinction Lossky draws between the church and a debating society. Lossky complains that

> if theological quarrels and discussions were the norm of dogmatic life [and] the only way to knowledge of the Truth, there would never have been Church Fathers, and Orthodoxy would not have existed; there would have been opinions, wandering in the dark, a multiplicity of commissions investigating and discussing particular propositions, a huge literature, the preparation of materials for a 'future Council' – and an abandoned flock of faithful left to the 'winds of doctrine,' not knowing whom to follow or what to believe,

[35] *Spor o Sofii*, pp. 10–12.

[36] John Meyendorff's personal assessment of the Russian school on this point is pertinent. 'As you know, my own personal theological "development" is rather based on the "neo-patristic" style of Lossky and Florovsky. However, as I grow older, my reaction against Solovievian sophiology is directed rather against Soloviev's, and Florensky's, and Bulgakov's use of historical and traditional arguments in favor of some of their positions. But the positions themselves are often legitimate, and interesting, and creative.' Private correspondence, July 30, 1990.

waiting for the 'well-founded judgment' of a Council which could still 'turn out to be a Robbers' Council,' as Father S. Bulgakov puts it.[37]

The confused and weak-minded handling of disciplinary issues in some Protestant and Anglican churches in recent years could be cited as evidence that Lossky's nightmare was not totally off the mark, even if it was overdrawn. Applied to Orthodoxy, however, Lossky's complaint was and is far likelier to encourage neo-traditionalism and authoritarianism than a welcome clarification of values. Lossky believed that modern intellectual freedom could be a negative force in the church. He was right. But his Orthodox contemporaries did not need him to tell them this; they believed it already. They needed to hear the other half of the story, namely, that intellectual freedom and the procedures supporting it can play a positive role in the life of the church. Kartashev's concern for procedures, which invites comparison with other process categories in the thinking of the Russian school, is worth underscoring here. The famed anti-juridicalism of Orthodoxy notwithstanding, a little more due process would not have done a bit of harm in an ecclesiastical milieu shaped by centuries of authoritarianism.

Not all of the concerns of the Russian school found expression in *Living Tradition*. There is no article on apocalyptic theology, for example, although the topic lends itself to the critique of tradition. Apocalyptic prophecy concerns that which is to come 'after this' (Rev. 1:19, 4:1); it goes beyond the limits of what is already known and mastered.

As it approached the end of its historical path, the Russian school did not lose interest in apocalyptic. Bulgakov's last book, published posthumously in 1948, was a commentary on the Revelation of John.[38] This seems fitting, given what we have seen of Bulgakov's character and outlook. By the time he commenced his commentary he was over seventy years old, he had lost his voice and was dying of cancer; yet he applied himself with a kind of youthful enthusiasm to the most futuristic material in the Christian canon.

[37] *Spor o Sofii*, p. 12.
[38] *Apokalipsis Ioanna: opyt dogmaticheskogo istolkovaniia* (Paris: YMCA-Press, 1948).

To see how Bulgakov's commentary serves the purposes of the Russian school one must keep in mind the difference between apocalyptic and other forms of eschatology. All Christian theology, including traditio-centric theology, contains an eschatology of some sort; but not all theologians take seriously the particular approach to eschatology embodied in apocalyptic. Traditional eschatology for the most part commends a spiritual orientation of radical verticalism. That is to say, eschatological reality is presented as standing in perpendicular, antithetical relation to the world at hand. Apocalyptic prophecy, by contrast, horizontalizes eschatology to some extent by envisioning a series of concrete historical events erupting in linear time. Certainly these events belong to endtime, but they are not disconnected from the historical process for that reason. On the contrary, apocalyptic prophecy acquires its specific character from the presumed historicity of that which is to come. The axioms of apocalyptic are that 'humanity is immersed in history and cannot fail to think about it,' and that 'the church has its own historical destiny which it cannot fail to seek out.'[39] This double engagement with history explains the Russian school's abiding interest in apocalyptic, an interest related to the school's concern with cosmodicy. Historiodicy, if the term is admissible, is the issue at the heart of apocalyptic prophecy everywhere.

The thousand-year reign of Christ, or millennium, is the perfect paradigm of the apocalyptic mentality. John the Theologian foresees an epoch when the martyrs of the church will come to life in a 'first resurrection' and rule the world with Christ for a thousand years (Rev. 20:4–5). The millennial kingdom, like the chain of events leading up to it (Rev. 5–19), is mysteriously revealed to the prophet from heaven; but it is not a mystery about heaven. It is a mystery about earth, about the end of world history. If the earthly element is completely spiritualized, the prophecy loses its apocalyptic character and becomes generic eschatology. Apocalyptic prophecy – perhaps all biblical prophecy in that the canon is sealed by an apocalyptic book – is historical in this sense. As Bulgakov says, speaking of Genesis and Revelation, 'the world not only begins in history, it also

---

[39] *Apokalipsis Ioanna*, p. 16.

ends in history.' The Revelation of John deals with 'the Christian philosophy of history, a historiosophy bordering on eschatology and passing over into it.'[40]

The fact apocalyptic theology forces theologians to run beyond the limits of tradition is one of the reasons why traditional theology has tended to keep its distance from the subject. What Bulgakov says about the millennium applies to apocalyptic prophecy as a whole: 'the historical church ... has not taken *any* definite or definitive dogmatic and exegetical position on it.' The church possesses eschatological dogmas but few apocalyptic dogmas, and certainly no dogma concerning the millennium. Despite the fact the millennial prophecy is 'a clear and blinding star on the dogmatic horizon ... one gets the impression that the teachers of the church do not just fail to notice it but do not wish to notice it; they close their eyes to it as if they, well, fear it.'[41]

The timidity of traditional theology is an obstacle which every commentator on the apocalypse must surmount. As Father Aleksandr Men observes, 'many people suppose that it is impossible and even spiritually dangerous for the ordinary person to read the Revelation of John ... as if a part of Holy Scripture was not written for human beings but was put in place for some purpose unknown to us.' He suggests also that the deeply Judaic idiom of apocalyptic has discouraged study. Apocalyptic prophecy is more resistant to spiritualization than most parts of the New Testament. To make sense of the Revelation of John the reader must grasp that 'its author lived and thought totally by means of the concepts and images of the Old Testament, which he knew by heart.'[42] The apocalyptic seal on the Christian canon shows that the church is bound to Israel not only in its historical roots but also in its historical destiny, a fact which most Christians have been slow to recognize.

By putting apocalyptic on the theological agenda the thinkers of the Russian school made another distinctive contribution to modern Orthodox theology. They could deal with the subject

[40] *Apokalipsis Ioanna*, pp. 15–16.
[41] *Apokalipsis Ioanna*, p. 188.
[42] Aleksandr Men', *Apokalipsis: Otkrovenie Ioanna Bogoslova* (Riga: Fond im. Aleksandra Menia, 1992), p. 47.

because they recognized the limits of tradition. Apocalyptic prophecy threatens settled arrangements. It challenges the historic to come to grips with the historical, the fixed with the unhinged, the old with the new. Bulgakov's commentary is pervaded by a sense of excitement about these confrontations, excitement about the newness of the gospel. His attitude inspires some enchanting formulations. The Revelation of John is 'a kind of *vetus testamentum in novo*,' 'a kind of fifth Gospel,' 'the newest testament in the New Testament.'[43] It has 'its own particular, apocalyptic image of Christ,' which must be taken seriously by dogmatic theologians. Each section of the book has 'its own heavenly music.'[44]

The millennium in particular fascinates Bulgakov. The whole church confesses the resurrection of the dead at the end of the world, but Bulgakov observes the Revelation of John attests not one resurrection but two: the millennial reign of Christ and the saints, and the second or general resurrection. Similarly, the prophecy contains two revelations about the end of the world: 'the first [end] is immanent-historical, a maturing from within; the second is transcendent-catastrophic, connected with the Parousia.' Bulgakov proceeds here as he did at the very beginning of his career as a dogmatic theologian in *St Peter and St John*. Finding unexamined complexities in the tradition (two primacies, two resurrections, two ends of the world), he calls for 'a fresh look' (*trebuetsia peresmotr*) at traditional concepts.[45] He invites us to theologize in a new key.

Methodologically Bulgakov's apocalypse commentary is a great improvement over Archimandrite Feodor's. He abandons the attempt to schematize world history and focuses on the canonical text. He also brings a more seasoned sense of how to integrate apocalyptic with church tradition than Soloviev evinced in the colorful yet idiosyncratic personages of Mr Z and the monk Pansofy in *Three Dialogues*. But one mistakes the character of Bulgakov's commentary completely if one regards it as a work of critical-historical exegesis. While the author pays

---

[43] *Apokalipsis Ioanna*, pp. 11, 18, 194.
[44] *Apokalipsis Ioanna*, pp. 20, 22.
[45] *Apokalipsis Ioanna*, pp. 192–3.

close attention to the historic text, his chief interest is the historical process, the process which forms the ultimate frame of reference for text, commentator and church alike. Bulgakov was committed to 'philosophy of the end,' to inquiry into 'the destiny of the whole world and the Church in their interconnected history.'[46] *The Revelation of John* is the last, unfinished volume of his church-and-world dogmatics. Bulgakov's method may be more sober than Bukharev's or Soloviev's, but his purpose is as evangelical as ever. There is no domestication of transcendence.

Tradition is grand, but the gospel is grander. This was the outlook of the Russian school. For Bulgakov as for Soloviev, it was not enough to say that dogma must develop because the world around the church is always changing. The gospel itself is expanding. Or if one prefers, our understanding of the gospel is expanding (which is to say the same thing in another way). All-embracing to begin with, the gospel grows more capacious as the world-historical process goes on falling into its divine-human future. There is always more to know about the gospel, more to discover in it, more to draw out of it, more to incorporate into it, more to do with it. To locate, assess, express and invest this cascading surplus is the business of theology in a new key. The thinkers of the Russian school were unsurpassed masters of the art of evangelical kataphasis.

It is too early to make pronouncements about the legacy of the Russian school. Its significance will be clarified only as the Orthodox world, ravaged in the twentieth century, reconstructs itself in the twenty-first. But it stands to reason that, as reconstruction proceeds, the ideas of Orthodox reconstructionists of the not-too-distant past will prove relevant to the tasks at hand. One should not look for mere imitation or reiteration, of course, nor would the thinkers discussed in this volume have approved of such an appropriation of their work. The Russian school is

---

[46] *Apokalipsis Ioanna*, pp. 17–18. Cf. p. 189: 'The historical process [*prodolzh-aiushchaiasia istoriia*] is an unfolding historico-dogmatic commentary on the Revelation of John which we should be able to grasp, though it is far from clear whether the time for this has arrived.' In effect these words justify Bukharev's apocalypticism, while allowing one to question the timing and particulars of his (and perhaps any) scheme.

honored not by imitation, much less by canonization, but by new theological projects inspired by same theological eros which animated its own.

Projects of this sort can already be found on the Orthodox theological scene, especially (as one would expect) in Russian theology. The work of Father Aleksandr Men (1935–90) is the most obvious example. Men's legacy is huge, and it will take years to sort it out; but there is no doubt about the Solovievian roots of his intellectuality. His was a mature Solovievianism, certainly, enriched by an erudite biblicism and decades of experience as a parish priest. But these enhancements simply show the Solovievian seed had marvelous growth potential on Orthodox soil. A thinker should be judged in part by the sort of students and continuators he attracts. If the case of Bulgakov as we have presented it does not suffice to prove the deep compatibility of Soloviev's philosophy with Orthodox faith, Father Aleksandr Men may be cited as a second and, one hopes, decisive example. All three men were, as Evgeny Rashkovsky has written of Men, 'a testimony to the complex but vital interconnection between spiritual tradition and freedom.'[47]

Numerous other projects in contemporary Orthodox theology bear the stamp of the Russian school. Michael Meerson is reviving the religious intellectuality of the Russian Silver Age with his reconstructionist trinitarianism.[48] Hegumen Innokenty (Pavlov), with his introduction to the history of Russian theology, reminds us of the extraordinary complexity of the Orthodox intellectual tradition in his country.[49] His book prompts dreams of a new *Paths of Russian Theology* composed by an author who would walk the same terrain as Florovsky, only with binoculars set at wider range.

Sergei Khoruzhy's *Towards a Phenomenology of Asceticism*

---

[47] E.B. Rashkovskii, 'Protoierei Aleksandr Men': intellektual'nyi oblik,' *Voprosy filosofii*, 1994/2: 174. For an introduction and brief sampler of Men's work in English, see *Christianity for the Twenty-First Century: The Prophetic Writings of Alexander Men*, eds Elizabeth Roberts and Ann Shukman (New York: Continuum, 1996).

[48] See Introduction, note 2 above.

[49] Innokentii (Pavlov), *Vvedenie v istoriiu russkoi bogoslovskoi mysli* (Moscow: Krutitskoe patriarshee podvor'e, 1995).

is another kind of contribution.[50] At first glance this important book appears to be a work of neo-hesychasm, but closer examination shows Khoruzhy's project is much more complicated. While steeped in the primary sources and the indispensable studies of Palamite theology by Lossky, Meyendorff and others, Khoruzhy integrates this material into a highly original intellectual scheme which owes as much to continental phenomenology and modern Russian philosophy as to patristic tradition. Khoruzhy's aim is to construct 'a discourse of synergy' with which to talk about 'the arena of Divine-human collaboation and dialogue' (*Bogochelovecheskogo sotrudnichestva-dialoga*) which is life in the world.[51]

Finally, Vladimir Zelinsky's refined and haunting essays on the awakening of faith may be cited. Zelinsky's theology of the Word owes much to modern Protestant theology and to the idiom of Karl Barth in particular. But at the heart of his thought is the humane, ontological universalism of Orthodoxy:

> The human being is endowed with a certain spark, a bud of Mystery, a 'not-I' coiled tightly within him in which in his own way – be it directly or in distant echoes – he hears Another ... [The Other] reveals itself to us as the light which enlightens every human being, as the Word which became flesh and dwells among us ... The Word can speak to us anonymously (for it knows a thousand languages) until we finally recognize it as incarnate in a human face, in the human destiny of Jesus Christ; for 'He is the Word in whom the whole human race participates' (Justin Martyr).[52]

Archimandrite Feodor initiated the project of the modern Russian school by seeking to discern in every human being and every honest human endeavor the light that enlightens every human being who comes into the world. Zelinsky, like so many others who found their way to faith from the ideologized depths of Soviet reality, reminds us the Light continues to shine.

---

[50] Sergei Khoruzhii, *K fenomenologii askezy* (Moscow: Izdatel'stvo gumanitarnoi literatury, 1998).
[51] Khoruzhii, *Posle pereryva*, p. 12.
[52] Vladimir Zelinskii, *Otkrytie slova* (Moscow: Put', 1993), pp. 40–1. See the related citation of John 1:9 on p. 20

Bibliography

English translations of titles are supplied for works by Bukharev, Soloviev and Bulgakov; titles of edited collections and other sources are not translated.

WORKS BY ALEKSANDR MATVEEVICH BUKHAREV

(ARKHIMANDRIT FEODOR)

'Chetyre sluchainykh razgovora po "krest'ianskomu voprosu" ' [Four Casual Conversations Concerning the 'Peasant Question']. In *O sovremennykh dukhovnykh potrebnostiakh mysli i zhizni*, pp. 275–319.

Issledovaniia Apokalipsisa [Studies on the Apocalypse]. With two portraits and three autographs of A.M. Bukharev. Izdanie redaktsii 'Bogoslovskogo vestnika'. Sergiev Posad: Tipografii Sviato-Troitskoi Sergievoi Lavry, 1916.

Neskol'ko statei ob apostole Pavle [Essays on the Apostle Paul]. St Petersburg: V tipografii Koroleva i komp., 1860.

'Neskol'ko zamechanii po povodu stateiki v "Nashem vremeni" o mnimom lzheproroke' [Observations on an Article in 'Our Time' Concerning an Imagined False Prophet]. In I. Pryzhov, *Zhitie Ivana Iakovlevicha, izvestnogo proroka v Moskve*, pp. 31–45. St Petersburg, 1860.

O dukhovnykh potrebnostiakh zhizni. Ed. with intro. and notes by Kapitolina Koksheneva. Russkie dukhovnye pisateli. Moscow: Izdatel'stvo 'Stolitsa', 1991.

'O Filarete, mitropolite moskovskom, kak plodotvornom dvigatele razvitiia pravoslavno-russkoi mysli' [Metropolitan Filaret of Moscow as an Effective Promoter of the Development of Orthodox Russian Thought]. *Pravoslavnoe obozrenie*, 1884, 1: 717–49.

O novom zavete gospoda nashego Iisusa Khrista [On the New Testament of Our Lord Jesus Christ]. St Petersburg: V tipografii Iosafata Ogrizko, 1861.

'O poslanii apostola Pavla k Filippiitsam' [On the Letter of the

Apostle Paul to the Philippians]. *Pribavleniia k izdaniiu tvorenii sviatykh ottsev v russkom perevode*, pt 13: 121–35. Moscow: V tipografii V. Got'e, 1854.

O pravoslavii v otnoshenii k sovremennosti, v raznykh stati'akh [On Orthodoxy in Relation to the Modern World, in Various Articles]. Izdanie 'Strannika'. St Petersburg: V Tipografii Torgovogo Doma S. Strugovshchikova, G. Pokhitonova, N. Vodova i Ko., 1860.

'O romane Dostoevskogo "Prestuplenie i nakazanie" po otnosheniiu k delu mysli i nauki v Rossii' [On Dostoevsky's Novel 'Crime and Punishment' with Regard to Thought and Science in Russia]. In *O dukhovnykh potrebnostiakh zhizni*, ed. Koksheneva, pp. 213–50.

'O sobornykh apostol'skikh poslaniiakh' [On the Catholic Epistles]. Ed. Arkhimandrit Anatolii (Kuznetsov). *Bogoslovskie trudy* 9 (1972): 149–225.

O sovremennykh dukhovnykh potrebnostiakh mysli i zhizni, osobenno russkoi [On Contemporary Needs of Thought and Life, Especially in Russia]. Moscow: Izdanie knigoprodavtsa Manukhina, 1865.

'O vtoroi chasti knigi sv. proroka Isaii' [On the Second Part of the Book of the Prophet Isaiah]. *Pribavleniia k izdaniiu tvorenii sviatykh ottsev v russkom perevode*, pt 9: 79–131. Moscow: V tipografii V. Got'e, 1850.

'O vtorom psalme' [On Psalm 2]. *Pribavleniia k izdaniiu tvorenii sviatykh ottsev v russkom perevode*, pt 8: 353–403. Moscow: V tipografii V. Got'e, 1849.

'Pis'ma arkhimandrita Feodora (A.M. Bukhareva) k Varvare Vasil'evne Liubimovoi i Antonine Ivanovne Dubrovinoi.' *Bogoslovskii vestnik*, 1917, nos 2–3.

'Pis'ma arkhimandrita Feodora k o. protoiereiu Valerianu Viktorovichu Lavrskomu i supruge ego Aleksandre Ivanovne.' *Bogoslovskii vestnik*, 1917, nos 4–5.

'Pis'ma k A.A. Lebedevu.' *Bogoslovskii vestnik*, 1915, nos 10–12.

'Razbor dvukh romanov, kasaiushchikhsia vazhnykh zatrudnenii i voprosov sovremennoi myslitel'nosti i zhizni: "Chto delat" g. Chernyshevskogo i "Ottsy i deti" g. Turgeneva' [Analysis of Two Novels Bearing on Important Difficulties and Issues of Modern Intellectuality and Life:

Chernyshevsky's 'What Is To Be Done?' and Turgenev's 'Fathers and Sons']. In *O dukhovnykh potrebnostiakh zhizni*, ed. Koksheneva, pp. 148–83.

Sv. Iov mnogostradal'nyi: obozrenie ego vremeni i iskusheniia, po ego knige [Job the Long-Suffering: A Survey of His Time and His Temptation, According to His Book]. Moscow: Izdanie knigoprodavtsa A.I. Manukhina, 1864.

Sv. prorok Daniil: ocherk ego veka, prorocheskogo sluzheniia i sviashchennoi knigi [The Prophet Daniel: A Sketch of His Age, Prophetic Service and Sacred Book]. Moscow: Izdanie knigoprodavtsa A.I. Manukhina, 1864.

Tri pis'ma k N.V. Gogoliu, pisannye v 1848 godu [Three Letters to N.V. Gogol, written in 1848]. St Petersburg: V tipografii morskogo ministerstva, 1860.

WORKS BY VLADIMIR SERGEEVICH SOLOV'EV

Chteniia o bogochelovechestve [Lectures on the Humanity of God]. *SSVSS* 3: 1–181.

[Vladimir Solovyov] *The Crisis of Western Philosophy (Against the Positivists)*. Trans. Boris Jakim. Hudson, New York: Lindisfarne Press, 1996.

'Dogmaticheskoe razvitie tserkvi v sviazi s voprosom o soedinenii tserkvei' [The Development of Dogma in the Church in Connection with the Question of Church Union]. *SSVSS* 11: 1–67.

'Evreistvo i khristianskii vopros' [The Jews and the Christian Question]. *SSVSS* 4: 135–85.

Filosofskie nachala tsel'nogo znaniia [The Philosophical Principles of Integral Knowledge]. *SSVSS* 1: 250–407.

'Ideia chelovechestva u Avgusta Konta' [The Idea of Humanity in Auguste Comte]. *SSVSS* 9: 172–93.

Istoriia i budushchnost' teokratii (Issledovanie vsemirnoistoricheskogo puti k istinnoi zhizni) [The History and Future of Theocracy (Investigation of the World-Historical Path to True Life)]. *SSVSS* 4: 241–633.

'Kratkaia povest' ob antikhriste' [A Brief Tale of the Anti-Christ]. See *Tri razgovora*.

Kritika otvlechennykh nachal [The Critique of Abstract Principles]. *SSVSS* 2: v–xvi, 1–397.

Krizis zapadnoi filosofii (Protiv pozitivistov) [The Crisis of Western Philosophy (Against the Positivists)]. *SSVSS* 1: 27–170.

[Vladimir Solovyov] *Lectures on Divine Humanity*. Trans. Boris Jakim. Hudson, New York: Lindisfarne Press, 1995.

'Mitologicheskii protsess v drevnem iazychestve' [The Mythological Process in Ancient Paganism]. *SSVSS* 1: 1–26.

'Nepodvizhno lish' solntse liubvi …': stikhotvoreniia, proza, vospominaniia sovremennikov. Ed. with intro. by Aleksandr Nosov. Moscow: Moskovskii Rabochii, 1990.

'O filosofskikh trudakh P.D. Iurkevicha' [On the Philosophical Works of P.D. Yurkevich]. *SSVSS* 1: 171–96.

O khristianskom edinstve. Moscow: Rudomino, 1994.

Opravdanie dobra: nravstvennaia filosofiia [The Justification of the Good: Moral Philosophy]. *SSVSS* 8: 3–516.

'Pervyi shag k polozhitel'noi estetike' [The First Step Toward a Positive Esthetics]. *SSVSS* 7: 69–77.

Pis'ma Vladimira Sergeevicha Solov'eva. Ed. E.L. Radlov. 3 vols. St Petersburg: Tipografiia t-va 'Obshchestvennaia Pol'za', 1908–11.

Rossiia i vselenskaia tserkov' [Russia and the Universal Church]. Trans. from the French by G.A. Rachinskii. Moscow: Tovarishchestvo tipografii A.I. Mamontova, 1911.

[Vladimir Soloviev] *Russia and the Universal Church*. Trans. Herbert Rees. London: Geoffrey Bles – The Centenary Press, 1948.

[Vladimir Soloviev] *La Russie et l'Église universelle*. 4th ed. Paris: Librairie Stock, 1922.

'Smysl liubvi' [The Meaning of Love]. *SSVSS* 7: 3–60.

Sobranie sochinenii Vladimira Sergeevicha Solov'eva [SSVSS, Collected Works of Vladimir Sergeevich Soloviev]. Eds S.M. Solov'ev and E.L. Radlov. 2nd ed. 10 vols. St Petersburg, 1911–14. Reprint, Brussels: Foyer Oriental Chrétien, 1966. Supplementary vols 11–12. Brussels: Izdatel'stvo Zhizn' s Bogom, Foyer Oriental Chrétien, 1969–70.

Sochineniia v dvukh tomakh. Ed. with intros by A.F. Losev and A.V. Gulyga. Filosofskoe nasledie, vols 104–5. 2 vols.

Moscow: Akademiia nauk SSSR. Institut filosofii. Izdatel'stvo 'Mysl'", 1988.

[Vladimir Soloviev] *'La Sophia'* et les autres écrits français. Ed. François Rouleau. Lausanne: La Cité-L'Age d'Homme, 1978.

'Talmud i noveishaia polemicheskaia literatura o nem v Avstrii i Germanii' [The Talmud and the Recent Polemical Literature on It in Austria and Germany]. *SSVSS* 6: 1–32.

'Teoreticheskaia filosofiia' (Theoretical Philosophy). *SSVSS* 9: 87–166.

Tri razgovora o voine, progresse i kontse vsemirnoi istorii, so vkliucheniem kratkoi povesti ob antikhriste i s prilozheniiami [Three Dialogues on War, Progress and the End of World History, with a Brief Tale of the Anti-Christ]. *SSVSS* 10: 81–221.

'Tri rechi v pamiat' Dostoevskogo' [Three Speeches in Memory of Dostoevsky]. *SSVSS* 3: 185–223.

'Tri sily' [Three Forces]. *SSVSS* 1: 227–39.

'Velikii spor i khristianskaia politika' [The Great Schism and Christian Politics]. *SSVSS* 4: 3–114.

[Vladimir Solovyov] *War, Progress, and the End of History: Three Conversations. Including a Short Story of the Anti-Christ.* Trans. Thomas R. Beyer, Jr. Hudson, New York: Lindisfarne Press, 1990.

'Zhiznennaia drama Platona' [The Drama of Plato's Life]. *SSVSS* 9: 194–241.

WORKS BY SERGEI NIKOLAEVICH BULGAKOV
(PROTOIEREI SERGII BULGAKOV)

Agnets bozhii [The Lamb of God]. Pt 1 of *O bogochelovech-estve.* Paris: YMCA-Press, 1933.

Apokalipsis Ioanna: opyt dogmaticheskogo istolkovaniia [The Revelation of John: A Dogmatic Interpretation]. Paris: YMCA-Press, 1948.

Avtobiograficheskie zametki. Posthumous ed. Preface and notes by L.A. Zander. Paris: YMCA-Press, 1946.

'Chto daet sovremennomu soznaniiu filosofiia Vladimira Solov'eva?' [What Does Vladimir Soloviev's Philosophy Offer the Modern Mind?]. In *Ot marksizma k idealizmu*, pp. 195–262.

Dokladnaia zapiska Mitropolitu Evlogiiu prof. prot. Sergiia Bulgakova po povodu opredeleniia Arkhiereiskogo sobora v Karlovtsakh otnositel'no ucheniia o Sofii Premudrosti Bozhiei. Prilozhenie k zhurnalu 'Put". Paris: YMCA-Press, 1936.

Drug zhenikha (Io. 3:28–30): o pravoslavnom pochitanii Predtechi [The Friend of the Bridegroom (John 3:28–30): On the Orthodox Veneration of the Forerunner]. Paris: YMCA-Press, 1927.

'Dushevnaia drama Gertsena' [Herzen's Spiritual Drama]. In *Ot marksizma k idealizmu*, pp. 161–94.

Dva grada: issledovaniia o prirode obshchestvennykh idealov [Two Cities: Investigations on the Nature of Social Ideals]. 2 vols. Moscow: Tovarishchestvo tipografii A.I. Mamontova, 1911.

Filosofiia khoziaistva [The Philosophy of Economy]. Moscow: Izdatel'stvo 'Put", 1912. Reprint, New York: Chalidze Publications, 1982.

'Filosofiia kn. S.N. Trubetskogo i dukhovnaia bor'ba sovremennosti' [Prince S.N. Trubetskoi's Philosophy and the Spiritual Struggle of the Modern World]. In *Dva grada*, 2: 243–59.

'Geroizm i podvizhnichestvo (Iz razmyshlenii o religioznoi prirode russkoi intelligentsii)' [Heroism and Humility: Reflections on the Religious Nature of the Russian Intelligentsia]. In *Vekhi: sbornik statei o russkoi intelligentsii*, pp. 23–69. 2nd ed. Moscow: Tipografiia V.M. Sablina, 1909. Reprint, Frankfurt am Main: Izdatel'stvo 'Posev', 1967.

Ikona i ikonopochitanie: dogmaticheskii ocherk [The Veneration of Icons: A Dogmatic Sketch]. Paris: YMCA-Press, 1931.

'Ipostas' i ipostasnost': Scholia k *Svetu Nevechernemu*' [Hypostasis and Hypostaseity: Scholia to *The Unfading Light*]. In *Sbornik statei posviashchennykh Petru Berngardovichu Struve ko dniu tridtsatipiatiletiia ego nauchno-publitsisticheskoi deiatel'nosti, 1890–1925*, pp. 353–71. Prague, 1925.

'Ivan Karamazov (v romane Dostoevskogo "Brat'ia Karamazovy") kak filosofskii tip' [Ivan Karamazov (in Dostoevsky's Novel 'The Brothers Karamazov') as a Philosophical Type]. In *Ot marksizma k idealizmu*, pp. 83–112.

Kapitalizm i zemledelenie [Capitalism and Agriculture]. 2 vols. St Petersburg: Tipografiia V.A. Tikhanova, 1900.

Khristianstvo i evreiskii vopros. Paris: YMCA-Press, 1991.

Kupina neopalimaia: opyt dogmaticheskogo istolkovaniia nekotorykh chert v pravoslavnom pochitanii Bogomateri [The Burning Bush: A Dogmatic Interpretation of Some Features of the Orthodox Veneration of the Mother of God]. Paris: YMCA-Press, 1927.

Lestvitsa iakovlia: ob angelakh [Jacob's Ladder: On the Angels]. Paris: YMCA-Press, 1929.

Nevesta agntsa [The Bride of the Lamb]. Pt 3 of *O bogochelovechestve.* Paris: YMCA-Press, 1945. Reprint, Gregg International Publishers Limited, 1971.

O bogochelovechestve [On the Humanity of God]. 3 vols. Paris: YMCA-Press, 1933–45. See *Agnets bozhii, Uteshitel'* and *Nevesta agntsa.*

O chudesakh evangel'skikh [The Gospel Miracles]. Moscow: Russkii put', 1994.

'O pervokhristianstve: o tom, chto bylo v nem i chego ne bylo. Opyt kharakteristiki' [On Early Christianity: What It Did and Did not Contain. A Characterization]. In *Dva grada,* 1: 234–303.

O Sofii premudrosti bozhiei: ukaz moskovskoi patriarkhii i dokladnye zapiski prof. prot. Sergiia Bulgakova Mitropolitu Evlogiiu. Paris, 1935.

'Ob ekonomicheskom ideale' [On the Economic Ideal]. In *Ot marksizma k idealizmu,* pp. 263–87.

[Sergius Bulgakov] *The Orthodox Church.* Foreword by Thomas Hopko. Trans. Lydia Kesich. Crestwood, New York: St Vladimir's Seminary Press, 1988.

[Sergius Bulgakov] *Orthodoxy and Modern Society.* With a bibliography of Bulgakov's works in English. Ed. Robert Bird. Variable Readings in Russian Philosophy, no. 4. New Haven, Conn.: The Variable Press, 1995.

Osnovnye motivy filosofii khoziaistva v platonizme i rannem khristianstve. [Fundamental Motifs of Philosophy of Economy in Platonism and Early Christianity]. Vol 1, pt 3 of *Istoriia ekonomicheskoi mysli,* ed. V.Ia. Zheleznov and A.A. Manuilov. Moscow: Moskovskii nauchnyi institut, 1916.

'Osnovye problemy teorii progressa' [Fundamental Problems of the Theory of Progress]. In *Ot marksizma k idealizmu*, pp. 113–60.

Ot marksizma k idealizmu: sbornik statei (1896–1903) [From Marxism to Idealism: A Collection of Essays]. St Petersburg: Tovarishchestvo 'Obshchestvennaia Pol'za', 1903. Reprint, Frankfurt am Main: Posev, 1968.

[Serge Boulgakof] *Le Paraclet*. Vol. 2 of *La Sagesse divine et la théanthropie*. Trans. Constantin Andronikof. Paris: Aubier, Éditions Montaigne, 1946.

'Priroda v filosofii Vl. Solov'eva' [Nature in the Philosophy of Vladimir Soloviev]. In *Sochineniia v dvukh tomakh*, 1: 15–46.

Sergii Bulgakov: Towards a Russian Political Theology. Ed. Rowan Williams. Edinburgh: T&T Clark, 1999.

Sochineniia v dvukh tomakh. Eds S.S. Khoruzhii and I.B. Rodnianskaia. 2 vols. Moscow: Izdatel'stvo 'Nauka', 1993.

[Sergius Bulgakoff] 'Social Teaching in Modern Russian Orthodox Theology.' The Twentieth Annual Hale Memorial Sermon. Evanston, Illinois: Seabury-Western Theological Seminary, 1934.

Svet nevechernii: sozertsaniia i umozreniia [The Unfading Light: Contemplations and Speculations]. Ed. V.V. Sapov. Afterword by K.M. Dolgov. Moscow: Izdatel'stvo 'Respublika', 1994.

Sviatye Petr i Ioann: dva pervoapostola [St Peter and St John: The Two Primary Apostles]. Paris: YMCA-Press, 1926.

Uteshitel' [The Comforter]. Pt 2 of *O bogochelovechestve*. Paris: YMCA-Press, 1936.

[Serge Boulgakof] *Du Verbe incarné. (Agnus Dei)*. Vol 1 of *La Sagesse divine et la théanthropie*. Trans. Constantin Andronikof. Paris: Aubier, Éditions Montaigne, 1943.

[Sergius Bulgakov] *The Wisdom of God: A Brief Summary of Sophiology*. Preface by the Rev. Frank Gavin. New York: The Paisley Press, Inc.; London: Williams and Norgate Ltd, 1937.

OTHER SOURCES

Akulin, V.N. 'S.N. Bulgakov: vekhi zhizni i tvorchestva.' In S.N. Bulgakov, *Khristianskii sotsializm*, ed. V.N. Akulin, pp. 5–24. Novosibirsk: 'Nauka', Sibirskoe otdelenie, 1991.

Arkhimandrit Feodor (A.M. Bukharev): Pro et contra: Lichnost' i tvorchestvo arkhimandrita Feodora (Bukhareva) v otsenke russkikh myslitelei i issledovatelei. Antologiia. Eds B.F. Egorov, N.V. Serebrennikov, and A.P. Dmitriev. Seriia 'Russkii Put''. St Petersburg: Izdatel'stvo Russkogo Khristianskogo gumanitarnogo instituta, 1997.

Aulén, Gustav, Karl Barth, Sergius Bulgakoff, M.C. D'Arcy, T.S. Eliot, Walter M. Horton and William Temple. *Revelation*. Eds John Baillie and Hugh Martin. New York: The Macmillan Company, 1937.

Barth, Karl. *The Humanity of God*. Trans. John Newton Thomas and Thomas Wieser. Richmond, Virginia: John Knox Press, 1960.

Behr-Sigel, Elisabeth. *Alexandre Boukharev: Un Théologien de l'Église orthodoxe russe en dialogue avec le monde moderne. Introduction et Lettres à Valérien et Alexandra Lavrski.* Preface by Olivier Clément. Paris: Éditions Beauchesne, 1977.

Belorukov, A.M. 'Vnutrennii perelom v zhizni A.M. Bukhareva.' *Bogoslovskii vestnik*, 1915, nos 10–12.

Bethea, David M. *The Shape of Apocalypse in Modern Russian Fiction*. Princeton, New Jersey: Princeton University Press, 1989.

Blane, Andrew, ed. *Georges Florovsky: Russian Intellectual and Orthodox Churchman*. Crestwood, New York: St Vladimir's Seminary Press, 1993.

Boswell, John. *Same-Sex Unions in Premodern Europe*. New York: Villard Books, 1994.

Bowie, Andrew. *Schelling and Modern European Philosophy: An Introduction*. London and New York: Routledge, 1993.

Brown, Robert. 'Resources in Schelling for New Directions in Theology.' *Idealistic Studies* 20 (1990): 1–17.

Browne, C.G. and J.E. Swallow. *Christology of the Later Fathers*. Ed. Edward Rochie Hardy in collaboration with

Cyril C. Richardson. The Library of Christian Classics, vol. 3. Philadelphia: The Westminster Press, 1954.

Carlson, Maria. 'Gnostic Elements in the Cosmogony of Vladimir Soloviev.' In *Russian Religious Thought*, eds Kornblatt and Gustafson, pp. 49–67.

Congar, Yves M.-J. *Dialogue Between Christians: Catholic Contributions to Ecumenism*. Trans. Philip Loretz. London and Dublin: Geoffrey Chapman, 1966.

——. *Diversity and Communion*. Trans. John Bowden. Mystic, Connecticut: Twenty-Third Publications, 1985.

Copleston, Frederick. *Fichte to Hegel*. Vol 7, pt 1 of *A History of Philosophy*. Garden City, New York: Doubleday & Company, Inc., Image Books, 1965.

——. *Philosophy in Russia: From Herzen to Lenin and Berdyaev*. Notre Dame, Indiana: Search Press, University of Notre Dame, 1986.

——. *Russian Religious Philosophy: Selected Aspects*. Notre Dame, Indiana: Search Press, University of Notre Dame, 1988.

Crum, Winston F. 'Sergius N. Bulgakov: From Marxism to Sophiology.' *St Vladimir's Theological Quarterly* 27 (1983): 3–25.

Cunningham, James W. *A Vanquished Hope: The Movement for Church Renewal in Russia, 1905–1906*. Crestwood, New York: St Vladimir's Seminary Press, 1981.

Davydov, Iu. N. 'Veber i Bulgakov (khristianskaia askeza i trudovaia etika).' *Voprosy filosofii*, 1994/2: 54–73.

Dostoevskii, F.M. *Sobranie sochinenii*. Eds L.P. Grossman *et al.* 10 vols. Moscow: Gosudarstvennoe izdatel'stvo khudozhestvennoi literatury, 1958.

Dostoevsky, Fyodor. *The Karamazov Brothers*. Trans. with intro. and notes by Ignat Avsey. Oxford and New York: Oxford University Press, 1998.

Elena, Monakhinia. 'Professor Protoierei Sergii Bulgakov (1871–1944).' *Bogoslovskie trudy* 27 (1986): 107–194.

Evlogii, Mitropolit. *Put' moei zhizni: Vospominaniia Mitropolita Evlogiia (Georgievskogo), izlozhennye po ego rasskazam T. Manukhinoi*. Moscow: Moskovskii rabochii, Izdatel'skii otdel vsetserkovnogo pravoslavnogo molodezhnogo dvizheniia, 1994.

Evtuhov, Catherine. 'The Church in the Russian Revolution: Arguments for and against Restoring the Patriarchate at the

Church Council of 1917–1918.' *Slavic Review* 50 (1991): 497–511.

——. *The Cross and the Sickle: Sergei Bulgakov and the Fate of Russian Religious Philosophy*. Ithaca and London: Cornell University Press, 1997.

Fedotov, George P. *The Russian Religious Mind: Kievan Christianity*. Cambridge, Massachusetts: Harvard University Press, 1946. Vol. 2: *The Middle Ages, the Thirteenth to the Fifteenth Centuries*. Ed. with a foreword by John Meyendorff, 1966.

Florensky, Pavel. *The Pillar and Ground of the Truth*. Trans. and annotated by Boris Jakim. Intro. by Richard F. Gustafson. Princeton, New Jersey: Princeton University Press, 1997.

Florovskii, Georgii. *Puti russkogo bogosloviia*. 3rd ed. Preface by J. Meyendorff. Paris: YMCA-Press, 1983.

Florovsky, Georges. *The Collected Works of Georges Florovsky*. Ed. Richard S. Haugh. 14 vols. Belmont, Massachusetts: Nordland Publishing Company; Vaduz: Büchervertriebsanstalt, 1972–89.

Freeze, Gregory L. *The Parish Clergy in Nineteenth-Century Russia: Crisis, Reform, Counter-Reform*. Princeton: Princeton University Press, 1983.

——. 'Die Laisierung des Archimandriten Feodor (Bucharev) und ihre kirchenpolitischen Hintergründe: Theologie und Politik im Russland der Mitte des 19. Jahrhunderts.' *Kirchen im Osten: Studien zur osteuropäischen Kirchengeschichte und Kirchenkunde* 28 (1985): 26–52.

——. 'The Orthodox Church and Serfdom in Prereform Russia.' *Slavic Review* 48 (1989): 361–87.

Gachev, Georgii. *Russkaia duma: portrety russkikh myslitelei*. Moscow. Novosti, 1991.

Gaut, Greg. 'Christian Politics: Vladimir Solovyov's Social Gospel Theology.' *Modern Greek Studies Yearbook* 10/11 (1994/95): 653–74.

——. 'Can a Christian Be a Nationalist? Vladimir Solov'ev's Critique of Nationalism.' *Slavic Review* 57 (1998): 77–94.

Glagolev, S. 'Golubinskii Feod. Aleksandr.' *Bogoslovskaia entsiklopediia*. St Petersburg, 1900–11.

Gogol, Nikolai. *Selected Passages from Correspondence with*

Friends. Trans. Jesse Zeldin. Nashville: Vanderbilt University Press, 1969.

Gorodetzky, Nadejda. *The Humiliated Christ in Modern Russian Thought*. London: Society for Promoting Christian Knowledge; New York: The Macmillan Company, 1938.

Gulyga, Arsenii. *Shelling*. Moscow: Izdatel'stvo 'Molodaia Gvardiia,' 1984.

Guroian, Vigen. *Incarnate Love: Essays in Orthodox Ethics*. Notre Dame, Indiana: University of Notre Dame Press, 1987.

Gustafson, Richard F. 'Soloviev's Doctrine of Salvation.' In *Russian Religious Thought*, eds Kornblatt and Gustafson, pp. 31–48.

Hedda, Jennifer Elaine. 'Good Shepherds: The St Petersburg Pastorate and the Emergence of Social Activism in the Russian Orthodox Church, 1855–1917.' PhD dissertation, Harvard University, 1998.

Herman, Maxime. *Vie et oeuvre de Vladimir Soloviev*. Collection Prémices. Éditions Universitaires Fribourg Suisse, 1995.

Himmelfarb, Martha. 'The Apocalyptic Vision.' In *The Oxford Study Bible: Revised English Bible with the Apocrypha*, eds M. Jack Suggs, Katharine Doob Sakenfeld and James R. Mueller. Articles, pp. 181–9. New York: Oxford University Press, 1992.

Hopkins, C. Howard. *John R. Mott, 1865–1955: A Biography*. Grand Rapids: William B. Eerdmans Publishing Company, 1979.

Hopko, Thomas, ed. *Women and the Priesthood*. Crestwood, New York: St Vladimir's Seminary Press, 1983.

Il'in, I.A. *Filosofiia Gegelia kak uchenie o konkretnosti Boga i cheloveka*. 2 vols. Moscow: V tipografii A.I. Mamontova, n.d. [1918].

Innokentii (Pavlov). *Vvedenie v istoriiu russkoi bogoslovskoi mysli*. Moscow: Krutitskoe patriarshee podvor'e, 1995.

Iurkevich, P.D. *Filosofskie proizvedeniia*. Eds V.S. Stepin *et al.* Moscow: Izdatel'stvo 'Pravda', 1990.

Iz-pod glyb: sbornik statei. Paris: YMCA-Press, 1974.

Jaeger, Werner. *Early Christianity and Greek Paideia*. Cambridge: The Belknap Press, Harvard University Press, 1961.

Kelly, J.N.D. *Early Christian Doctrines*. 2d ed. New York: Harper & Row, Publishers, 1960.

Khoruzhii, S.S. *Posle pereryva: puti russkoi filosofii*. St Petersburg: Izdatel'stvo 'Aleteiia', 1994.

——. *K fenomenologii askezy*. Moscow: Izdatel'stvo gumanitarnoi literatury, 1998.

Kniazeff, Alexis. *L'Institut Saint-Serge: De l'Académie d'autrefois au rayonnement d'aujourd'hui*. Paris. Éditions Beauchesne, 1974.

Kornblatt, Judith Deutsch. 'Solov'ev's Androgynous Sophia and the Jewish Kabbalah.' *Slavic Review* 50 (1991): 487–96.

——. 'Soloviev on Salvation: The Story of the "Short Story of the Antichrist."' In *Russian Religious Thought*, eds Kornblatt and Gustafson, pp. 68–87.

Kornblatt, Judith Deutsch and Richard F. Gustafson, eds. *Russian Religious Thought*. Madison and London: The University of Wisconsin Press, 1996.

Kostalevsky, Marina. *Dostoevsky and Soloviev: The Art of Integral Vision*. New Haven and London: Yale University Press, 1997.

Lavrskii, V.V. 'Moi vospominaniia ob arkhimandrite Feodore (A.M. Bukhareve).' *Bogoslovskii vestnik*, 1905, nos 7–8; 1906, nos 5, 7–8, 9, 11.

Lazarev, V.V. 'Filosofiia Vl. Solov'eva i Shelling.' In *Filosofiia Shellinga v Rossii*, ed. V.F. Pustarnakova, pp. 477–99. St Petersburg: Izdatel'stvo Russkogo Khristianskogo gumanitarnogo instituta, 1998.

The Lenten Triodion. Trans. Mother Mary and Archimandrite Kallistos Ware. London and Boston: Faber and Faber, 1984.

Losev, A. *Vladimir Solov'ev i ego vremia*. Ed. L.V. Blinnikov. Moscow: Izdatel'stvo 'Progress', 1990.

Losskii, V. *Spor o Sofii: 'Dokladnaia Zapiska' prot. S. Bulgakova i smysl Ukaza Moskovskoi Patriarkhii*. Paris, 1936.

Lossky, Vladimir. *The Mystical Theology of the Eastern Church*. London & Cambridge: James Clarke & Co. Ltd, 1957.

Lowrie, Donald A. *Saint Sergius in Paris: The Orthodox Theological Institute*. London: SPCK, 1954.

Luk'ianov, S.M. *Materialy k biografii V.S. Solov'eva*. Petrograd, 1916–21.

Meehan, Brenda. 'Wisdom/Sophia, Russian Identity, and

Western Feminist Theology.' *Cross Currents* 46 (1996): 149–68.

Meerson, Michael A. 'Sergei Bulgakov's Philosophy of Personality.' In *Russian Religious Thought*, eds Kornblatt and Gustafson, pp. 139–53.

——. *The Trinity of Love in Modern Russian Theology: The Love Paradigm and the Retrieval of Western Medieval Love Mysticism in Modern Russian Trinitarian Thought (from Solovyov to Bulgakov)*. Quincy, Illinois: Franciscan Press, 1998.

Meerson-Aksenov, Michael and Boris Shragin, eds. *The Political, Social and Religious Thought of Russian 'Samizdat': An Anthology*. Trans. Nickolas Lupinin. Belmont, Massachusetts: Nordland Publishing Company, 1977.

Men', Aleksandr. *Apokalipsis: Otkrovenie Ioanna Bogoslova*. Riga: Fond im. Aleksandra Menia, 1992.

Meyendorff, John. *Living Tradition: Orthodox Witness in the Contemporary World*. Crestwood, New York: St Vladimir's Seminary Press, 1978.

——. 'The Russian Bishops and Church Reform.' In *Russian Orthodoxy under the Old Regime*, eds Nichols and Stavrou, pp. 170–82.

Mochul'skii, K. *Vladimir Solov'ev: zhizn' i uchenie*. 2nd ed. Paris: YMCA-Press, 1951.

Naumov, Kliment. *Bibliographie des oeuvres de Serge Boulgakov*. Preface by Constantin Andronikof. Bibliothèque russe de l'Institut d'études slaves, vol. 68/1. Paris: Institut d'études slaves, 1984.

Newman, Barbara. 'Sergius Bulgakov and the Theology of Divine Wisdom.' *St Vladimir's Theological Quarterly* 22 (1978): 39–73.

Nichols, Aidan. 'Bulgakov and Sophiology.' *Sobornost* 13/2 (1992): 17–31.

Nichols, Robert L. and Theofanis G. Stavrou, eds. *Russian Orthodoxy Under the Old Regime*. Minneapolis: University of Minnesota Press, 1978.

Nygren, Anders. *Agape and Eros*. Trans. Philip S. Watson. Philadelphia: The Westminster Press, 1953.

A Patristic Greek Lexicon. Ed. G.W.H. Lampe. Oxford: The Clarendon Press, 1961.

Pauck, Wilhelm. *Harnack and Troeltsch: Two Historical Theologians*. New York: Oxford University Press, 1968.

Pelikan, Jaroslav. *The Vindication of Tradition*. New Haven and London: Yale University Press, 1984.

——. *Christian Doctrine and Modern Culture (since 1700)*. Vol. 5 of *The Christian Tradition: A History of the Development of Doctrine*. Chicago and London: The University of Chicago Press, 1989.

Placher, William C. *The Domestication of Transcendence: How Modern Thinking About God Went Wrong*. Louisville: Westminster John Knox Press, 1996.

Poole, Randall Allen. 'The Moscow Psychological Society and the Neo-Idealist Development of Russian Liberalism.' PhD dissertation, University of Notre Dame, 1995.

Pribavleniia k tvoreniiam sv. ottsev. 48 vols. Moscow, 1843–91.

Problemy idealizma: sbornik statei. Ed. P.I. Novgorodtsev. Moscow: Moskovskoe Psikhologicheskoe Obshchestvo, 1902.

Pryzhov, I. *Zhitie Ivana Iakovlevicha, izvestnogo proroka v Moskve*. St Petersburg, 1860.

Raeff, Marc. 'Enticements and Rifts: Georges Florovsky as Russian Intellectual Historian.' In *Georges Florovsky: Russian Intellectual and Orthodox Churchman*, ed. Blane, pp. 219–86.

——. 'Georgij Florovskij historien de la culture religieuse russe.' *Cahiers du monde russe et soviétique* 29 (1988): 561–5.

——. *Russia Abroad: A Cultural History of the Russian Emigration, 1919–1939*. New York: Oxford University Press, 1990.

Rashkovskii, E.B. 'Protoierei Aleksandr Men': intellektual'nyi oblik.' *Voprosy filosofii*, 1994/2: 166–74.

Roberts, Elizabeth and Ann Shukman, eds. *Christianity for the Twenty-First Century: The Prophetic Writings of Alexander Men*. New York: Continuum, 1996.

Rodnianskaia, Irina. 'Sergei Nikolaevich Bulgakov.' *Literaturnaia Gazeta*, 27 September 1989, no. 39, p. 6.

Rosenthal, Bernice Glatzer. 'The Nature and Function of Sophia in Sergei Bulgakov's Prerevolutionary Thought.' In *Russian Religious Thought*, eds Kornblatt and Gustafson, pp. 154–75.

——. 'The Search for an Orthodox Work Ethic.' In *Between Tsar and People*, eds Edith W. Clowes, Samuel E. Kassow and

James L. West, pp. 57–74. Princeton: Princeton University Press, 1991.

Samosoznanie: sbornik statei. Eds P. Litvinov, M. Meerson-Aksenov and B. Shragin. New York: Izdatel'stvo 'Khronika', 1976.

Scheibert, Peter. *Die Petersburger religiös-philosophischen Zusammenkünfte von 1902 und 1903.* Berlin, 1964.

Schelling, F.W.J. *Philosophie der Offenbarung 1841/42.* Paulus-Nachschrift. Ed. Manfred Frank. Frankfurt am Main: Suhrkamp Verlag, 1977.

Scherrer, Jutta. *Die Petersburger religiös-philosophischen Vereinigungen: Die Entwicklung der religiösen Selbstverständnis ihrer Intelligencija-Mitglieder (1901–1907).* Berlin, 1973.

Schmemann, Alexander. 'Role of Honour.' *St Vladimir's Seminary Quarterly* 2 (1954): 5–11.

——, ed. *Ultimate Questions: An Anthology of Modern Russian Religious Thought.* New York, Chicago, San Francisco: Holt, Rinehart and Winston, 1965.

——. 'Russian Theology: 1920–1972, An Introductory Survey.' *St Vladimir's Theological Quarterly* 16 (1972): 172–94.

Shanin, Teodor. *The Awkward Class: Political Sociology of Peasantry in a Developing Society: Russia 1910–1925.* Oxford: The Clarendon Press, 1972.

——. *The Roots of Otherness: Russia's Turn of Century.* Vol. 1, *Russia as a 'Developing Society'.* Vol. 2, *Russia, 1905–07: Revolution as a Moment of Truth.* New Haven and London: Yale University Press, 1985–6.

Shaw, Lewis. 'John Meyendorff and the Heritage of the Russian Theological Tradition.' In *New Perspectives on Historical Theology: Essays in Memory of John Meyendorff,* ed. Bradley Nassif, pp. 10–42. Grand Rapids, Michigan and Cambridge, UK: William B. Eerdmans Publishing Company, 1996.

Shestov, Lev. *Speculation and Revelation.* Trans. Bernard Martin. Athens, Chicago, London: Ohio University Press, 1982.

Shevzov, Vera. 'Pravoslavnoe obozrenie 1860–1870: An Overview.' Unpublished paper, Yale University, 1987.

——. 'Pravoslavnoe obozrenie and the Academic Theologians' View on Orthodoxy and "Modernity" in the 1860's.' Paper presented at the Second International Scientific and Ecclesiastical Conference on the Millennium of the Baptism of Russia, Moscow, June 1987.

Slesinski, Robert. *Pavel Florensky: A Metaphysics of Love.* Crestwood, New York: St Vladimir's Seminary Press, 1984.

Solov'ev, S.M. *Zhizn' i tvorcheskaia evoliutsiia Vladimira Solov'eva.* Brussels: Izdatel'stvo Zhizn' s Bogom, 1977.

Solzhenitsyn, Alexander *et al. From Under the Rubble.* Trans. A.M. Brock *et al.* under the direction of Michael Scammell, with intro. by Max Hayward. Boston and Toronto: Little, Brown and Company, 1975.

Stone, Jerome Arthur. 'Tillich and Schelling's Later Philosophy.' In *Kairos and Logos: Studies in the Roots and Implications of Tillich's Theology,* ed. John J. Carey, pp. 3–35. Macon, Georgia: Mercer University Press, 1984.

Stone, Ronald H. *Paul Tillich's Radical Social Thought.* Atlanta: John Knox Press, 1980.

Strémooukhoff, D. *Vladimir Soloviev et son oeuvre messianique.* Publications de la Faculté des Lettres de l'Université de Strasbourg, fasc. 69. Paris: Société d'Édition, Les Belles Lettres, 1935.

——. *Vladimir Soloviev and His Messianic Work.* Eds Philip Guilbeau and Heather Elise MacGregor. Trans. Elizabeth Meyendorff. Belmont, Massachusetts: Nordland, 1980.

Struve, Nikita. 'S. Bulgakov et la question juive.' *Cahiers du monde russe et soviétique* 29 (1988): 533–42.

Stumme, John R. *Socialism in Theological Perspective: A Study of Paul Tillich 1918–1933.* American Academy of Religion Dissertation Series, no. 21. Missoula, Montana: Scholars Press, 1978.

Sutton, Jonathan. *The Religious Philosophy of Vladimir Solovyov: Towards a Reassessment.* New York: St Martin's Press, 1988.

Tareev, M.M. *Iskusheniia Bogocheloveka, kak edinyi iskupitel'nyi podvig vsei zemnoi zhizni Khrista, v sviazi s istorieiu dokhristianskikh religii i khristianskoi tserkvi.* Moscow: Izdanie Obshchestva liubitelei dukhovnogo prosveshcheniia, 1892.

——. *Osnovy khristianstva.* 4 vols. Sergiev Posad: Tipografiia Sv.-Tr. Sergievoi Lavry, 1908.

Tataryn, Myroslaw. 'Sergius Bulgakov (1871–1944): Time for a New Look.' *St Vladimir's Theological Quarterly* 42 (1998): 315–38.

Tillich, Paul. *Dynamics of Faith*. New York: Harper & Row, Publishers, 1957.

——. 'Kairos.' In *The Protestant Era*, abridged ed., trans. James Luther Adams, pp. 32–51. Chicago: The University of Chicago Press, 1957.

——. *Christianity and the Encounter of the World Religions*. New York and London: Columbia University Press, 1963.

——. *The Construction of the History of Religion in Schelling's Positive Philosophy: Its Presuppositions and Principles*. Trans. with intro and notes by Victor Nuovo. Lewisburg: Bucknell University Press; London: Associated University Presses, 1974.

Trubetskoi, Evgenii. *Mirosozertsanie Vl.S. Solov'eva*. 2 vols. Moscow: Izdanie avtora, 1913.

Trubetskoi, Sergei Nikolaevich. 'Etika i dogmatika.' In *Sobranie sochinenii Kn. Sergeia Nikolaevicha Trubetskogo*, 2: 134–60. Moscow: Tipografiia G. Lissnera i D. Sobko, 1908.

Valliere, Paul. 'The Idea of a Council in Russian Orthodoxy in 1905.' In *Russian Orthodoxy Under the Old Regime*, eds Nichols and Stavrou, pp. 183–201.

——. 'M.M. Tareev: A Study in Russian Ethics and Mysticism.' PhD dissertation, Columbia University, 1974.

——. 'Solov'ev and Schelling's Philosophy of Revelation.' In *Vladimir Solov'ev: Reconciler and Polemicist*. Eds Wil van den Bercken, Manon de Courten and Evert van der Zweerde. Selected Papers of the International Conference on Vladimir Solov'ev 15–18 September 1998. Eastern Christian Studies, vol. 2. Leuven: Peeters, in press.

——. 'Sophiology as the Dialogue of Orthodoxy with Modern Civilization.' In *Russian Religious Thought*, eds Kornblatt and Gustafson, pp. 176–92.

——. 'Tradition.' *The Encyclopedia of Religion*, ed. Mircea Eliade, 15: 1–16. New York: Macmillan Publishing Company, 1987.

Vekhi: sbornik statei o russkoi intelligentsii. 2nd ed. Moscow: Tipografiia V.M. Sablina, 1909. Reprint, Frankfurt am Main: Izdatel'stvo 'Posev', 1967.

Vostryshev, M. *Patriarkh Tikhon.* Moscow: Molodaia gvardiia, 1997.

Vysheslavtsev, B.P. *Etika preobrazhennogo erosa.* Intro. and notes by V.V. Sapov. Moscow: Izdatel'stvo 'Respublika', 1994.

Walicki, Andrzej. *A History of Russian Thought from the Enlightenment to Marxism.* Trans. Hilda Andrews-Rusiecka. Stanford, California: Stanford University Press, 1979.

——. *Legal Philosophies of Russian Liberalism.* Oxford: Clarendon Press, 1987.

White, Alan. *Schelling: An Introduction to the System of Freedom.* New Haven and London: Yale University Press, 1983.

Wielenga, Bastiaan. *Lenins Weg zur Revolution: Eine Konfrontation mit Sergej Bulgakov und Petr Struve im Interesse einer theologischen Besinnung.* Munich: Chr. Kaiser Verlag, 1971.

Zander, L.A. *Bog i mir (Mirosozertsanie ottsa Sergiia Bulgakova).* 2 vols. Paris: YMCA-Press, 1948.

Zelinskii, Vladimir. *Prikhodiashchie v tserkov'.* Paris: La Presse Libre, 1982.

——. *Otkrytie slova.* Moscow: Put', 1993.

Zen'kovskii, Vasilii. 'Delo ob obvinenii o. Sergiia Bulgakova v eresi (glava iz neizdannykh vospominanii).' *Vestnik russkogo khristianskogo dvizheniia* 149 (1987): 61–5.

Zenkovsky, V.V. *A History of Russian Philosophy.* Trans. George L. Kline. 2 vols. New York: Columbia University Press, 1953.

Zernov, Nicholas. *The Russian Religious Renaissance of the Twentieth Century.* New York and Evanston: Harper & Row, Publishers, 1963.

——. 'The Eastern Churches and the Ecumenical Movement in the Twentieth Century.' In *A History of the Ecumenical Movement 1517–1948*, eds Ruth Rouse and Stephen Charles Neill, pp. 645–74. 2nd ed. with revised bibliography. Philadelphia: The Westminster Press, 1967.

Zhivoe predanie: pravoslavie v sovremennosti. Moscow: Sviato-Filaretovskaia moskovskaia vysshaia pravoslavno-khristian-skaia shkola, 1997.

Znamenskii, P.V. *Istoriia kazanskoi dukhovnoi akademii za*

pervyi (doreformennyi) period ee sushchestvovaniia (1842–1870 gody). 3 vols. Kazan: Tipografiia imperatorskogo universiteta, 1891–2.

———. 'Pechal'noe dvadtsatipiatiletie.' *Pravoslavnyi sobesednik*, 1896. See Znamenskii, 'Vmesto vvedeniia.'

———. *Bogoslovskaia polemika 1860–kh godov ob otnoshenii pravoslaviia k sovremennoi zhizni*. Kazan, 1902. See Znamenskii, *Pravoslavie i sovremennaia zhizn'*.

———. *Pravoslavie i sovremennaia zhizn': polemika 60–kh godov ob otnoshenii pravoslaviia k sovremennoi zhizni (A.M. Bukharev)*. Moscow: 'Svobodnaia Sovest'', 1906.

———. 'Vmesto vvedeniia. O zhizni i trudakh Aleksandra Matveevicha (arkhimandrita Feodora) Bukhareva.' In Arkhimandrit Feodor (A.M. Bukharev), *O pravoslavii v otnoshenii k sovremennosti*, pp. v–xxviii. St Petersburg: Sinodal'naia tipografiia, 1906.

Index